RELATIONS OF PRODUCTION

Marxist Approaches to
Economic Anthropology

Relations of Production

Marxist Approaches to Economic Anthropology

Edited by
DAVID SEDDON

Translated by
HELEN LACKNER

FRANK CASS

First published 1978 in Great Britain by
FRANK CASS AND COMPANY LIMITED
Gainsborough House, Gainsborough Road,
London, E11 1RS, England

and in the United States of America by
FRANK CASS AND COMPANY LIMITED
c/o Biblio Distribution Centre
81 Adams Drive, P.O. Box 327, Totowa, N.J. 07511

ISBN 0 7146 3000 4

GN 448
.2
.R44
1978

Typeset by Preface Ltd., Salisbury, Wilts.
Printed in Great Britain by

T. J. Press (Padstow) Ltd., Padstow, Cornwall

Contents

Preface

This book reflects both a personal intellectual 'crisis' and the more general 'crisis' in social anthropology of the last ten or so years. The former is in part a consequence of the latter. During the last year of my own anthropological fieldwork in north-east Morocco (carried out between 1968 and 1970) I was introduced by a Danish sociologist friend to a book that had an immediate and profound effect on my thinking about the study of society and in particular of social and economic changes: *Capitalism and Underdevelopment in Latin America*, by A. G. Frank. Firstly, it seemed to suggest an approach to the study of 'underdeveloped' countries that was sharp and powerful and which, in contrast to the majority of studies by 'bourgeois' economists, sociologists and anthropologists, denied the conventional dichotomy between 'modern' and 'traditional' sectors and developed an essentially holistic and dynamic approach to the phenomenon of underdevelopment; secondly, it appeared to apply quite remarkably directly to what I knew of Morocco, the history of its progressive involvement in the international capitalist economy over the last few centuries, and the transformations undergone by the pre-capitalist social and economic formations of the Maghreb.

On my return to England I took up a post as lecturer in African anthropology at the School of Oriental and African Studies, where one of the courses I taught was 'economic institutions', or 'economic anthropology'. While making use of those standard works of social anthropology available in English that concentrated on economic aspects of 'primitive society' and also of the conventional literature on the major debates in economic anthropology, I also began to follow the direction indicated initially by Frank and sought out studies that adopted a Marxist approach, for it seemed to me that such an approach was likely to prove particularly fruitful.[1] I found that there was virtually no work in English that dealt systematically with social and economic life in 'primitive', 'tribal' and 'peasant' societies – the main object of economic anthropology, as of any branch of anthropology – from a Marxist theoretical standpoint; and certainly not within the domain of anthropology itself. There was, of course, the work of Marx himself, of which the most immediately relevant text was the *Pre-Capitalist Economic Formations* (which appeared in English in 1964 with an introduction by Eric Hobsbawm), and that of Engels, of which *The Origin of the Family, Private Property and the State* seemed the most useful. But these works, although extremely valuable and most stimulating, clearly required further development and elaboration[2] and I was unable to find more than a handful of attempts in English to do this.[3] Within British social anthropology there was nothing – with the possible exception of Worsley's re-evaluation of Fortes' work on the Tallensi and his comparative study of 'cargo cults'[4] – from a Marxist perspective, while in American anthropology those adopting an 'evolutionary' or 'cultural materialist' approach (like White, Steward, Harris, Service and Sahlins), although clearly drawing on Marxist theory, diverged from it in certain significant ways.[5]

In French, however, I discovered a body of fascinating and directly relevant literature revealing the development of a lively and critical discussion which directed its attention primarily at the investigation and analysis of pre-capitalist formations – the general 'field' of economic anthropology. Beginning with the work of Jean Suret-Canale and developed in various somewhat different directions by Maurice Godelier and Claude Meillassoux this discussion had produced, by the end of the 1960s, a considerable body of extremely important work which asked, among other things, the 'key questions' referred to by Frankenberg[6] which British and American anthropology had rarely and unsatisfactorily asked.

By the beginning of the 1970s the crisis in anthropology and the other social sciences had begun to lead to a search for alternative approaches; one manifestation of this was a preparedness to look outside the conventional confines of the disciplines and outside the conventional literature, in particular towards what some have called the 'new' Marxism. My discovery of the French Marxists' work on pre-capitalist formations was thus part of a general rediscovery of Marxist theory clearly reflected in Britain and the U.S.A. in the growing number of translations of Marxist works into English from French and German during the past five or six years.

This particular collection of essays by nine French Marxists is concerned essentially with the investigation and analysis of pre-capitalist social and economic formations, through the modes of production which characterise them, and of their transformation. It is intended to provide the English-speaking reader with an introduction to the important, and exciting, discussion that has been developing over the last ten or so years in France, which raises fundamental questions about the way in which a truly scientific study of society should be conducted, and which goes some considerable way towards answering those questions. Much, however, remains to be done, and it is hoped that the publication of this collection of articles translated from the French will help to stimulate, in the English-speaking countries, original work which will take this discussion even further towards its objective: the discovery of the laws that underlie the development of those social and economic formations now studied by historians, sociologists, political scientists, anthropologists and economists within their separate disciplines.

In so far as a significant part of this discussion has concentrated on pre-capitalist formations and on the relations of production characteristic of these formations, that part of it may be said to fall within the sphere of what non-Marxists refer to as 'economic anthropology'. But, although some of the authors whose work is represented here have in the past used the term 'economic anthropology' and have certainly drawn heavily on the work of those 'liberal' anthropologists whose epistemology they do not share (e.g. Bohannan, Dalton, Firth, Polanyi, Salisbury), there is now growing agreement among them that use of this term is misleading and ultimately incompatible with their general concerns and objectives as determined by their theoretical position. As Maurice Godelier has observed in the foreword to his recent book *Horizon, trajets marxistes en anthropologie* (presented in this collection as a postscript to an earlier piece), 'the task of discovering, by a process of thought, the modes of production which have developed, and are still developing, during the course of history, is both *more* and *something other* than that of constructing an economic anthropology, or any other discipline with a similar label' (*my translation*). And yet, in that earlier work (presented here, pp. 49–102) he draws heavily on the work of 'liberal' econonomic anthropologists and makes use of the term 'economic anthropology' himself.

In a recent review of Emmanuel Terray's book *Marxism and 'Primitive' Societies* John Taylor suggests that the work of Claude Meillassoux is not 'economic anthropology' but rather 'an application of the concepts of historical materialism to primitive social formations', despite the use of the term by Meillassoux himself, both in his early work *Anthropologie économique des Gouro de Côte d'Ivoire*, and in more recent discussions.[7]

Taylor points out that 'there is a clear disjuncture between the objects of historical materialism and anthropology; on the one hand, the social formation as a number of relatively autonomous super-structures determined in the last instance by the articulation in dominance of at least two modes of production, and on the other, the expressive totality'.[8] He suggests that the object of anthropological discourse is essentially 'the primitive society', conceived as an expressive totality, following the discussion set out in *Reading Capital* and in Terray's book,[9] and that Terray's work 'is not, therefore, anthropology; it is a theoretical analysis of primitive modes of production, which is part of a general theory of modes of production and their combinations'.[10]

It can, therefore, be argued that to talk of 'Marxist approaches to economic anthropology' is, in a very real sense, to introduce a contradiction in terms. One should speak rather of 'approaches to the study of precapitalist formations', which presupposes that such approaches are made in terms of a developing and coherent theory of modes of production directed at understanding the laws underlying the evolution and transformation of *all* modes of production, both past and present (and even future), and of the associated social and economic formations. It will be clear, however, from the essays in this collection and from the references given that, until about 1972, at least some of the leading contributors to the analysis of pre-capitalist formations have considered themselves to be working in the field of 'anthropology', and particularly of 'economic anthropology', although their theoretical position was different from that of their 'liberal' colleagues (for whom anthropology constituted a distinct discipline with a distinctive object) and their mode of analysis quite different. Others, however, would probably not agree that their investigations and analyses were 'anthropological' in so far as this term implies a totally distinct and incompatible mode of analysis and theoretical position from that which involves the application of the concepts of historical materialism to pre-capitalist formations and their transformation under capitalism (e.g. Coquery-Vidrovitch, Rey, Suret-Canale). This latter point of view is becoming more prevalent. It seems likely that this shift is to some extent related to the fact that, as the discussion has developed, and the body of theoretical and practical work has grown, it has become less necessary to refer to the work of 'liberal' anthropologists and economists; Marxists carrying out their own investigations in the field, in Africa and elsewhere, and working on historical documents, have begun to generate their own distinctive corpus of work.

This collection is intended to provide an introduction to the discussion so far. It is conceived less as a 'primer' or 'first steps in . . .' than as a preliminary view of what, for many, will be new territory and where many important journeys and discoveries remain to be made. The collection is structured so that the reader will be able to appreciate the essentially dialectical and cumulative nature of the discussion. The collection as a whole is introduced by a brief general discussion of 'Marxism and anthropology'; each individual essay is preceded by a short explanation for its inclusion in the collection and either preceded or followed by a longer comment by the author himself placing it in the context of his own intellectual and theoretical development since the time of writing. It is hoped that these introductions, comments, auto-critiques and post-scripts will serve to involve the reader in this continuing and evolving discussion.

*   *   *

This book was first conceived in the early 1970s and the manuscript, including the above section of the preface, completed in 1974. Between that time and its reaching print the influence of the French Marxists and their work has grown significantly both in Britain and the USA, and the number and quality of contributions from within the English-speaking countries to the continuing and evolving discussion has increased correspondingly. There is insufficient space, nor would it be entirely appropriate, to provide here a detailed commentary on, and assessment of, this new work in English – or to analyse developments that have taken place within French Marxist 'anthropology' since 1974; but some indication of crucial texts and sources is required if readers of this collection are to be able to proceed further into the debate. A select bibliography is provided at the end of this collection to give an indication of such texts in English, and a quick perusal of the publisher's list produced by Maspero of Paris will reveal the more recent work of those French Marxists represented in this collection or referred to in the text.

In Britain, probably the most significant development has been the publication of the theoretical work *Pre-Capitalist Modes of Production* by Paul Hirst and Barry Hindess, a text strongly influenced by the thinking of Louis Althusser and yet original in certain critical respects. Of major importance too is the appearance of Perry Anderson's two volumes: *Passages from Antiquity to Feudalism* and *Lineages of the Absolutist State*, in which pre-capitalist social formations and their transformation are considered within a problematic differing in important respects from that of Hindess and Hirst. The review of Anderson's work by Hirst, and that of Hindess and Hirst by Talal Asad and Harold Wolpe, both in the journal *Economy and Society*, reveal some of the crucial differences, and some of the theoretical weaknesses, of these major projects. In the last couple of years the two journals, *New Left Review* and *Economy and Society* – which have been until recently the sources for articles relating to the discussion represented in this collection – have been joined by others, notably *Critique of Anthropology* in which original essays and analyses increasingly compete with translations from French and other languages. The appearance of this journal marks, in a sense, an important stage in the emergence in Britain of an alternative 'anthropology'. However, as has already been stressed above, to characterise the recent developments in theory, and their manifestations in the production of articles and other texts, as Marxist 'anthropology' is to reduce their stature and their significance and to isolate them artificially, and misleadingly, from developments in Marxist theory more generally.

What is beginning to emerge is a genuine debate whose objective is the construction of a historical social science capable of explaining, and of helping to bring about, the transformation of concrete social formations, whether capitalist or non-capitalist. Evidence that this debate is not limited to the domain of 'anthropology' may be found in the journals mentioned above, as well as in others, such as the *Journal of Peasant Studies*, the *Journal of Contemporary Asia*, the *Review of African Political Economy, Race and Class*, and many others; evidence may also be found in the papers presented to seminars and workshops held in universities and polytechnics throughout the country – as for example in the contributions to the 'peasants' seminar held at the Centre for International and Area Studies in London, or those to the British Sociological Association's 'Sociology of Development' Group. The debate, furthermore, is not merely confined to the formal institutions of higher education and to the academic or semi-academic journals but spills over into more self-consciously and explicitly political organisations and groups, revealing as it does so the wider implications of theoretical activity within the Marxist tradition.

DAVID SEDDON

Overseas Development Group
University of East Anglia

NOTES

1. Frank, A. G., *Capitalism and Underdevelopment in Latin America*, Penguin, 1972; Frank, A. G., *Latin America: Underdevelopment or Revolution*, Monthly Review Press, New York, 1969; Laclau, E., 'Feudalism and capitalism in Latin America', *New Left Review*, 67, 1971; pp. 19–38.

2. Hobsbawm, E. in Marx, K., *Pre-Capitalist Economic Formations*, Lawrence and Wishart: London, 1964 (Introduction); Meillassoux, C., 'From reproduction to production', *Economy and Society*, vol. 1, no. 1, 1972

3. Lichtheim, G., 'Marx and the "Asiatic mode of production"', *St. Antony's Papers, no. 14, Far Eastern Affairs, no. 3*, London, 1963; Meillassoux, C., 'Social and economic factors affecting markets in Guro land', in Bohannan, P. and Dalton, G. (eds), *Markets in Africa*, Northwestern University Press, 1962; Meillassoux, C., Introduction to Meillassoux, C. (ed), *The Development of Indigenous Trade and Markets in Western Africa*, International African Institute, Oxford University Press, 1971; Meillassoux, C., 1972, *op. cit.*; Thorner, D., 'Marx on India and the Asiatic mode of production', *Contributions to Indian Sociology*, no. IX, December 1966

4. Worsley, P. M., 'The kinship system of the Tallensi: a revaluation', *Journal of the Royal Anthropological Institute*, vol. 86, pt. 1, January–June, 1956; Worsley, P. M., *The Trumpet Shall Sound: a study of 'Cargo' cults in Melanesia*, Paladin, Granada Publishers Ltd., London, 1970 (first published 1957)

5. Harris, M., *The Rise of Anthropological Theory: a history of theories of culture*, Routledge and Kegan Paul, London, 1969, pp. 217–249 and 634–687

6. Frankenberg, R., 'Economic anthropology: one anthropologist's view', in Firth, R. (ed), *Themes in Economic Anthropology*, Tavistock Publications, 1967, p. 84

7. Meillassoux, C., *Anthropologie économique des Gouro de Côte d'Ivoire: de l'économie de subsistance à l'agriculture commerciale*, Mouton, Paris, 1964; Meillassoux, C., 1972, *op. cit.*

8. Taylor, J., 'Marxism and anthropology', *Economy and Society*, vol. 1, no. 3, 1972, p. 348

9. Althusser, L. and Balibar, E., *Reading Capital*, New Left Books, London, 1970; Terray, E., *Marxism and 'Primitive' Societies*, Monthly Review Press, New York and London, 1972, pp. 180–14

10. Taylor, 1972, *op. cit.*, p. 348

In the social production which men carry on they enter into definite relations that are indispensable and independent of their wills; these relations of production correspond to a definite stage of development of their natural powers of production. The sum total of these relations of production constitutes the economic structure of society – the real foundation, on which rise legal and political super-structures and to which correspond definite forms of social consciousness. The mode of production in material life determines the general character of the social, political and spiritual processes of life. It is not the consciousness of men that determines their existence, but, on the contrary, their social existence determines their consciousness. At a certain stage in their development, the material forces of production in a society come in conflict with the existing relations of production, or – what is but a legal expression for the same thing – with the property relations within which they had been at work before. From forms of development of the forces of production, these relations turn into their fetters. Then comes the period of social revolution.

Karl Marx

According to the materialist conception of history the determining element in history is *in the last instance* the production and reproduction in real life. More than this neither Marx nor I have ever asserted. If therefore somebody twists this into the statement that the economic element is the *only* determining one, he transforms it into a meaningless, abstract and absurd phrase. The economic situation is the basis, but the various elements of the superstructure – political forms of the class struggle and its consequences, constitutions established by the victorious class after a successful battle, etc. – forms of law – and then even the reflexes of all these actual struggles in the brains of the combatants: political, legal, philosophical theories, religious ideas and their further development into systems of dogma – also exercise their influence upon the course of the historical struggles and in many cases preponderate in determining their *form*.

Friedrich Engels

Marxism and Anthropology:
A Preliminary Survey

Jean Copans and David Seddon

THE 'CRISIS' IN THE SOCIAL SCIENCES

It now seems clear that the late 1960s and early 1970s have constituted a period of major upheaval and change, involving unprecedented self-criticism and radical rethinking, in the various established disciplines of Western social and human science. Recognition of the association between the inadequacy of previous approaches to the study of society and what some have termed the present 'crisis' in the social sciences has come from many different quarters, and it appears to be generally agreed that the 'crisis' is, in some way, moral as well as theoretical and practical (i.e. that it has to do with values) and that it is intimately related both to the fundamental economic and political changes that have taken place in 'the real world' since the mid-1950s and to the inability of the social sciences to explain adequately or even to take full account of these changes and their implications. In other words, that it is a political, theoretical and practical crisis.

Despite this broad agreement on its main features and general context, the precise origin and nature of the 'crisis', the specific inadequacies and limitations of the social sciences, the extent of rethinking required to transcend earlier inadequate modes of analysis, and the implications of the crisis for the future of social science, have been very differently perceived, assessed and presented, according to the theoretical (and ideological) perspective of the commentator. One aspect of the crisis, however, has been a growing disillusionment and dissatisfaction with what might be termed 'the traditions of liberal scholarship', its theories and its methods, and it is significant that the most far-reaching criticism and most effective critique of the social sciences as they are presently constituted has come from the radical left, and in particular from Marxists, whether in France, Britain or the U.S.A. It is the Marxists, more than any other group of scholars, who offer not only a critique of, but also a powerful alternative to, the present fragmented and admittedly unsatisfactory approaches through the established disciplines and traditions of 'liberal' scholarship to the study of society. The full meaning of the suggestion that the crisis in the social sciences is a political, as well as a theoretical and practical crisis, only becomes clear in the Marxist critique.

The crisis is not confined to any one country, nor is it confined to any one discipline, although economics, sociology and anthropology are those in which the origin and nature of the crisis have been most minutely examined. In the Marxist critique all of the social sciences suffer from the same basic defects, explicable in essentially similar fashion, and in all cases the alternative is clear: a dismantling of the current fragmented, ideological and inadequate social sciences and their replacement by a new, integrated social science constructed along the lines provided by Marxist theory.

The editors of the British journal *Economy and Society*, for example, believe that all the social sciences are in a state of crisis. In their view the manifestations of this crisis, which include 'intellectual sterility' and 'the neglect of fundamental theoretical and philosophical work', and 'which are more or less characteristic of the main body of work in sociology, political science, economics and history, are the product of the empiricist conceptions which dominate the social sciences in academic institutions in Britain today'. *Economy and Society* rejects the view that it is sufficient to describe societies as aggregations of discrete institutions. Rather it is committed to a theoretical approach which is holistic and which concentrates on systems of production and the division of labour, and on the related systems of domination and control, as the primary or core sectors of society. 'A theoretical approach of this nature differs from current empiricist modes of investigation and analysis in that it does not take the "common sense" definitions of social groups and institutions as given, but attempts to specify and analyse them in its own theoretic terms. A social science which defines social reality in this way constitutes, at least implicitly, a challenge to current ideological modes of defining reality. . . . In this sense, the approach advocated is a radical, critical one.' It seems clear that the emphasis on whole societies and the focus on what would conventionally be termed 'economic and political processes' leads to an elimination of the distinctions between sociology, political science, anthropology and economics. The editors also argue that 'such an approach is also necessarily historical and thus breaks the conventional boundaries between history and the social sciences'.[1]

In a recent collection of essays aiming at providing 'a critique of economic theory'[2] the editors observe that the entire school of economic theory going back to the 1870s is now under attack and see this as part of the insurgence now sweeping the social sciences

— in literature, political science, sociology, history and economics — which can only be understood as an aspect of the general crisis of cold-war liberal ideology. For such radical 'economists' the internal crisis in economics is firstly part of a wider crisis in the social sciences in general and secondly related to fundamental changes in the real world, particularly in the nature of operation of national and international capitalism, and in national and international politics, during the late 1950s and the 1960s. For them, 'all things cry out give us new forms, new ways of thinking: a new political economy! A New Political Economy that encompasses economics, sociology, history, art, literature, poetry. The negation of the atomistic compartmentalization of development economics, labour economics, industrial economics, statistical economics, business economics. . . A science of the purely human, universal basis of the production of material wealth for human needs'.[3]

Within the last few years many sociologists have spoken of the present or coming crisis in Western sociology. For some radicals the fundamental re-thinking of the discipline precipitated by this crisis is 'based on an awareness that the academician and university are not simply put upon by the larger world, but are themselves active and willing agents in the dehumanizing of this larger world'.[4] The recognition of the involvement of intellectuals, willy-nilly, in the real world and the questioning of the traditional distinction between 'subjective' and 'objective' that has played such a crucial role in the supposedly value-free science of liberal scholarship is vital, but it may be argued that such an awareness, and the development of a truly reflexive or self-aware sociology, is impossible without a complete understanding of the way in which sociology itself is a product of a particular intellectual tradition that was, and is still, largely determined by the nature of the society in which it has developed. For the Marxist, the liberal intellectual by definition cannot fully understand sociology as a component part of bourgeois social thought as it has developed; for the Marxist the answer is not the apparently simple assertion that the sociologist must become self-aware, but the 'overcoming' of sociology as a discrete discipline and the development of a new and revolutionary theory. 'The real crisis of capitalism, of which the crisis of Western sociology is a part, is giving birth to the spectre of a revolutionary theory and practice which will overcome the fragmentation of social being and social consciousness that is capitalism'.[5]

In anthropology, as in the other social sciences, a crisis has been identified, and this crisis is again seen to consist of two interdependent elements: the theoretical and the political. In his discussion of 'the crisis of British anthropology', Banaji focuses on

what he terms the internal crisis of British anthropology. He attacks
the 'unscientific' approach of functionalism which has remained
central to much anthropological 'theory', arguing that 'the arrested
development of pre-war anthropology was the natural product of
the sterilizing impact of a functionalism which never developed
theoretically, because it was in its essence a pseudo-theory, a hand-
book of practice disguised as theory.'[6] He recognises the impact of
'structuralism' — originating in France with the work of Claude Lévi-
Strauss — but argues that the structuralist impact in Britain is
conspicuous for its unevenness. The endogenous crisis of British
anthropology is thus, he argues, the unity of two conditions: the
acute theoretical stagnation of functionalism, born as a practice and
transformed surreptitiously into a 'theory'; and the marginal,
distorted and uneven development of structural anthropology. But,
in addition to its own specific crisis — the failure to constitute itself as
a science — British anthropology is affected by the global crisis of
anthropology. Anthropology is not, he suggests, only stagnating as a
theory, it is also threatened as a practice because of the disruption
and transformation of 'the "primitive totality" which formed social
anthropology's traditional object'[7] under the impact of Western
capitalism. For Banaji two events have transformed the background
of post-war anthropology: 'the colonial revolution leading to the rise
of struggles against imperialism, now on the defensive, and, at a
different level, the growth of structural anthropology. The one
reflects the other. . . .'[8]

A 'NEW' ANTHROPOLOGY OR 'THE END OF ANTHROPOLOGY'?

It is not only radical and Marxist scholars who have recognised the
major upheaval and re-thinking in the social sciences characteristic
of the late 1960s and early 1970s. Among anthropologists, Ardener,
for example, drew the attention of his 'positivist' colleagues (in his
Malinowski Memorial Lecture of 1971) to the fact that '. . .
something has already happened to British social anthropology (and
to international anthropology in related ways) such that for practical
purposes textbooks which looked useful, no longer are; monographs
which used to appear exhaustive now look selective; interpretations
which once looked full of insight now appear mechanical and
lifeless'.[9] It is a sign of the times and an expression of growing
interest among British anthropologists in the work of certain French
Marxists that Ardener expressed this 'something' in terms of 'an
epistemological break (a *coupure* as Althusser would have put it) of
an important kind'.[10]

For Ardener this 'break' is one that divides 'the later stages of functionalism' from 'the new anthropology'. Ardener's 'new anthropology' is a kind of structuralism, although he does 'not feel the need specifically to adopt the label "structuralist".' It is evident, he argues, that we are not merely concerned with an internal 'revolution', like Malinowski's discovery of fieldwork, from the world-wide intellectual interest not only in structuralism itself, but in almost any writing that reflects or resembles it — even in corrupt or distorted forms. For Ardener, there are important affinities between 'the new anthropology' and what he terms 'the new Marxism', for 'if we look now at Lévi-Strauss' structuralism, stripped of all its trendy accretions, we can see that it truly has affinities with Marxism as well as with various versions of psychoanalysis. It is certainly *not* either, but it is an entity of a similar sort. . . .'[11]

The widespread fascination with structuralism in general and with the work of Lévi-Strauss in particular may be seen, in part, as a consequence of the general crisis in the social sciences and in particular of the theoretical bankruptcy of 'traditional' anthropology. As the editors of *Economy and Society* have remarked, 'the search for new orientations has led to revived interest in Marxism, Structuralism, and Phenomenology in its various forms, to attempts to create a "critical" sociology or "critical" theory and to a demand for "relevant" as well as inter-disciplinary research. These new interests, however, have tended to be unsupported by serious scholarship and have consequently too often degenerated into blind dogmatism, confused eclecticism or mere polemic.'[12] But structuralism must be, and indeed has been, taken extremely seriously and its relationship with Marxism considered in some detail. Maurice Godelier, for example, argued in 1966 that a new situation was emerging, one of the aspects of which was the resumption of a dialogue between structuralism and Marxism. This was hardly surprising, he suggested, as Marx himself, a century ago, described the whole of social life in terms of 'structures', advanced the hypothesis of the necessary existence of correspondences between infrastructures and superstructures characterizing different 'types' of society and, lastly, claimed the ability to explain the 'evolution' of these types of society by the emergence and development of 'contradictions' between their structures. For Marx the scientific understanding of the capitalist system consisted in the discovery of the internal structure hidden behind its visible functioning. 'Thus, for Marx, as for Claude Lévi-Strauss, "structures" should not be confused with visible "social relations" but constitute a *level of reality* invisible but present behind the visible social relations. The logic of the latter, and the laws of social practice more generally, depend on the functioning of these hidden structures and the discovery of these last should allow us to "account for all the facts observed"'.[13] Godelier emphasises here the importance of Lévi-Strauss' methodological principles and conclusions in the epistemo-logical sphere, referring to his work on 'the elementary structures of kinship', which rejects in principle Radcliffe-Brown's functionalist structuralism and, in general, the whole of Anglo-Saxon empirical sociology, for which structure is part of empirical reality.[14]

Others have drawn attention to certain crucial differences between 'structuralism' and 'historical materialism'. Banaji for instance argues that structuralism, or at least Lévi-Strauss, has separated historical and structural analysis and assigned to each a discrete sector of reality. 'But by the very logic of this disjunction or dualism, Lévi-Strauss is forced to vacillate between two options: that of stressing the *complementarity* of historical and structural analysis, and that of asserting their opposition. Thus the infrastructures can both be "primary" (*historically* determinant) *and yet* remain, after all, an expression of the more basic Reality of the codes underlying all the levels of the social formation'.[15] Structural anthropology has oscillated, in Banaji's opinion, between two models, one of which recognises the primacy of the infrastructure and the other of which dissolves it in the 'expressive circularity' defined by the example of mythical transformations. He identifies the elements of a scientific theory of history in the work of Lévi-Strauss but points out that this is never developed or operationalised because of the circularity of the second, dominant model. 'The limits of structuralism are determined by the limits of its dominant model, an expressive totality imposed by a dualist theory of knowledge in which the super-structures *coexist* with the infrastructure. . .'[16] Thus, he argues, because it postulates, or assumes, a complete equivalence between its parts, that is, never postulates an asymmetry in their articulation, the structuralist totality can never become the basis of a general theory of precapitalist modes of production.

In a more recent work[17] Godelier returns to the problem of structuralism, history and Lévi-Strauss, and points out that Lévi-Strauss appears to accept 'the undoubted primacy of infrastructures' when he argues that 'it is of course only for the purposes of exposition and because they form the subject of this book that I am apparently giving a sort of priority to ideology and superstructures. I do not at all mean to suggest that ideological transformations give rise to social ones. Only the reverse is in fact true. Men's conceptions of the relations between nature and culture is a function of modifications of their own social relations.'[18] Yet, despite this, he can say 'the development of the study of infrastructures proper is a task which must be left to history — with the aid of demography, technology, historical geography and ethnography. It is not principally the ethnologist's concern, for ethnology is first of all psychology'.[19] As Godelier observes, here we are back at the positions held by functionalist empiricism: 'history is concerned with changes, ethnology with structures' — and this because changes, or processes, are conceived not as analytical objects but as the particular way in which a temporality is *experienced* by a *subject*', an empiricist view that is profoundly contrary to the thesis of the 'law of order' of social changes which Lévi-Strauss took from Marx.[20]

Historical materialism unlike structuralism provides a radical solution to the problems posed by the fragmentation and theoretical inadequacy of the social sciences. In particular it provides the basis for a theory of social change and social development that is not limited, as in functionalist approaches to social change, to change that is determined by and takes place within the existing 'social structure', or by the 'impact' of outside forces, but which explains the evolution of different 'types of society' as well as changes within a particular 'type of society' by the emergence and development of contradictions within them — a sort of endogenous dynamics. Thus, according to the Marxist understanding of evolution, not only does the social structure permit or give rise to some social change, as in the functionalist conception, but more importantly the ongoing process of social change determines the social structure of the moment.

To go further than the 'structural morphology' of Lévi-Strauss it is necessary to account for the forms, functions, mode of articulation and conditions of transformation of the social structures within the concrete societies studied by the historian and the anthropologist. It is precisely in order to accomplish this complex task, which pre-supposes a combination of several theoretical methods, that Marx's hypothesis of the determination in the last instance of the forms and the evolution of societies by the conditions of production and reproduction of their material life is needed as the central hypothesis. 'From this standpoint it will no longer be possible to go on counterposing anthropology to history or to sociology as three fetishised separate domains, nor to present economic anthropology or economic history as mere specialized lines of research belatedly added to other specialized domains that are more advanced.'[21]

Here, once again, Marxist critics of 'traditional' anthropology and of the 'new' anthropology alike join in arguing the inadequacy of the present division of social science into distinct domains or disciplines and of the theoretical perspectives that make this division possible. What is needed, in effect, is not a 'new' anthropology but the 'overcoming' of anthropology and the end of anthropology.[22] And, indeed, Emmanuel Terray has claimed, it is the present task of

Marxist scholars to 'annex the reserved domain of social anthropology to the field of application of historical materialism . . . the aim is to replace social anthropology by a particular section of historical materialism consecrated to socio-economic formations where the capitalist mode of production is absent'.[23] Certainly, Marxist scholars, by bringing the field so far reserved for social anthropology within the ambit of historical materialism, will finally eliminate the last refuge of that ideology of the 'expressive totality' which has come to define the very subject matter of anthropology, and bring about the end of anthropology.

MARXISM AND ANTHROPOLOGY IN BRITAIN

In Britain, as in the U.S.A. and France, there is a growing interest among social scientists in Marxist theory and in Marxist approaches to the study of society. This interest is still essentially embryonic in the traditional domain of anthropology but there is evidence that here too a number of scholars, particularly among the younger generation, are finding existing Marxist studies both illuminating and challenging when applied to their own investigations, and are beginning to produce original and provocative studies of their own.[24]

The almost complete absence of any explicit discussion or consideration of the work of Marx or of Marxism in British social anthropology until the last few years is, however, quite striking. In a recent general survey of 'social anthropology and Marxist views on society', Raymond Firth observes that 'for sociologists and economic historians, consideration of Marx's ideas has long been a commonplace. R. H. Tawney once said that no historian could write as if Marx had never existed. Yet some anthropologists have evaded a parallel conclusion. . .'[25] He points out that Marx's arguments claim to go to the roots of man's economic life, yet economic anthropology has largely ignored his views. Marx propounded a revolutionary theory of social change, yet general works by anthropologists have cheerfully dispensed with all but minimal use of Marx's ideas on the dynamics of society. He notes, finally, that, while some American works do refer to Marx and Engels and quite a number clearly draw on Marxist theory, references to Marx in British social anthropology have usually been brief. In fact, they have not only been brief, they have been extraordinarily few and far between, and Firth is too mild when he suggests that 'some anthropologists' have written as if Marx had never existed; *most* have done so, at least in Britain. Indeed, Firth's own discussion, although demonstrating a number of misunderstandings of Marx and Marxism for which Frankenberg has taken him to task,[26] is probably the first in British social anthropology devoted to a consideration of Marxism and anthropology.

This is not to say that British social anthropology developed in total ignorance of Marx or Marxist approaches to the study of society; for a variety of reasons (which Firth attempts to identify)[27] they have tended to avoid or dismiss the work of Marx and Engels, even where it has been directly relevant to their investigations and analyses of pre-capitalist societies. As far as we know, there has been no explicitly Marxist analysis of 'primitive', 'tribal' or 'peasant' society in British social anthropology until the 1970s, although a number of the influential social anthropologists in Britain were clearly aware of Marx's work and even made use themselves occasionally of 'Marxist concepts', although they tended generally (and continue) to misunderstand or to distort those concepts because of their unwillingness or inability to consider, in detail, the body of theory from which those concepts derive.

Virtually the only piece of work in British social anthropology which takes a systematically 'Marxist approach' before the 1970s is Worsley's re-evaluation of Fortes' analysis of the Tallensi,[28] for most social anthropologists would probably consider both Frankenberg's work on communities in Britain and Worsley's survey of 'the Third World' as 'sociology', while Worsley's important comparative historical study of 'cargo cults' in Melanesia, although clearly formed from a Marxist viewpoint, sometimes appears uncertain as to whether a 'Marxist' or a 'Weberian' approach is the most fruitful.[29]

It is perhaps significant that both Frankenberg and Worsley have worked in Manchester, for the social anthropologists and sociologists who have often been referred to as 'the Manchester School' all demonstrate a relatively detailed acquaintance with Marxism that is reflected in their published work and in that of their students, even if it is generally distorted and corrupted by the dominant influence of structural-functionalism. The interest in conflict and 'contradiction' shown by Gluckman, Turner and others of the 'Manchester School' is all too often, however, a concern with the way in which conflict at one level leads to cohesion at another. As Frank has pointed out, 'functionalists have always incorporated a part of social conflict into the very basis of structure-functionalist theory. We need only recall Simmel on conflict, Gluckman on custom and conflict, Leach on political systems, Durkheim and Merton on alienation, or even the most integralist of functionalists, Radcliffe-Brown, on joking relationships or mother's brothers. However, the function of social conflict for functionalists is only social integration. All other social conflicts — revolution and social disintegration — are off-limits for functionalist theory and practice.'[30]

Of the more influential British social anthropologists a number do refer to Marxist theory, although usually to emphasise its 'shortcomings' or simply to spurn it. Leach, for example, who is clearly aware of the main directions of Marxist theory, writes, in his discussion of the political systems of highland Burma: 'the concepts which are discussed in the present section (on Property and Ownership) are of the utmost importance for my general argument for they provide the categories in terms of which social relations are linked with economic facts. In the last analysis the power relations in any society must be based upon the control of real goods and the primary sources of production, but this Marxist generalization does not carry us very far.'[31] One cannot but wonder, with Godelier, 'at the inconsequence of the conclusion, a pirouette by which the author shrugs off an hypothesis "of the utmost importance", and applicable to "any society", so as not to seem to be casting doubt on the non-Marxist thesis of the functionalists.'[32] Other influential British social anthropologists who have drawn upon and made explicit reference to the work of Marx and Engels include Peter Lloyd, Raymond Firth and Jack Goody.

In the case of Lloyd this amounts to little more than a recognition of the fact that 'much of modern conflict theory derives ultimately from Karl Marx', the adoption of an essentially 'conflict model' based approach and a central concern with historical change, development, evolution and transformation.[33] Firth, perhaps more than any other British social anthropologist, has been aware of the fundamental inadequacies of 'classical' structural-functionalism in coping with the question of social change, of the need to go beyond the confines of the discipline of social anthropology to reduce this inadequacy, and of the existence of Marxist theory. As early as 1954 he wrote: 'we are hardly yet on the threshold of any general theory of a dynamic kind which will enable us to handle comprehensively the range of material within our normal anthropological sphere.'[34] He argued the need to consider the work of other social scientists: 'from Durkheim and Max Weber to Talcott Parsons, Robert Merton, and Kingsley Davis — not disdaining also the less polemical aspects of Karl Marx and Friedrich Engels — we have much to learn still about the interpretation of our material in its more dynamic aspects.'[35] In his 'comment on dynamic theory in social anthropology' of 1964 he returned to this theme, discussing in some detail the possible contribution of Marxist theory to anthropology. He concluded that, even 'if the answers be not acceptable, the questions have been very relevant' and that 'several major features of the Marxist scheme which are well known are, I think, still worth serious reconsideration.'[36] In this same work he also considered the possible reasons for the 'lukewarm response' of social anthropologists to the challenge of Marx's ideas and also the conditions that 'may tend to promote a growing anthropological interest in Marxist theses.' He argued that modern social anthropologists 'now require a more developed and more massive social theory to account for the phenomena which they observe, and they cannot pretend to supply that theory wholly from within their own resources. They are likely to seek elements of the theory in an eclectic way, and will be searching *inter alia* in historical sociology.'[37]

It is certainly true that, over the last two decades, British social anthropologists have become increasingly dissatisfied with the 'classical' structural-functional approach with its inherently static form of analysis, and have drawn, in eclectic fashion, on the other social sciences, and even on ideas and techniques from outside the social sciences. It is also true, as Firth observes, that, especially since the war, there has undoubtedly been much diffusion of Marxist thought in Western social anthropology, but this diffusion has resulted, generally, in the dilution and distortion of Marxist theory and in an emphasis on the value of 'insights' derived from Marxist theory considered eclectically and not holistically or even systematically. Of those who have worked mainly within the general framework of structural-functionalism and who would be included in the list of influential British social anthropologists, only Jack Goody has attempted to draw explicitly upon Marxist concepts in the discussion and analysis of particular pre-capitalist formations.[38] Despite certain misconceptions regarding Marxism and certain significant shortcomings in his approach from a Marxist point of view, which lead him towards a technological interpretation of history, Goody's study demonstrates the fruitfulness of an investigation which utilises a Marxist approach, and it is to be hoped that this work, together with the comments made in its review by Meillassoux[39] will stimulate others to draw upon Marxist theory but also to appreciate the inherent inadequacy of an eclectic approach.

In his recent survey Firth is concerned to explain both what he refers to as 'caution towards' Marx and Marxism by British social anthropologists and also the recent growth of interest in, and even, in a few cases, espousal of, Marxist theory and practice. Frankenberg, in commenting on Firth's discussion and drawing attention to some of the misconceptions and false assumptions implicit or explicit in it, argues that 'the fact that British social anthropologists took Marx less seriously and misunderstood him when they did take his views into account does not require very special explanation, since by and large this was true of all but a handful of British academics.'[40] It will certainly not be possible to explain the avoidance of Marx and Marxist approaches to the study of society by social anthropologists until anthropology, both as theory and practice, is placed in its general context, in the history of thought in the social and human sciences in Britain during the nineteenth and twentieth centuries, in the economic and political history of Britain during the same period, and in the relationship between social processes and social thought, in the manner of Bernal's *Science in History*.[41]

It is significant, for example, that no British author of comparable status to Durkheim or Weber emerged in their generation. While the reasons for this are no doubt complex, it is unquestionably true that *one* factor responsible was the absence, in Britain, of a veritable revolutionary socialist movement as existed, for instance, in Germany and France. In both of those two countries, in the late nineteenth century, the influence of Marx's thought was far more than purely intellectual in character; Marx's writings became the primary impetus within a vital and dynamic political movement. Marxism, and 'revolutionary socialism' more generally, formed a major element in the horizon of Durkheim and Weber; such an element was hardly visible on the horizon of British intellectuals, whether sociologists, economists, political scientists or social anthropologists.[42] Since the last decades of the nineteenth century, with the formation of the Independent Labour Party and the Fabian Society, the role of theorists of the socialist movement in Britain was taken over not by Marxists but by Fabians and since that time until very recently Marxism has failed to provide more than a marginal influence, either politically or theoretically, on developments in Britain.

Bernal has suggested that in Britain, in accordance with traditions that go even further back than the Industrial Revolution, abstract theory never played such an important role as in Europe, and, accordingly, social science and practical politics were never entirely distinct. 'The British, more particularly the English . . . prided themselves on being practical and having no use for theory or metaphysics, especially on social matters'[43] and he notes that 'the characteristics of Fabian sociology were avoidance of fundamental theory and attention to facts.'[44] With such a traditional approach to social problems, Marxism, a revolutionary theory as well as a revolutionary practice, has had little chance of appealing to the majority of 'bourgeois' intellectuals or even of appearing relevant to their major concerns. It was this belief in the value of pragmatism and a certain hostility towards pure theory that led nineteenth century British anthropologists to emphasise the practical utility of anthropology for colonial administrators and missionaries and which also led, eventually, to the acceptance by the colonial administration of this argument (whether in fact valid or not) for the practical value of anthropological work. During the first half of the present century social anthropology came to be considered, both by social anthropologists – the majority of whom considered themselves as 'radical' or at least 'liberal' in outlook – and by colonial administrators, as being of considerable utility (although not always in the same way) in ensuring the peaceful and enlightened administration of 'native' peoples. In British social anthropology furthermore, as it emerged during the 1920s and 1930s, the work of Durkheim, born out of a European continental philosophical tradition and European continental social and political history, was assimilated to a distinctively British tradition of philosophical empiricism and political reformism which underlay the attitude of many early anthropological fieldworkers and affected both their 'theory' and 'practice', albeit often unconsciously.[45] This tradition has affected not only social anthropology but social thought in general in Britain.

It is not surprising, in view of the intellectual traditions in Britain, the social origins of the anthropologists, the particular nature of British society and of British colonialism, that the 'practice' of anthropology in the field appeared to produce a theoretical orientation in which the essential problem was that of social order and the way in which it was maintained, and that this theoretical orientation was considered valuable by the colonial administration. Nor is it surprising that the great majority of British social anthropologists working during the 1930s and 1940s were concerned primarily with 'government', 'politics' and 'social control'. There has, however, been a tendency, among critics of British social anthropology as well as among its defenders,[46] to over-value the practical contribution of social anthropology. Firstly, it can be argued that, despite the belief of many contemporary anthropologists that British structural-functionalism in the colonial period provided a powerful and effective analytical approach to the study of society, it was in fact partial and inadequate, its widespread adoption and persistent influence being explained more by the prevailing intellectual and political climate in Britain and the colonies, than by its own inherent 'power' as a scientific theory. Secondly, it can be argued that, while it provided additional 'scientific' and academic legitimation, in certain cases, for particular approaches and attitudes towards 'native' society (whether 'exploitative' or 'protective') anthropology provided little more than a marginal influence on the administration of the colonial territories and a useful body of data. For the colonial administration sometimes had its own version of functionalism, unaided by anthropologists and certainly had its own views of 'native society'. Indeed, as Gellner has pointed out, '. . . it would have been surprising if this idea (functionalism) had been novel, for after all it had been the stock in trade of conservative political theory for quite some time. . . . Far from it being the case that anthropologists obligingly supplied the colonial administration with an ideology for using the tribes against the emergent, disrupted and hence revolutionary classes, it might well be that the anthropologist had brought back his functionalism in part *from* the district officer, who had picked it up from a conservative political background.'[47]

Any attempt to understand the development of social anthropology in Britain must clearly take into consideration both the prevailing intellectual climate in Britain and also the *total* social and political context within which social anthropologists have worked and taught. The general neglect or avoidance of Marxism in British social anthropology must be seen in this context. The growth of interest in Marxist theory during the last few years, which has resulted in a growing demand for translations into English, must be analysed in similar fashion, as must the fact that this growth of interest is still confined, in Britain even more than in France or the U.S.A., to a relatively small number of intellectuals, and to a tiny handful of social anthropologists.[48]

MARXISM AND ANTHROPOLOGY IN THE U.S.A.

The dissatisfaction with 'traditional' approaches in social anthropology expressed by many British anthropologists during the 1950s and 1960s differed profoundly, in many ways, from the fundamental criticism and, in some cases, outright rejection of 'traditional' approaches in anthropology expressed in the writing of radical anthropologists in the U.S.A. during the 1960s. There were some similarities, however, the most obvious of these being the fact that, in both cases, the dissatisfaction with the theory and practice of anthropology was the result of the confrontation of the academic discipline with major political changes in the real world — in particular with the struggles for national liberation — which revealed its inadequacy as a tool for understanding and explaining the origins and nature of these changes. But, while the dissatisfaction of British anthropologists with structural-functionalism failed to generate an adequate diagnosis of the discipline's failure and the causes – both political and theoretical – of this failure, or to produce any real alternative until the 1970s, in the U.S.A. the theoretical inadequacy of the mainstream of both British and American anthropology was located during the 1960s within a more general moral, political and theoretical context, and the crisis in American anthropology, in particular, identified as part of a crisis both of 'liberal scholarship' and of 'liberal politics', both related to the internal and external crisis of American capitalism and imperialism.[49]

Although the coincidence of protest against the Indo-China war and protest against racialism and poverty within the U.S.A. was no accident, and served to underline the intimate relationship between the situation within the country and the situation abroad (and the involvement of intellectuals in both), it was the war in Vietnam above all which precipitated the crisis in the social and human sciences, most notably in anthropology, and which has played a crucial role as a stimulus to the development of a critique, both of the discipline and of the traditions of scholarship which endorsed the idea of a value-free and morally neutral science while ignoring actual political involvement if it supported the status quo. The involvement of anthropologists in counter-insurgency programmes in Asia and Latin America also served to highlight this paradox and to intensify feeling that anthropology, in particular, required a fundamental re-thinking and re-directing.

Probably the best-known and one of the most outspoken critics of 'traditional' anthropology has been Kathleen Gough whose discussion of 'anthropology and imperialism' has been widely disseminated.[50] She identifies a number of weaknesses in anthropology in general but situates them within the American political and institutional context as well as within the intellectual context of Western anthropology as a whole. Anthropology, in her view, has been weak in two major respects: firstly, anthropologists have failed to analyse the structure of Western imperialism as an international system and an interconnected political economy, or to investigate the general and the particular features of its impact on the non-Western world; secondly, anthropologists, when studying social change, have tended to produce essentially factual accounts and to remain at a very low level of theoretical elaboration, producing only limited hypotheses regarding the impact of 'the outside world' on local communities. She suggests that the excessively empiricist approach of anthropology is related to its failure to consider the total system of which its traditional object — primitive society — was an integral part when the anthropologists first studied it. This failure to develop an adequate theoretical framework for the analysis of imperialism is particu.. ly striking in view of the very considerable literature available on the question of imperialism, most, though not all, influenced by Marx and Marxist approaches to the problem. She notes that 'such books tend in America to be either ignored or reviewed cursorily and then dismissed. They rarely appear in the standard anthropological biblio-graphies. I can only say that this American rejection of Marxist and other "rebel" literature, especially since the McCarthy period, strikes me as tragic. . . . It is heartening that in recent years the publications of the Monthly Review Press, International Publishers, "Studies on the Left", and other left-wing journals have become a kind of underground literature for many graduate students and younger faculty in the social sciences.'[51]

Gough is certainly correct when she identifies a general unwillingness in the U.S.A. to recognise the value or significance of Marx or Marxist theory for anthropology. Harris has suggested: 'there is no doubt that a consensus exists among contemporary anthropologists that Marx and Engels are irrelevant to the history of anthropological theory. Robert Lowie did not even permit these names to appear in his index: while T. K. Penniman allots Marx a few disjointed lines, and A. I. Hallowell mentions Comte and Buckle but not Marx. According to Alfred Meyer, cultural anthropology "developed entirely independently from Marxism".'[52]

Nevertheless, it is quite clear that anthropology in the U.S.A. did not develop 'entirely independently from Marxism', for two different reasons. Firstly, as Wright Mills pointed out in the early 1960s, 'in the United States, the intellectual influences of Marxism are often hidden; many of those whose very categories of thought are influenced by Marx are often unaware of the source of their own methods and conceptions';[53] and, secondly, it would be truer to say that, in so far as it developed as a result of conscious deliberation, anthropology developed in reaction to, rather than independently of, Marxism.

This reaction originated with the adoption of the scheme of historical social development constructed by Lewis Henry Morgan in his *Ancient Society* by Engels in his *Origin of the Family*. Engels argued that Morgan had, in his own way, 'discovered afresh in America the materialistic conception of history discovered by Marx forty years ago, and in his comparison of barbarism and civilization it had led him, in the main points, to the same conclusions as Marx.'[54] 'With Morgan's scheme incorporated into Communist doctrine', writes Harris, 'the struggling science of anthropology crossed the threshold of the twentieth century with a clear mandate for its own survival and well-being: expose Morgan's scheme and destroy the method on which it was based.'[55] This attack on Morgan, and indirectly on Marx, Engels and Marxist approaches to the study of society as a whole, was to have as its consequences the abandonment of the comparative method, the rejection of any serious attempt to consider history from a nomothetic standpoint and the postponement for forty years of what Harris terms 'the cultural-materialist strategy'. From 1880 to the present, the history of the criticism, defence and interpretation of Morgan's work runs through the history of American anthropology as a strong thread. But in general, hostility towards Marxism was associated both with ignorance and with misrepresentation of the work of Marx and Engels, as well as of later Marxists. One of the more influential of the 'historical particularist school' in America, Melville Herskovits, for example, praised the work of Franz Boas with the words, 'he was obviously no Marxist — we have seen how vigorously he rejected any simplistic explanation of social phenomena, whose complexity none recognised better than he.'[56]

During the last two decades of the nineteenth and the first half of the twentieth centuries, anthropology in the U.S.A. was characterised by a strong avoidance of theoretical syntheses and an overwhelming concern with ethnography and fieldwork. The label 'historical particularism' has been used to characterise this period and 'school' of thought in American anthropology. The founder of this 'school' was Franz Boas and his students included Alfred Kroeber, Robert Lowie, Melville Herskovits, E. Adamson Hoebel, Ruth Benedict and Margaret Mead. 'Historical particularism' dominated American anthropology until the mid-twentieth century, although the influence of British structural-functionalism and that of the 'culture and personality school' had some effect.

Beginning in the mid-1930s, however, there began to emerge a new concern for comparative research and a growing interest in the problems of origins and causality in the study of society. A prominent participant in this revival, and one whose indebtedness to the historical method of Marx is obvious, was Karl Polanyi, an economic historian whose range of interests embraced both economics and anthropology, as is shown by the subjects of his three principal works. *The Great Transformation* was concerned with the structure of nineteenth century capitalism and the enormity of its social consequences; the second major work, *Trade and Market in the Early Empires*, created a theoretical framework for the study of economies which were neither industrialised nor organised by market institutions; and the third work, published posthumously, on *Dahomey and the Slave Trade*, analysed the internal economic organisation of the eighteenth century West African kingdom, and the organisation of its external trade in slaves with Europeans.[57] His influence on the development of economic anthropology, particularly in the U.S.A., has been very considerable and his work is much admired by the French Marxist 'economic anthropologists'.[58] Within anthropology one line of attack on the followers of Boas and his approach, led by Julian Steward and Leslie White, 'explicitly embraces the strategy of techno-environmental and techno-economic determinism, although it has for the most part either obfuscated or shied away from an acknowledgment of its debt to Marx.'[59] Others, however, while adopting a kind of 'economic determinism', were explicitly opposed to 'socialism', pointing out that 'belief in some of the Marxian positions, together with entire distrust in the plan for their application, does not make one a socialist or a communist. . . .'[60] It is clear, nevertheless, that Leslie White, for example, was deeply influenced by Marxism although, for both political and theoretical reasons, he managed to avoid placing his critique of historical particularism within what Harris refers to as 'the arena of Marxist disputation'.[61] Steward who, like White, is concerned to reintroduce evolution and problems associated with the development of social forms and their variations, was particularly concerned with the articulation between production processes and habitat which he himself terms 'the method of cultural ecology'.[62] This approach had a considerable influence during the late 1950s and the 1960s as evidenced by the earlier work of Sidney Mintz, Eric Wolf, Morton Fried, Elman Service, Marshall Sahlins, Andrew Vayda and others. In almost all cases there is clear evidence of ideas derived ultimately from Marx and Engels but rarely any explicit recognition of this fact.

The avoidance of reference to Marx and Marxism characteristic of much of the work (during the 1950s and early 1960s) of those influenced, whether directly or indirectly, by Marxist thought is clearly a political phenomenon in the U.S.A. as much as a theoretical one. As Wright Mills pointed out in the early 1960s, 'in capitalist societies, the ideas of Marx are ignored or worse, ignorantly identified with "mere communist ideology". Thus, here too, the work of Marx, and of his followers, has become "marxism-leninism" — an official target of confused and ignorant abuse, rather than an object of serious study.'[63]

The crisis of liberalism, recognised by Wright Mills and others as early as around 1960, but becoming more acute and manifest during the second half of the decade, was associated with both the development of the New Left and the emergence of an increasingly explicit authoritarianism, both in American political life and in the social sciences. In this situation there was increasing reference to, and use of, the works of Marx, Engels, Lenin and other Marxists by both Left and Right.[64] In anthropology the debate centred on three related 'areas': the interpretation of Morgan's *Ancient Society*, the discussion of the distinction between various 'evolutionary' and 'materialist' approaches to the study of society, and the debate focused on the relationship between anthropology and imperialism, the last of which is the most widely known and probably the most widely discussed outside the U.S.A. as well as within it.

These three central concerns of the late 1960s were intimately related to each other in a systematic fashion and are also connected to developments outside the U.S.A., as well as inside, as is made clear, for example, by Eleanor Leacock in her recent introduction to *The Origin of the Family*. She refers to the disenchantment with positivist or purely pragmatic approaches in the social sciences common to most Western countries in the last decade and a growing interest in theory, particularly in Marxist theory, the need for re-thinking Marxist theory demonstrated by events in the socialist countries and the Third World, and the emergence of the 'primitive peoples' studied by anthropologists as members of new nations. All this, she points out, has contributed to the growth of an active and influential 'neo-evolutionary' wing of American anthropology, and a wide acceptance of the fact that broad evolutionary trends have given form to mankind's history. The result, however, has not been entirely salutary. ' "Evolution" has been and continues to be many things to many people. The conscious application of dialectics to a materialistic view of history is a far cry from the strong current of economic determinism characteristic of contemporary evolutionism in the United States. Nor have issues been clarified by the popular but theoretically flabby formula of "multilinear" evolution, a supposed correction to the straw man of "unilinear" evolution ascribed to Morgan (and by implication Marx and Engels).'[65] She concludes, however, that the stage has at least been set for the redefinition and re-examination of the issues.

As in Britain, many of those who have considered the relevance of Marx and Marxism for the development of anthropological theory have, perhaps largely by definition, been non-Marxists, and have frequently misunderstood or misrepresented not only 'what Marx said' but also the essential characteristics of the Marxist approach and of Marxist theory. It is also true that the work of applying systematically the concepts of Marxism either in the 'traditional' areas of anthropology or else in the new field for anthropologists as identified by Gough, Frank and others, has really only just begun in the U.S.A.; for despite the clear head-start on Britain in both theoretical and political re-thinking in anthropology there is still in the U.S.A. nothing really comparable with the theoretical development that has taken place in France. Work has, however, started on a number of 'areas', including the general characterisation of the relations of dependence and exploitation associated with colonialism and imperialism, on the analysis of the peasantry, on the reconsideration of the work of Morgan, on ideology and anthropological 'theory' and on a number of other subjects. Interestingly, some of the pre-occupations of the 'older' Marxist or 'Marxism-oriented' American anthropologists — for example, Leacock's defence of a 'materialist' Morgan[66] and Sahlins' new exploration of the so-called 'domestic mode of production[67] — parallel the interests and concerns of the French Marxist anthropologists – for example, Terray's discussion of Morgan and the work of Godelier, Meillassoux and others on the modes of production in pre-capitalist social and economic formations. On the whole, however, it would seem that the growing body of younger Marxist or 'Marxism-oriented' anthropologists are working on a wide range of problems only some of which are directly related to the major pre-occupations of the French scholars represented in this collection; this is partly because there are quite simply more radical anthropologists in the U.S.A. than in France or in Britain with a wider range of interests and partly because of a very different theoretical and political tradition on the left.

It would also seem that the situation in the U.S.A. differs from that in France in another respect, namely that political involvement *within* the context of anthropology is more advanced in the U.S.A. than in France. Since 1971 the Association of American Anthropologists has devoted several sessions to symposia on Marxism each year and the number of those attending and presenting work has grown significantly[68] over the last few years. In addition to this development within the central professional association one may point to the formation of a group of 'anthropologists for radical political action' (ARPA) which produces a quarterly newsletter and which grew out of a major political struggle within the A.A.A. following a report made to the Association on counterinsurgency in Thailand.[69]

THE DEVELOPMENT OF ANTHROPOLOGY IN FRANCE

The history of French anthropology is still relatively unexplored when compared with that of British or American anthropology, the self-consciousness that generates such exercises in historiography having developed only fairly recently, with a few notable exceptions.[70] A full study of the development of anthropology in

France, which considers not merely the history of ideas but also attempts to relate the evolution of anthropological theory both to the intellectual traditions of nineteenth and twentieth century France and to the economic and political history of France, at home and abroad, during the same period, remains to be undertaken. What is presented here is a brief sketch.

In 1859 Paul Broca founded the Société d'Anthropologie, with the intention of bringing together a variety of scholars interested in various aspects of the study of man; and in 1879 he founded the Ecole d'Anthropologie where courses were given in anatomical anthropology, ethnology, prehistory, linguistics, demography and geography.

In France, as in Britain and the U.S.A., anthropology during the nineteenth century was broadly-conceived as a comparative science whose object (or subject-matter) was considered to be all human populations, both past and present, studied from a biological and also from a social and cultural point of view. During the latter part of the century this comparative science came to adopt a general evolutionary perspective, similar to that which prevailed elsewhere in Europe and the U.S.A. There gradually developed a split between those who studied human populations primarily from a biological point of view and those who considered them from a social and cultural point of view, although the intellectual links between the two were never completely severed. By the end of the century the term 'anthropology' (*anthropologie*) was being used, almost exclusively, for what in Britain came to be called 'physical anthropology'.

'Ethnography' (*ethnographie*) gradually came to be associated with the detailed collection of firsthand material relating to the social and cultural life of native peoples. This association, which is similar to the English usage, remains to the present day. 'Ethnology' (*ethnologie*) came to be used towards the end of the nineteenth century, to refer to the synthesis and analysis, on a comparative basis, of ethnographic data collected from a number of different peoples or groups. 'Sociology' (*sociologie*), a term coined by Comte around 1830, had, by the last decades of the nineteenth century, become 'the study of society as a comparative discipline'. Thus ethnology (the rough equivalent of the British social anthropology and American cultural/social anthropology) came to be conceived of as a branch of sociology.

The development of sociology around the turn of the century in France is indissolubly associated with Emile Durkheim and his colleagues and collaborators on the *Année Sociologique*. Although the theoretical development of sociology and ethnology by the

'Durkheim school' during the last decade of the nineteenth century and the first two decades of the twentieth was remarkable and had a considerable influence on the ethnography of the period,[71] it is striking that the professional sociologists and ethnologists relied, to a very large extent, on others for the collection of ethnographic data. While the philosophical pragmatism of the British led quite early on to fieldwork proper by professional anthropologists associated with universities, in France, by contrast, the professionals remained largely concerned with what one might term 'armchair' research into certain particular aspects of social life: 'the elementary forms of the religious life', 'the theory of magic' and 'the mental functions in inferior societies', for example.[72] Also, despite the ethnological preoccupations of many members of the 'Durkheim school' of sociology, including Mauss, Hertz, Lévy-Bruhl, Bouglé and Durkheim himself, the acceptance of ethnology as a valid scientific concern by the universities was long-delayed.

In France ethnography remained almost entirely in the hands of colonial administrators and missionaries until the formation of a discipline of ethnology. The philosophical training of Durkheim, Mauss and Lévy-Bruhl provides an explanation, at least in part, for the lack of fieldwork on the part of the 'Durkheim school' and for their particular concern with 'representations'.[73] Lévi-Strauss has argued that in other countries the development of theory was far behind descriptive studies and that the French sociologists and ethnologists provided advances to balance this lack; he also has suggested that, had it not been for the first world war ethnographic research might have been carried out by such ethnologists as Robert Hertz.[74] None of the 'Durkheim school' did carry out fieldwork among non-literate peoples, however, although they drew upon the ethnographic work of colonial administrators, and Mauss even argued that ethnographic missions should be sponsored by the colonial government. The problems of ethnography in France, he stated, lay to a large extent in the fact that her colonial officers and missionaries for a long time were neither encouraged nor aided in the observation of the customs of colonial peoples.[75]

From the very beginning there were tendencies within the 'Durkheim school' towards a division between those who studied the institutions of Western society and those who were more concerned with the institutions and representations of non-Western societies. This division was to become more pronounced, particularly after the death of Durkheim himself whose work was essentially comparative. Maurice Halbwachs, Jean Ray, Paul Frauconnet, Georges Davy and François Simiand are examples of scholars primarily interested in the study of Western society; in contrast, Marcel Mauss, Henri

Hubert, Robert Hertz and Lucien Lévy-Bruhl concentrated their attention on non-Western societies, for the most part. The founding of the Institut d'Ethnologie of the University of Paris by Mauss, Lévy-Bruhl and Paul Rivet helped to formalise this division between 'sociology' on the one hand and 'ethnology' on the other — a division which parallels that between sociology and social anthropology in Britain and which is maintained even today. Thus, Mauss, who became the first director of the new Institute, presided over the disintegration of the Durkheimian comparative sociology and established a distinct academic discipline which was, henceforward, to integrate the hitherto separate fields of ethnography and ethnology.

The direction taken by French anthropology in the first few decades of its existence was undeniably a distinctive one, and strikingly different in some respects from that taken by British or American anthropology, although it resembled other schools of anthropology in its concentration upon 'primitive society' as an expressive totality.[76] The 'total social phenomenon' of Mauss, for example, has had an immense theoretical impact on scholars as different as Lévi-Strauss and Balandier, and there is surely, in this idea of a 'phenomenon' reflecting the totality of social relations and social structures, in which 'all kinds of institutions find simultaneous expression. . .',[77] a large dose of Hegelian idealism. Furthermore, while Durkheim had emphasised that the laws governing collective representations exist on a social level, Mauss pioneered an approach which was based on the belief that the same human behaviour can be understood most adequately from both a psychological and sociological perspective, the two approaches being complementary and not exclusive.[78] The intellectual predilections of French ethnology (which empiricists have often, although wrongly, characterised as metaphysical) were made clear from the start; the great names of the discipline since its beginnings — Emile Durkheim, Marcel Mauss, Marcel Griaule and Claude Lévi-Strauss — confirm this orientation. To what extent the concern with individual and collective representations was associated with the absence of a tradition of fieldwork in the early years of French ethnology and to what extent to the strength of a particular philosophical tradition is not clear, but the fact remains that, by the time fieldwork began to form an essential part of the practice of professional French ethnology, its intellectual direction was already strongly established.

The new Institute of Ethnology provided for the training of professional ethnologists as well as of colonial administrators and missionaries. It began with twenty-six students in 1926, had expanded to one hundred and sixteen by 1930 and by 1935 had one hundred and seventy-one students.[79] During the first ten years of its existence nearly one thousand students in all received training and ethnographic research was carried out under its auspices in Africa, Asia, the Near East, Latin America, Oceania and Europe. In the Americas, for example, Robert Richard, Francois Weymuller and Jacques Soustelle did work in Mexico, while Metraux worked in thē Chaco and Lévi-Strauss in the Matto-Grosso of Brazil, Vellard worked in Brazil, Venezuela and Paraguay, and Odden, Devereux and Dijour in the U.S.A. In Africa, the Dakar-Djibuti ethnographic mission, which took place during 1931-1933, included Michel Leiris, Eric Lutten, Jean Mouchet, Andre Schaeffner, Deborah Lifschitz and Marcel Griaule, and was the first of many such missions initiated by Griaule. The decade immediately before the war thus saw the initiation of a tradition of fieldwork by professional ethnologists, through teaching and research.[80]

Lévi-Strauss has observed that the first generation of professionally trained ethnologists produced by the Institute almost entirely neglected theoretical work;[81] they were either not interested in high level theorisation or comparison or else were almost anti-theoretical. It is probably largely true that this almost exclusive pre-occupation with ethnographic research to the exclusion of theoretical concerns was mainly the result of a reaction against the situation which existed earlier when theoretical formulations outstripped empirical research, although the dominant concerns of French colonialism are likely to have had some effect as well.[82] This position is clearly manifested in the work of those ethnologists associated with Griaule and his ethnographic missions to the Sudan. These ethnologists acquired not a theoretical position nor even a desire to carry out theoretical work but, as Griaule himself observed,[83] a passion for ethnographic research.

In contrast with the straight-forward pragmatism and empiricism of the British social anthropologists, however, French ethnology between the wars came to synthesise, in a paradoxical fashion, two distinct tendencies. On the one hand, a tradition which was concerned with the study of world views (conceptions du monde), collective representations and 'social facts' expressing — in the manner of the Hegelian logic — the totality of social relations. This approach sought the 'principles' of social organisation, not the nature of social relations or social systems; it is well exemplified in the work of Griaule himself.[84] On the other hand, thanks to the establishment of the Musée de l'Homme, a considerable interest had developed in museum collection work and in the production of monographs which were largely ethnographic catalogues with no explicit problematic or theoretical concern. Both these tendencies, demonstrating the defects of a certain philosophical idealism, had in common their total neglect of history and a complete disregard of the colonial situation within which the fieldwork was carried out. This, then, was the prevailing trend in French ethnology before the second world war, although broader historical and comparative investigations were attempted here and there in the early Durkheimian tradition.[85] It was to be at least ten to fifteen years before French ethnology became interested in such fields as 'government and politics', the study of social and cultural change and 'economic anthropology', which had been established in Britain even before 1940.

These major concerns of French ethnology before the war — which led to the avoidance of any analysis of the social, economic and political structures of the so-called 'primitive' societies, or rather a tendency to believe that the simple description of the infrastructure and material culture, because of its 'lack of preconceptions',[86] was the most valuable form of research — left an enormous gap in the coverage of the discipline, which explains, in part, the emergence after the war of a 'Third World sociology' concerned primarily with the areas ignored by pre-war ethnology. The 1950s provided both continuity and a break with the pre-war period. The continuity lay in the pursuit of a 'descriptive ethnography' associated with the study of both material culture and the dominant concerns of the 'Griaule team'. The continuity was also implicit, in certain respects, in the development of the work of Claude Lévi-Strauss. The growing pre-occupation with superstructural phenomena, such as mythology and 'primitive thought' (*pensée sauvage*) and the emphasis on its intellectual descent from Mauss led this new theoretical current to renew, in another form and with a different formulation, the essential tradition of French ethnology.[87]

The break came with the recognition of the importance of social, political and economic structures, which, in turn, stemmed from a recognition of the colonial situation. Here there is an interesting difference from the development of British social anthropology, which had been, in a sense, obliged to study these problems because of the institutional framework within which many British anthropologists worked, but which had, nevertheless, accepted the colonial framework as given for the most part and failed to subject it to the same scrutiny that was applied to those 'primitive' societies that were (in fact) a part of that colonial structure.

The questioning of the current themes and concerns of French ethnology that took place during the 1950s was stimulated firstly by influences from outside the discipline, through the analysis of the 'modern' sector and the consequences there of colonialism. This perspective made it possible to reformulate the approach to the study of 'traditional' societies, that is to say, to ethnology. Perhaps the best example of this theoretical development and of the work associated with it during the 1950s and early 1960s is that of Balandier;[88] the approach might be best termed 'the theory of de-colonisation'. Even with this major re-orientation in concerns and in theoretical approach the strength of the French traditions in ethnology and sociology is shown by the fact that many of the studies in this new perspective still concentrated on the ideological sphere: on messianism, syncretism and the new political 'ideologies' of independent ex-colonies. It was essentially a phenomenon of late colonialism, and, despite its introduction of history, its analysis of colonialism and of the concomitants of domination, it remained sceptical of the possible contribution of Marxism to the study of colonialism and imperialism. It was largely for this reason that the 'economic' remained subordinated to the 'political'.

After the earlier colonial ethnology (or rather the a-colonial ethnology) and after the sociology/ethnology of de-colonisation, there remained, inevitably, the problem of economic neo-colonialism. Recognition of this phenomenon was made possible by the existence and availability to scholars in the social sciences of a 'de-Stalinised' Marxism; of a 'new' Marxism conceived as a methodological and conceptual tool designed to investigate and analyse, not only the structures of capitalism but also lesser known or even unknown social structures, that is to say, the structures of pre-capitalist formations.

RE-THINKING MARXISM OR A 'NEW' MARXISM?

It is unlikely that any Marxist would disagree with Godelier's emphasis on the need 'to carry out a theoretical revolution in the humane sciences, a revolution that becomes daily more urgent if we are to rescue these sciences from the dead-ends of functionalist empiricism or the helplessness of structuralism in the face of history', nor with his suggestion that 'such a revolution must today proceed by way of reconstruction of these sciences on the basis of a Marxism that has been radically purged of all traces of vulgar materialism and dogmatism.'[89] But does this suggestion imply a need for a re-thinking of Marxism, or the construction of a fundamentally 'new' or 'neo-' Marxism, as some, particularly non-Marxists, have argued?

Both Ardener and Firth, for example, have suggested that the work of the French Marxists — Althusser, Godelier, Meillassoux and Terray — constitutes something essentially 'new'. Ardener describes the work of Louis Althusser, one of the most brilliant and influential of the French Marxists, as involving a 'modern re-thinking of Marx' and as constituting a 'new Marxism', which he contrasts with the 'old-style materialist' views of Marvin Harris; '. . . under Althusser', he suggests, 'the crude errors of Marxist materialism are averted' and he appears surprised 'that Althusser's[90] brilliance is satisfied with the limited ends of the Marxist problematic. . . .' Firth argues that many Marxists now recognise that much of Marx's theory in its literal form is outmoded, and, although he recognises that 'some of his major issues and his conclusions are still with us' and suggests that 'Marx's insights . . . embody propositions which must be taken for critical scrutiny into the body of our science', he is more interested in the recent and more 'sophisticated' work of those Marxists who reject the 'crude', 'older Marxism' and who are producing work that 'refreshingly puts Marx's thought in its proper light as material for scientific use'.[91] 'The work of these "cerebral" Marxists — some of it clearly revisionist — can be best exemplified from French anthropology, which has opened up problems of a highly theoretical order', for their approach 'is critical, of Marx as well as of others; concepts are reformulated in a lively systematic way'.[92]

More radical scholars have also identified a 'crisis in world Marxism' expressed in the 'growing variety of neo-Marxisms', and it has been asked 'how much further can Marxism be opened without itself undergoing a radical transformation?'.[93] Gouldner has drawn attention to the growing differentiation in interpretations of Marxism which he relates to the diversity of the national experiences and interests of Marxists in various cultures. Where, as in China, Cuba and Yugoslavia, they came to power largely by their own revolutionary efforts, with little or no Soviet aid, this is commonly taken as a basis for theorising that is independent of and divergent from the Soviet model. Also underlying the crisis of Marxism is the blunting of its own 'critical' impulse after it became the official theory and ideology of the Soviet State and of the mass communist parties of Western Europe.

Even avowed Marxists have sometimes adopted the use of the term 'neo-Marxist' 'as a useful and necessary term for distinguishing a sub-set of Marxist thought: namely, that which has attempted mainly since 1945 to come to terms with the now notorious paradox of Marxism's practical success in underdeveloped countries and its comparative failures in more developed ones'.[94] Foster-Carter, for example, distinguishes between a 'neo-' as against a 'palaeo-' Marxism: the former open-minded, viewing the world inductively and bringing in Marxian elements by way of explanation, the latter clinging dogmatically to a Marxist *Weltanschauung* and deducing scholastically from this what the world 'must be' like. He suggests that 'neo-' Marxism adopts a distinctive approach to a whole range of crucial problems: imperialism, nationalism, class, feudalism, 'the national bourgeoise', 'the petit bourgeoise', the proletariat, the 'lumpenproletariat', the peasantry, revolution, communism, 'self-transformation', relations between town and country, and ecology.[95]

While rejecting this extreme caricature and the suggestion that 'neo-Marxist' is a useful and necessary term, it is, nevertheless, essential to recognise that a number of major developments in world history, particularly since 1955-1956, have had a powerful effect on the directions taken by Marxist analysis and have contributed to the growth of concern in several areas relatively neglected or discussed in dogmatic terms by Marxists until the last twenty years. Three 'areas', especially, have been subjected to reconsideration and further investigation, largely as a result of these historical developments: (1) pre-capitalist formations and the various schema of social evolution, (2) the nature and role of the peasantry, and (3) relations between 'developed' and 'under-developed' countries in the context of colonialism and imperialism. These three 'areas' are distinguished as a matter of convenience but they are not distinct or discrete domains, even if there is often a tendency for certain scholars to concentrate their attentions on one 'area' at the expense of the others; they are inter-related and inter-penetrating and together constitute a significant portion of the total object of historical materialism. Two further developments in Marxist analysis, associated with the undoubted emergence of differing interpretations of Marxism, have been (4) detailed consideration of the role of the State under capitalism and socialism, and (5) a profound and self-conscious reconsideration of the works of Marx, and also of Engels and Lenin, focusing, in particular, on the elaboration of the relationship between science and ideology, on the one hand, and of the relationship between the Marxist science of history (historical materialism) and Marxist philosophy (dialectical materialism), on the other.

The 'area' that relates most centrally to the primary concerns of the authors representing in this collection is that of pre-capitalist formations; but, significantly, it has been argued that Marx's approach to pre-capitalist formations is a relatively superficial one. Meillassoux, for example, suggests that '. . . the main contribution of Marx and Engels to the study of pre-capitalist formations was to demonstrate their specificity and to stress the necessity of discovering the appropriate concepts needed for the analysis of their functioning. But besides some indications of these concepts, which allowed the elaboration of a sketchy and rather loose typology,

Marx did not try, as he did for capitalism, to find out the law of the inner functioning of pre-capitalist formations. Furthermore, except for the passage from feudalism to capitalism, Marx did not give any clue as to the transformation of the anterior formations. . .'.[96] He criticises those Marxists who seem to have followed Marx in the weakest area of his analysis and indulge in the endless reconstruction of a succession of hypothetical precapitalist formations, and suggests that the task of Marxism is elsewhere. 'It is to investigate along lines drawn by Marx in his most mature work, *Capital*, and not to dwell for ever on the draft of the *Grundrisse*, in spite of a constant tendency of Marxicologists to divert our attention to this early and unsatisfactory work'.[97] Others (e.g. Godelier), while agreeing with Meillassoux that it is of vital importance that Marxists carry out fieldwork on contemporary societies, would nevertheless argue that a reconsideration and analysis of what Hobsbawm has called Marx's 'most systematic attempt to grapple with the problem of historic evolution'[98] (i.e. the *Formen*), is a necessary and most productive piece of work.

In practice, research has been carried out in both directions over the last few years; in discussions of the general problems of historical periodisation and of specific pre-capitalist formations, particularly with reference to the 'Asiatic' mode of production, reintroduced into Marxist schema of social evolution after the death of Stalin,[99] and also in fieldwork and the discussion and criticism of methods and conclusions of fieldwork.[100]

Meillassoux has also argued that Marx's study of the contemporary period is almost entirely focused on the development of capitalist countries and that he pays little attention to the impact of this development on the colonised areas, or to the role played by the exploitation of the colonised countries in the growth and prosperity of capitalism.[101] Despite the work represented by the collection of writings *On Colonialism*, this is probably just, although the importance of Lenin's work on *Imperialism* should not be underestimated; but a considerable body of work in this 'area' has accumulated over the years (notably that of Amin, Baran, Emmanuel, Frank, Kemp, Magdoff and Sweezy) although much of it is highly controversial.[102] Here again, some of the French Marxists have made important contributions, in particular to the understanding of the effects of the development of capitalism particularly on the colonised and 'underdeveloped' areas of Africa.

The third 'area' that has recently been subjected to reconsideration and further investigation is that of the peasantry. Since the end of world war two the under-privileged rural majority have emerged not merely as the numerical majority of mankind but also as one of the major social and political forces in the world, particularly in the Third World. As a result of these developments social scientists in the West, Marxists included, have begun to rediscover the peasantry and to reconsider their social, political and economic status and their historical role. Marx and many of the early Marxists were often disparaging and negative on the subject of the historical role of the peasantry, seeing them as 'non-existent, historically speaking'.[103] The importance of the revolutionary practice of many peasant movements and of the revolutionary theoretical contributions of such major political figures as Mao Tse Tung, Ho Chi Minh, Kim Il Sung, Franz Fanon, 'Che' Guevara, Fidel Castro and Amilcar Cabral have obliged social scientists in the West to re-think the earlier formulations and to reconsider the 'peasant question' in the light of recent history. As yet, however, contemporary Western scholars, Marxists included, have made few significant theoretical contributions to the analysis of 'the peasantry'.

The consideration of the peasantry has tended to overlap with that of two other new 'areas', for while the peasantry may be considered, in the Marxist tradition of class analysis, as the suppressed and exploited producers of pre-capitalist society now constituting a sort of left-over from an earlier social formation and considered as such, it is also possible to consider the peasantry in the context of their transformation under the peripheral capitalism of the Third World and the process of class formation in contemporary Africa, Asia and Latin America. The work of most Marxists today, however, while showing some awareness of the dangers inherent in a split between the analysis of pre-capitalist formations and the analysis of the development of peripheral capitalism and the underdevelopment of the Third World, nevertheless tends often to favour one concentration at the expense of the other; most Marxist 'anthropologists' have so far favoured the former (pre-capitalist formations) and left the latter to 'sociologists' and 'economists'.

Whether there has or has not developed, since the early 1960s, a *fundamentally* 'new' Marxism, following an epistemological 'break' of the kind referred to by Althusser in his analysis of the work of Marx himself, is by no means clear and is, at the very least, arguable. What is abundantly clear, however, is that there is a real need to re-think and reconsider, making use of the impressive foundations and constructions already available, in order to develop and refine the existing body of Marxist theory. It is equally clear that this re-thinking is now taking place, with all the difficulties, false starts, controversy, misunderstandings and disagreements that this, of necessity, involves. This may be seen from the tremendous growth of Marxist literature and the very considerable number of scholars turning their attention to this task of re-thinking Marxism over the last few years. A great deal of the most important work has come from France.

MARXISM AND ANTHROPOLOGY IN FRANCE

Despite the long history of the diffusion of socialist and communist ideas in France, and despite the long-standing tradition of a powerful workers' movement, the recognition of Marxism as a theoretical instrument for social analysis is comparatively recent in France. This situation, at first sight paradoxical, is explained by three major factors: (1) the absence of a *theoretical* tradition associated with the French communist and workers' movement, in contrast with the German, Russian or Italian workers' movements, which had Marx and Engels, Kautsky, Rosa Luxemburg, Plekhanov, Lenin, Labriola and Gramsci;[104] (2) the importance of the Stalinist dogma, which was deep-rooted within the French Communist Party (P.C.F.) and, as a result, among the intellectuals, who were more or less committed to it and who were among those most involved in the diffusion of Marxist ideas — during the Stalinist period proper (1930-1956) there were no Marxists who were not members of the P.C.F.; and (3) the fundamental conservatism and mentalism of the French universities and the associated hostility towards sociology and ethnology, which remained relatively insignificant within the universities until as late as the 1950s. Indeed, it was really only in the latter part of the 1950s that this situation was transformed by the combination of a number of factors and Marxism could begin to penetrate the 'social sciences'.

Three major features characterised Marxist anthropology — in so far as it existed — in France before around 1960: (1) in the theoretical sphere it was dominated by the Stalinist schema of five inevitable stages of social evolution, and anthropology contented itself with the investigation of the first of these stages, 'primitive communalism'; (2) its approach placed almost exclusive emphasis on the 'material culture' of the social and economic formations considered, hence the technological, archaeological and crude ethnographic aspect of this kind of anthropology; and (3) the only 'valid' anthropology was that derived from the U.S.S.R., any other kind being considered idealist, reactionary and bourgeois. It was largely because of these characteristics that the majority of French anthropologists regarded 'Marxist anthropology' (to some extent correctly) as both mechanistic and Machiavellian.[105]

Marxist anthropology, in turn, considered the theoretical basis and methodology of mainstream French ethnology as questionable

and unsatisfactory. Thus Marxism, or at least Marxist
anthropology, remained essentially marginal to the broad trends in
the development of French ethnology, although one of the students
of the Institute of Ethnology who was to become the most prominent
and influential of French anthropologists, Claude Lévi-Strauss, was
himself deeply influenced by Marxism and has explicitly identified
Marx as the point of departure of his thought.[106] Any consideration
of the relationship between Marxism and anthropology in France,
or in any European country, must take heed of the fundamental
'break' between the Stalinist and the post-Stalinist situation, and
recognise that this break was not just a matter of chronology. During
the late 1950s and early 1960s the situation of Marxist thought
underwent considerable change. At the theoretical level the work of
Jean-Paul Sartre should certainly be mentioned, although his
questions were possibly more productive than his answers;[107] but it
was above all the reconstruction and renaissance initiated and
brought about by Louis Althusser and his colleagues which opened
up genuine theoretical alternatives to the previous dogma.[108]
Marxism now began to acquire the full status of an instrument of
analysis. The theoretical developments just mentioned
corresponded to major political changes in the world, of which the
growth of national liberation movements and the associated
struggles were among the most important, which had a major impact
on the development of thought in France. Particularly important
was the war in Algeria between 1954 and 1962. Finally, the rapid
development of ethnology as a discipline, its growing institutional
respectability and its intellectual prestige among students and non-
ethnologists provided Marxists and Marxism with new possibilities
of intervention in the mainstream of French ethnology. The
situation of Marxism with respect to anthropology was no longer as
it had been during the preceding period. The U.S.S.R. (and therefore
its Marxism and its ethnology) was no longer the sole and obligatory
point of reference; Marxism had become polycentric. Discussion
began among Marxists with regard to the lines of evolution
(unilinear or multilinear?) that human society had taken and the
debate on the 'Asiatic' mode of production, which began in the late
1950s and continued during the 1960s, served to crystallise these
questions.[109] New problems also preoccupied the French
ethnologists: myths, political organisation, pre-colonial history,
economic and demographic transformations. In the case of some
Marxists fieldwork in Africa or elsewhere provided an important
source of inspiration for the elaboration or reformulation of certain
Marxist concepts.

The elaboration of a Marxist problematic was, at first, the work of a few isolated scholars; and even today it remains the preoccupation of a small minority and involves individuals of varying persuasions. The theoretical divergences between Marxists are almost as numerous as those which exist between Marxists and non-Marxists. It is also, unfortunately, true that many call themselves 'Marxists' for reasons of fashion (much as others refer to themselves as 'structuralists') without even having read Marx. It is therefore true to say that there is not, in effect, a 'school' of Marxist anthropology in France, but rather a number of scholars who claim kinship with Marxism. This observation could, in fact, be applied to the other human sciences and it is important that we do not create a myth; there is merely a tendency or a 'current' in the professional and institutional domain of anthropology which considers itself Marxist, not a theoretical 'school', like functionalism, culturalism and structuralism.

The elaboration of the problematic ranges over the traditional fields of anthropology and sociology, concerned on the one hand with the explanation of 'traditional' social structures in Marxist terms (e.g. mode of production, social inequality, exploitation, ideological function, etc.), and on the other with the definition of the inegalitarian relations of the colonial situation in the terminology of imperialism, as a global system of economic and political exploitation. In so far as the development of Marxist thinking itself has been, and remains, the driving force behind this elaboration, the latter has suffered the effects of a number of general divergences of an ideological, political or truly theoretical nature. Thus, the theoretical reflections of Althusser, Godelier and Bettelheim have had more or less contradictory effects. In any case, it is impossible to understand the significance of certain divergences, apparently of a purely scientific or theoretical nature, unless one takes into consideration the far larger discussion taking place among Marxists in general.[110]

It is unfortunate that the 'workers'' dogmatism of the Stalinist period has been followed by a kind of university dogmatism. The success of Marxism in anthropology has stemmed partly from the fact that the societies labelled 'primitive' were a virgin field for Marxist theoreticians. Their university experience led them to treat both the Marxist knowledge acquired and the anthropological practice itself in a bookish fashion. The fact that the word of the 'founders' (Marx and Engels) was weak in this area meant that divergent elaborations developed and different interpretations became more and more refined. This theoretical development has certain definite limitations. In particular, it is confined to the university and to anthropology and is not really associated with any political practice, either in the field or in the professional institutions within which the various scholars work.

Chronologically it was Suret-Canale who initiated new Marxist research in Africa. This was in 1958, and, since that time, he has devoted himself largely to the study of African colonial and post-colonial history and to the question of the applicability of the concept of 'Asiatic' mode of production to social formations in Black Africa, although he has also considered the relationship between structuralism and economic anthropology.[111] But a Marxist 'economic anthropology' really began with the work of Claude Meillassoux.[112] At much the same time, but from a somewhat different perspective, Maurice Godelier also began to apply himself to the elaboration of a Marxist 'economic anthropology'.[113] Since 1965 a number of scholars has joined this new tendency or 'trend'.[114]

The penetration of Marxism into ethnology in France has produced an 'economic anthropology' quite naturally. The lack of anything that could be termed 'economic anthropology' was a striking lacuna in the work of French ethnology, which had never been systematically affected by the dominant themes of British functionalist pragmatism nor those of the American neo-evolutionary 'cultural ecology'. The growing political and subsequently theoretical sensitivity of the younger scholars of the decade 1956-65 towards Marxism led to the consideration of the whole subject matter of ethnology from the direction of this neglected field; to the analysis of the structures of production, distribution and consumption and their links with the social and cultural totality. The use of the term 'economic anthropology', both among Marxists and non-Marxists, derives in part from the simple adoption of the English term and in part from a desire (often unconscious) to break with the old ethnology which claimed no theoretical concern, or problematic. The adoption of the term 'anthropology' rather than 'ethnology' by Lévi-Strauss has facilitated this usage and equally that of 'political anthropology'.[115] Finally, it is felt to imply a comparative approach — something that Godelier has emphasised often.

'Economic anthropology' in France is seen, above all, as involving the systematic investigation through fieldwork of certain social relations previously virtually ignored. Of course, earlier professional studies, and those by colonial administrators, contained some description of 'economic activities' and of the material and spatial aspects of the 'way of life' (*genre de vie*). Indeed, this tendency is still found, to a certain extent, in some geographical works, which describe the factors of production and their use; but their contribution is largely from the point of view of land tenure and agricultural development.[116] But these kinds of studies were still very superficial; they were not concerned to discover the structure of production and still less to analyse its correspondence with the total sum of social relations, in particular from the perspective of 'determination in the last instance'.[117]

This theoretical systematisation introduced by the Marxist scholars did not question, at first, the empirical division of social reality. Thus, the 'ethnic' framework finds itself quite naturally confirmed by the approach of the 'economic anthropologist': the Guro, the Punu, the Soninke and the Baruya are still the object of monographs which take for granted the 'ethnic group' or 'tribe' and yet are primarily 'economic'. Marxist anthropologists have not yet fully analysed the 'ethnic group' or 'tribe' or compared it with the concepts of mode of production, or social and economic formation, although Godelier has made a start on it.[118]

In fact the research reveals at least three objects each of which implies distinct, or convergent, lines of theoretical reflection. The first level is that of the definition and description of the different economic structures and sets of economic relations. The questions asked here are those identified by Frankenberg[119] as the 'key questions': how are the units of production constituted? What is the nature and form of work? Is its organisation associated with relations of hierarchy, subordination, co-operation or exploitation? How are products distributed and consumed? One leads from here into forms of non-market exchange, the role of reciprocity and of markets. To ask these new questions is also to envisage 'primitive' social relations in a new fashion also. For Marxist 'economic anthropology' finds itself obliged to investigate not only 'economic' relations and structures, but also those of kinship, of politics and even of ideology. The analysis of units of production, or redistribution of products and of relations in work leads inevitably to a consideration of relations between seniors and juniors, of matrimonial exchanges (involving marriage settlements — dowry and brideprice — and surplus) and of the internal organisation of family units. At the village or tribal level the same investigator confronts a whole series of political and religious questions. Is there or is there not payment of tribute to higher social strata or to other social entities? Is there any political control over exchanges? does social stratification define groups of producers and of non-producers — holders of rare goods and slaves? To what extent do states of peace and of war also involve economic relations — predatory economies and long-distance trade of complementary products? How much does the operation of religious or political institutions actually 'cost'? The 'economic anthropologist' ends by discovering social groups with predominantly economic functions, like merchants or casted producers.

But for the Marxist anthropologist this set of questions and problems makes sense only in the context of a theory which enables him to discover the logic and coherence of these economic groups and economic structures. Two complementary approaches are available to him: the reconstruction of the 'primitive' economy and the identification of the effects of colonialism and of capitalism on this economy. It is at this point that the different interpretations arise, for it is necessary not merely to synthesise the data but also to define theoretically the mode or modes of production involved and the ways in which they are articulated. It is around these themes that the diversity and differences among the French Marxist 'economic anthropologists' develop; but it is here too that the most fruitful work may be done. An example is the debate initiated more or less by Terray's dissection of Meillassoux's work on the Guro which is concerned with important questions of method and interpretation. This debate has remained largely informal but has become quite heated at times and the direct or indirect contributions to the argument have given Marxist 'economic anthropology' the appearance, for the moment, of a battlefield.[120]

PRESENT PROBLEMS AND THE COMING 'CRISIS IN MARXIST ECONOMIC ANTHROPOLOGY'

A central problem for Marxist 'economic anthropology', and one which has also occupied non-Marxist social anthropologists,[121] is that of the role of kinship in 'primitive' society. It is here, perhaps more than anywhere else, that the different approaches and interpretations arise. For the Marxist the concern with kinship follows from the question: how can one define the mode(s) of production of a 'primitive' society? The systematisation of a forgotten remark of Marx's, notably by Althusser, indicates one type of reply: it is necessary to distinguish between *determination in the last instance by the economy* and the *dominance of other social relations (or instances)*. Thus, just because kinship *dominates* the reproduction of social relations this does not mean that the economy is not *determinant*. From this point of departure develop several different positions, which differ, not over the principle, which is generally accepted, but over the precise application of this principle.

Godelier, for example, observes that, in an 'archaic' society, 'the kinship relations of individuals and groups seem to be the source of their rights to use land and products, their obligation to work for others, to make gifts and so on. They likewise seem to be the source of the political and religious functions exercised by certain individuals within the group. In a society like this, kinship relations dominate social life. How, then, are we to understand the "ultimately" determining role of the economy?'[122] He answers this by suggesting that 'we need, in fact, to analyse more closely these kinship relations, for if they determine the places occupied by individuals in production, their rights to land and goods, their obligations in respect of work and gifts, etc., then they *function* as production-relations, just as they function as political, religious, etc., relations. Kinship is thus here *both* infrastructure and superstructure. Accordingly, the correspondence between productive forces and production-relations is *at the same time* correspondence between economy and kinship.'[123]

For Terray things are more complex and he argues that 'it is inadequate to say that kinship relations "function as relations of production, in the same way as political, religious, etc., relations function" and that "kinship is thus both infrastructure and superstructure". To stop at this is simply to apply new terms to that functional polyvalence of "primitive" institutions which has long been known to classical anthropology, and in fact to thus adopt the structuralist position.'[124] He suggests that 'concrete kinship relations must be seen as the product of a triple determination operating on a given substratum' and as 'the complex result of the combined effect of the economic, juridico-political and ideological instances of the mode of production.'[125] What then, he asks, is the correct status of kinship in such a situation? It is a typical case of super-determination (or over-determination) as defined by Althusser: 'super-determination is used to designate . . . the conjunction of different determinations in a single object, and the variations in dominance between the determinations within their very conjunction.'[126]

Meillassoux sees relations of production as 'built on the basis of genealogical kinship relations, which are themselves subject to constant modification and renewal. The kinship relations revealed to us are the result of these changes.'[127] In his view the lineage system, of the Guro, for example, 'realises' the relations of production and the superstructural relations associated with simple co-operation, but kinship relations, as concrete relations, are an expression of relations of production. He also discovers, in the fact that, in an agricultural society, the workers of one agricultural cycle are indebted for seeds and food to the workers of the previous one, thus providing a cyclical renewal of the relations of production over time (and, eventually, from generation to generation), the material and temporal bases of the emergence of the family as a productive and cohesive unit and of kinship as an ideology.[128] He also points out that in such societies social control of the community over its members is realised through control over subsistence and that control over subsistence is not control of the means of production but of the means of physiological reproduction — in other words control over women. Thus, control of women is the central pre-condition in 'self-sustaining social and economic formations' for the reproduction of social relations, although relations between seniors and juniors reflect this central precondition. Rey, on the other hand, argues that the central relationship in such societies is the relationship of exploitation that exists between seniors and juniors; for him, 'kinship is merely a light veil which hides, but may easily be made to reveal, the process by which the dominant class brings the producers under its control'.[129]

This ultra-schematic presentation serves to demonstrate the difficulties experienced by the Marxist anthropologists in reaching a common position on this fundamental problem. In fact, besides the theoretical divergencies there are several additional objective reasons for this debate — whether they are made explicit or not. These include an unwarranted degree of theorisation based on a particular system of kinship (and one that is sometimes insufficiently analysed itself), occasional confusion between the structure of kinship as such and the concrete relations of kinship realised in the process or production and other economic processes, and the allocation of a dominant position to descent, alliance, residential unity, circuits of matrimonial exchange, and so on, depending on the particular case from which theorisation takes off. The characterisation of the mode of production depends, obviously, on the theoretical direction or orientation adopted, but also it depends on the type of society analysed. One thing is certain, and that is that 'primitive communalism' is no more than a 'marginal' mode of production within the series of pre-capitalist modes of production identified: cynegetic (or hunting) mode of production, lineage and segmentary mode of production, tribal-village mode of production, tributary mode of production, 'Asiatic' mode of production and 'African' mode of production. This list has no necessary 'evolutionary' significance; it is merely a list of modes of production identified by French Marxist anthropologists — most of the labels are in fact preliminary and rather crudely empirical. Finally, it is necessary to note that the identification of these modes of production is based very largely on fieldwork in Africa alone, the predominance of Africanists among Marxist anthropologists merely reflecting the state of affairs in French ethnology generally.

This research into modes of production and their identification and characterisation — which is not, incidentally, taken up by all (Godelier, for example, whether rightly or wrongly, has not identified the dominant mode of production among the Mbuti or the Baruya or assigned it a label) — is made more complicated by the fact of the history of colonial and capitalist transformations. The precise nature of these transformations constitutes another problem for Marxists.

As a general rule, their kind of anthropology has been able to avoid the trap of 'external dynamism', or what Frankenberg refers to as 'exogenous comparative statics' and 'exogenous dynamics'.[130] This has enabled it to construct, albeit in a somewhat unsatisfactory fashion, the articulation both between the various pre-capitalist modes of production themselves, and between them and the peripheral capitalism that has developed in Africa, as elsewhere in the Third World.[131] The problematic of the articulation of pre-capitalist and capitalist modes of production involves the elaboration of a new set of concepts centred on the category of 'social and economic formations'.[132] Godelier, Rey and Terray have all attempted to contribute to this elaboration in very different fashions, Terray by applying it to the Guro formation as described by Meillassoux, Rey with respect to the development of colonial capitalism in the Congo and Godelier to the historical example of the Incas.[133] But this 'area' of theoretical work has received less attention so far than the previous one. One further crucial problem that has received relatively little attention from French Marxist 'economic anthropology' is that of the determination of the level of productive forces and of the precise correspondence between the forces of production and the relations of production that constitutes a determinate mode of production or modes of production.

How can one summarise the present state of French Marxist 'economic anthropology'? It has clearly come to the end of a period of preliminary 'breaking ground', for, whatever his theoretical orientation — and therefore the state of his agreements and disagreements with others — each scholar has identified, more or less, the dead-ends and the impasses — the empirical and theoretical constraints peculiar to a Marxist anthropology. That a certain distinct phase has been completed is manifest in a number of different ways. Firstly, there is widespread recognition in French ethnology, or anthropology, of a domain defined as 'economic'. Economic anthropology has become a legitimate concern, or field, for non-Marxists and even for non-anthropologists. This development and the corresponding increase in the range of information analysed cannot but be helpful in the refinement and de-dogmatisation of earlier approaches. The development of economic anthropology has also been, and will continue to be, associated with the development of Marxism within anthropology, for to choose to work in the field of economic anthropology in France is now tantamount to choosing to acquire a working understanding of Marxism. Secondly, there are emerging new concerns and theoretical pre-occupations among Marxists, which direct work towards new problems, reflected in the growing interest in the nature and role of superstructures, including ideology and politics, on the one hand, and in the significance and the effects of neo-colonial and imperialist domination, including the development of social classes and the nature of the State, on the other.

The development of new theoretical concerns and the enlargement of the domain of analysis is precipitating a two-fold crisis in Marxist economic anthropology. Firstly, the potential split between those most concerned with pre-capitalist formations and those concerned with the recent and contemporary transformation of these pre-capitalist formations under capitalism (colonial and imperialist) and with the global system of domination associated with 'development' and 'underdevelopment' is becoming more apparent as a threat. Secondly, it raises a fundamental, and related question, that has been largely avoided by French Marxist anthropologists until recently: is it possible to speak, as a Marxist, of 'economic anthropology'?[134] Is it possible, in other words, to construct an empirical domain of this kind, given the theoretical perspective of Marxism? Even more generally, it is now being asked, whether it could ever be possible to elaborate a 'Marxist anthropology' in the strict sense of the term. To agree would be to accept the disciplinary division traditional in the social and historical sciences; but this has no theoretical validity for an approach based on historical materialism. In a recent work, Godelier has tried to reply to the question, 'is an economic anthropology possible?'; and he concludes that 'it is no longer possible to close in on oneself, to constitute, in an autonomous, fetishised domain, the analysis of economic relations and economic systems. It is not therefore possible, in the Marxist perspective which we adopt, to find place for what we generally understand by economic anthropology, whether it be formalist or substantivist. The task of discovering, by a process of thought, the modes of production which have developed, and are still developing, during the course of history, is both *more* and *something other* than that of constructing an economic anthropology, or any other discipline with a similar label'.[135]

In this way the holistic approach of Marxism is maintained. If it continues merely to fill in the gaps left by the mainstream of traditional anthropology Marxism runs the risk of being allocated, as its theoretical object, merely the explanation of 'the economic', ignored until recently for ideological reasons. However, in developing, first of all, a Marxist 'economic anthropology' the French Marxists have made it possible to establish the fundamental conditions for a systematic and global analysis of elementary pre-capitalist formations and their transformation within the theoretical tradition of historical materialism. It is this project — the only one really agreed on by all — that will determine, to an ever greater extent, the directions of French anthropology and sociology in the decade to come.

NOTES

1. Editorial, *Economy and Society*, vol. 1, no. 1, 1972, pp. iii-iv
2. Hunt, E. K. and Schwartz, J. G. (eds), *A Critique of Economic Theory*, Penguin, London, 1972
3. *Ibid.*, p. 32-3
4. Gouldner, A. *The Coming Crisis of Western Sociology*, Heinemann, London, 1972, p. 512
5. Shaw, M., 'The coming crisis of radical sociology' in Blackburn, R. (ed), *Ideology in Social Science: readings in critical social theory*, Fontana, London, 1972
6. Banaji, J., 'The crisis of British anthropology', *New Left Review*, 64, November-December, 1970, p. 72
7. *Ibid.*, p. 85
8. *Ibid.*, p. 71
9. Ardener, E., 'The new anthropology and its critics', *Man* (NS), vol. 6, no. 3, September 1971, p. 449
10. *Ibid.*, p. 464
11. *Ibid.*, pp. 460-1
12. *op. cit.*, Economy and Society, 1972
13. Godelier, M., 'Structure and contradiction in *Capital*', in Blackburn (ed), 1972, *op. cit.*, p. 336 (originally published in 1966 as 'Système, structure et contradiction dans le Capital', *Les Temps Modernes*, October-November)
14. *Ibid.*, pp. 340-1
15. Banaji, 1970, *op. cit.*, p. 83
16. *Ibid.*, p. 84
17. Godelier, M., *Rationality and Irrationality in Economics*, New Left Books, London, 1972, Foreword.
18. Lévi-Strauss, C., *The Savage Mind*, Weidenfeld and Nicolson, London, 1966, p. 117
19. *Ibid.*, pp. 130-1
20. Godelier, 1972, *op. cit.*, pp. xxxvi-xxxvii
21. *Ibid.*, p. xlii
22. Banaji, 1970, *op. cit.*, p. 85; Worsley, P. M., 'The End of Anthropology?', paper prepared for the Sixth World Congress of Sociology, 1966
23. Terray, E., *Marxism and 'Primitive' Societies*, Monthly Review Press, New York and London, 1972, p. 184; see also Firth, R., 'The Sceptical Anthropologist? Social anthropology and Marxist views on society', *Proceedings of the British Academy*, vol. lviii, 1972, p. 32

24. See Select Bibliography and the journals mentioned in the second part of the preface.

25. Firth, 1972, *op. cit.*, p. 5

26. Frankenberg, R., 'Where speculation ends? Marxism and the social anthropology of real life', paper presented to the 1973 Conference of the Association of Social Anthropologists, pp. 1–15

27. Firth, 1972, *op. cit.*, pp. 5–8

28. Worsley, P. M., 'The kinship system of the Tallensi: a revaluation', *Journal of the Royal Anthropological Institute*, vol. 86, part 1, January-June, 1956

29. Frankenberg, R., *Communities in Britain: social life in town and country*, Penguin, London, 1966; Worsley, P. M., *The Third World*, Weidenfeld and Nicolson, London, 1967; Worsley, P. M., *The Trumpet Shall Sound: a study of 'cargo' cults in Melanesia*, Paladin, Granada Publishers, London, 1970

30. Frank, A. G., 'Functionalism and Dialectics', in his *Latin America: Underdevelopment or Revolution*, Monthly Review Press, New York and London, 1969, p. 103

31. Leach, E. R., *Political Systems of Highland Burma*, G. Bell and Sons, London, 1964, p. 141

32. Godelier, 1972, *op. cit.*, p. xxxi

33. Lloyd, P. C., *Africa in Social Change*, Penguin, London, 1967; Lloyd, P. C., 'Conflict, Theory and Yoruba Kingdoms', in Lewis, I. M. (ed), *History and Social Anthropology*, Association of Social Anthropologists Monograph no. 7, 1968

34. Firth, R., 'Social Organization and Social Change', Presidential address to the R.A.I., *Journal of the Royal Anthropological Institute*, vol. 84, pp. 1–20

35. Firth, R., *Essays on Social Organization and Values*, Athlone Press, London, 1964, p. 57

36. Firth, R., 'Comment on "dynamic theory" in Social Anthropology', in Firth, 1964, *op. cit.*, p. 19

37. Firth, 1964, *op. cit.*, pp. 21–2

38. Goody, J., *Technology, Tradition and the State in Africa*, International African Institute, Oxford University Press, London, 1971

39. Meillassoux, C., review of Goody, 1971, *op. cit.*, in *Africa*, vol. xli, no. 4, 1971

40. Frankenberg, 1973, *op. cit.*, p. 2

41. Bernal, J. D., *Science in History*, 4 vols., Penguin, London, 1969

42. Giddens, A., *Capitalism and Modern Social Theory: an analysis of the writings of Marx, Durkheim and Max Weber*, Cambridge University Press, London, 1971, p. 185

43. Bernal, 1969, *op. cit.*, p. 1095

44. *Ibid.*, p. 1098

45. Goddard, D., 'Anthropology: the limits of functionalism', in Blackburn (ed), 1972, *op. cit.*

46. E.g. Firth, 1972, *op. cit.*, p. 26; Stauder, J., 'The Function of Functionalism: the adaptation of British social anthropology to British colonialism in Africa', paper presented at meetings of the American Anthropological Association in New York, November, 1971

47. Gellner, E. A., 'Sociology and Social Anthropology', ms., March 1966, pp. 34–6

48. At the 1973 Association of Social Anthropologists Conference on 'new directions in social anthropology' there was a session on 'Marxism', but only three papers were presented by British anthropologists.

49. Chomsky, N., *American Power and the New Mandarins*, Penguin, London, 1969; Roszak, T. (ed), *The Dissenting Academy: essays criticizing the teaching of the humanities in American universities*, Penguin, London, 1969

50. Gough, K., 'Anthropology and Imperialism', *Monthly Review*, April 1968;

Gough, K., 'Anthropology, Child of Imperialism', *School of Oriental and African Studies, Third World Study Group*, 1968; Gough, K., 'New Proposals for Anthropologists', *Current Anthropology*, 'social responsbilities' symposium, May 1968; Gough in Roszak (ed), 1969, *op. cit.*

51. Gough, K., 'Anthropology, Child of Imperialism', *op. cit.*, p. 8.
52. Harris, M., *The Rise of Anthropological Theory: a history of theories of culture*, Routledge and Kegan Paul, London, p. 228
53. Wright Mills, C., *The Marxists*, Dell Publishing Co., New York, 1962, p. 11
54. Engels, F., *The Origin of the Family, Private Property and the State*, Lawrence and Wishart, 1972, p. 71
55. Harris, 1969, *op. cit.*, p. 249
56. Herskovits, M., *Franz Boas*, Scribner, New York, 1953, p. 118
57. Polanyi, K., *The Great Transformation*, Rinehart, New York, 1944; Polanyi, K., Arensberg, M., and Pearson, W. H. (eds), *Trade and Market in the Early Empires*, The Free Press, Glencoe, 1957; Polanyi, K., *Dahomey and the Slave Trade*, American Ethnological Society series, University of Washington Press, Seattle, 1966. Also see Dalton, G. (ed), *Primitive, Archaic and Modern Economies: essays of Karl Polanyi*, Doubleday and Co., New York, 1968
58. E.g. Meillassoux, C., 'From reproduction to production', *Economy and Society*, vol. 1, no. 1, 1972, p. 96. Also see references in this collection.
59. Harris, 1969, *op. cit.*, p. 606
60. Keller, A. G., *Societal Evolution: a study of the evolutionary basis of the science of society*, Macmillan, New York, 1931, pp. 249–50
61. Cf. Barnes, H. E. in Dole, G. and Carneiro, R. (eds), *Essays in the Science of Culture*, T. Crowell, New York, 1960, Foreword.
62. Cf. Steward, J., *Theory of Culture Change*, University of Illinois Press, Urbana, 1955
63. Wright Mills, 1962, *op. cit.*, p. 22. For an insight into this question see the unpleasant debate between Betty Meggers, Morris Opler and Marvin Harris — Harris' comments in Harris, 1969, *op. cit.*, pp. 637–40
64. Cf. Cruise O'Brien, D., 'Modernization, Order, and the Erosion of a Democratic Ideal: American Political Science, 1960-1970', *Journal of Development Studies*, vol. 8, no. 4, 1972
65. Leacock, E. B. in Engels, 1972, *op. cit.*, pp. 17–8 (Introduction)
66. Leacock, E. B., 'Morgan and Materialism: a reply to Professor Opler', *Current Anthropology*, vol. 5, no. 2, 1964, pp. 109–10; Leacock, 1972, *op. cit.*, pp. 61–6 (where she criticises Marvin Harris' *Rise in Anthropological Theory*)
67. Sahlins, M., *Stone Age Economics*, Aldin-Atherton, New York, 1972. Sahlins, although not a Marxist, has drawn on Marxist theory increasingly over the last few years, particularly as a result of his period of teaching in Paris between 1967-1969
68. Firth, 1972, *op. cit.*, p. 25; pers. comm. Faris, J., September 1973; cf. details of symposia in A.A.A. annual meetings programmes: 13 papers in two sessions (science, history and materialism; anthropology and imperialism) in 1971; 26 papers and one general discussion in five sessions (anti-imperialist teaching; contemporary political struggles of tribal peoples: divide and rule — racism, sexism, etc.; critique of theory; analyses of imperialism) in 1972
69. Lee, R. B., 'Notes on the prehistory of the ARPA', *ARPA Newsletter*, no. 1, November 1972
70. Balandier, G., 'Tendances de l'ethnologie française', *Cahiers Internationaux de Sociologie*, vol. xxvii, 1959; Balandier, G., 'The French tradition of African research', *Human Organisation*, vol. 19, 1960; Lévi-Strauss, C., 'French sociology', in Gurvitch, G. and Moore, W. (eds), *Twentieth Century Sociology*, The Philosophical Library, New York, 1945; Mauss, M., 'L'ethnographie en

France et à l'étranger', *La Revue de Paris*, September-October, 1913; Mercier, P., *Histoire de l'Anthropologie*, Paris, 1966; Poirier, J., *Histoire de l'Ethnologie*, Paris, 1969

71. E.g. the ethnography of North Africa around the turn of the century and later, cf. Montagne, R., *The Berbers: their social and political organisation*, Frank Cass, London, 1973, Introduction by Seddon, D.

72. Titles of books by Durkheim, Mauss and Lévy-Bruhl respectively.

73. Cf. Mauss, M., *The Gift*, Cohen and West, London, 1970, p. vii (Introduction)

74. Lévi-Strauss, 1945, *op. cit.*, p. 522

75. Mauss, 1913, *op. cit.*, p. 834

76. '(The expressive totality) presupposes in principle the whole in question to be reducible to an *inner essence*, of which the elements of the whole are then no more than the phenomenal forms of expression, the inner principle of the essence being present at each point in the whole, such that at each moment it is possible to write the immediately adequate equation: such and such an element (economic, political legal, literary, religious, etc. in Hegel) = the inner essence of the whole.' Althusser, L. and Balibar, E., *Reading Capital*, New Left Books, London, 1970, pp. 186-7

77. Mauss, 1970, *op. cit.*, p. 1

78. Bender, 1965, 'The Development of French Anthropology', *Journal of the History of the Behavioural Sciences*, vol. 1, pp. 139-151, p. 144-5; Lévi-Strauss, 1945, *op. cit.*

79. Rivet, P., *L'Espèce Humaine*, vol. vii, *Encyclopédie Français*, Librairie Larousse, Paris, 1936, 08-2

80. Mauss taught a course in ethnographic field methods at the Institute of Ethnology between 1926 and 1929. Cf. Mauss, M., *Manuel d'Ethnographie*, Payot, Paris, 1947

81. Lévi-Strauss, 1945, *op. cit.*, p. 522

82. Although much has been written about the difference between the British and the French systems of colonial rule and the importance of ethnographic data for the system usually associated exclusively with the British — Indirect Rule — the French colonial administration was often equally as concerned as the British to obtain accurate and useful information about the peoples under colonial rule. Indirect Rule was a feature of French colonial rule at several times in different territories. Cf. Montagne, R., 1973, *op. cit.*, Introduction.

83. Griaule, M., 'Jeux Dogons', *Travaux et Mémoires de l'Institut d'Ethnologie*, vol. 32, 1938, p. vii

84. Cf. Lettens, D., *Mystagogie et Mystification. Evolution de l'oeuvre de Marcel Griaule*, Presses Lavigerie, Bujumbura, 1971; also Copans, J. discussion in *Cahiers d'Etudes Africaines*, vol. xiii, no. 49, 1973

85. E.g. Montagne, R., 1973, *op. cit.*

86. Cf. Durkheim, E., *The Rules of the Sociological Method*, Free Press, New York, 1938

87. Lévi-Strauss, C., *The Savage Mind*, Weidenfeld and Nicolson, London, 1966; Lévi-Strauss, C., *Totemism*, Merlin Press, London, 1964
Also cf. Durkheim and Mauss, *Primitive Classification*, Routledge, London, 1963

88. Balandier, G., *Sociologie des Brazzavilles noires*, Paris, 1955; Balandier, G., *Sociologie actuelle de l'Afrique noire*, Paris, 1955; Balandier, G., *Sens et Puissance*, Paris, 1971

89. Godelier, 1972, *op. cit.*, pp. xii-xiii

90. Ardener, 1971, *op. cit.*, pp. 464-5

91. Firth, 1972, *op. cit.*, pp. 38-39

92. *Ibid.*, p. 32

93. Gouldner, 1972, *op. cit.*, pp. 450–1
94. Foster-Carter, A., 'Neo-Marxist approaches to development and under-development', paper presented at the British Sociological Association Conference on Sociology and Development, York, 1972, p. 1
95. *Ibid.*, pp. 13–24
96. Meillassoux, C., 1972, *op. cit.*, p. 97
97. *Ibid.*, p. 98
98. Hobsbawm, E., in Marx, K., *Pre-Capitalist Economic Formations* Lawrence and Wishart, 1969, p. 10 (Introduction)
99. Cf. *Sur le 'Mode de Production asiatique'*, C.E.R.M., Editions Sociales, Paris, 1969
100. E.g. Terray, E., *Marxism and 'Primitive Societies'*, Monthly Review Press, 1972, pp. 95–186; Rey, P.Ph., *Colonialisme, néo-colonialisme et transition au capitalisme*, Maspero, Paris, 1971, pp. 32–69
101. Meillassoux, 1972, *op. cit.*, p. 97
102. E.g. Frank, A. G., 'The myth of feudalism in Brazilian agriculture', in Frank, 1969, *op. cit.*, and Laclau, E., 'Feudalism and capitalism in Latin America', *New Left Review*, 67, 1971; also Emmanuel, A., *Unequal Exchange: a study of the imperialism of trade*, New Left Books, London, 1972 and Pilling, G., 'Imperialism, trade and 'unequal exchange': the work of Aghiri Emmanuel', *Economy and Society*, vol. 2, no. 2, 1973
103. Cf. Mitrany, D., *Marx against the Peasant*, Collier, London, 1961
104. Cf. Althusser, L., *For Marx*, Penguin Books, London, 1969, Introduction
105. The debate between Claude Lévi-Strauss and Maxime Rodinson has become notorious in this regard. Cf. Lévi-Strauss, C., *Structural Anthropology*, Basic Books, New York, 1963.
106. Lévi-Strauss, C., 1966, *op. cit.*, final chapter.
107. Sartre, J.-P., *Critique de la Raison Dialectique*, Gallimard, Paris, 1960
108. Althusser, L., 1969, *op. cit.*; Althusser, L., and Balibar, E., *Reading Capital,* New Left Books, London, 1970; Althusser, L., *Lenin and Philosophy and Other Essays*, New Left Books, London, 1971
109. Cf. Suret-Canale, J., *Afrique noire*, Editions Sociales, Paris, 1958, vol. 1, p. 94; Tokei, F., 'Les conditions de la propriété foncière dans la Chine de l'époque des Tcheou', *Actes de l'Académie des Sciences hongroises*, vol. vi, nos. 3–4, 1958. Cf. also the journal *La Pensée*, between 1960 and 1968 for discussions of the 'Asiatic' mode of production.
110. It is, for example, by no means irrelevant that Jean Suret-Canale was a member of the central committee of the PCF until December 1972 but is so no longer; that Emmanuel Terray supported the Maoist tendency of the PSU but has recently left to work with an autonomous Maoist group; and that Claude Meillassoux has followed neither of these two directions.
111. Suret-Canale, J., *Afrique noire occidentale et centrale*, Editions Sociales, Paris, 1961 (2nd ed); Suret-Canale, J., *Afrique noire occidentale et centrale: l'ère coloniale*, Editions Sociales, Paris, 1964; Suret-Canel, J., 'Les sociétés traditionelles d'Afrique et le mode de production asiatique', *La Pensée*, no. 117, October 1964; Suret-Canale, J., 'Sur la notion marxiste de "mode de production asiatique" '. *Cahiers de communisme*, March, 1966; Suret-Canale, J., 'Problèmes théoriques de l'étude des premières sociétés de classes', *Recherches Internationales*, 57–58, 1967; Suret-Canale, J., 'Structuralisme et anthropologie économique', *La Pensée*, no. 135, 1967; Suret-Canale, J., 'Les sociétés traditionelles d'Afrique et le mode de production asiatique', in *Sur le 'mode de production asiatique'*, C.E.R.M., Editions Sociales, Paris, 1969; Suret-Canale, J., *Afrique noire occidentale et centrale: de la colonisation aux indépendances*, Editions Sociales, Paris, 1972

112. Meillassoux, C., 'Essai d'interprétation du phénomène économique dans les sociétés traditionnelles d'autosubsistance', *Cahiers d'Etudes Africaines*, 4, 1960; Meillassoux, C., 'Social and economic factors affecting markets in Guro land', in Bohannan and Dalton, (eds), *Markets in Africa*, Northwestern University Press, 1962; Meillassoux, C., *Anthropologie économique des Gouro de Côte d'Ivoire: de l'économie d'autosubsistance à l'agriculture commerciale*, Mouton, Paris, 1964

113. Godelier, M., 'Les structures de la méthode du *Capital* de Karl Marx' *Economie et Politique*, nos. 70, 71, 80, 1960–61; Godelier, M., 'Economie politique et philosophie', *La Pensée*, October-November 1963; Godelier, M., 'Le mode de production asiatique', *La Pensée*, no. 114, April 1964, no. 122, August 1965; Godelier, M., 'Economie politique et anthropologie économique', *l'Homme*, vol. iv, no. 3, 1964; Godelier, M., 'La notion de mode de production asiatique et les schemas marxistes d'évolution des sociétés', in the Cahier Spécial du C.E.R.M., 1969, *op. cit.*

114. This somewhat heterogeneous group includes: M. Godelier, C. Meillassoux, E. Terray, G. Dupré, P. Ph. Rey, J. Copans, P. Bonnafé, R. Waast, M. Augé, J.-P. Olivier de Sardan, J.-L. Amselle, G. Althabe.

115. Balandier, G., *Political Anthropology*, Penguin Books, London, 1970

116. Cf. the journal *Etudes Rurales*, 1970

117. A phrase used by Engels in his letter to Joseph Bloch of 22.9.1890

118. Godelier, M., *Horizon, trajets marxistes en anthropologie*, Maspero, Paris, 1973, pp. 93–131

119. Frankenberg, R., 'Economic anthropology: one anthropologist's view', in Firth (ed), *Themes in Economic Anthropology*, Tavistock, London, 1967, p. 84

120. Cf. particularly Terray, E., 1972, *op. cit.*, pp. 95–186 and Rey, P. Ph., 1971, *op. cit.*, pp. 32–69

121. Cf. the debate in the journal *Philosophy of Science* and in *Man*: Gellner, E., 'Ideal language and kinship structure', *P of S* vol. xxiv, 1957; Needham, R., 'Descent systems and ideal language', *P of S*, vol. xxvii, 1960; Gellner, E., 'The concept of kinship', *P of S*, vol. xxvii, 1960; Barnes, J. A., 'Physical and social kinship', *P of S*, vol. xxviii, 1961; Gellner, E., 'Nature and society in social anthropology', *P of S*, vol. xxx, 1963; Schneider, D., 'The Nature of kinship', *Man*, vol. lxiv, November-December, 1964; Sahlins, M. D., 'On the ideology and composition of descent groups', *Man*, vol. lxv, July-August, 1965. See also the remarks of Leach in Leach, E. R., *Pul Eliya*, Cambridge University Press, London, 1965, conclusion

122. Godelier, M., 1972, *Rationality and Irrationality in Economics*, *op. cit.*, p. 93

123. *Ibid.*, pp. 93–5

124. Terray, E., 1972, *op. cit.*, p. 143

125. *Ibid.*, p. 143

126. Quoted in Terray, *ibid.*, p. 144

127. Meillassoux, C., 1964, *op. cit.*, p. 168

128. Meillassoux, C., 1972, *op. cit.*, pp. 100–1

129. Rey, P. Ph., 1971, *op. cit.*, p. 210

130. Frankenberg, R., 1967, *op. cit.*, p. 83

131. Cf. Amin, S., *Le Développement Inégal: essai sur les formations sociales du capitalisme périphérique*, Editions Minuit, Paris, 1973

132. Cf. *La Pensée*, 1971

133. Terray, 1972, *op. cit.*, pp. 95–186; Rey, 1971, *op. cit.*; Godelier, 1973, *op. cit.*, pp. 83–92

134. Godelier, 1973, *op. cit.*, pp. 13–82

135. *Ibid.*, p. 80

PART ONE

Explorations in Theory

The Object and Method of
Economic Anthropology

Maurice Godelier

The essay with which this collection begins is not the earliest of those we have selected, in a chronological sense, but it provides an ideal starting point, for it represents an arrival and a departure, both personal and more general; an arrival at anthropology first from philosophy and then economics, and a departure from 'liberal' anthropology towards the elaboration of a distinctively Marxist approach to the study of pre-capitalist formations. It represents the stage reached by Godelier in 1965, after some six years of research and thought on the questions formulated most clearly in his Foreword to the English edition of Rationality and Irrationality in Economics. *These questions were: what is the rationality of the economic systems that appear and disappear throughout history — in other words, what is their hidden logic and the underlying necessity for them to exist, or to have existed; and what are the conditions needed for a rational understanding of these systems — in other words, for a fully developed comparative economic science? It is with such questions that the journey begins. How far one may travel is indicated by Godelier's postscript to this early survey of economic anthropology, which is taken from the Avant-Propos of his recent book,* Horizon, trajets marxistes en anthropologie.*

Economic anthropology[1] has as its object the comparative theoretical analysis of different economic systems, actual and possible. In order to work out this theory, economic anthropology derives its material from the concrete information provided by the historian and the ethnologist on the functioning and evolution of the societies they study. Alongside 'political economy', which appears to be devoted to the study of modern industrial societies, both commodity-producing and planning, economic anthropology sees itself as a sort of 'extension' of political economy to the societies that the economist neglects. Or at any rate, by its very conception, economic anthropology paradoxically causes political economy, both old and new, to appear as one of its own special spheres, illuminating the particular mechanisms of modern industrial societies. In this way economic anthropology takes upon itself the task of constructing a general theory of the various social forms of man's economic activity, for comparative analysis must necessarily result one day in anthropological knowledge of a general character.

Today, however, the comparative study of economic systems is something more than and something different from a theoretical necessity imposed by abstract concern to widen the field of political economy and unify it under the body of principles of a hypothetical general theory.

The concrete and imperative urgency of the transformation of that part of the world which has remained 'under-developed' gives a practical character to the need to understand the economic systems of other societies. It should be remembered that this twofold need, theoretical and practical, to compare different economic systems was manifested at the very birth of political economy and even constituted the reason why it was born.

For the Physiocrats, seeking the principles of an economy that would be 'rational' because 'natural',[2] the economic structures and rules of the *ancien régime*, inherited from feudalism, seemed so many obstacles to the progress of trade and production, and therefore to the welfare and harmony of society. It became necessary to change or destroy the old 'irrational' economic edifice, in order to bring the world into line with the principles of natural reason. From the beginning, economic reflexion was thus engaged in the twofold task of explaining 'scientifically' the different functioning of two historical economic systems, one of which was still in process of being born from the womb of the other, and of justifying 'ideologically' the superiority of one of them over the other — proving its 'rationality'. Adam Smith and Ricardo followed along this dual path. Consequently, political economy was both science and ideology, and so placed in an ambiguous situation which it has constantly to overcome by ridding itself of its ideological element in order to reconquer itself as a scientific domain that grows greater each time this is done. In this way the socialist critique of liberalism and its apologia for a society that the principles of *laissez-faire* and competition were to maintain mechanically in a state of social harmony, resulted in exposing some of the ideological content of classical political economy, demanding from the latter a new, scientific answer to problems which, in the absence of ideological criticism, it was unable to see or appreciate properly: the problems of under-employment, economic inequality, cyclical crises, etc.

Consequently it is understandable why the idea of 'rationality', situated at the heart of all economic reflexion, should be the most necessary and yet the most challenged of all the categories of political economy. If economic anthropology is an enlargement of political economy, it must lead the latter to a renovation of the idea of economic rationality. This, however, will happen only as the outcome of its replies to a series of questions that are as formidable as they are inevitable.

What domain of human activities forms the distinctive object of economic science? What is an economic 'system'? What is meant by an economic 'law'? Are there laws that are 'common' to all systems? And, finally, what is meant by economic 'rationality'?

It goes without saying that I shall be able to do more than make a first approach, in these few pages, to these very large topics, and that I wish only to offer my reflexions as mere hypotheses submitted for challenge and criticism.

1. THE IDEA OF AN ECONOMIC SYSTEM AND ANALYSIS OF ITS WORKING

The domain of the 'economic'

The object of economic anthropology, the study of economic systems, seems at first sight to be a domain with clear-cut limits that one ought to be able to define without difficulty. Before considering, however, what is meant by a 'system', what social activities does the term 'economic' enable us to mark off from other social relations, bound up with politics, kinship, or religion? Have we to do with a domain of specific activities or with a specific aspect of every human activity?

The production of capital goods in the USA, the collective clearing away of scrub from a field by the men of a village in New Guinea, the conduct of the Fugger bank in the 16th century, the storing of agricultural and craft products in state storehouses and the distribution of these products under the Inca Empire, the nationalization of the subsoil in the USSR, household consumption in Abidjan — all these seem to be specifically economic activities. But the presenting of gifts between clans that give, and clans that receive, wives among the Siane of New Guinea, the struggle for prestige and the competition in gifts and counter-gifts in the potlatch of the Kwakiutl Indians, the daily offering of consecrated meals to the Egyptian gods — these seem to be social realities with many-sided significance, the essential purpose of which is not economic and in which the economic is only one facet of a complex fact. Is there then a common element that can bring together in the same domain, under the same definition, a particular *field of activities* and also a particular *aspect of all human activities* that do not fall within this field?

To answer this question means to become involved in the dark maze of definitions of what is economic, and to desire to put an end to the ceaseless, vain clashes between these definitions. The economic was first defined, from Plato[3] to Adam Smith, as the material wealth of societies. This definition relates to the structures of the real world, and for this reason Karl Polanyi calls it 'substantive'.[4] To reduce economic activity to the production, distribution and consumption of goods means, however, to cut off from it the huge field constituted by the production and exchange of services. When a musician receives fees for a concert, he has produced not any material article but an ideal 'object' for consumption — a service. The old definition of what is economic, while not wholly mistaken, is nevertheless inadequate to bring together in a single domain the two groups of facts which it has to account for.

On the other hand, some have wished to see in the economic an aspect of *all* human activity. Every action that combines scarce means so as the better to attain an objective is said to be economic. The formal property of all purposive activity, namely, possession of a logic than ensures its effectiveness in face of a series of constraints, becomes the criterion of the economic aspect of every act. This criterion has been adopted by Von Mises,[5] Robbins[6] and, nearer to the present time, Samuelson,[7] among the economists, and by Herskovits,[8] Firth,[9] Leclair[10] and Burling[11] among the economic anthropologists — followed, to some extent, by Polanyi and Dalton.

Certainly, the behaviour of an entrepreneur or of a firm that strives to maximize its profits, and organizes accordingly the strategy of its production and selling, is relevant to this criterion and seems to testify unanswerably in its support. But if we take Robbins' definition of economics as 'the science that studies human behaviour as a relation between ends and scarce means that have alternative uses', we see that it does not grasp the economic as such, but dissolves it in a formal theory of purposive action in which it is no longer possible to distinguish between economic activity and activity directed towards obtaining pleasure, power or salvation. At this rate, while all purposive action comes to be called economic in principle, no action actually remains economic in fact.

The absurdity of this thesis has been shown by one of its most subtle advocates, R. Burling, who says:

> If all behaviour involving allocation is economic, then the relationship of a mother to her baby is just as much an economic one, or rather has just as much of an economic aspect, as the relationship of an employer to his hired laborer.... There are no specifically economic techniques or economic goals. It is only the relationship *between* ends and means, the way in which a man manipulates his technical resources to achieve his goals, that is economic (Burling, op. cit., p. 811).[12]

This attitude leads him logically to see in the Freudian theory of the personality ruled by the pleasure principle, in Leach's[13] analysis of Burmese political systems, in Lasswell's[14] theory of power, and in Zipf's[15] essay on 'least effort', so many expressions of the 'economic' principle of the optimum use of scarce means.[16] The road indicated by this abstract criterion leads him, as happens with Hegel's 'bad' formalism, to mix up what needs to be distinguished, in a twilight in which 'all cats are grey'.

It is no paradox to claim that the proof of the radical helplessness of the formal theory of action to define the economic as such lies in the very fruitfulness of that operations research which has so perfected in recent years the practical tools of economic management. The formal theory certainly sees in this an apodictic proof of its correctness: but operations research is not a branch of economics, it is a set of mathematical calculation procedures that enable one to minimize or maximize the value of an objective function. Whether the objective be the maximum destruction of the strategic points of an enemy's military system, the optimum circulation of the Paris bus services, the transmission of a flow of information, the 'rational' management of the stock of a department store, or a game of chess, the mathematical procedures remain 'indifferent' to the 'objects' they manipulate, and the logic of the calculation remains the same throughout. Thus, operations research defines the economic no better than it defines the art of war or the theory of information. On the contrary, in order to find employment it has to presuppose that these 'objects' already exist and have been defined, and that manipulating them presents the type of problem than it can solve.[17] Now, the principle governing the practices of operations research, that of achieving the best combination of limited means in order to attain a quantifiable objective, is precisely the formal principle invoked by Robbins, Samuelson and Burling to define specifically what is economic. If operational research cannot define the objects it manipulates, the principle that is its norm and basis cannot do this either.

And so here we are, after these two analyses, faced with a 'real' definition which is inadequate because it is incomplete and onesided, and a general 'formal' definition that fails directly to come to grips with its object.[18]

The way to make progress seems plain — to get away completely from the dead end of formalism and push along the path of realism, already half-opened. Since the 'realistic' definition was inadequate because it removed from the economic sphere the reality of services, can we construct a unifying definition by saying that economics is the theory of the production, distribution and consumption of goods and services?

It is not hard to see that now we fall, for the opposite reason, into the same helplessness as the formal theory suffers from. If the production of services is economic, then economics absorbs and explains the whole of social life, religion, kinship, politics, science. Again, everything becomes economic in principle while nothing remains economic in fact.

Are we condemned, as Burling ironically suggests, to say that what is economic is the production, distribution and consumption of 'economic' services, and shut ourselves up for good in this splendid tautology? No: the realistic definition is wrong when it assigns the *whole* of the production of services, all the aspects of a service, to the economic sphere, whereas only *one aspect* of any service belongs to this sphere.[19] Let us again take the example of a musician, or a singer. What is there that is 'economic' in his recital — the work by Mozart that he interprets, the beauty of his voice, the pleasure it gives, the prestige he derives from it? What is economic is the fact that we pay to hear the singing, and that the singer receives some of this money that we pay. This is what gives an economic aspect to the social relation between the singer and his public, between the producer and the consumers of that ideal object, the opera *Don Giovanni*.

With this fee the singer will perhaps be able to live, to maintain his family, to improve his skill, to obtain some or all of the goods and services that he wants or needs. This money is therefore, for him, the virtual equivalent of the practical conditions for the satisfaction of his needs and desires. The size of the fee also serves him as an indicator of his success with the public. But it is hard to claim that the first objective of a performer is to maximize his gains. Rather is it the striving to achieve greater perfection in his art, and acknowledge-ment of this perfection through the favour and the aesthetic emotion of the public. For the listener, the price of his seat constitutes the economic aspect of his taste for music. This assumes that he has a choice in the use he makes of his income, and that he distributes it, in accordance with a personal scale of preference, over a series of objects of consumption. As for the owner of the concert-hall and organizer of the performance, his aim is certainly to get the biggest possible return from the sale of a service to a body of customers, and this determines his choice of performer, the price he charges for seats, the frequency of performances, and so on. But it is also possible to assume that the concert is free, the opera-house a state enterprise, and the cost of the performance covered by the state without its getting any profit therefrom in money terms.

Instead of the opera-singer we could take as our example a Malian 'griot' who sings before a Keita prince of the exploits of Sundyata, the legendary king of old Mali.[20] The economic aspect of his activity will not, in this case, appear in the form of money earned but in the gifts and favours that the master of the house will heap upon him. It is not only for these gifts that the 'griot' sings well and draws wonderful sounds from the 'kora'; but it is because he sings and plays so well he is laden with presents. For the prince, the fame of the 'griot' is the mirror of his own prestige, and the magnificence of his gifts is the outward symbol of his own power.

In the same way one can analyse the offering of a priest to his god, or the gifts of the faithful to this priest, or the presents given by a clan that receives wives to a clan that gives them. In each of these social relations, whether or not money plays a part, the economic aspect is that of the exchange of a service for goods and services.[21] Thus, *provided* we do not reduce the significance and function of a service to its economic aspect, or deduce that significance and function from this aspect, the economic can be defined, without risk of tautology, as the production, distribution and consumption of goods and services. It forms both a domain of activities of a particular sort (production, distribution, consumption of material goods: tools, musical instruments, books, temples, etc) and a particular aspect of all the human activities that do not strictly belong to this domain, but *the functioning of which involves the exchange and use* of material means. The economic thus appears as a particular field of social relations which is both external to the other elements of social life and also internal to them, that is, as a part of a whole that is at once external and internal to the other parts, a part of an organic whole. The economic anthropologist's task is to analyse both this external and this internal aspect, and to penetrate to the depths of the domain, until the latter opens on to other social realities and finds there that part of its meaning that it does not find in itself. The more complex a society's economy the more it seems to function as a field of autonomous activity governed by its own laws, and the more will the economist tend to concentrate on this autonomy, treating the other elements of the social system as mere 'external data'. The anthropological viewpoint, however, as Dalton emphasizes,[22] forbids description of the economic without showing its relation to the other elements of the social system.

The idea of a 'system'

Now that the economic domain has been recognized, we must account for one of its 'properties', that of appearing as a 'system'.[23] Other domains of nature and culture possess this same property, since we speak of a nervous system, a political system, a philosophical system. We must therefore define this property that is common to any and every system of possible 'objects'.

I propose to understand by a 'system': 'a group of structures interlinked by certain rules (laws)'. We are thus referred back to the idea of 'structure', by which we mean: ' group of objects interlinked by certain rules (laws)'.[24] I will explain later this mysterious doublet rule (law)'. By 'object' I mean any reality whatever: individual, concept, institution, thing. By 'rules' I mean the *explicit* principles whereby the elements of a system are combined and related, the norms *intentionally* created and applied in order to 'organize' social life: rules of kinship, technical rules of industrial production, legal rules of land-tenure, rules of monastic life, and so on. The existence of these rules allows us to suppose that, in so far as they are followed, social life already possesses a certain 'order'. All anthropological investigations, undertaken from the angle of history, economics, ethnology, etc., lead us to the assumption that no society exists without organizing its different activities in accordance with the principles and logic of a certain willed order. The task of the social sciences is to compare these rules with the facts, so as to bring out 'laws'. Before dealing with the idea of the 'law' of a system's functioning, let me go back to the idea of 'system' and 'structure', so as to bring out an essential characteristic of their definitions from which I shall draw my first methodological principles of scientific analysis.

These definitions are actually 'homogeneous' in two ways. They both refer to combinations of objects in accordance with rules, that is, realities such that one can dissociate only by abstraction the objects-in-relation from the relations between the objects. Unrelated objects constitute a reality deprived of meaning, and objectless relations a meaning deprived of existence. Thus, all systems and all structures have to be described as 'mixed', contradictory realities made up of objects and relations that cannot exist separately — such, in other words, that their contradiction *does not exclude* their unity.

Both ideas refer to relations between a whole and its parts. A structure and a system are wholes in relation to their parts. A structure is thus both a whole in relation to its parts (objects plus relations) and a part in relation to the system (structures plus relations) to which it belongs. The same is true of a system in so far as it is included in a totality larger than itself. An economic system is thus an element of the social system, or, to use Parsons'[25] expression, a 'sub-system' of the social system. These remarks bring us to the point where we lay it down as a principle that we must distinguish *levels* in every domain of 'objects', and carry out our analysis of a level (structure of system) in such a way as always to be able to see its links with other levels, to see it as part of a whole, even if, at the start, for convenience of study, such connexions have been 'abstracted', 'left out'. The need to take seriously both the specificity of the levels and the relations between them within the same totality forbids us to analyse them in such a way that one level can be *reduced* to another, or *deduced* from it. We must therefore tackle the problem of the laws of correspondence between structures without allowing ourselves to be affected by any implicit philosophy of causality in the social domain, any pre-conceived ways of approaching each level, such as the idea that the non-economic can be reduced to the economic, or deduced from it — or the other way round.[26] Armed with this principle we are able, since a system is an organic totality of objects in relation, to make clear what is meant by studying the laws of the functioning of a system.

The laws of the functioning of a system

When he studies a system, the investigator is faced with a twofold task. He has to find out what the elements of this system are and what their relations are, at a given time (t) in the evolution of this system (synchronic analysis). He has also to find out how these elements and their relations have been formed and have evolved during (*dia*) the time that this system has lasted (diachronic analysis, which is theory both of the origin and of the evolution of a system).

The use of the terms 'synchronic' and 'diachronic' has the advantage of putting in the forefront the *fact* of time (*chronos*)[27] and avoiding the impression that a structure can really be analysed without analysing its evolution. In this way one gets rid of the old ambiguous manner of talking that contrasted a 'structural analysis' with a 'dynamic analysis', as though one could exist without the other; as if time were a variable external to the functioning of a system which could be introduced into this functioning 'after the event'.

The study of a system, then, should enable us to know its 'laws'. What is meant by a 'law'? The moment has arrived to take up and clarify the relation between 'rule' and 'law'. While there are laws of social life, these cannot in my view, be confused with the 'rules', that is, the explicit, willed principles of organization of a society. To do so would presume that consciousness governs completely the movement of social reality. Conversely, experience forbids us to suppose that the social world functions without consciously willed norms playing a part. The investigator's task is to compare norms and facts so as to bring out *through their relations* a certain necessity that is expressed in the laws of the synchronic and diachronic functioning of the system.

To move from description of the rules to establishment of the laws, by way of knowledge of the facts, means passing from the intentional to the unintentional and analysing the relation between them: it means theoretically conceiving social reality as it manifests itself and as everyone experiences it, as a reality that is both willed and not-willed, performed and suffered, as a 'mixed' reality, to employ the expression Plato used[28] when referring to this world of ours.

If social life is subject to certain laws, these must make themselves felt in practice. This happens through the successive readjustments that a society makes in its own 'rules' of functioning when the situation, or in other words the facts, demand that this be done. By these readjustments, which take over and modify the relations between the rules and the facts, a society submits to its own laws without necessarily having a completely explicit or adequate theoretical awareness of them.

Scientific cognition strives to become explicit theoretical awareness. But this does not depend only upon a rigorous theoretical problematic. It presupposes no less the existence of a certain quantity and quality of information about the process of becoming of the societies concerned, so as to try to reconstitute their functioning with an adequate approximation to reality and for a sufficiently long period. Without a certain quantum of information, especially about the origin and transformations of a system, a scientific undertaking cannot be accomplished. It is possible, if one has collected a few rules and a few facts about a society, to rough out a synchronic analysis, to sketch a 'model' of what this society 'might' be, and if one has a number of successive pictures of this society, to attempt a diachronic analysis by offering diagrams of 'transition' from one state to another of the reconstituted system.

Thus, despite the shortcomings of their methodological equipment, prehistorians, historians, and ethnologists occasionally prove capable of completing the investigation and establishing of 'laws'. Perhaps the history of France between 1760 and 1815[29] has been sufficiently explored for this undertaking to be attempted. Perhaps Firth's work on Tikopia,[30] carried on during more than a quarter of a century, will provide a similar 'opportunity' in ethnology. The small number of these 'favourable' cases at once shows the imperative need to multiply historical work and ethnological investigations on the ground.

I have suggested abstract definitions of the nature of a system and tried to clarify somewhat the ultimate objective of all scientific knowledge, which is knowledge of laws. I must now apply these definitions more closely to the specific domain of economics. Two paths are possible for such an 'application'. One could describe the concrete elements of an actual system, supported by adequate information, and find the most probable 'explanation' of its functioning, the 'logic' that shows most respect for the sequence of events running through its evolution. In the context of our present study, this path is barred, for it is that of the specialist in a particular society and epoch. There is, however, another path, the one which explores not an actual system but a 'possible' one, the path of formalism.

The formal model of a possible economic system

What do we mean by a 'possible system'? The representation of the element that is common to every possible case of the kind of system under consideration. The reconstitution, for example, of the 'totemic operator' that Lévi-Strauss[31] gives us is the representation of the formal element common to every possible system of totemic thinking. A common formal element is an 'invariable' that persists all through every one of the possible varieties and variations of the system envisaged. Formalism is an 'eidetic'[32] approach, by which thought is detached from every *actual* system so as to give us all the *possible* systems, and to rediscover the actual in them as a 'realized possibility'.

To the extent that, in order to construct the formal model of a possible economic system, thinking 'ignores the difference' between actual systems, the formalist approach does not, strictly speaking, give knowledge of *any* actual system, but rather an explanation of some of the *conditions of possibility* of this knowledge, through revelation of the *formal structures* of all possible economic systems. The formalist approach thus belongs to the sphere of epistemological reflexion by economic science upon itself, through the formal properties of its subject-matter.

Edward Leclair's[33] mistake lies not in constructing a model of this kind but in believing that in doing so he has produced a 'general theory' and proved, in opposition to Dalton, that the laws of political economy, worked out for our system of capitalist commodity production, constitute the heart of this general theory, thereby acquiring universal validity. Only the study of real systems will enable us to 'decide' whether the laws of one system are applicable to another, and to work out a typology, first, of the different varieties of a given system, and then of the different varieties of system. We may assume that, stage by stage, the conditions will eventually be assembled for the creation of a 'general theory' that will not be 'formal' in character. At the beginning of the road, the formal approach will have enabled us to prepare a series of questions to be put to the facts, in order to guide investigation towards the discovery of certain information — in other words, to avoid falling into the rut of empiricism and to establish a 'problematic'. This will likewise enable us to avoid the vain speculative illusions of *a priori* deduction. For, if the general theory is not the formal theory of systems, this is because it is not possible either to 'deduce' the actual from the formal or to 'reduce' the actual to the formal. These precautions having been taken, what are the formal components of an economic system?

Since we have defined the economic activity of a society — the totality of *operations* whereby its members obtain, distribute and consume the material means of satisfying their individual and collective needs — an economic system is the combination of three structures, those of production, distribution and consumption.

If *what* is produced, distributed and consumed depends on the *nature* and *hierarchy* of needs in a given society, then economic activity is organically linked with the other activities — political, religious, cultural, family — that along with it make up the content of the life of this society, and to which it provides the material means of realizing themselves: for instance, the 'cost of living' of the dead among the Etruscans[34] and the Egyptians, the means of ensuring the prosperity of the lamaseries of Tibet,[35] etc.

The structures of production

Production is the totality of the operations aimed at procuring for a society its material means of existence.[36] So defined, the concept of production opens out on to all possible forms of operation of this kind, those that are characteristic of economies of food-gathering, hunting and fishing, in which a territory is 'occupied' and the resources needed are 'found' there, and also those that are characteristic of agricultural and industrial economies, in which what is needed is 'produced' by 'transforming' nature. An economic system may, moreover, combine food-gathering, hunting, agriculture and craft work. Historically, many societies have evolved from an occupying economy to an economy that transforms nature.[37]

Comparing these economies makes it possible to outline a typology of forms of material life which is both chronological (historical) and functional (logical). Formally, the forms of production resemble each other in that producing signifies combining, in accordance with certain technical rules (T), resources (R), instruments of labour (I) and men (M) so as to obtain a product (P) that can be used socially. Production, the functional combination of three sets of variables (the factors of production R — I — M) assumes different forms depending on the nature of the variables and the possible ways of combining them. The relation between the variables is reciprocal. The raw materials used (R) depend on the instruments of labour (I) and the knowledge and skill (M) that make it possible to use them. Reciprocally, the instruments of labour and the knowledge and skill available reflect adaptation to a certain type of usable resources. There are thus no resources as such, but only possibilities of resources provided by nature in the context of a given society at a certain moment in its evolution.

All exploitation of resources thus presupposes a certain awareness of the properties of the 'objects' and of their necessary relations under certain 'conditions', and the application of a body of technique which 'uses' these necessities in order to produce an expected result. Productive activity is thus an activity 'governed' by technical 'norms' which reflect the necessities to which this activity has to submit in order to succeed. Hunting techniques, for example, imply a detailed knowledge of the habits of the animals being hunted,[38] their relations with the fauna and flora of their *milieu*, in other words, a 'science of the concrete'[39] that is hard to reconcile with the 'pre-logical'[40] mentality that only yesterday was ascribed to primitive hunting peoples.

Every production-process thus constitutes an ordered series of operations, the nature and succession of which are based on the necessities that are submitted to in order to obtain the expected ultimate product. These operations thus develop on the basis of a given natural *milieu* and of the given social realities which form the 'constraints' to which the technological system of production is subjected, constraints that 'limit' and determine the 'possibilities' of the system, its effectiveness.

The less complex its production structures, the more the effectiveness of a technological system will be dependent on the diversity of the natural conditions in which it operates.[41] The productivity of a system will be the measure of the ratio between the social product and the social cost that it implies. In so far as production operations combine quantifiable realities (resources, instruments of labour, men) and require a certain time to be completed, qualitative, conceptual analysis of a system leads on to numerical calculation.

Combination of the factors of production is carried out within the setting of what are called 'production units'.[42] These may be the small family holding, the village community, an industrial enterprise, etc. The setting thus depends on the nature of the work undertaken and of the means available (I, M) to undertake it. In 'primitive' economies some work requires the co-operation of all the men in the village community — e.g. the clearing of a field by the Siane of New Guinea — or, even, for tasks exceeding the power of separate communities, the mobilization of the whole tribe, or of even wider groupings. The construction of huge irrigation systems, or the undertaking of terrace cultivation by the great agrarian civilizations of Egypt[43] or pre-Columbian America[44] presuppose complex division of labour and centralized control of it. Hunting economies, such as that of the Blackfoot Indians,[45] knew forms of co-operation on the tribal scale. They practised two types of hunting, depending on whether the bison were grouped in huge herds (spring and summer hunts) or scattered in small groups (autumn and winter hunts). The summer hunt required the co-operation and concentration of the entire tribe, the winter hunt that of much smaller groups operating over traditionally-fixed territories. The regrouping of the whole tribe in the spring opened the season of major political and religious ceremonies. Thus, close adaptation to the habits of the animals they hunted entailed a vast systole-diastole movement of economic and social life. The technical relation with nature is achieved through a division of roles among the economically active individuals, that is, through the relations between the 'economic agents' of this society within the setting of the production units. This setting must be compatible, to a certain degree, with the pursuit of the production-objectives. For example, mechanization of agriculture usually presupposes the existence of large-scale agricultural enterprises, owned either by an individual or by a community (the state). In the case of the great works carried out by the Incas, a more complex compatibility is to be seen between economic and political structures (centralized government). To show the possible ways in which non-economic social structures may function in the social organization of production, here is an abstract example. Let us assume that, in an agricultural village community, there is a lineage who live by their rights to use a certain number of plots of land, which are cultivated successively year by year. It is of little importance whether these cultivators produce for their own subsistence or for a market. We will merely assume that the family's labour-force and means of production (M, I) are insufficient to carry out certain production-operations of the agricultural cycle: clearing, enclosing, etc. In order to obtain the necessary complement of factors of production, the head of the family then calls upon his relatives by blood or marriage, or upon a certain age-group, upon persons dependent on him, perhaps upon wage-labourers. Consequently, the productive work is organized with the aid of personal services rendered (either spontaneously or, sometimes, under coercion) by these workers who are additional to the members of the family, for the sake of their kinship, political or religious relations with this family. The work is at one and the same time an economic, political and religious act, and is experienced as such. Economic activity then appears as activity with many different meanings and functions, differing each time in accordance with the specific type of relations existing between the different structures of a given society.[46] The economic domain is thus both external and internal to the other structures of social life, and this is the origin and basis of the different meanings assumed by exchanges, investments, money, consumption, etc., in different societies, which cannot be reduced to the functions that they assume in a capitalist commodity society and that economic science analyses.

Our example has shown us the economic aspect of the functioning of non-economic relations, but if we proceed further we find that the economic is not to be reduced to the functioning of these relations, and cannot be wholly understood on the basis of these relations. It is not at the level of these relations that we grasp the necessity of combining the factors of production in a certain way so as to obtain the products needed, in the given ecological (R) and technological (I) conditions. Economic science is neither ecology nor technology, nor is it dissolved in the study of kinship, religion, etc.

It begins with study of the social relations that operate in production and also, as we shall see, in distribution and consumption. This opens up several directions for investigation. One may note that the more complex the division of labour, the more does the kinship group or local community lose part of its economic function.[47] A part of production develops outside the family or village framework, in different organizations that depend on wider social groupings (the tribe, the state, etc.)[48] In new economic conditions, the kinship relations and the political and religious relations play a new role. It is the logic of the reciprocal modifications of the elements of the social structure that forms the object of the scientific study of societies. In the setting of Western capitalist society, the economy seems to be governed wholly by its own laws. Polanyi bases himself on this appearance in distinguishing societies in which the economy is 'embedded' in the social structure from those in which it is said not to be, in which it is 'disembedded', as with commodity societies.[49] This distinction seems to me to be a questionable one, since the term 'disembedded' could suggest an absence of internal relation between the economic and the non-economic, whereas this relation exists in every society. Actually, the conditions characteristic of the functioning of an industrial commodity economy confer on the economy (during the 19th century, at least) a very extensive autonomy in relation to the other structures (the state, etc.) and lead to the disappearance of direct control over the product by the direct producers or the owners. In this particular historical context, in which the factors of production are commodities that are appropriated individually, the optimum combination of these factors appears to their owner as that which maximizes his profits in money terms. It is at this very point that we encounter the problem, which I shall analyse later, of the nature and possible forms of economic 'rationality'.[50] Maximizing an individual profit in money appears as the particular social form of economic rationality that is characteristic of capitalist commodity societies. This rationality is that of competing individuals who may or may not be owners of the factors of production. It cannot be reduced to 'purely' economic significance, because it also means a particular way of functioning of the family, the state, etc., in these societies, and because its aim, the accumulation of wealth in money form, creates possibilities for the individual of playing a role in the political, cultural, etc., structures of his society. In other societies, at other moments of history, economic rationality would have a quite different content. The prodigality in giving that is shown in potlatch contests will prove to be the best form of saving in other societies, ensuring for the givers security for the future and social and political prestige in the present. We shall discover this internal relation between social structures when we analyse forms of distribution.

The structures of distribution

Distribution operations are those that determine in a given society the forms of appropriation and use of the conditions of production and of its outcome, the social product. Appropriation of these 'objects' is subject, in every society, to explicit rules which define the rights (written or unwritten) that the various members of this society possess in relation to these objects.

The first category of rules governing appropriation and use relates to the factors of production (R,I,M.). The rules governing the appropriation of resources — land, raw materials—can assume a variety of forms, such as those analysed by the theory of systems of ground rent.[51] One may instance the collective ownership of a hunting territory by a community of hunters,[52] the common ownership of the land by the Inca *ayllu*, with right to periodical or hereditary use of plots, the collective ownership of the sub-soil in a socialist state, alienable private property, the *dominium eminens* of Pharaoh over the lands of the village communities, and so on. Ownership may relate to water, as with the rules about use of the reaches of the Niger among the Bozo and Somono fishermen, or the rules about using the irrigation canals in the *huerta* of Valencia. The rules may relate to tools, canoes, machines, *daba* (hoes) or anything else, including men.[53] Thus, the Greek or Roman slave-owner owned the labour-power of his slave and also his person, whereas the modern employer buys the use of his workers' labour-power but has no claim on their persons. The private owner of the land may not be the same person as the owner of tools and of labour-power with whom he associates himself in order to constitute a unit of agricutural exploitation (tenant-farming), and so on.

In a society, the rules about appropriation and use of the factors of production may differ for each type of object, and combine into a complex and coherent whole. Thus, among the Siane[54] of New Guinea the rules about appropriation of material objects (land, axes, clothing) or of nonmaterial ones (knowledge of ritual) are of two kinds:

(1) A person has rights over an object that are like the rights of a father (*merafo*) over his children. He is responsible for them before the community and before his ancestors. This is the rule that applies to appropriation of the land, of sacred flutes, and of knowledge of ritual, goods that are under one's protection and cannot be transferred.[55]

(2) A person has rights over an object if he is like the shadow (*amfonka*) of this object. Such objects may be articles of clothing, pigs, planted trees, axes, needles. These goods are appropriated personally and may be transferred.

There is a relation of order between these two types of rules. If someone stands in *merafo* relation to the land, then only the work carried out in planting trees confers the right to individual appropriation (*amfonka*) of these trees. The existence of this relation of order between these two types of right reveals membership of the group as the foundation of the system of rights, and control by the clan over other dependent groups (men's houses, lineages), and over the individual, as the directing principle of this system. The system as a whole harmoniously combines the interests of the group and those of the individual, limiting, through the absolute priority of the former over the latter, the contradictions that could arise in connexion with control of scarce resources.

The second category of rules of appropriation and use concerns the effects of production, the ultimate product, whether in the form of goods or of services. This category itself includes two types of rules, depending on whether the motive of distribution is directly or indirectly economic. For directly economic motives, a share must be taken from the social product in order to renew the factors of production (R, I, M) and ensure continuity of production and of the material conditions of social existence. If this share during one period (t2) is greater than it was in the previous period (t1), then society, all other things being equal, has carried out an 'investment' and expanded its possibilities of production. If the share is less, it has reduced these possibilities. At this level we can see outlined certain forms of the dynamic of an economic system. Thus, it is necessary to take from a year's agricultural product the grain and seed for the following year, and to store these. Another reason for building up reserves is the fact that agricultural production is often seasonal, and months have to pass before the fruits of labour can be harvested. In some economies that produce sweet potatoes and *taro*, cultivation and harvesting are continuous operations, both for agrotechnical reasons and because of the lack of methods of storage. This is the case with the Chimbu of New Guinea.[56]

Also, in every society, it is necessary to care for those who are not yet producing (the children) and for those who are no longer producing (the aged and the sick).[57] Part of the product is set aside for their use, the amount depending mainly on the productivity of labour and the margin of surplus exceeding the producers' mere subsistence needs. Here we are at the intersection of rules with a direct and rules with an indirect economic motive.[58] The maintenance of chiefs, of gods, of the dead, of priests, the festivals that mark birth, marriage and death, warlike expeditions — all these social activities presuppose the use by society of material resources and of part of disposable time.

Thus, among the Incas,[59] the lands of the village communities were divided into three groups: those left at the disposal of the members of the *ayllu*, those reserved for the Inca, and those reserved for the gods, and in particular for Inti, the Sun God. The lands of the Inca and the gods were cultivated collectively, by virtue of the *mita*, labour-service in which every married man had to take part. The product of these lands was stored in state granaries and serviced to maintain the nobility, the clergy, the army, the workers who built the roads, the irrigation systems, the temples, etc. A body of specialized officials, the Quipu-Kamayoc, drew up statistics to evaluate the wealth of communities and households and calculate the quantities of agricultural and craft products and the size of labour-force necessary for the maintenance of the 'ruling caste', the carrying out of large-scale public works and the waging of war. The framework for these statistics was a division of the entire population into 'ten categories, approximately defined by apparent age and aptitude for work'.

One could also cite the forms of ground rent, in labour, in kind and in money, levied by the feudal lord.[60] The amount of this rent generally depended on the unstable relation of strength between lords and peasants. Depending on this relation, the peasants were able to enlarge to a greater or less extent the share of their own labour that they appropriated, and to improve their agricultural holding. Another example is provided by the forms of share-cropping and tenant-farming lease which lay down how the product is to be shared between the owner of the land (R) and the owner of the instruments of labour (I) and of labour-power (M). Similarly, through the mechanisms of the formation of wages and profits, the national income is distributed among the classes and social groups of an industrial capitalist country.

If we analyse distribution operations as a whole, we note that some of them distribute to the non-economic activities of social life — politics, religion, culture, etc. — the material means necessary for the practice of these activities. Here, too, the economic is internal to all non-economic activity, and constitutes *an* aspect of *every* human activity, and, reciprocally, the non-economic activities are linked organically with the economic activities to which they give meaning and purpose. At the same time, the development of non-economic activities presupposes the existence of an economic surplus — meaning not what is 'redundant',[61] an absolute surplus, but what exceeds the level that is socially recognized as necessary for the subsistence of all members of a society. In his book *From Stone to Steel*, in which he describes the conditions and effects of the replacement of the stone axe by the steel axe among the Siane of New Guinea, R. F. Salisbury calculates that the subsistence activities that took up 80 per cent of the labour-time of men equipped with stone axes required only 50 per cent of this time when they used steel ones.

The time 'gained' was devoted by the Siane not to increasing their material means of subsistence but to increasing their extra-economic activities — festivals, wars, travels. This choice between different uses of their time reflects the hierarchy of the values attributed by the Siane to their various activities.[62] An example such as this, resembling that of the Tiv, as described by Bohannan,[63] confirms certain analyses made by Polanyi and his followers Pearson[64] and Dalton, but refutes their essential thesis, which makes the idea of surplus an analytical assumption that 'explains' social arrangements *ex post*, like a *deus ex machina*, and is condemned to remain without empirical proof or disproof.

Pearson and Dalton are quite right in seeking to ascertain the precise circumstances and nature of the existence of a surplus — is it accidental or permanent, is it recognized as such, and so on — especially in emphasizing strongly that what the consequences of the existence of a surplus will be depends entirely on the given institutional framework. In the case of the Siane, these people have appreciated and measured perfectly well the time that they have gained through the diffusion of the steel axe among them, and have devoted this time to the pursuit of those ends which are most highly valued in their eyes, because they ensure the prestige of individuals within the clan community. But this intensification of the most highly esteemed activities, which already constitutes a change as compared with tradition, even if it does not affect the overall structures, has been made possibly by a technological change. It is in this sense that it is assumed that the appearance of a surplus makes possible — which does not mean 'necessary' — structural transformation in a society. And there is no relation between this statement and the claim that economic activity historically *precedes* other human activities and *must* necessarily be *valued more highly* than they are. The contribution made by Dalton and Pearson is, in fact, to bring out the errors of a crude materialism which postulates a mechanical causality between social facts the dialectic of which it cannot grasp. When, however, Dalton and Pearson allege that the idea of surplus is a mental construction that lacks any practical implications, the whole of economic practice and theory cries out against their view.

Before our eyes, the rapid transformation of the 'underdeveloped' countries underlines the priority of productive investment in development, in other words, the need to withdraw from immediate consumption the means for increasing future consumption. And by consumption we mean the ending of mass illiteracy, the training of skilled workers, the multiplication of services, as well as the infrastructure of agriculture and industry. For industrialization, a labour-force is needed that will be made available by the increase in agricultural productivity. This logic of facts, guided by the strategies of (forced) saving and investment, does not differ in kind from the 'take-off'[65] of industrial capitalism and its gigantic growth during the 19th century. From the analyses of Smith, Ricardo and Marx[66] to the statistics of historians like Mantoux[67] and Labrousse, the mechanism of the 'accumulation of capital' is described as a phenomenon of forced saving on the part of the working people and of investment in 'capital goods' by the bourgeoisie. These economists and historians, supporters of the idea of surplus, were the first to point out that institutional transformations in the spheres of law, the state and culture stimulated economic changes, and did not see in this role played by institutions any proof that the idea of surplus was essentially metaphysical. Actually, the metaphysics is to be found among those who were looking for a 'surplus in itself' and who do not know what to do with the idea of surplus when they come upon what actually exists, namely, 'relative' surpluses.

Furthermore, the idea of surplus is still obscured by the notion that many people still hold that there is a necessary causality between the existence of a surplus and that of the exploitation of man by man. This raises the general problem, not of the mechanisms but of the 'principles' of distribution, since the latter can be either equal or unequal among the members of a society. One and the same society may, moreover, follow different principles, depending on the objects that are to be distributed. The Siane ensures equal access for everyone to the use of the land and to subsistence foodstuffs. Luxury goods, however, such as tobacco and salt, depend on the initiative of each individual. As for actual wealth — feathers, shells, pigs — the material basis for ceremonial acts and for access to women, these are controlled by the elders of the families and the important men (*bosboi*), whose prestige and power they symbolize. But this inequality does not signify at all that there is exploitation of some by others.

Similarly, in a community divided into specialized and complementary groups — cultivators, fishermen, craftsmen — the exchange of their products enables everyone to have access to the totality of resources without there being any phenomenon of exploitation. From this standpoint, the sharing of products between those who have produced them and the individuals who are consecrated to the affairs of politics and religion is at first a form of exchange between manual workers and mental workers without any exploitation of the former by the latter. This exchange corresponds to a service rendered to the community, a communal function that has been taken upon themselves by particular persons. Exploitation of man by man begins when this service ceases to be rendered, and products go on being levied by the non-producers without anything being done in return for them. It is generally very difficult to determine where the authority of function stops and the authority of exploitation begins, in societies in which social contradictions, conflicts between groups, are not highly developed. This was the case with the kingdoms of Ghana and Mali, where an aristocracy carried out religious, political and military functions on behalf of the whole tribe, and slightly exploited the free men of the village communities.[68] Often the development of the power of a minority is a powerful factor in economic and social development, at least for a certain period. The unification of Egypt under Menes, the first Pharaoh, made possible the control of Nile irrigation, to the benefit of the village communities.[69]

Karl Polanyi, drawing his inspiration from Marcel Mauss,[70] has attempted to subsume the mechanisms of distribution under three principles: reciprocity, redistribution, exchange. An illustration of the first of these is the game of gifts and counter-gifts, the *potlatch*, of the Kwakiutl; of the second, the redistribution of products by order from above in the Inca Empire; and of the third, the universal circulation of the commodities land, labour or other objects in capitalist economy. This thought-provoking analysis would be more fruitful if it sought to isolate the different criteria of the 'value' that is attributed to the objects given, redistributed or exchanged, for these criteria would enable us eventually to analyse the differing forms of social equality and inequality.[71] On this point, analysis of the different categories of structures of distribution has shown us the strategic role played in the functioning of societies by the operations and norms of the distribution of the factors of production. It is these that control, in the last analysis, the possibilities of action that a social system offers to the individuals and groups who operate it and are subject to it — possibilities, equal or unequal, of power, of culture, of standard of living. As we shall see in our conclusion, it is these possibilities of different systems that are contrasted in the arguments about economic 'rationality'. When the French bourgeoisie abolished, in the course of revolutionary struggles, the structures of the *ancien régime*, it did this in the name of 'reason', aware that it was opening for itself and for the other classes of society possibilities of economic, social and cultural development that could not flourish under the *ancien régime*. Ultimately, it is the rules of distribution that govern the structures of consumption.

The structures of consumption

Consumption of the factors of production — resources, equipment, labour — is nothing other than the actual process of production, the existence and continuity of which it ensures. It is thus subject to the technical rules of production and to the social rules governing appropriation of the factors of production. It operates within the framework of the production units. Personal consumption, in its individual and social forms, operates within the framework of consumption units,[72] which may sometimes coincide with production units, as in the case of an agricultural small-holding.[73] Often the basis for the establishment of consumption units is kinship. The nuclear family, the enlarged family, the clan, the tribe, all may provide the framework of consumption, depending on circumstances. Among the Siane the wife prepares the food and takes it to her husband, who distributes it among all the members of the men's house. Another part of the food is consumed by the wife, her unmarried daughters and her sons who have not been initiated. Thus, all the 'values' of the social system are expressed in consumption, through the preferences and prohibitions affecting food, for example. Once again, 'the economic' does not possess all of its meaning and purpose entirely within itself.

With the process of consumption we conclude the description of the formal components of every possible economic system. This 'model' provides the guide-lines for a 'problematic' of economic analysis, that is, a series of questions giving direction to one's interrogation of the facts. What are the technological methods employed by a society? What is their effectiveness? What are the rules governing the appropriation and use of factors of production, and of products? What are the units and forms of consumption? What is the inner unity of these structures, their relation with the other structures of social life?

In the end we see that all production is a twofold act subject to the technical norms of a certain relation between men and nature and to the social norms governing the relations between men in their use of the factors of production. The organic solidarity of the structures of an economic system appears through the complementary and circular character of the process — production making consumption possible and consumption making production possible.

Synchronic and diachronic analysis of economic systems can now be defined with more precision in the context of this problematic. Synchronic analysis will seek to reconstitute, at a certain moment in the evolution of a system, the functioning of the structures of production, distribution and consumption. Diachronic analysis will seek to reconstruct the genesis of the elements of the system and of their relations, and then to follow the evolution of their functioning through a series of synchronical pictures of the system. By comparing the rules with the facts it will then try to determine the conditions under which the system changes or remains constant, and to work out the laws by which it functions.

I shall use this problematic in order to deal briefly with the two problems that have loomed at the intersection of all the paths we have followed hitherto. Why is a formal theory not a general theory? And has the idea of 'economic rationality' any scientific content?

2. THE PROBLEM OF A 'GENERAL THEORY' AND OF THE RIGHT TO 'EXTEND' THE CATEGORIES AND LAWS OF POLITICAL ECONOMY

In building my formal 'model' of a possible economic system, I deliberately *ignored all the differences* that exist between the actual systems. This method enables one to isolate the formally identical elements that are common to all these systems. 'Formally', however, does not mean 'really'. At the level of a formal analysis which, on principle, proceeds by ignoring real differences, no 'criterion' is available for *deciding* whether two systems are really identical or different. To decide this one has to analyse the systems as they are, so as to find out whether they belong to the same actual kind of system. This analysis therefore proceeds by subjecting itself to the concrete facts, which cannot be deduced from formal principles. By this road progress is made towards a genuine general theory that undertakes to picture both the identity *and* the difference between systems.

Using this method one can hope to be able genuinely to decide whether the laws of one system 'apply' to others, and whether there are 'real' laws common to all the systems.[74] This shows well enough that the elaboration and the actual content of a general economic theory are identical with the ultimate aim of economic anthropology as R. Firth once defined it:

> What is required from primitive economics is the analysis of material from uncivilised communities in such a way that it will be directly comparable with the material of modern economics, matching assumption with assumption and so allowing generalizations to be ultimately framed which will subsume the phenomena of both civilized and uncivilized, price and non-price communities into a body of principles about human behaviour which will be truly universal.[75]

If, as ordinary experience indicates, economic systems are both identical and different — as, for example, in our own day, the capitalist and socialist systems — representing their reality cannot mean reducing or eliminating their contradictions. If we see only the difference between systems, we perhaps respect their singularity, but while this is preserved, intelligibility is lost, for thought is then left confronted with a diversity of radically heterogeneous realities, opaque to any attempt at comparison. If, on the other hand, we see only the resemblances, intelligibility seems to be preserved, but singularity is lost in a homogeneous totality in which only slight shades of difference can be discerned. By depicting reality as it is with all its contradictions, economic theory can hope to escape from this ceaseless and inescapable to-ing and fro-ing between two half-truths that when brought together, do not even make one — in other words, it can hope to cut the Gordian knot of the old paradoxes of the kind of historical thinking that was unable to conceive the structure and the event together, to conceive time.

The predominant attitude among economists and anthropologists, however, is to reduce or deny the differences between economic systems and, as they imagine, to rid their domain of its contradictions. This attitude seems to find firm support upon facts that have been collected empirically. In primitive economies we find division of labour, external trade, money, credit, calculation, just as in our modern commodity economies. Consequently, Herskovits, or Leclair, seems to have every right to postulate that:

> Practically every economic mechanism and institution known to us is found somewhere in the non-literate world. . . . The distinctions to be drawn between literate and non-literate economies are consequently those of degree rather than of kind.[76]

The general theory appears to have been found before even being sought for, since it was there already. If there is no difference other than one of degree between all the economies known to us, then the laws of commodity economy discovered by classical political economy have universal validity and are 'found again' in every possible system. The higher explains the lower, the complex is the development of the simple, in which it was already pre-formed, in germ. The conclusion was firmly drawn long since by Goodfellow — economic anthropology will be either 'liberal' political economy or it will be nothing at all:[77]

> The proposition that there should be more than one body of economic theory is absurd. If modern economic analysis, with its instrumental concepts, cannot cope equally with the Aborigine and with the Londoner, not only economic theory but the whole of the social sciences may be considerably discredited. For the phenomena of social science are nothing if not universal. . . . When it is asked, indeed, whether modern economic theory can be taken as applying to primitive life, we can only answer that if it does not apply to the whole of humanity then it is meaningless. For there is no gulf between the civilized and the primitive; one cultural level shades

imperceptibly into another, and more than one level is frequently found within a single community. If economic theory does not apply to all levels, then it must be so difficult to say where its usefulness ends that we might be driven to assert that it has no usefulness at all.[78]

I shall have no difficulty in showing that in trying to deny the 'real' differences between economic systems and rid this domain of its contradictions, Herskovits and others have brought their thinking into flagrant contradiction with the facts and with itself. Their attitude is ultimately based upon a prejudice relating both to the nature of primitive economies and to the Western market economy, and this prejudice sanctifies *a certain way of seeing* (or not seeing) the Western economy, and the other economies *through this conception*. Despite his efforts, Herskovits, having already set out side by side the two definitions of the economy, formal and real, asserts and questions at the same time that the laws of political economy apply to every system, renouncing through this double compromise the task of undertaking a real theoretical elaboration of the facts.

Let me resume my argument. In the first place, to allege, as Goodfellow and Rothenberg do,[79] that political economy applies to every economic system because the theory of prices applies to every such system means willfully to reduce political economy to the theory of prices which, to be sure, was dominant from Malthus to Marshall. It means cutting off from political economy a number of fruitful developments like Keynes's theory that full employment does not automatically prevail in a decentralized market economy. The basic reason why this amputation is made is, as Dalton has pointed out, that anthropologists are well aware, even though they do not admit it, that the essential pre-condition for Keynes's doctrine to 'apply' is missing, because the income of a primitive economy is not mainly derived from or dependent on the sale of products on a market.

Reducing classical political economy to the theory of prices means shutting oneself up in the practical helplessness of economists to analyse the mechanisms of our own Western economy when these are based on exchanges of goods and services that do not go through a market and are therefore not 'measured' by a price. As Burling has emphasized, the economist is obliged to leave out of his statistics of the national economy the domestic work performed by housewives.[80] An anthropologist, on the contrary, will see in the work done by women in the home in a 'primitive' society a reality that belongs to the economic sphere. Reducing political economy to the theory of prices thus means taking things 'as they appear', or as they are dealt with empirically, and not as they are, even in our market economies. A reality may be economic without being a commodity. To think otherwise is to make a theoretical fetish of the commodity. Already we can see how the anthropological perspective enables political economy to see itself better, through being subjected more faithfully to social reality in all its singularity and concreteness.

Besides, even if, in our societies, the giving of a price to goods and services *seems* to be the criterion that defines the latter as economic facts, in other societies the giving of a price is a rare and limited fact that cannot constitute the decisive criterion by which economic activity is to be distinguished from the other activities of a society. For Burling, if economics just means price-theory, then it is an incredible contradiction to talk of primitive 'economics', since the latter uses money in a very limited way, or even uses it not at all, and especially because, as Moore has pointed out, land and labour are never, or hardly ever, the object of transactions through a market mechanism. Nevertheless, even in face of these facts, some economists do not lay down their arms, and in order to 'save' the right to apply to primitive economies the corpus of principles of the market economy, describe the economies as being marked by 'inelastic' supply and demand, and so subject to the particular group of principles of the theory of prices that apply to situations of inelasticity in a market. Dalton shows that thereby analysis of the facts is guided by the prejudice that the market structure, or its functional equivalent, exists universally.[81] For the theory of elasticities to be applicable and verifiable, however, it is further necessary that the inelastic resources and products be bought and sold through a market mechanism, which does not exist in a primitive economy.

Ultimately, the controversy is resumed again and again around the way in which most of the economists and anthropologists manipulate the master-concepts of political economy, those of *capital* and *money*. The definitions they give to these form the essential justification for the 'right' that many of them claim to extend the laws of commodity economies to every possible economy, as proclaimed by Salisbury:

> The traditional western economic concept potentially most applicable and useful in understanding the Siane material is that of 'capital'.[82]

Now, what is the nature of 'capital'? Three definitions seem to emerge from the plentiful and contradictory economic literature.

First we have Thurnwald's (1932):

> If by 'capital' is meant commodities which, by their own inherent nature, can not only maintain themselves but increase themselves, ... [this] occurs in two main forms: capital in plants and capital in domestic animals, especially cattle.[83]

The second is that given by Firth and taken over by Salisbury:

> Firth [in *A Primitive Polynesian Economy*, p. 273] stressed that capital is a stock of goods and services which is used in the productive process by being 'immobilized' (i.e. not used by the entrepreneur for immediate consumption) and 'used ... to meet any ... changes in the productive situation' (Salisbury, *From Stone to Steel*, p. 141). 'In real terms, then, capital will be defined as a stock of goods, present before a productive act is performed, used in production, and "immobilized" from direct consumption while the act is in progress' (Salisbury, op. cit., p. 142).

The last, in the line of classical thought, is given by Max Weber:

> ' "Capital" is the sum of money in terms of which the means of profit-making which are available to the enterprise are valued.'[84]

In all these three definitions capital is defined as an object — cattle, plants, tools, money — and this object possesses the property of growth. Capital is thus taken as it 'appears' in the most diverse material forms and in its apparent 'functioning'. A theoretical attitude like this gives rise to a whole sheaf of paradoxes. The fact that thinkers in Antiquity described the use of money as capital *by analogy* with the relations between certain elements of nature, animal or vegetable species, gives no-one the right to take this analogy for an 'identification'. If money was called in Latin *pecus*, from a word that also meant, and had meant for a longer period, 'herd' or 'flock', or if *tekhos* means in Greek the 'interest' on capital lent, and also the 'little one', the young offspring of an animal, this is merely a way of describing a 'cultural' object by analogy with a structure observed in nature. For an animal to become capital it must be bought and sold, that is, *a certain social relation*, a certain type of exchange, must be established between persons through the intermediary of the exchange of things — flocks, money, etc. To the first paradox, taking an analogy for an identification, is added a fundamental inability to see in capital more than a set of things, instead of essentially a social relation.

The consequences are logical and absurd. Since capital is a thing, or a property of certain natural objects, any society which uses these things (plants, animals) uses capital. Capital, a fact specific to societies with a commodity and money economy, thus turns up in every agricultural or pastoral society. Here indeed is a paradox, for an anthropologist to be unable to see a social relation beneath its material appearances, and so to transform something social into a 'fact of nature'.

In the case of Firth and Salisbury the thesis is a more complex one. Capital is still a set of 'things', but now they are withdrawn from consumption and so used in a 'social' process; but, alas, the definition actually belongs to another concept, that of 'factors of production'.[85] And this concept, as we have seen, applies to any form of economy, commodity or not, that needs, in order to produce, to use material and human means (R, I, M), without these necessarily having to assume the particular form of capital. The concept of capital has thus been 'extended' and maintained for the analysis of every society, after its distinctive monetary character and the specific social relations of commodity exchange that it implies have been taken away from it. At this cost it becomes applicable to every society, without defining any of them, and obscuring all of them. One may well wonder what the underlying reason can be for this obsessive obstinacy in introducing the idea of capital into every kind of society.

If capital presupposes the existence of money and commodity economy, is Max Weber's definition fully satisfactory? No, if money is regarded as something that brings in profit by virtue of its mere existence; yes, if money is used as capital only through certain social relations. To summarize the problem briefly, for a thing to be used as capital, two conditions are needed:

The first, necessary but not sufficient, is that this thing be bought and sold. Anything can become capital if it becomes a commodity for its owner. When land, labour and goods becomes commodities, the production and circulation of commodities become general, and money takes the form of all-purpose currency, a currency in universal use.

But not all money functions as capital. It may serve as a mere means for the circulation of commodities. Money functions as capital when the using of it brings its owner something more than its initial value — a surplus-value, a profit.

If we separate these two conditions we restrict ourselves to the appearance of things and fall into Thurnwald's paradoxes. In its essence, capital is not a thing but a relation between men realized by means of the exchange of things. It is a social fact.

From this angle, Marx, following Ricardo,[86] analysed the circuit of the 'metamorphoses' of an industrial capital[87] and showed that under the different successive appearances of a capital there lay one process only, the development of an invested capital. Before it is invested, a capital appears (1) as a certain amount of money, M. This money is transformed (2) into factors of production the use of which creates (3) commodities of one kind or another, the sale of which (4) brings in a profit, Δ M. By way of these four stages, M has thus become M′ (M + Δ M). If we compare M with M′ we recognize Weber's definition of capital; if, however, we consider stages 2 and 3, capital appears as means of production, *à la Firth*, or as some sort of commodity to be sold; thus, under the diversity of successive material forms, there is the functional identity of one and the same capital which is fructifying, and this presupposes that labour and the other factors of production can be bought and the product sold — that is, it presupposes the existence of certain social relations, and it is within this social structure that material things become capital.[88]

The classical economists showed that all the forms of capital — financial, commercial, industrial — presupposed the existence of exchange and of a currency of some kind, used in different ways (loan of money, buying and selling of commodities, productive investment) in order to make a profit (interest, commercial profit, entrepreneur's profit). They also pointed out that the financial and commercial forms of capital had an antediluvian existence, in some cases going back to very ancient times in certain Asiatic societies, whereas industrial capital, typical of modern capitalist societies, had become a dominant economic fact only late in history.

These already old-established analyses illuminate two apparently paradoxical features that are often mentioned by anthropologists when they describe 'primitive' societies: the absence of capitalism animated by a 'spirit of enterprise'[89] (even when the existence of capital in the given society is alleged — meaning means of production) and the presence in economies where there is exchange, with or without the use of a currency, of certain forms of behaviour that are formally very close to that of a financier who seeks to maximize the return on his loans (the potlatch, among the Kwakiutl, and interest-bearing loans on Rossel Island) or that of a trader who makes money by 'bargaining' over his purchases and sales. (Cf. the Gim Wali of the Trobrianders, the exchange which accompanies the Kula but is distinct from it by the nature of the objects exchanged and the bargaining that takes place in connexion with their exchange.)

But this resemblance, as we shall see, has limits based on the very nature of the exchanges and of the circulation of goods and currency (when this exists) in primitive societies, and these limits forbid us to mix up these phenomena with those of developed commodity societies, or to interpret them entirely on the basis of classical political economy. In primitive societies, goods are classified in distinct and hierarchically ordered categories, and their exchange and circulation are strictly compartmentalized. It is in general impossible and unthinkable to exchange one article for *any* other article *at all*, regardless. The economic structure of primitive societies is thus, as Bohannan puts it, 'multicentric',[90] unlike capitalist economies centred upon a market. The 'multicentric' character of the economic structure is determined by the particular relation that obtains between the economic and the non-economic in primitive societies, and expresses this relation. The compart-mentalizing and hierarchical arrangement of goods arises from their use for the functioning of distinct social relations — kinship, politics, religion — relations that each possess a distinct social importance. In entering into the functioning of these many and various relations, goods and currency acquire *utilities and significances* that are multiple and hierarchically ordered.[91] Consequently, currency and other economic phenomena, being directly determined by the relation between all the structures of society, constitute a reality that it is a more complex task to analyse theoretically than the economic realities of capitalist societies, because it is socially *pluridetermined*. The compartmentalized and hierarchical classification of goods thus expresses the specially dominant role played in a particular society by relations of kinship and marriage (e.g. the Siane), or political and religious relations (e.g. the Incas) — that is, it expresses the dominant aspect of the social structure. These observations enable us to appreciate better a number of features of the economic mechanisms of primitive societies.

The hierarchy of goods is organized in accordance with increasing scarcity. The category of scarcest goods contains those that enable men to attain the social roles that are most highly valued and for which competition between members of the society is keenest, because they procure the maximum social satisfaction to those who obtain them. The restricted number of these dominant roles necessitates that social competition, in its economic aspect, shall be effected through possession of the scarcest goods. On this basis one could analyse theoretically the existence of scarcities that seem to be 'artificial' in certain societies: some shells brought from far away, pigs' teeth that have been artificially made to grow in a spiral shape, the existence of *limited* series of shells (Rossel Island) and of coppers (Kwakiutl), each item having its own name and history,[92] and so on.

Everything happens as though society had 'instituted' a scarcity by choosing unusual objects for certain exchanges.

This would also explain the principle behind the exclusion of subsistence goods from the field of objects that enter into social competition. By excluding these goods from competition and ensuring relatively equal access by everyone to the use of them (the land being, moreover, excluded from any competition between the members of the group), the group safeguards the survival of its members and its own continuity.[93] Competition within the group begins beyond the level of problems of subsistence, and involves not the loss of physical existence but only the non-attainment of social status. Consequently one might seek to explain that subsistence goods, when they enter into social competition on the occasion of ceremonial feasts, must acquire the 'scarcity needed' for them to play this role, and that this scarcity is created by an exceptionally large accumulation of them that must inevitably result in their destruction, their economic non-use. This 'purposeful waste', far from being 'irrational' economic behaviour, would then possess its necessity in the actual content of social relations.

Similarly, the fact would be explained that in certain complex primitive societies (Tiv, Trobiand, Kwakiutl), whereas subsistence goods can hardly ever be converted into anything else, certain rigorously defined possibilities are allowed for converting among themselves the goods belonging to other categories, so as in the end to command those goods of the highest value that give access to women, to political or religious authority, and so on.[94] At the same time, since these scarce goods bring prestige, or the satisfaction desired, only if they are generously redistributed or ostentatiously destroyed, social competition can continue to operate, and social inequality remains relatively limited and can be challenged continually. The theoretical problem is therefore to know how, in societies of this type, inequality becomes more serious and firmly established, how it actually ceases to be challenged (except ritually and symbolically when the ruler dies), how a social minority is able to benefit *permanently* by an *exceptional* situation, even if it continues to redistribute part of its possessions. This is the problem of the conditions for the transition to the state, of the birth of a class structure within a tribal society, the problem that was raised, and mispresented, by Morgan in the 19th century, but which today dominates all political anthropology.

There is another possible consequence, economic this time; it seems that if subsistence goods enter only indirectly into social competition within primitive societies, there is no need for production of these goods to be carried on by the members of these societies beyond the limit of their socially necessary wants. The functioning of the social structure, which does not require maximum use of the available factors of production determines the intensity of the incentives to developing the productive forces involved in the production of subsistence goods. This social limit on incentives to develop the productive forces explains the generally slow pace of development of these forces in such societies[95] and the absence of individuals animated by a 'true spirit of enterprise' — in other words, the motivation of an industrial capitalist.[96] This absence and this limitation, far from being 'irrational', express once again the logic of social relations and are neither a 'psychological' problem nor a problem of human 'nature', whether savage or civilized. On the contrary, this situation expresses the *conscious control* that 'primitive or ancient societies' habitually exercise over themselves, a control that quickly disappears with the development of commodity production.[97] The *optimum* of production of subsistence goods in a primitive society thus does not correspond, here any more than elsewhere, to the *maximum* of possible production, but this optimum expresses the 'social necessity' of this production, its relative 'social utility', compared with the utilities of the other purposes, accorded different values, that are recognized as 'socially necessary' and are based on the actual structure of social relations.[98]

The economic optimum here appears as that organization of economic activities (production, distribution, consumption) which is most compatible with the realization of socially necessary objectives, and so that which is best adjusted to the functioning of the social structure. The economic optimum thus appears, for the moment, as the result of an intentional organization of economic activity (allocation of resources, combination of factors of production, rules of distribution, etc.) directed towards the better functioning of all the social structures (kinship, politics, religion, etc.), and this result is meaningless unless reference is made to the functioning of these structures.[99] The economic optimum is thus the economic 'aspect' of a wider, 'social' optimum.[100] This intentional activity, which is aimed at achieving the best possible combination of means to attain alternative ends, is strictly what I shall call the conscious, intentional aspect of economic rationality, to be later distinguished from 'unintentional' rationality. Thus the 'rationality' of the economic behaviour of the members of a society is seen as an aspect of a wider, fundamental rationality, that of the functioning of societies. There is therefore no economic rationality 'in itself', nor any 'definitive' form of economic rationality.

This confirms my analysis of the theoretical inadequacy of the formal definition of what is economic that is currently accepted by economists. In every society the 'intelligent' behaviour of individuals appears 'formally' as the organization of their means in order to attain their ends. It is clear that if this attitude is described as one of 'economizing' their means, then all purposive activity becomes 'economic', or has an economic aspect. The 'formal' properties of 'rational' economic behaviour therefore do not suffice either to distinguish economic from non-economic behaviour or to define the real content of economic rationality proper to each type of society, a rationality that is only an aspect of a wider, social, overall rationality. As it is not possible either to *reduce* the economic rationality of a society to these formal principles or to *deduce* it from these principles, the formal definition of what is economic is not only incapable of defining its object but also remains practically useless for analysing the real problem it presents — that of the best *form of organization* of the economy in the framework of a given society. This analysis presupposes a scientific explanation of the *raison d'être* of the ends that are socially recognized as necessary, of what their foundation is in the structure of the societies in question. This scientific explanation is still only in its infancy.

If we return from this analysis of the intentional aspect of economic rationality, to our starting-point, the critique of the notion of capital, the existence of compartmentalized categories of goods, currency and forms of exchange and their significance in the working of competition within a primitive society, we can assume that in every society, whether primitive or not, there is a definite field open to social competition, a field structured by the dominance of certain social relations over others (kinship, religion, etc.). It is this field that offers individuals the *possibility* of acting so as to maximize those determined and hierarchically ordered social satisfactions the *necessity* of which is based upon the particular way the social structure functions.[101]

This would illuminate both the fact that one can regard the formal principles of the rational attitude as being universal and the fact that the real content of economic rationality differs from one type of society to another. To put forward, as do so many economists, the maximizing of the money gains of individuals as the sole rational attitude possible, an absolute and exclusive model, is to forget that this form of economic rationality is the product of a special historical evolution,[102] and is characteristic of developed capitalist societies in which the control and accumulation of capital constitute the strategic point of social competition. Furthermore, the capitalist form of economic rationality differs fundamentally from the forms of rationality of primitive societies in that in it the structure of the field open to social competition is such that the struggle for control of the factors of production plays the decisive role, so that quite a different content is given to social inequality.

The assumption can be made that the development of new possibilities for production in tribal societies shifts the strategic centre of social competition from the domain of the distribution of the most highly valued elements of the social *product* to that of the distribution of the *factors* of production among the members of society — without competition over the distribution of the product ceasing to play a part.[103] Social inequality becomes greater, and may become permanent when a minority has exceptional rights of control over the conditions of production: control of land and hydraulic arrangement among the Egyptians or the Incas, rights over the labour of slaves in Greece, labour-services rendered by peasants, and so on. All possible combinations of unequal distribution of the product and of factors of production need to be explored by economic and political anthropology in order to explain how the transition has taken place from primitive tribal societies to new forms of society including a class structure, whether embryonic or well developed, and in which the old principles of reciprocity and redistribution either disappear or no longer play the same role.[104]

Thus, the explicit content of the idea of economic rationality is that of the problem of the basis for the organization of production and distribution in different types of society. Within this dual content the organization of distribution (of the products or of the factors of production) plays the dominant strategic role. On the epistemological plane, these analyses enable us to define more closely the conditions for working out a 'general theory of economic systems'. Since, as we have seen, it is not possible to deduce from formal principles the content of different economic rationalities, nor to reduce this content to these principles, the general theory will be neither a formal theory nor the projection into all societies of the structures and laws of functioning of capitalist societies (or of any other type of society taken as *absolute* term of reference). Neither a formal theory nor an extension of political economy, this general theory in process of construction would be *the theory of laws of functioning of the economy within different types of possible social structures, and of the basis of these laws*, and this scientific knowledge is bound up to a large extent with theoretical knowledge, at present very unevenly developed, of the bases of the other social structures — kinship, religion, politics.

In order to see for a last time the sort of paradox to which a certain use of categories of political economy can lead us in the study of primitive societies, we will analyse the practical consequences of Salisbury's use of the idea of 'capital', before setting out the conclusions of L. Lancaster on the functioning of currency and credit on Rossel Island, which seems formally very similar to the working of financial capitalism.

Having defined capital as Firth defines it, and resolved to discover the 'capital' of the Siane, Salisbury still had to 'measure' it, since there is no science without measurement. Now, he had no price-indicators he could use for this task, since neither land or labour, nor the bulk of the products, were exchanged on a market. One criterion alone was left to him, a single analysable datum: the amount of social labour that the production goods and services had required. He calculated, for example, that making a stone axe took on the average six hours of labour, a needle one day, a large 'men's house' five days' labour by a team of thirty men, one day's labour by a team of six men, and one day's labour by a team of thirty women, or 186 days' labour altogether. . . .

This information is very useful, but what it measures is the productivity of the Siane system of production, not its 'capital'. Salisbury was thus *really* measuring the productivity of the system while *believing* that he was measuring a capital, without criticizing his own concepts. Long since we have been taught by physics, for example, to separate science from belief, to isolate the positive achievements of Newton from the ideas that Newton held regarding the existence of an absolute Space and Time, and to explain both the real achievements and the mistaken ideas. The misadventures of Salibury's method illustrates the dangers of an uncritical attitude in theory. In measuring the social cost of goods, Salisbury, somewhat horrified at what he was doing, took the path of doctrinal *lèse-majesté* in relation to the 'prevailing ideas' of the economists. For to measure the 'value' of goods by the social labour necessary to produce them is to go back to the fundamental theses[105] of the founders of political economy and of Marx,[106] who was their disciple on this point, theses long since rejected as useless by the economists of the marginalist inspiration.[107] By a strange fate, the thesis of labour-value, formerly the basis for analysis of modern commodity societies, has become 'good' for analysing a primitive non-commodity society. The paradox is that every economy presupposes the combination and consumption of factors of production, and only labour realizes this combination. Thus the value theory of the classical economists possessed in principle a capacity for universal, anthropological explanation, and could be applied to every society, ancient or modern, commodity or not, liberal or planned. Unfortunately, the idea that this principle of explanation is outdated and obsolete has prevented many from recognizing one of the universal theoretical assumptions of political economy.

Nevertheless, I do not think that the labour theory of value explains by itself how prices are formed in a market economy. The category of 'price' is much more complex than that of value and expresses both the cost of production and the social utility of an article, measured through the working of supply and effective demand. It is this last point that marginalism has developed. However, as Marshall pointed out long ago, in the long run the evolution of prices does follow the line of evolution of costs of production. One might perhaps be tempted to find a relation between the social utility of goods, their exchange-'value', and the labour necessary to produce them, or to produce their equivalent, in a primitive society, when they are obtained in a regular exchange (cowries, etc.). Actually, the most highly valued goods are the scarcest, and possess a status equivalent to luxury articles in our societies. Often it has required a considerable amount of labour to obtain them or to accumulate their equivalent. Steiner has analysed the Yap currency, in the form of huge stones, as described by Furness in 1910. Others have estimated the amount of labour and foodstuffs needed for breeding pigs in New Guinea. These goods represent an exceptional direct or indirect levy upon the society's resources in labour and subsistence goods. At the same time, owing to their scarcity, they are called upon to play an essential role in social competition, in which they acquire their manifold significance and their exceptional social utility.

Actually, it seems to me, political economy cannot be, or is not adequate to form a general theory, because the economic phenomena in a primitive society, though simpler than the economy of a modern society, are *socially more complex*, and consequently have *neither the same significance nor the same content*.

In order to finish with this essential point I will take up again the analysis of the ultimate master-concept of political economy, the last excuse for discovering the laws of political economy in primitive societies: the concept of money. We find examples of 'primitive money'[108] in the writings of Armstrong, Bohannan, Guiart, Lancaster, Salisbury and Wilmington.[109] These examples present great differences but they bring out one negative characteristic common to all these 'primitive moneys': they cannot be exchanged for absolutely anything whatsoever — they are not 'all-purpose currencies'.

Bohannan[110] has shown the existence among the Tiv of Nigeria of three categories of objects: subsistence goods, prestige goods (slaves, cattle, metal), and women. Within each category one object can be exchanged for another. Between the second and third categories certain principles of conversion make possible access to women on the basis of brass rods, but goods of the first category cannot be converted into those of the second — nor, and especially not, into the third. There is thus no money serving as common denominator between these three categories, and labour and land remain outside them.[111] When European money was introduced, its role of universal equivalent was seen as a threat to the traditional social structure, and the Tiv tried to save the 'model' of their exchanges by adding a fourth category to the other three, in which European money was exchangeable for goods imported from Europe, or for other European money. This attempt soon collapsed.

Salisbury's work on the Siane enables us to get closer to understanding the properties of a primitive currency and to present a theoretical interpretation of it.

Among the Siane, goods were divided into three heterogenous categories: subsistence goods (products of agriculture, food-gathering, the crafts); luxury goods (tobacco, palm oil, salt, pandanus nuts); and precious goods (shells, bird-of-paradise feathers, ornamented axes, pigs) forming part of ritual expenditure on the occasion of weddings, initiations, treaties of peace, religious festivals. No article in one category could be exchanged for an article in any other. Substitutions were effected only within a category. There was not one currency, but several currencies, not a general exchange of goods and services, but limited and compartmentalized exchanges. When European money appeared, the principle of non-convertibility of goods was applied to it: coins were placed in category 2, notes in category 3. The reciprocal convertibility of coins and notes, correlative of the convertibility of money into any other article at all, was neither understood nor accepted by the Siane for a long time. I am going to try to explain why this had to be. It seems to me that the absence of a universal currency among the Siane was due, on the one hand, to the limited character of exchanges, the lack of real commodity production (this was the negative reason), but also, on the other, to the need to regulate access to women within a clan and to balance the circulation of women among the clans (this being the positive reason). This second reason, arising from the kinship structures, made it imperative, it seems to me:

(1) To *choose*, among the available resources, certain types of goods, in order to make these correspond to women, and these goods had to be limited in quantity, so as to correspond to the scarcity of women, and to demand greater effort and be more difficult of access than other goods:

(2) To *sever* the mode of circulation of these goods (pigs, shells, etc.) radically from the mode of circulation of other goods, which means setting up a scale of goods arranged in several heterogeneous and non-substitutable categories.

The absence of an all-purpose currency thus appears doubly necessary. An analysis inspired by classical political economy would grasp only the negative reason, the absence of commodity production: an anthropological analysis adds the positive reason. This twofold way of looking at the situation clarifies both the fact that, for a Siane, the significance of an all-purpose currency could not be spontaneously recognizable, since it had neither meaning nor necessity in his own social system, and the fact that the introduction of this currency entailed a threat to his social system.[112] Here we come to the general problem of the relations between economic structures and kinship structures, and one may ask what modifications are made in the long run to the axioms of a kinship system as a result of the development of generalized commodity production and all-purpose currency.[113]

The existence of a currency thus has not the same meaning in a primitive economy as in a Western commodity economy. One and the same reality may take on different and unexpected significances through belonging to different social wholes. Once again, the structure gives a meaning to the elements that compose it, and if one's method is a good one it is not the same element that has to be sought in several structures, in order to prove functional identity, but *the same relation between the elements* of one structure and those of another. My interpretation leads to the same conclusion as that of Dalton. The differences between economic systems are no less important than the similarities, and the differences are due to the different social structures within which the same element functions.

To complete this argument, let us look at the system of currency and credit existing in Rossel Island, as described by Armstrong[114] and interpreted by Lancaster.[115] On Rossel Island there was a currency made up of two series of shells, the Ndap and the Nkö. Each series contained a limited number of coins, arranged in 22 categories in the case of the Ndap and 16 in that of the Nkö. No value was a multiple of a basic unit. The Ndap series had the highest value. Values 1 to 18 were used in ordinary transactions, but those from 19 to 22 figured in exceptional transactions only, being handled by the chiefs in accordance with a certain ritual. Coins of category 22 were handed down in the male line of a family of powerful chiefs. Through the intermediary of this system of values a complicated credit system was established. The island's life revolved around a set of social obligations involving transactions in money. In order to carry out a certain transaction it was necessary to possess a certain kind of coin. If one did not possess it then it had to be borrowed, and at the end of a certain period one had to pay it back. In order to do this one could hand over either a coin of the same value, plus some coins of an inferior value, or else a coin of a higher value. Thus there existed an interest, related to time, the rate of this interest being fixed in ritual discussions. Each individual sought to invest his coins, so as at the end of a certain time to obtain coins of a higher value. A financier, the *ndeb*, borrowed and discounted the coins of owners of 'liquid' assets, and took care of the repayment rituals. Everyone thus sought to derive profit from the circulation of money and acted as though he wished to maximize his individual advantages. With this example (and with that of the Malekula currency described by J. Guiart),[116] we seem very close to the modern idea of financial capital. Everyone competes with everyone else to maximize the profits that he draws from the use of a currency. However, Lancaster has shown that this closeness is deceptive. Actually, in the society of Rossel Island, the accumulation of wealth in the hands of certain individuals *did not lead* to an increase in the overall wealth of society, unlike what happens in a Western economy where the credit mechanism is directly a factor of growth through the role it plays in the financing of productive investment.[117] This money and this credit are imbricated in a system that is closed in upon itself and is based not upon commodity exchange but upon a system of 'giving' dominated by the principle of reciprocity. Unlike Mauss,[118] who took Armstrong as his authority for alleging that the operations of credit and giving were identical, Lancaster sees them as two distinct manifestations of the same principle: whoever is in possession of certain goods at the end of a transaction that calls for an eventual 'return' is in the situation and under the obligations of a beneficiary, and this is socially a state of dependence. The cycle of the transaction is closed by the repayment of the debt, with interest, but in the meantime a social relation is created which, in a primitive economy, belongs to a social dimension that goes far beyond the relation between debtor and creditor in a Western economy and gives it a different meaning (social obligations and ritual requirements on the occasion of funerals, weddings, successions — the debt conferring, so to speak, authenticity upon the event).

Lancaster's conclusion regarding Armstrong's materials is thus the same as mine in relation to Salisbury's. The theories of political economy are insufficient to explain a primitive economy, because the latter is socially more complex, and the *uncritical* application of these theories *obscures* the primitive economy more than it illuminates it, as it provides only superficial resemblances while concealing significant differences. Indeed, even the greatest anthropologists have not been able to avoid the snares of deceptively obvious words and apparently 'explanatory' analogies. Boas expressed himself in these terms in his well-known description of the potlatch:

> The economic system of the Indians of British Columbia is largely based on *credit*, just as much as that of civilized communities. In all his undertakings, the Indian relies on the help of his friends. He promises to pay them for this help at a later date. If the help furnished consists in valuables, which are measured by the Indians by blankets as we measure them by money, he promises to repay the amount so loaned with interest.[119]

Such words suggest a close equivalence between potlatch and credit, but Dalton, relying on Boas himself and on Irving Goldman,[120] has shown that here too the differences were more important than the similarities. In the market economy, credit has a variety of functions, the most important being the financing of 'enterprises' through short-term and long-term loans. The borrower uses this all-purpose currency in a materially productive way so as to be able to pay back the loan together with the interest charge upon it, while still retaining some profit. This is not the case with the Kwakiutl. In a market economy, the apparatus that creates debt and credits is an element in the institution of the market. Rates of interest are variable, depending on supply and demand on the money market. There is no law in a market economy that 'constrains' anyone to borrow, and to borrow only from the group to which his family belongs. Among the Kwakiutl, blankets are a currency of very limited usage. The sphere of the potlatch is that of transactions in certain goods and with special currencies that are not used in other spheres and remain distinct from the sphere of everyday life. In our economy the essential elements of everyday life are acquired through the market, and to the same market belongs the mechanism of debit and credit. The mechanism by which the debt is created, the conditions for repayment, the penalties for failing to repay, are entirely different from what they are among the Kwakiutl. In our economy the debtor always takes the initiative in contracting the debt, but in the potlatch it is the 'creditor' who takes the first step, obliging his rival to accept his gifts. And, most important, the chief motive of the potlatch is the seeking of honorific prestige, not the accumulation of material wealth, and the ultimate conclusion of the potlatch code of honour is the destruction of wealth in order to show one's worth and thereby to crush one's rival.

Through the analysis of these four examples (Tiv, Siane, Rossel, Kwakiutl) we can perhaps make out a sort of general law. The more complex the division of labour, the more do economic activities acquire relative autonomy in the social totality and the easier is it to define elementary economic categories, that is, categories and laws that are 'simply' economic. Contrariwise, the simpler a society is, the less possible it is to isolate the economic from the other elements in social life, and the more complex will be the analysis of an apparently economic mechanism, since the entire social configuration is directly present at the heart of this mechanism. In a certain way, the simplicity of the categories of thought seems to be in inverse ratio to the complexity of the structures of social reality. In this sense it is because it produces 'simple' concepts that 'the higher explains the lower', that political economy is the *starting-point* of economic anthropology. At the other end of the journey, however, economic anthropology finds that political economy is not enough for its purposes, and that it can itself provide political economy with the angle of vision that the latter usually lacks, in order to mark out its limits, its field of theoretical and historical validity, and perhaps to suggest to it the need to clear up its *terrae incognitae*, its uncultivated areas, to explore its own world in the manner of an ethnologist.[121]

By wishing to see political economy[122] as already the general theory of 'what is economic', one ends up losing sight of the sociological and historical dimension of the facts, transforming a social fact into a natural one, denying or distorting the facts found in primitive societies, even deceiving oneself about the actual functioning of our own economic system, and eventually one forgets that good rule of method that allows for one and the same element to take on a different meaning in wholes that are structured differently. Facts, method, science, all are lost, and this because one has lost the anthropological point of view, the comparative point of view, because one is following the 'natural' bent of a culture by taking one's own society as 'absolute' point of reference. Uncritically, one is taking the rationality of Western economy as the only possible rationality. In other words, one is *justifying* it while analysing it, something that is characteristic of ideological thinking. Can the concept of economic rationality escape from the realm of ideology and possess a scientific content? Is there even such a thing as *an* 'economic' rationality?

3. TOWARDS A RENOVATION OF THE IDEA OF 'ECONOMIC RATIONALITY'

'The Greeks lived formerly as the Barbarians live today' — (Thucydides, I, 6, 6)

I will limit myself to taking a little further the problematic that I have already outlined for this idea — the most difficult of all, and calling for very extensive development. Science, as we have seen, is lost where ideology begins, and ideology begins when a society takes itself as the absolute point of reference and as centre of perspective, whether initial or ultimate. To take one's own society as one's centre of perspective is, indeed, the procedure followed spontaneously by every consciousness; but scientific knowledge begins when the affirmations of spontaneous awareness are challenged and transcended.

Economic science itself was born when the generally-accepted and 'obvious' idea that the *ancien régime* must be upheld was challenged, and when the rules of functioning of an industrial and commercial capitalist economy were taken as the object of analysis and seen as the principles of a 'rational' society. From the beginning, political economy was involved in criticizing, explaining and justifying. And this criticism and this justification were held to be absolute, this explanation was seen as decisive, since the rules of the new economy were, it was believed, in accordance with the principles of 'natural Reason', transcending every historical contingency. History had been led astray through ignorance of the true principles: now that these were known, the reign of Reason would begin.

In this way the mechanisms of commodity economy were both described and 'given value'. Facts became 'norms'. The new economic system was presented and 'felt' as being a 'model' before which the rules of the *ancien régime* and of other societies were indicted, judged and found guilty of 'irrationality'. Very soon after this, with Fourier and Saint-Simon, later with Marx,[123] and nowadays with the upheavals of decolonization and the confrontation between systems on a world scale, criticism of the principles of free enterprise developed, producing as evidence the exploitation of the workers, the wastage of resources, crises, colonial imperialism, etc. It is no longer obvious that the pursuit of private interest automatically promotes the public interest. With the same idea of conferring value upon a 'model', the ancient Greeks treated foreigners as 'barbarians', and only yesterday the sociologists discovered that primitive peoples had a 'pre-logical' mentality. In discussing the subject of rationality are we doomed to compile a doxography of the prejudices of men and societies?[124] Is there nothing but prejudice, ideology, illusion, in this perpetual motion of complementary and successive ascription and denial of value to different forms of behaviour? Can there be scientific knowledge of the rationality characteristic of a particular system, and can this be compared with other systems?

What meaning is accorded implicitly to the idea of economic rationality? To find the answer, I will proceed *a contrario*, by recalling the content that underlay the charge of 'irrationality' brought against the *ancien régime*: briefly, that system was accused of *being an obstacle to technical and social progress*.[125] Thus, the idea of economic rationality is organized around two poles of significance. By a 'rational' economy is meant one that is 'efficient' and 'just'. 'Efficiency' relates to the technical structures of production, in other words, to the greater or less domination by man over nature, while 'justice' relates to relations between men in their access to resources and to the social product. If we compare these two fields of meaning with the state of our present theoretical knowledge, we observe a dissymmetry between them. Technical efficiency is the subject-matter of thorough-going research, aided by processes of calculation. Operational research provides some of these methods, which make it possible to raise the productivity of various combinations of factors of production. 'Social justice', however, is a sphere of apparently insoluble conflicts, and it is not easy to see when the equation between justice and welfare will be satisfactorily settled, despite all the 'welfare' theoreticians.[126] Nevertheless, we can see that these two fields of meaning are in fact one. The best combination of factors of production is not sought after merely in order the maximize the personal profit of their owner. If the question of rationality relates to these two themes, productivity and justice-welfare, then clearly it lies at the heart of everyday life as an inevitable and permanent question, which calls for an answer not only in theory but also in practice. A closer analysis reveals that the question of the technical and social efficiency of a system is the question of this system's potentialities — more precisely, of the *maximum potentialities* that this system has for bringing about the economic and social changes that are necessarily imposed upon it. It is not possible here to analyse the potentialities of all actual systems known to history, past and present, but it is possible to tackle the problem 'formally', that is, to outline the 'problematic' of such an analysis. How does one tackle the analysis of a system's 'potentialities'? I think we have to distinguish between two planes — the plane of consciously created, willed potentialities, and that of potentialities that are submitted to, whether consciously or not — and two levels of rationality, the intentional and the unintentional.

Willed rationality is seen first in the use that a society makes of its environment. Every technique, as we have seen, makes use of the potentialities of a *milieu*, and assumes a knowledge, whether rudimentary or complex, of the properties of the objects forming this *milieu*, and of their relations. Schlippe[127] has shown, for example, that, behind the appearance of chaos presented by the itinerant agriculture of the Azande, there lies a rigid, hidden order. The scattered arrangement of cultivated plots, the different forms of association for purposes of cultivation, represent close adaptation to ecological possibilities. The work of Conklin,[128] Viguier[129] and Wilbert[130] has shown that the ratio between cultivated and fallow land among practitioners of extensive agriculture revealed an exact knowledge of the regeneration cycle of the fertility of soils. G. Sautter has shown that the ratio between land cultivated continuously and land cultivated discontinuously, as expressed by the concentric arrangement of the cultivated land in West Africa, depended on the possibilities of producing manure and the means for transporting it. The potentialities of a *milieu* thus constitute alternatives that can be exploited under certain conditions and which always necessitate a conscious effort if they are to be exploited.[131]

Hackenberg[132] has studied the economic alternatives offered to the Pima and Papago Indians by their territory, situated in the central desert and the south-west of Arizona. He classifies these alternatives in accordance with an increasing gradient of technological intervention in the given facts of the *milieu*, a gradient that arranges in logical order: (1) Hunting and food-gathering, (2) Marginal agriculture, (3) Pre-industrial agriculture, (4) Industrial agriculture. In the 17th century the Papago, living in dry mountain valleys, drew 75 per cent of their resources from hunting and food-gathering, whereas for the Pima, in the basin of the Gila River, the corresponding figure was 45 per cent. The rest of their resources was obtained — to a greater extent by the Pima than by the Papago — from marginal agriculture which exploited with a very simple technique, the fertility of the soil maintained by the rain and the natural irrigation of the Gila River. Among the Pima, in contrast to the Papago, the fields were permanent and the way of life was that of fixed settlement. The differences became much greater when the Pima went over to pre-industrial agriculture. By co-ordinating their efforts they improved their hydraulic system. The introduction of wheat, a winter grain-crop, by the Spaniards completed the cycle of harvests and ensured the subsistence of the communities, thanks to agriculture, all through the year. Consequently, the Pima were now completely freed from their former dependence on hunting and food-gathering. The Papago, on their more arid terrority, were never able to produce agricultural resources in sufficient quantity to replace hunting and food-gathering. The white men introduced industrial agriculture, producing cotton. They brought the Gila River under control by building dams and big reservoirs. This meant effecting a far-reaching change in the *milieu*, which presupposed the use of machines and a market economy to give an outlet for the produce. This potentiality the Pima, and *a fortiori* the Papago, had been unable to realize.

The potentialities of a *milieu* are thus actualized or developed through the techniques of production. It seems that the lower the technological level of a society, the simpler the economic system, the fewer 'alternatives' exist for an economic 'choice' and the smaller is the maximum production that the society will be able to attain. The fluctuations of this maximum depend very much more upon the variations in constraints external to the system than upon internal variations within it. If, for example, we analyse the units of land measurement that were used in the Middle Ages — the acre, the ploughland and so on — we see that they express the largest area that could be cultivated by a plough-team in one day or one year. This maximum depended on the conditions of the terrain — valley, hill-slope, heavy soil, light soil — and the agrarian metrology adapted itself flexibly to these variables.

Maximization of production is meaningless, however, without reference to the hierarchy of needs and values that are imposed upon individuals in a given society, having their basis in the nature of the structures of this society. The maximizing of production is only one aspect of the overall strategy of maximizing social satisfactions which is imposed upon individuals and groups within this society. In connexion with Amatenango, a community of the Indians of the State of Chiapas, in Mexico, Nash[133] has shown that none of them is unaware of the rules for maximizing monetary gain, but that the ends that each one seeks to maximize are objectives to which value is accorded otherwise than in accordance with this economic magnitude. Every man endeavours to pass through the entire cycle of communal offices, civil and religious, that will confer on him an important rank in the group's hierarchy. Every man therefore practises a complex set of forms of behaviour, co-operating and competing with the other members of the group, allowing for the prestige and wealth of his family and marriage-connexions. These examples show us that the intentional rationality of a social system is revealed in the form and through the purposive acts by which individuals combine means in order to attain their ends. But this 'formal' analysis says nothing about the nature of these means and these ends. Above all, it does not allow us to analyse certain properties of a system that are neither willed by nor, often, even known to its agents, an unintentional level of rationality.

When theoretical consciousness arrives at knowledge of this level, it has passed from rules to laws, from the known properties of a system to those of its properties that were unknown at the start. We will deal with this delicate point by means of a few examples. Hackenberg points out that when the Pima adopted the cultivation of wheat and went over to a system of permanent agriculture, they greatly transformed, without wishing to, and, probably, at first without knowing it, the wild flora and fauna of their environment, the basis of their old economy of food-gathering and hunting. After a certain time, any return to these old forms of economy became, first difficult and then impossible. The Pima had thus destroyed one of their economic possibilities, and cut off all retreat in that direction.[134] Furthermore, population increase, connected with the development of agriculture, made such a path fundamentally inadequate to their needs. Thus, by adopting a new economic system, a society acquires some new possibilities, while depriving itself of others. All determination is negation, as Spinoza and Hegel said. And this deprivation is not aimed at by any consciousness, anyone's intention. It is not the deliberate act of any person taken separately, but the unconscious work of all. At the same time, however, the new possibilities that a society opens to itself have their own objective limits, their own shutting-off mechanism.

Conklin, Viguier and many others have shown that, in a system of extensive agriculture on patches of denshered land, there was a *necessary ratio* between land cultivated and land left uncultivated, in order to ensure maintenance of the fertility of the soil and reproduction of the productive system at the same level of efficiency.[135] When this ratio is exceeded, the 'equilibrium' of the system is upset,[136] a process of defertilization and deterioration of the soil sets in, yields decline, social difficulties begin. If no solution is found, the vicious circle of extensive cultivation sets in: when yields fall, cultivated areas expand, and when cultivated areas expand, yields fall. The functioning of the system is thus incompatible with certain rates of population growth, or with the necessity of extending cultivated surfaces so as to produce industrial crops and obtain income in money form. The problem then arises of how to change the system so as to break the vicious circle it engenders and resolve the contradiction between production and consumption,[137] means and needs. This example throws up a number of theoretical problems, and offers some light for their solution.

Sometimes, as we have just seen, the very success of a system creates the conditions for its failure. Extensive agriculture makes possible in general a higher rate of population increase than is offered by an economy of food-gathering or hunting, but beyond a certain point, this density of population is incompatible with the maintenance of conditions for the proper functioning of the system, or at least the rules that yesterday were effective and rational are no longer so in this new situation. Thus we obtain the hypothesis that there is a functional correspondence between the working of a system and a certain type and a number of external and internal conditions for this working. There is thus no economic rationality 'in itself', definitive and absolute. The evolution of a system may, in certain conditions, develop contradictions that are incompatible with maintenance of the essential structures of the system, and reveal the limits to the possibilities of the system's 'invariance'.

What is meant by the 'invariance' of a system? Not the invariance of the elements combined in the system but the *invariance of the relation* between these elements, the invariance of its fundamental structures. The hypothesis can be advanced that, beyond a certain point, variation in the variables of a system dictates variation in the functional relation between these variables. The system must then evolve towards a new structure. In this connexion an objective dialectic of the relation between 'structure' and 'event' becomes apparent. A structure has the property of tolerating and 'digesting' certain types of event up to a certain point and time when it is the event that digests the structure. A social structure can thus dominate an evolution and contradictions both internal and external up to a certain point which is not known in advance and is not a property of the 'consciousness' of the members of the society defined by this structure but a property of their social *relations*, both conscious and unconscious. The conscious action of the members of a society to 'integrate and neutralize' the event or the structure that threatens or injures their social system has been strongly emphasized by anthropologists, and shows the inner bond between the intentional and unintentional rationalities of the system.[138] We have seen, for example, the Tiv and Siane seeking to integrate European money and the new commodity exchanges into a supplementary category and thereby to preserve, while giving it a wider field of action, their traditional system of circulation of goods. We have also seen these attempts fail after a certain time. The contradiction that developed here did not come from inside the system, like the contradiction between population growth and extensive agriculture, but from outside it. Nevertheless, it also reveals what the internal possibilities of this system are. There is thus, when it comes to forming a science of societies, no theoretical superiority of non-acculturated societies as compared with acculturated societies, or vice versa. The former are needed in order to understand the latter, and the latter throw light on the former. This reciprocity enables us to attempt an analysis of the possibilities of invariance of the different social systems.

The resolution of a contradiction that is incompatible with the invariance of a system does not necessarily result in the mutation and destruction of this system. When a crisis breaks out in a community of slash-and-burn cultivators, if there is plenty of land available around this community, it can break up and, so to speak, expel the contradiction by hiving off daughter-communities around it. This solution maintains the economic system and multiplies it, while endowing it with great stability of evolution. When hiving off is impossible, the contradiction has to be resolved on the spot by producing more from the same area and going over to more intensive forms of agriculture. Some writers, such as Richard-Molard[139] and G. Sautter explain in this way the presence of intensive agriculture among the Palaeo-Negritic peoples of Africa, who were probably driven from their original area by invaders and confined to their places of refuge, where, in order to survive, they were obliged to exploit a limited territory intensively.[140]

Besides, the existence of contradictions within a system does not mean that this system is doomed to paralysis. Some contradictions are constituent features of a system, and give it its dynamism for a certain period. Thus, under the *ancien régime*, peasants and lords were both opposed to each other and in solidarity with each other. The contradiction between them *did not rule out* their unity like the contradiction between a master and his slaves. The struggles between peasants and their lords, far from weakening the system, gave it a stronger stimulus. When the peasants succeeded in forcing their lord to reduce labour-services and rents, they then had more time and means available to develop their own resources. The peasant communities became richer, exchanges became livelier — and the lords benefitted from this prosperity. Some have supposed that the economic, social, cultural and demographic dynamism of feudal Europe between the 11th and 13th centuries had its source in the possibilities of growth that were contained in the contradiction of the lord-peasant relationship, at least so long as the lords were still 'entrepreneurs of production' and had not yet become almost exclusively mere 'drawers of ground-rent' and a parasitical class.[141] There are thus contradictions that act as driving forces of economic and social development, or periods when the social order and the economic system can evolve rapidly without being held up by acute contradictions. Perhaps the difference between the contradictions of a primitive community — the unity of the working of competition and co-operation — and those of a class society is that the former do not entail economic and social changes *directly*, or at the same pace as the latter. In order to verify this point, exact investigations and statistical inventories would have to be made. In any case, however, if a system functions only under certain conditions, the optimum of its functioning corresponds to a 'state' and a 'moment' of the evolution of this system in which its internal and external contradictions are best 'dominated' — which does not necessarily mean 'excluded.' For, while excluding the surplus population of a society of slash-and-burn cultivators means resolving its contradiction, destroying the relation between master and slave, or between lord and peasant, does mean really 'changing' the system, abolishing it, in the way that the night of 4 August, 1789, saw the 'abolition of privileges and of the *ancien régime*'. But we ought not to consider the optimum functioning of a system in the manner of Montesquieu seeking the date of the highest 'grandeur' of the Romans before they fell into irremediable decadence, or Toynbee describing the death-throes of civilizations strewing the arena of history with their remains. At each moment of a system's evolution there is an optimum practice that can be employed in order to dominate the contradictions of that moment, and those who are called great leaders are precisely the men who find the 'necessary' transformations. One may assume, however, that a system is at the optimum of its functioning during the period when the compatibility of the social structures that compose it is at its maximum.

Thus the idea of functional compatibility and incompatibility leads us towards an operations research and cybernetics of economic systems, towards a logic — not formal but 'real' — of the evolution of systems which is the proper theoretical task of economic anthropology.[142] Our last analyses, however, may have left the impression that an 'economic' rationality capable of isolation does exist. The analyses of Nash and Lancaster gave us a glimpse of individuals pursuing a wider, social rationality, which covers and organizes the totality of social relations. This sets us on the path to a compatibility much broader than the compatibility between an economic structure and an event or a structure that is also economic, on the path to a functional 'correspondence' between economic and non-economic structures.

Hackenberg has shown that the development of a pre-industrial agriculture among the Pima resulted in the development of six features that were unknown to the Papago, and created a difference that was now a difference of 'kind' between their two social systems. The habitat of the Pima became concentrated and definitively settled. Co-operation developed between several villages, for organizing water-resources. The economy was finally liberated from food-gathering and hunting. An agricultural surplus could be exchanged with other tribes. The employment of a labour-force from outside (the Papago), which had become necessary, had begun a process of social differentiation. Finally, and above all, the political and social structure had become much more complex within the extensive Pima communities than it was among the Papago. A tribal authority had been formed, headed by a single chief.

This example raises the general problem of intentional and unintentional correspondence between all the structures of a social system, of 'social' rationality. Ember[143] has tried to show, by a statistical analysis, the general relation of correspondence between economic and political development. For primitive or pre-industrial societies the indicators of economic development cannot be direct, since we have no prices with which to measure the value of goods and services. Economic specialization is a valid indicator, but is hard to pin down in usable form, amid the materials provided by ethnographic and historical writing. Ember, following Naroll,[144] selected two indirect indicators of both economic specialization and economic development: the larger size of the social community (connexion between productivity and population-growth), and the relative importance of agriculture as compared with hunting, food-gathering and stock-breeding. As indirect indicators of political development he selected the degree of differentiation of political activity, measured by the number of different functions connected with the task of government, and the level of political integration of the society, measured in terms of the most extensive territorial groups on whose behalf one or more activities of government were carried on.

He took at random a sample of 24 societies from the list drawn up by Murdock[145] of 565 cultures, contemporary and historical, and studied the correlation between his four indicators. It emerged as a strong one in a non-linear relationship. The complexity of social systems seems, to employ Naroll's expression, to increase in geometrical progression, like the complexity of biological systems. Ember interprets the relation between economics and politics by adopting the assumption that politics plays a necessary and decisive role in a society as regards control of resources and the product, or, in other words, in operations and redistribution. And this role increases with the importance of the surplus that the economy produces. In a society of food-gatherers the distribution of products is direct. It is no longer the same in a more complex economy. But examination of the deviant cases in Ember's sample shows us that we must not seek a mechanical, linear connexion between economic and political systems, and that the nature of the economic system counts less than the dimensions of the surplus that it can produce, in other words, its productivity. Among the Teton Indians, who were bison-hunting horsemen, community sizes were relatively large, despite the absence of agriculture, and political complexity and integration had also reached a high level. In fact, at the period when the high plains of the North were relatively underpopulated, bison-hunting on horseback obtained more resources than primitive agriculture. In a different set of conditions, a fishing economy like that of the Kwakiutl of British Columbia could provide a production per head greater than that of an agricultural society.

These deviant cases bring out the fact that it is not possible mechanically to deduce a political system from an economic one, nor to reduce a political system to its economic functions, for a political system assumes other functions, too, such as defence, which do not belong to the economic sphere. Thus, among the Pima, at the moment when they were going over to permanent agriculture, the menace of the Apaches contributed to hasten the regrouping of the habitat and the political integration of the villages under the authority of a single chief. It is in a complex and subtle context like this that the idea of surplus has been taken up by the prehistorians[146] in order to explain the appearance of the great Bronze-Age societies of the Near East, or the great pre-Columbian empires of Mexico and Peru.

Through the hypothesis of a correspondence between economic and political structures[147] we meet again the idea of a wider rationality, a correspondence between all the structures of a social system — kinship, religion, politics, culture, economics. There is thus no strictly economic rationality, but instead an overall, totalizing rationality — an historical, social rationality. Max Weber already in his day attempted to show a correspondence between the Protestant religion, merchant capitalism, and modern forms of law and of philosophical thought. This task demands, if it is to bear fruit, the organic collaboration of different specialists in social facts, and such collaboration implies a methodology that has not yet been elaborated.

On the basis of this overall social rationality revealed by anthropological analysis, the economic mechanisms can be reinterpreted and better understood. A kind of economic behaviour that seems to us 'irrational' is found to possess a rationality of its own, when set in its place in the overall functioning of society. Nash showed that the Amatenango community, while not unaware of the rules of monetary gain, was unable to experience real economic expansion owing both to the low technological level and to the lack of land that dragged down the whole society, and also to the fact that accumulated wealth was periodically drained away in the carrying out of the religious and secular functions of the community instead of being invested for productive purposes. The absence of 'spirit of enterprise' and incentive to invest is therefore not explicable by a merely economic necessity but also has its *raison d'être* in the actual structure of the Indian community. The economic behaviour of this community may seem 'irrational' to us, but this view reflects two attitudes — one, ideological, due to our taking Western society as absolute centre of reference, and the other which notes an objective limit to the Amatenango social system's ability to ensure continued technical progress and an evolution of its members' standard of living. It is clear that these two distinct attitudes reinforce one another, so far as the uncritical spontaneous consciousness is concerned.

By way of all these analyses and distinctions some theoretical conclusions can be gathered together. There is no rationality 'in itself', nor any absolute rationality. What is rational today may be irrational tomorrow, what is rational in one society may be irrational in another. Finally, there is no exclusive economic rationality. These negative conclusions challenge the preconceptions of 'ordinary' consciousness and are remedies against the 'temptations' that these present. In the end, the idea of rationality obliges us to analyse the basis of the structures of social life, their *raison d'être* and their evolution. These *raisons d'être* and this evolution are not merely the achievement of men's conscious activity but are the unintentional results of their social activity.[148] While there is some rationality in the social development of mankind, the subject of this rationality is not the isolated and absurd individual of a timeless human nature and psychology, but men in all the aspects, conscious and unconscious, of their social relations. Synchronic and diachronic analysis of past and present social systems would enable us to get an inkling of the 'possibilities' of evolution inherent in these systems, their dynamism; it would illuminate retrospectively the particular circumstances of the *uneven development* of these societies, and would give us a new conception of the contrasts that exist between societies today. The history of societies is not accomplished in advance, today any more than yesterday. The idea of a linear evolution leading all societies mechanically through the same stages by the same paths is a dogma that has quickly foundered, despite Morgan's[149] authority, in the insoluble quarrels of dogmatic Marxism.[150] It seems to me that the assumption of a certain unintentional and intentional rationality in the evolution of societies leads to a 'multilinear' evolutionism that seeks, in that laboratory of social forms called history, to reconstitute the precise conditions for the opening or the closing of different possibilities.[151] And this multilinear evolutionism that will come into being seems to be nothing else but the general theory of economic systems, the ultimate task of economic anthropology.

I have tried to bring out some methodological principles for critical use of the categories of economic science. These are only hypotheses, needing to be checked. But economic science, like the other social sciences, is still caught in the labyrinth of a method that is incapable of conceiving the identical *and* the different, the intentional *and* the unintentional. It will need to find the Ariadne's thread of its future by getting as close as possible to the literal content of the empirical material provided by anthropology and ridding itself constantly of any temptation to project upon history the phantom of our modern societies, transforming the relative into an absolute. If this is done, scientific consciousness will become what it should be, both internal and external to its object.

POSTSCRIPT

There is no longer any fixed point of reference which any one of us could use to attain once again, even in its simplest form, the structure of knowledge and thus, to suggest its limits. The temptation is there, but the instrument allowing us to give in to it convincingly is lacking. It is impossible today to find material to fulfil and complete a totalising discourse either in the field of the Subject, the Concept, or in that of Nature. It is best to come to terms with this and to give up fighting an anachronistic, rearguard action on this issue.

Jean Desanti[152]

In 1958 we posed ourselves two questions and to answer them we were compelled to follow a peculiar route, from philosophy to economics and then to anthropology.[153] The two questions were: 'What is the *hidden* logic of economic systems, and the *necessity* underlying their emergence, reproduction or disappearance in the course of history?' and 'What are the epistemological preconditions for the theoretical knowledge of this logic and these necessities?' These amount to the same thing, since we can recognise in them two aspects of the problem of economic rationality — a vast question whose answer we have sought not in the philosophy of economics or of history, but within the various fields of knowledge that are included in economic studies. In 1965, our conclusion on the progress we had achieved was that 'purely economic rationality did not exist' and that the problem was to construct the structural analysis of social relations in such a way that the 'causality of the structures'[154] upon each other could be analysed, in particular that of modes of production on the other social structures, and thereby to be able to understand the mechanisms of their reproduction and transformations. In this postscript we should like to present an outline of the steps which in our view, in 1973, must necessarily be taken to progress in this task.

The task of discovering and reconstructing in thought the modes of production which have developed, and are still developing, during the course of history, is *larger* than and *different* from the elaboration of an economic anthropology or any discipline which may be similarly labelled. It is essential to the completion of this task to take up one by one all the theoretical problems posed by knowledge of societies and of their history, that is, the problems of the discovery of laws, not of 'History' in general, which is a concept without any corresponding object, but those of the various economic and social formations studied by historians, anthropologists, sociologists or economists. These laws exist, they express the unintentional structural properties of social relations, and their hierarchy and articulation on the basis of given modes of production.

By contrast with the form of Marxism commonly practised, which soon turns into vulgar materialism, we assert that Marx's distinction between infrastructure and superstructure and his assumption that the deep logic of societies and of their history was, in the final analysis, dependent on the transformations of their infrastructure, threw light for the first time on a hierarchy of functional distinctions and structural causalities, without in any way prejudging either the *nature* of these structures which, in each case, are responsible for these functions (kinship, politics, religion . . .) or the *number of functions* which a structure can sustain. To unveil this deep logic, it is necessary to go beyond the structural analysis of the forms taken by social relations and by thought, to attempt to discover the 'effects' the structures have on each other through the various processes of social practice and to indicate their real place in the hierarchy of causes which determine the working and reproduction of a social and economic formation.

Choosing Marx's materialism as the epistemological horizon for theoretical work in the social sciences requires us to uncover and explore by as yet uninvented trajectories the invisible causal network which connects the forms, the functions, the mode of articulation, the hierarchy and the emergence and disappearance of given social structures.

Commitment to these paths is evidence of a desire to reach a point where the distinctions and oppositions between anthropology and history will be abolished, where it will no longer be possible to turn the analysis of economic systems and relations into an autonomous, fetishised field, i.e. to a point beyond the powerlessness of functionalist empiricism and the limits of structuralism.

Choosing these paths is not a question of 'returning to Marx' nor, for the anthropologist, does it mean taking up and defending all Marx's ideas on primitive and early class societies, although, as we have shown in our tentative critical summary,[155] their live elements have a considerable advantage over the dead ones. Marx's contribution to our progress is primarily an open set of hypotheses and methods, invented for analysing the structures and conditions for the emergence and development of *one particular* mode of production, the capitalist mode of production, and, corresponding to it, of bourgeois *society*, but which also have a more general, exemplary, value. We shall show why this open set of hypotheses and methodological procedures not only belongs to the contemporary epistemological horizon, but constitutes its main direction.

Indeed, for Marx the starting point of science does not lie in appearances, in the visible, in the spontaneous representations of the nature of things, of themselves and of the universe which the members of a society create. For him — and in this he differs from empiricists and functionalists — scientific thought cannot hope to discover the true connection and internal relation of things by starting from their apparent connections and visible relations. Therefore it turns away from them, not to leave them unexplained and outside rational knowledge, but to return to them later and explain them according to the principles of the internal connection of things, and in this movement of returning, the illusions of the spontaneous consciousness of the world dissolve one by one.

But in this movement from the visible to the invisible, what scientific thought discovers is that relations between things, material goods, precious objects and values are in fact relations between men, relations which they simultaneously express and conceal. To discover within relations between things the presence and the determination of relations between men is to set off a process which every anthropologist should 'understand' and in which he cannot help but recognise the very object of his theoretical work. Marx's greatness is that, while analysing commodities, money, capital, etc. he 'correctly understood' the facts which are presented inside out — in the daily practice and representations of individuals who live and act within the capitalist mode of production — and he demonstrated the phantasmic character of social relations.

The theory of modes of production must therefore be constructed, since the precise nature of relations of production cannot be read directly in the visible web of social relations. But, and it is in our view necessary to stress this point once again, Marx has not established a doctrine of what infrastructure and superstructure must be once and for all. He did not allocate in advance an invariable form, content and place to what can function as a relation of production. What he did establish is a distinction of functions and a hierarchy in the causality of social structures as they concern the working and evolution of societies. It is therefore impossible to use Marx's name, as some Marxists do, to refuse to see relations of production in kinship relations or, on the other hand, to use this phenomenon as an objection to, even a refutation of, Marx, as is done by some functionalists or structuralists. It is necessary therefore to go beyond the morphological analysis of social structures to analyse their functions and the transformations of these functions and structures.

But the fact that a structure may sustain a number of functions does not sanction either confusion between the structural levels nor failure to give serious consideration to the relative autonomy of the structures. The latter is nothing other than the autonomy of their internal properties. Marx's thought is neither a reductionist materialism which reduces all reality to the economy, nor a simplistic functionalism which refers all the structures of a society back to that which at first sight seems to dominate it, be it kinship, politics or religion. It is by taking this distinction of functions and the relative autonomy of structures as a starting point that it is possible to tackle correctly the problem of the causality of one structure on another, of one level on the others. But insofar as a structure has *simultaneous* effects on all the structures with which it forms an original society liable to reproduce itself, it is necessary to try and discover at different *places* and *levels*, thus with a *different content* and *form*, the presence of the *same* cause, i.e. the necessary and simultaneous effects of a specific set of unintentional properties of particular social relations. This is not to 'reduce' structures to one another, but to demonstrate the different forms of the active presence of one of them in the very working of the others. Any metaphor of container-contained, interior-exterior is obviously incapable of correctly expressing these mechanisms of the intimate articulation and reciprocal action of structures.[155]

But a materialism which takes Marx as its starting point cannot consist merely in the difficult search for the networks of structural causalities without, in the final analysis, attempting to evaluate the specific and unequal importance which these various structures can have on the working, that is, primarily, on the conditions of *reproduction* of, a social and economic formation. In this analysis of the hierarchy of the causes which determine the reproduction of a

social and economic formation this materialism takes seriously
Marx's fundamental hypothesis that the causality of the mode or
modes of production which make up its material and social infrastructures is, 'in the last instance', determinant for the reproduction
of this formation. Of course, taking this hypothesis seriously does
not imply transforming it into a facile dogma or recipe, accompanied
by incantatory and potentially terrorist language which
unsuccessfully conceals its author's ignorance beneath an
unqualified denunciation of the bankruptcy of the 'bourgeois'
sciences. To draw up an inventory of the number and complexity of
the problems which have to be faced by anyone wishing to compare
societies whose subsistence is based on hunting and gathering, such
as those of Bushmen, Shoshone, the Australian Aborigines, would
be enough to show the ridiculous futility of such theoretical
attitudes.[156]

A particular remarkable example of the determining causality of
the modes of production on the organisation and reproduction of
societies is the formation of an original type of economy and society
which emerged from the seventeenth century onwards among the
Indians of the plains of North America. As Symmes Oliver has
shown, this type of society was governed by the constraints of a
hunting economy based on the use of the horse, and later of the gun,
and adapted to the particular economy of the bison which led to
individual bands being dispersed and independent in winter, and
close together and mutually dependent in summer.[157] What is
particularly striking in this case is the way in which identical
constraints produced the *convergence* and *uniformisation* of the
forms of social organisation among all the plains tribes. Originally
these tribes were very different. Those of the north and west, the
Cree, the Assiniboine, and the Comanche, came from groups which
had previously been hunters and gatherers and had lived in loosely
structured bands. Those of the east and south-east were originally
agricultural populations who, particularly in the south, lived in fixed
villages, under the centralised authority of hereditary chiefs and
priests.[158] Very quickly, within a century, and without any real
collapse or radical disappearance of original social relations, a new
mode of production and a nomadic way of life arose throughout
these tribes, transforming social relations by the addition of new
functions or the suppression of old ones: suppressions and additions
which corresponded to the constraints of the new conditions of
production and social life. Those groups, which originally were
settled horticulturalists organised in chiefdoms, were obliged to
adopt a far looser and more egalitarian social organisation because
of the periodic need to divide into nomadic bands in which personal

initiative played a great part. On the other hand, groups which were originally nomadic bands of hunter-foragers were obliged to adopt a more hierarchical organisation in order to impose the common discipline necessary to the success of the great collective summer hunts. As Marx and Engels have endlessly repeated, it is impossible to analyse and understand the forms and routes taken by the transition from one mode of production and social life to another without fully taking into consideration the 'premisses' from which this transition develops. Far from their disappearing from the scene of history at a stroke, it is these earlier relations of production and the other social relations which transform themselves, and we must start from them in order to understand the *forms* which the effects of the new conditions of material life will take and *places* where they will manifest themselves within the previous social structures.[159]

Thus the internal unintentional properties of the social structures are always manifest in these sequences and ruptures and the very contradictions which emerge between these structures are based on these properties. But on this point also — that of the analysis of the contradictions which characterise the functioning and evolution of social relations — Marx supplies us with valuable analyses and above all with the distinction between contradictions which are internal to a structure and constitutive of its functioning (just as capitalist-worker, or lord-peasant relations are constitutive of the capitalist and feudal modes of production) and contradictions between structures: interstructural contradictions. It is the interplay of these two types of contradiction which determines the specific conditions of reproduction of a given social and economic formation.[160]

Finally, whatever may be the nature of the causes and internal or external circumstances (e.g. the introduction of the horse in North America by Europeans) which bring about contradictions and structural transformations within a given mode of production and society, these contradictions and these transformations always have their basis in internal properties, *immanent* in the social structures, and realise unintentional necessities whose logic and laws must be uncovered. It is in these unintentional properties and necessities that human intention and action find their roots and the fullness of their social effects. If these structural transformations have laws, they are not 'historical' laws. In themselves these laws do not change, they have no history, since they are laws of transformation which refer to constant factors, because they refer to structural properties of social relations.

Thus history is not a category which explains but which is explained. Marx's general hypothesis on the existence of a relation of order between infrastructure and superstructure whch in the last instance determines the functioning and evolution of societies cannot allow us to determine in advance the specific laws of the functioning and evolution of the various economic and social formations which have emerged or are yet to emerge in history. That is because, on the one hand, there is no such thing as history in general and, on the other, because it is impossible to know in advance which structures function as infrastructures and super-structures within these various economic and social formations. The epistemological horizon which we have just drawn on the basis of Marx's work (and we must not conceal that it has been possible to make it explicit in parts only thanks to theoretical results achieved well after Marx's lifetime, in the fields of mathematics, linguistics, the theory of information, the structural analysis of kinship relations and myths) thus presents itself as an open set of methodological principles whose practice is on the whole very complex. The open character of this horizon precludes in advance any theoretical trajectory within its limits which might produce falsely totalising syntheses. On the other hand what it does allow is the indication, one by one, of the gaps which divide the fields of theoretical practice in these social sciences, and also the sifting out and elimination of assertions which 'close' these various gaps and these various fields in a false and ideological way.

To speak — in order to describe such theoretical practice which abandons any illusory totalisation but rigorously puts to work a very complex methodology for its more modest aim — to speak of Anthropology or History would only be a misuse of language. Beyond the fetishistic partitions and arbitrary divisions of the humanities, what is under discussion here is a science of man which truly attempts to explain history, that is, to put it back on the workbench, to put the past in the future; that is, to relocate history in the realm of the possible. 'The possible,' said Kierkegaard, 'is the heaviest of categories',[161] and we well know that the most difficult task of theoretical thought, as well as of practical action, is to draw up the inventory and analyse the possibilities which coexist at each moment.

As long as we are unable to reconstruct through scientific thought the *limited* number of possible transformations which any given structure or any given combination of structures can accomplish, history, yesterday's as well as tomorrow's, will tower over us like a gigantic mass of facts with the full weight of their enigmas, and their consequences. To give an example of these enigmas, certain Mbuti groups hunt with a net in groups of seven to ten hunters, while others hunt with a bow in groups of two or three and despise the use of the net with which they are very familiar, and yet others prefer to hunt with a spear. From the level of techniques of production onwards there are alternatives and choices. It is possible to do otherwise, but within certain limits. Meanwhile social relations and ideology are the same in all Mbuti groups. It would thus be necessary to take the analysis far enough to explain these possibilities of alternative action and their incidence or lack of it on other aspects of social life. Personally, we have been unable to go this far, but at least we have recognised the problem.

To conclude, we should like to come back to one of these ruptures, these gaps which remain in an unthought state in Marxist ideas and the human sciences. It is the problem of the phantasmic character of social relations, the problem of religion and beyond it, that of symbolic practice and of ideology in general. This problem is fundamental because our progress towards resolving it decides the possibility we have of understanding the various forms taken by relations of domination and the exploitation of man by man; and therefore also the possibility of reconstituting the various processes of emergence of the hierarchical caste and class societies which have gradually replaced the earlier primitive societies.

To deal with this problem we have first returned to a text of Marx's which remained unpublished for a long time: the *Formen*, which is part of the *Grundrisse* of 1857.[162] We have undertaken a critical analysis of this text to separate the live ideas in it from the dead ones.[163] By critical analysis we mean the work of reading a text in relation to its contexts, both that which is contemporary with it and that which is contemporary with ourselves.[164] But among these roughly outlined live ideas, there is one which has immense scope for discussion but whose theoretical consequences are only beginning to be drawn. It is the idea that in ancient societies, characterised by the Asiatic mode of production and by the exploitation of local villages and tribal communities dominated by a State personified by a 'despot', 'part of its surplus labour belongs to the higher community, which ultimately appears as a *person* . . . This surplus labour is rendered both as tribute and as common labour for the glory of the unity, in part that of the despot, in part that of the imagined tribal entity of the god.'[165] The main point of what Marx is describing is that fact that everything takes place 'as if' the conditions of reproduction of the mode of production and of the society, i.e. what ensures the *unity* and *survival* of the whole community and of each of its members or groups, really depended on the existence and actions of an imaginary tribal Being, of a God or of the person of a supreme despot who is thus placed above the common and made sacred. Thus we find here simultaneously a real and a phantasmic relation of men to their natural and social conditions of existence. But, what Marx adds to this is that previously the mechanisms through which 'the real conditions of life gradually take on an ethereal form' have remained unthought.

From this derives the exceptional importance of the text which Marx wrote a few years later in *Capital* to explain the content and the phantasmic character of the spontaneous representations elaborated by individuals on the essence of commodities, of money, capital, wages, etc.[166] In these representations everything is presented *inside out*; relations between people appear as relations between things and *vice versa* and what is cause appears as result.

What is immediately striking to the reader is the analogy between these mechanisms of the personification of things, the transposition of cause and effect and *vice versa* (which form the phantasmic character of commodity relations) and the forms of fetishisation of social relations which make an imaginary being, a god, appear as the living unity of a community, the source and the condition of its reproduction and well-being. But since in these primitive societies there are no developed commodity relations, and still less capitalist relations, through what possible mechanism could the objective conditions of social life acquire a mythical, phantasmic character? It is from this perspective that we have, on the one hand, questioned Lévi-Strauss's *The Savage Mind* and *Mythologiques* and, on the other, devoted a lengthy analysis to the content and form of religion among the Mbuti.[167] Thus we soon realised that there was a material base to religious practice among the Mbuti since worship consists primarily of a large cyclic of hunts which are more intensive than usual. Because of this intensified hunt and the greater quantity of game available for distribution, cooperation and reciprocity between members of the group, whatever their age and sex, are intensified and heightened, tensions decrease and temporarily exhaust themselves, without of course disappearing. In this way, religious practice really constitutes a form of practice, a political action on the specific social contradictions which are a permanent feature of their modes of production and social life, constantly threatened as they are with the separation and disintegration of the groups.

But at the same time this simultaneously material, political, symbolic and aesthetic (because of the dances and songs which necessarily accompany it) practice is directed towards a real and imaginary being, the Forest, to recall and celebrate its vigilant presence, accompanied by health, abundant game, social harmony and life and holding back epidemics, famine, discord and death. Thus religious practice is, above all, totally directed towards the conditions of reproduction of the Mbuti's mode of production and mode of life and constitutes a truly symbolic labour, an imaginary action on these conditions.

The Mbuti's religion is thus the point at which, in an imaginary form, is presented the invisible juncture which turns their various social relations into a totality liable to reproduce itself, into a society living in a given milieu. What is presented and concealed simultaneously in this mode of presence, or of representation, what is subjected to simultaneously positive and illusory action, is nothing else but the articulation, the invisible juncture of their social relations, their internal content and form, in the shape of the features and attributes of an omnipresent, omnipotent, and well-wishing subject, the Forest. The danger of reading a simple and direct relation of reflection-reflected to reflected-reality in analysing the content and function of religion among the Mbuti is clear. The phantasmic character of their social relations is due not only to the fact that their representation of their practice and the conditions of the reproduction of their mode of life is the reverse of the truth — since, indeed, everything happens as if hunters caught the game not because of their skill and techniques, but as if the catch were the gift of an omnipresent and well-wishing Person. But the phantasm is itself *part of the content* of these social relations and not merely the deviating and ridiculous reflection of a reality which exists beyond it.

This brief summary is sufficient to show how, using such analyses and their initial results as a starting point, the problem of the various forms taken by the relations of domination and exploitation of man by man in the course of the various processes of the formation of hierarchical and later caste or class societies can be tackled. It is important to notice that the Mbuti, whose society is very egalitarian, consider themselves to be all equally dependent on the continuous and favourable intervention of the Forest (this is objectively a correct position since, as they do not transform nature, they are entirely dependent on it to reproduce themselves). Among them everyone is a believer and a priest, and there is not even a shaman. They devote supplementary work to the glorification of the Forest, since they intensify their hunts and consume its product in feasts which claim the exceptional character of ritual life.

It can thus be imagined that, when conditions have given certain men, certain groups, the opportunity to personify *on their own* the common good or to have access to supernatural powers supposed to control the conditions of the reproduction of the universe and society, these men and groups have raised themselves above common men and become closer to gods, going further than other men into the area which, since earliest times, has separated men from gods. Out of this arises the fact that, in many societies in which there are hereditary chiefs who have no means of physical coercion over their dependents (e.g. the Trobriand Islanders studied by Malinowski) the form of ideological justification of these chiefs' powers are due primarily to the fact that they control the great rituals of fertility of the Earth and Sea, and that they appear as intermediaries between the clans, their ancestors and their gods. To keep aloof from men and dominate them, to get closer to gods and be obeyed by them may be no more than two *simultaneous* aspects of the *same* process, that which marks the beginning of the road towards class societies and the State. This road is marked by the immense figures of Assur King-God of his town, or Shinti the Inca, son of the Sun, who reigned on the Twantinsuyu, 'the empire of the four quarters'.[168]

But this time, what began by a peaceful domination has become ideological oppression and economic exploitation, supported or extended by armed violence. Maybe it is unnecessary, therefore, to see whether it is the political which takes a religious form or the reverse, since these are only two forms of the same process, two elements with the same content which exists *simultaneously* at many levels. However it is not irrelevant for the development of the caste and / or class relations, whether the religious elements dominate or the reverse. By working in this direction, Marxism will produce explanations which will answer the objections made to the hypothesis of the mode of production's determining responsibility in the last instance, by specialists like Louis Dumont who is right to suggest that in India, for example, it is the religious which dominated social organisation for millennia.

NOTES

1. The expression first appeared, according to Herskovits, in 1927, with the article by Gras on 'Anthropology and Economics' (Ogburn, *The Social Sciences and their Interrelation*, pp. 10–23).

2. Cf. Mercier de la Rivière: 'Personal interest drives every individual, vigorously and continuously, to improve and increase the things that he can sell, so enlarging the mass of satisfactions he can procure for others, in order to enlarge thereby the mass of satisfactions that others can procure for him in exchange. *The world thus goes by itself* (*L'Ordre naturel et essentiel des sociétés politiques*, 1767, chapter xliv: Daire's edition, p. 617). In 1904 Rist was still affirming: 'Free competition brings about justice in the distribution of wealth as well as maximum well-being in exchange and production' ('Economie optimiste et économie scientifique', *Revue de Métaphysique et de Morale*, July, 1904). See A. Shatz, *L'Individualisme économique et social*, Paris, A. Colin, 1907, ch. iv.

3. Plato, *The Republic*, ed. Budé, 369 b–73 d; Aristotle, *Politics*, Book I, chapters

2, 3 and 4, and *Economics*, Book II, chapter 1, Xenophon, *De l'économie* [*Oeconomicus*], ed. Hachette, 1859, pp. 137–96; Marshall, *Principles of Economics*, 8th edn, Macmillan, chapter 1, p. 1: 'Political economy or economics is a study of mankind in the ordinary business of life; it examines that part of individual and social action which is most closely connected with the attainment and with the use of the material requisites of well-being.' See, on the history of economic thought: Schumpeter, *History of Economic Analysis*, 1955, Part II, chapters 1, 2, pp. 51–142.

4. K. Polanyi, 'The Economy as Instituted Process', in *Trade and Market in the Early Empires*, Free Press, 1957. The definition of the economic as 'substantive' refers to 'an instituted process of interaction between man and his environment, which results in a continuous supply of want-satisfying material means' (p. 248).

5. Von Mises, *Human Action*, Yale, 1949.

6. Robbins, *The Subject-Matter of Economics, 1932.*

7. Samuelson, *Economics, an Introductory Analysis*, New York, 1958, ch. 2.

8. Herskovits, *Economic Anthropology*, New York, 1952, ch. 3.

9. Firth, *Primitive Polynesian Economy*, 1939.

10. Leclair, 'Economic Theory and Economic Anthropology', *American Anthropologist*, 1962, no. 64.

11. Burling, 'Maximisation Theories and the Study of Economic Anthropology', *American Anthropologist*, 1962, no. 64.

12. Firth was moving in the same direction when he said in *Elements of Social Organisation*, Watts, 1951, p. 130:
    'The exercise of choice in social situations involves economy of resources in time and energy. In this sense a marriage has an economic aspect . . . quite apart from the exchanges of goods and services that may go on. But by a convention the science of economics concerns itself with those fields of choice which involve goods and services.' By virtue of the obvious fact that man, like every other living creature, needs time to do anything at all, anything at all 'naturally' has an economic aspect.

13. Leach, *Political Systems of Highland Burma*, Cambridge (Mass.), 1954.

14. Lasswell, *Power and Personality*, New York, 1948.

15. Zipf, *Human Behaviour and the Principle of Least Effort*, Cambridge (Mass.), 1949.

16. In *Capitalism, Socialism and Democracy*, Schumpeter even claims that the 'logic' of economic activity is the basis of the principles of 'all' logic. This feat of reducing the non-economic to, or deducing it from, the economic is the usual outcome of 'economism', the naïve imperialism of one science in relation to the rest.

17. See F. N. Trefethen, 'Historique de la Recherche opérationnelle', in *Introduction à la Recherche opérationnelle*, by McCloskey and Trefethen, Dunod, 1959, pp. 7–20. More precisely, Pierre Massé wrote in his article 'Economie et Stratégie': 'Koopmans has defined the activity of production as the "best utilisation of limited means in order to achieve desired ends". However *different* our respective ends may be, it seems to me that this *definition* could apply *just as well* to the art of war' (in *Operational Research in Practice*, NATO, Pergamon, 1958, pp. 114–31. My emphasis, M.G.).

18. For this reason, the position taken up by Polanyi and Dalton, who claim to bring side by side under the same term the two definitions of the economic, one 'formal' and the other 'substantive', seems to me a theoretical failure (*Trade and Market*, pp. 245–50). The writers themselves admit that these two definitions bear no relation to each other, and that the formal definition expresses the logic of all 'rational' action. Their compromise position leaves them awkwardly placed in relation to the problem of 'scarcity'. Cf. Neil J. Smelser, 'A Comparative View of

Exchange Systems', in *Economic Development and Cultural Change*, 1959, Vol. 7, no. 2, pp. 176–7.

19. See in this connexion, Walter C. Neale, 'On defining "labour" and "services" for comparative studies', in *American Anthropologist*, December 1964, Vol. 66, p. 1305.

20. V. Monteil, 'Les empires du Mali', in *Bulletin du Comité d'Etudes historiques de l'A.O.F.*, 1929, Vol. XII, pp. 291–447.

21. When a professional singer sings at his brother's wedding, for the pleasure of the guests, his behaviour has no economic aspect. If he sings at a 'charity' function and waives his fee, his behaviour does have an economic aspect.

22. George Dalton, 'Economic theory and primitive society', in *American Anthropologist*, 1961, no. 63, pp. 1–25.

23. For many economists, the existence of 'economic systems' is a belated historical fact characteristic above all of the Western world in its recent phase. A. Marchal, in his textbook *Systèmes et structures économiques*, P.U.F., 1959, p. 210, writes: 'Patriarchal economy seems too primitive and unorganized to deserve the description of "system". In it, the father distributes tasks among the members of the family, enlarged by polygamy and slavery. Cattle-raising is the dominant activity, and exchange is restricted to mutual gifts of a ceremonial nature (potlatch) or a silent barter'.

24. Among the innumerable studies devoted to the idea of structure, let me mention: *Notion de structure*, XXe Semaine de synthèse, Albin Michel, 1957; the articles by Granger and Greef in the *Cahiers de l'ISEA*, December 1957; *Sens et usages du terme structure*, Mouton, 1962.

25. Parsons and Smelser, *Economy and Society*, Routledge, 1956.

26. The impossibility of reducing the different structures of social life to just one of their number, whether material or spiritual, rules out any linear, simplifying conception of causality in the sphere of the social sciences. Each type of society seems to be marked by a distinctive *relation* between the different social structures, and this relation determines the specific weight, in this society, of the economy, kinship, religion, etc. This relation between the social structures thus acts through and upon all the aspects of social life without it being possible to locate its efficacity anywhere, in any particular structure. Consequently, the influence of the overall social structure always enters in between one event and another, giving to each of them all its dimensions, whether conscious or not – in other words, the field of its effects, whether intentional or not. Between a cause and an effect there always lie the properties of the social structure, as a whole, and this rules out any simplified conception of causality.

27. For the problem of analysis of the different historical times appropriate to different social structures, see M. Halbwachs, 'La mémoire collective et le temps', in *Cahiers Internationaux de Sociologie*, 1947, pp. 3–31, and, especially, F. Braudel, 'Histoire et sciences sociales: la longue durée', in *Annales ESC*, Dec. 1958, pp. 725–53. See also J. Le Goff, 'Temps de l'Eglise et temps du marchand', in *Annales ESC*, June 1960, pp. 417–23, and G. Gurvitch, 'La multiplicité des temps sociaux', Paris, C.D.U.

28. Plato, *Timaeus*.

29. Cf. the works of G. Lefebvre, Labrousse, Soboul.

30. Firth, *We the Tikopia*, London, 1936, and *Social Change in Tikopia*, London, 1959.

31. Lévi-Strauss, *La Pensée sauvage*, 1963, chapters 5, 6. English trans., *The Savage Mind*.

32. Using Husserl's expression, when he defines phenomenology as an 'eidetic' science, in *Logische Untersuchungen* and *Ideen I*.

33. E. Leclair, 'Economic theory and economic anthropology', in *American Anthropologist*, 1962, no. 64, pp. 1187–8.
34. R. Bloch, *Les Etrusques*.
35. Stein, *La Civilisation du Tibet*, 1962, chapter on 'Economy and society'.
36. Wedgwood, 'Anthropology in the Field: A "Plan" for a Survey of the Economic Life of a People', in *South Pacific*, August, 1951, pp. 110, 111, 115. Productive activity is not, of course, restricted to 'subsistence'. Cf. Steiner and Neale, articles referred to; also R. Lowie, 'Subsistence', in *General Anthropology*, pp. 282–320.
37. Cf. I. Sellnow, *Grundprinzipien einer Periodisierung der Urgeschichte: Ein Beitrag auf Grundlage ethnographischen Materials*, Berlin, 1961. It must be remembered, however, that, in a hunting economy, for example, operations take place involving the transformation of nature: making tools, weapons, clothing, means of transport, etc.
38. Cf. Birket-Smith, *Moeurs et Coutumes des Eskimo*, Payot, 1955, ch. 4.
39. Lévi-Strauss, *La Pensée sauvage*, chapter 1.
40. Lévy-Bruhl, *La Mentalité primitive*, pp. 39–47, 85, 87, 104, 107, 520.
41. Daryll Forde, 'Primitive economics', in *Man, Culture and Society*, ed. Shapiro, 1956, p. 331.
42. Dalton, in his article: 'Traditional production in primitive African economies', in *Quarterly Journal of Economics*, 1962, Vol. LXXVI, no. 3, pp. 360–77, rejects the general use of the expression 'production unit' (p. 362), on the grounds that this means only the Western 'firm', an economic organization without any direct link with the political, religious and kinship structures of society, and that its use obscures analysis of primitive societies by distorting them. This point of view is connected with the theses of Karl Polanyi on economies that are 'embedded' or 'disembedded' in the social organization, theses that I discuss later. Nevertheless Dalton alleges the universal existence of 'production groups' (pp. 362, 364).
43. Hamdan, *Evolution de l'agriculture irriguée en Egypte*, UNESCO, 1961.
44. P. Armillas, 'Utilisation des terres arides dans l'Amérique pré-colombienne', in *Histoire de l'utilisation des terres des régions arides*, UNESCO, 1961, p. 279.
45. D. Forde, *Habitat, Economy and Society*, 1934, ch. IV.
46. Because of this, economic activity takes on the functions of social 'integration' to use the expression of P. Steiner, 'Towards a classification of labour', *Sociologus*, 1957, Vol. 7, pp. 112–30. Cf. also P. Bohannan, *Social Anthropology*, 1963, ch. 14. 'The economic integration of society', pp. 229–45.
47. Cf. Neil J. Smelser, 'Mechanism of change and adjustment to change', in *Industrialization and Society*, report of 1960, Chicago, symposium edited by Hoselitz and Moore, Mouton, 1966, pp. 32–54. Sociology has raised the question of the typology of forms of grouping, by making the distinction between 'Association' and 'Community', which has occupied the central place among the fundamental categories of sociology since *Gemeinschaft und Gesellschaft*, by Tonnies (1887), and Max Weber's *Wirtschaft und Gesellschaft*, 1922, Part I, chapters 1 and 2 and right down to MacIver, *Society, its Structure and Change*, New York, 1933, pp. 9–12, quoted by Dalton.
48. On tribal authority and the tribal economy, see Sahlins, 'Political power and the economy in primitive society', in *Essays in the Science of Culture*, ed. Dole and Carneiro, 1960, p. 412.
49. K. Polanyi, *Trade and Market in the Early Empires*, 1957, pp. 68, 71.
50. J. R. Firth, *Human Types*, 1958, chapter 3, 'Work and wealth of primitive communities', p. 62; W. Barber, 'Economic rationality and behaviour patterns in an under-developed area: a case study of African economic behaviour in the Rhodesias', in *Economic Development and Cultural Change*, April, 1960, Vol. 8, no. 3, p. 237. See the critique of Hoselitz's *Sociological Aspects of*

Economic Growth, 1960, by Sahlins, in *American Anthropologist*, 1962, p. 1068.

51. See, e.g. *African Agrarian Systems*, ed. Biebuyck, Oxford, 1963.

52. See R. Lowie, *Primitive Society*, chapter ix; Herskovits, *Economic Anthropology*, chapter xiv; and the dispute between Speck Hallowell, Schmidt and Leacock regarding the priority of private property or collective property among the Algonquin Indians — Aveskieva, 'The problem of property in contemporary American ethnography', in *Sovetskaya Etnografiya*, 1961, no. 4.

53. Cf. 'De jure personarum', in the Institutes of Justinian (in *Elements de Droit Civil Romain*, J. Heinnecius, 1805, vol. 4, pp. 90–107).

54. R. F. Salisbury, *From Stone to Steel*, Melbourne, 1962. For a detailed analysis of this book, see M. Godelier, *L'Homme*, Vol IV, ch. 4, pp. 118–32.

55. The idea of ownership has a field of application that extends considerably beyond the economic field. Cf. R. Lowie, 'Incorporeal property in primitive society', in *Yale Law Journal*, March, 1928, p. 552. It is significant that among the Siane the land is included in the category of inalienable sacred goods, the property at once of living people, their dead ancestors, and their descendants yet to be born. See also Hamilton and Till, 'Property', in *Encyclopaedia of the Social Sciences*, pp. 528–38.

56. P. Brown and H. C. Brookfield, *Struggle for Land*, Oxford, 1963.

57. The rules of distribution of the product need to be studied in their relation to different conjunctural situations: (1) plenty (+), (2) satisfactory position (±), (3) shortage (∓), (4) famine (—), and this over an annual cycle, as with the Eskimos, or over long cycles including whole years of plenty or of famine. Rules of distribution need to be distinguished in accordance with the nature of the goods (food, tools, luxuries, territory, etc.). Among the Eskimos, in situations of plenty or of famine the rules laid down for situations 2 and 3, which are the most usual, cease to apply. In a famine situation the group sacrifices the non-productive and reserves all its resources for the productive, upon whom the group's surival depends. This raises the problem of the relation between economic institutions and 'scarcity situations' (scarcity of game or of land, temporary or permanent scarcity, etc.). Cf. Smelser's criticism of Polanyi in 'A comparative view of exchange systems', art. cit., p. 177.

58. Herskovits, *Economic Anthropology*, p. 12. On the rules among the Chins for dividing up and distributing meat in accordance with kinship relations and the other social relations, see the festival of Khuang Twasi described by H. Stevenson in *The Economics of the Central Chin Tribes*, Bombay, 1944. In Samoa, pigs were divided into ten parts, destined for ten categories of persons of different status (Peter Buck, *Samoan Material Cultures*, Honolulu, 1939.)

59. A. Métraux, *Les Incas*, Paris, 1961. On the Aztecs, see the important article by A. Caso, 'Land tenure among the ancient Mexicans', in *American Anthropologist*, August, 1963, Vol. 65, no. 4, pp. 862–78.

60. Cf. Duby, *L'Economie rurale et la vie des campagnes dans l'Occident médiéval*, Vol. 1, p. 115.

61. Dalton, 'A note of clarification on economic surplus', in *American Anthropologist*, 1960, no. 62, pp. 483–90, replying to Marvin Harris: 'The economy has no surplus', in ibid., 1959, no. 61, pp. 185–99, and also: 'Economic surplus once again', in ibid., 1963, no. 65, pp. 389–93.

62. E. Fisk, in his article: 'Planning in a primitive society', in *The Economic Record*, Dec. 1962, pp. 462–78, points out, on the basis of Salisbury's research, that the Siane, even before the introduction of steel axes, produced what was economically necessary for their subsistence and their social life *without* having attained the *maximum* productive possibilities of their system. They were thus able to put up with a growth of population and an intensification of production

without causing a crisis of their system. Fisk calls this objective possibility a 'potential surplus'. Carneiro has shown the existence of such a surplus among the Kuikuru: 'Slash and burn cultivation among the Kuikuru and its implications for cultural development in the Amazon Basin', in *The Evolution of Horticultural Systems*, 1961, pp. 47–67.

This potential surplus must be distinguished from the idea of a potential surplus *already appropriated* by the landlords from the industrial capitalist, as propounded by Ricardo and Marx. For them, the already-appropriated surplus can serve development on condition that it is taken away from the landlords and invested productively.

Cf. the critical analysis of Paul Baran, *The Political Economy of Growth*, 1957, and by C. Bettelheim: 'Le surplus économique facteur de base d'une politique de développement', *Planification et croissance accélérée*, 1964, pp. 91–126. The analyses by Fisk and Bettelheim show clearly that the objective possibility of a surplus does not necessarily or automatically entail any economic and social development. For this, definite social conditions and stimuli are needed. If this is not seen, the idea of surplus explains nothing, and on this point Dalton is quite right.

63. Bohannan, 'Some principles of exchange and investment among the Tiv', in *American Anthropologist*, 1955, no. 57, pp. 60–70.
64. Pearson, 'The economy has no surplus: critique of a theory of development', in *Trade and Market in the Early Empires*, ed. K. Polanyi, 1957.
65. Rostow, *The Stages of Economic Growth*. Cf. the symposium of 1961 on *Social Development*, under the direction of R. Aron and B. Hoselitz.
66. *Capital*, I, chapters 26 to 33; III, chapter 47.
67. Paul Mantoux, *La Révolution industrielle au XVIIIe siècle*, Paris, 1961.
68. Mambi Sidebe, *Notes sur l'histoire de l'ancien Mali*, Bamako, 1962. See also Mauny, *Tableau géographique de l'Ouest africain au Moyen Age*, Dakar, 1961.
69. Willcocks-Craig, *Egyptian Irrigation*, London, 1913.
70. M. Mauss, 'Essai sur le don', in *Année sociologique*, 1925, pp. 30–186.
71. The organization of the redistribution of goods by a minority within a tribe creates the *possibility* of a certain exploitation of the majority of the members of the community by this minority, and through this process the possibility of the emergence of a dominant social 'class' in a tribal society. While performing religious and political services to the community and favouring an expansion of the production and circulation of goods, this minority controls the social product to some extent (Trobriand) and sometimes controls part of the factors of production (the land in Pharaonic Egypt, under the Incas, the Imerina of Madagascar, etc.) and manipulates them to its own particular advantage. The problem of the appearance of permanent social inequality and of the transition from a classless society to a class structure does arise here, but neither Polanyi, nor Sahlins nor Bohannan raise it when they analyse how the principle of redistribution works. Preoccupied, with justification in Sahlins' case, with rejecting the mistaken interpretations by Bunzel, Radin and others who 'found' 'capitalist' exploitation of man by man among the Chukchee or the Yurok, or, as in Murra's case, with challenging 'feudal' or 'socialist' interpretations of the Inca Empire, these writers see in redistribution a simple extension of the principle of reciprocity that presides over kinship and marriage relations. In doing so, it seems to me, they hide the real oppressive nature of the aristocratic authority — as indeed do the myths justifying this authority which present it as merely a special feature of the old mechanism of reciprocity. See R. Bunzel, 'The economic organization of primitive peoples', in *General Anthropology*, pp. 327–408; J. Murra, 'On Inca Political Structure', in *Systems of Political Control and Bureaucracy in Human Societies*, 1958, and 'Social Structure

and Economic Themes in Andean Ethnohistory', in *Anthropological Quarterly*, no. 34, April 1961, pp. 47–59; I. Shapera and J. Goodwin, 'Work and Wealth', in *The Bantu-Speaking Tribes of South Africa*, pp. 150 et seq.

72. The consumption unit for a product is the last social link at which the ultimate distribution of this product takes place before it enters into final consumption, whether individual or social. The consumption unit is not an empty social 'framework', as it is governed by a definite social *authority* (the head of a family, etc.), who has power to distribute and attribute.

73. Often, though, there is no coincidence. Cf. Daryll Forde, 'Primitive economics,' *art. cit.*, p. 335.

74. It is hardly necessary to point out that this problem faces those historians who are constantly tempted to project upon ancient or non-Western societies the categories of 'slavery', 'feudalism', 'capitalism', etc. As regards Antiquity, see the well-known controversy about 'capitalism' in the ancient world, and the views of E. Meyer and Von Pölmann analysed by E. Will: 'Trois quarts de siècle de recherches sur l'économie grecque antique', in *Annales E.S.C.*, March, 1954, pp. 7–22, and the addresses by M. Finley and E. Will on 'Trade and politics in the ancient world' at the World Economic History Congress in 1962, at Aix-en-Provence. As regards feudalism, let me recall the criticisms made by M. Bloch and R. Boutruche concerning the alleged 'exotic' feudalism of ancient Egypt, the Hittites, etc. (Japan being excepted). Cf. Boutruche, *Seigneurie et féodalité*, 1958, Vol. II, chapters 1 and 2. Similarly, in ethnology, it is customary to talk of 'African feudalisms' in connexion with the ancient states of Africa. E.g. J. M. Maquet, 'Une hypothèse pour l'étude des féodalités africaines', *Cahiers d'Etudes Africaines*, 1961, no. 6.

75. Firth, *Primitive Polynesian Economy*, 1939, p. 29.

76. Herskovits, *Economic Anthropology*, 1952, p. 488. See also Walker, 'The study of primitive economics', in *Oceania*, pp. 131–42.

77. Goodfellow, *Principles of Economic Sociology*, London, 1939, pp. 4–5.

78. Frank H. Knight, following Robbins, has taken this view to its logical conclusion: 'There are many ways in which economic activity may be socially organized, but the predominant method in modern nations is the price system, or free enterprise. Consequently, it is the structure and working of the system of free enterprise which constitutes the principal topic of discussion in a treatise on economics' (*Economic Organisation*, New York, 1951, p. 6).

79. Rothenberg, review of *Trade and Market in the Early Empires*, in *American Economic Review*, no. 48, pp. 675–8.

80. P. Bohannan, *Social Anthropology*, p. 220. More generally, it is hard for the Western economist to set out the national balance-sheet of an 'underdeveloped' nation, for 90 per cent of production is self-consumed and it is impossible to know what 'price' to attribute to it. Cf. P. Deane, *Colonial Social Accounting*, Cambridge, 1953, pp. 115–16.

81. See, e.g. Salisbury, *From Stone to Steel*.

82. Salisbury, op. cit., p. 4.

83. Thurnwald, *Economics in Primitive Communities*, 1932, pp. 108–9.

84. M. Weber, *The Theory of Social and Economic Organization*, 1947, p. 191.

85. Daryll Forde recognizes this explicitly in 'Primitive Economics' (with Mary Douglas), ch. XV of *Man, Culture and Society*, ed. Harry J. Shapiro, New York, 1956, p. 340: 'The simplest definition of capital, and one which is significant for any primitive economy concentrates on the tools and equipment for production.' Firth, in *Human Types*, p. 79, restricts the idea of capital to: 'certain types of goods [devoted] to facilitating production', but stresses that capital is rarely invested 'with the definite idea of getting a return from it'.

86. Ricardo, *Principles*, chapters 5 and 6.

87. *Capital*, II, chapter 1.
88. Marx, in *Wage-Labour and Capital*: 'A Negro is a Negro. He only becomes a slave in certain relationships. A cotton-spinning machine is a machine for spinning cotton. Only in certain relationships does it become *capital*. Torn from these relationships it is no more capital than gold in itself is *money* or sugar the *price* of sugar.'
89. This lack of the 'spirit of enterprise' is often regarded by the economists as proof of the 'irrationality' of the primitive people, their lack of 'economic principles' (Cf. R. Firth, in *Human Types*, p, 62). Other economists, inspired by Schumpeter's views, in *The Theory of Economic Development*, chapter 2, on the entrepreneur, present this lack as the most serious psychological obstacle to the rapid development of under-developed societies (Cf. Baumol, *Business Behaviour, Value and Growth*, New York, 1959, p. 87); Easterbrook, 'La fonction de l'entrepreneur', in *Industrialisation et Société*, 1962, pp. 54–69; and Leibenstein, *Economic Backwardness and Economic Growth*, 1957, p. 121, on 'requisites of an entrepreneur'.
90. P. Bohannan, *Social Anthropology*, chapter 15; also P. Bohannan and G. Dalton, *Markets in Africa*, introduction.
91. Maurice Leenhardt has listed in his article: 'La monnaie néo-calédonienne', in *Revue d'ethnographie et des traditions populaires*, 1922, no. 12, eighteen situations in which currency in the form of shells was used, and P. Métais took up the problem again in 1952: 'Une monnaie archaique: la cordellette de coquillages', in *Année sociologique*, pp. 3–142. I think it is worth pointing out that historians studying ancient Greece have raised the problem of the multiple significances of currency — religious, ethical, etc. — starting with B. Laum's book *Heiliges Geld: Eine historische Untersuchung über den Sakralen Ursprung des Geldes*, 1924. See Will, 'De l'aspect éthique des origines grecques de la monnaie', in *Revue historique*, 1954, pp. 212–31, and the most recent restatement of the question, by C. Kraay, 'Hoards, small change and the origin of coinage', in *Journal of Hellenistic Studies*, December 1964, pp. 76–91.
92. H. Codere, *Fighting with Property*.
93. C. Dubois, 'The wealth concept as an integrative factor in Tolowa-Tutunni Culture', in *Essays in Anthropology*, 1936.
94. Franz Steiner has sketched a theory of these principles of conversion (*Uebersetzung*), both negative and positive, in his article: 'Notes on comparative economics,' in *British Journal of Sociology*, 1954, pp. 118–29. P. Bohannan distinguishes between the principle of conversion of goods within the same category ('conveyance') and the principle of convertibility of an article from one category into an article from another ('conversion').
95. Each type of society has its own rate of evolution, based on the social structure itself. Historians have noted that, with changes in the type of society, there occur changes in rates of evolution (the flow of innovations, etc.).
96. Shea: 'Barriers to economic development in traditional societies', in *Journal of Economic History*, 1959, 4, pp. 504–27, and M. Nash, 'Some social and cultural aspects of economic development', in *Economic Development and Cultural Change*, 1959, pp. 137–51.
97. Regret for the passing of this control finds expression in Aristotle's violent criticism of 'money-making', the striving — absurd in Aristotle's view — for money for its own sake, which was in contradiction with the Greek ideal of family autarky, and was a source of many ills for the Greek community. Cf. *Politics*, 1257 a–b.
98. This is stressed by Fisk and Carneiro when they show that there is a potential surplus in the Siane and Kuikuru societies. In this sense Pearson and Dalton are right in showing that the existence of a potential surplus does not automatically

entail a transformation of the social structures. Among the Siane, after the introduction of steel axes, the production of subsistence goods was not expanded, but instead war, matrimonial exchanges and festivals were all conducted on a larger scale.

99. It is in this sense that Max Gluckman analyses the structure of the tribalization and detribalization process in Africa, and shows the logic of the attitude of the African worker who has to leave the subsistence sector and at the same time retain it, in order to possess security against the ups and downs of urban employment ('Tribalism in modern British Central Africa', in *Cahiers d'Etudes Africaines*, 1960, pp. 55–72).

100. Cf. J. Lesourne, 'Recherche d'un optimum de gestion dans la pensée économique', in *L'Univers Economique, Encyclopédie Française*, 1960. When recalling the idea of the optimum in Pareto's sense, as meaning a 'state defined by the impossibility of simultaneously improving the situation of all the individuals', many economists consider that this definition is a 'sociologically empty' form. It applies to any and every economic organization, capitalist or socialist (to confine ourselves to modern industrial societies). Mathematically, the problem is that of a 'bound' maximum, the solution of which is found by associating with each constraint of the form 'Fi' + constant a variable, 'fi', called the Lagrange multiplier. Lesourne shows that economic optimum is a 'restricted' optimum dependent on a 'social optimum'.

On this problem, see the writings of Allais, Lerner and Pigou, and especially Koopmans, *Three Essays on the State of Economic Science*, 1957, Essay I, section 2, 'Competitive equilibrium and Pareto optimality', and J. Rothenberg, *The Measurement of Social Welfare*, 1961, pp. 92–3, 95, 97.

101. Cf. the critique of Hoselitz by Sahlins in *American Anthropologist*, 1962, p. 1068; also Firth, *Elements of Social Organization*, pp. 137, 142 and 153.

102. Numerous Marxists, claiming to find support in Marx's ideas, continue to think that the idea of economic rationality came in with capitalism. Cf. O. Lange, *Political Economy*, chapter V, 'The principle of economic rationality'. Lange is content to make a few allusions to 'the customary and traditional character of economic activity under the conditions of natural economy', and rapidly refers to Herskovits. Sombart and Weber before affirming (p. 193) that 'the principle of economic rationality is the historical product of capitalist enterprise'. On Lange's views see Angelo Pagani, 'La razionalità nel comportamento economico', in *Antologia di Scienze Sociali*, Il Mulino, 1963, pp. 97–148; K. W. Rothschild, 'The meaning of rationality: a note on Professor Lange's article', in *Review of Economic Studies*, Vol. 14 (1), 1946–1947.

As a rule, the problem of economic rationality is confined to study of the forms of behaviour, decision and organization that are most likely to procure for individuals the maximum of expected satisfactions. It is generally assumed, for reasons of convenience of calculation, that the society being studied possesses an economy either of perfect competition or of centralized planning. The problem of rationality then seems to revolve entirely around psychology, the mathematical theory of probability, and the theory of information. In no case, however, has the idea of rationality every been worked out and criticized theoretically, and the problem of the basis of socially necessary wants is evaded, by means of vague statements about the arbitrary nature of subjective preferences.

The task is then restricted to seeing if the actual behaviour of the producers and consumers conforms or not to the principles of rational behaviour. If it does not, then the actual and the ideal are contrasted, and the irrationality or rationality of the individual and of the social world are discussed. In another direction an attempt is made to estimate the chances for a decision which is assumed to be rational to be followed by the expected effects, taking account of the degree of information possessed by the economic subject, the value of his forecasts. Then a 'science' of the organization of enterprises is hastily constructed, such as to enable the entrepreneur to possess the motivations and the information needed if he is to take the best 'management' decision — the rational decision.

103. D. Forde, 'Primitive Economics', art. cit., p. 338.
104. E.g. the control of the trade routes for gold, salt and slaves by the Sarakole aristocracy of the kingdom of Ghana in the 11th century, and the control of water and land by the King among the Imerina of Madagascar in the 18th century. Cf. G. Condominas, *Fokon'olona et les collectivités rurales en Imerina*, chapters 1 and 2.
105. Ricardo, *Principles . . .*, chapter I.
106. *Capital*, I, pp. 4–5.
107. M. Godelier, 'Théorie marginaliste et théorie marxiste de la valeur et des prix', *Cahiers de planification*, Ecole des Hautes Etudes, no. 3, 1964. P. Bohannan firmly rejects the labour theory of value: cf. *Social Anthropology*, chapter 14, p. 230. R. Firth in *Human Types*, p. 80, takes up a much more subtle attitude. In the same line of thought as mine is L. Johansen, 'Some observations on labour theory of value and marginal utilities,' art. cit.
108. Cf. on this problem the works of P. Einzig, *Primitive Money in its Ethnological, Historical and Economic Aspects*, 1949; Quiggin, *A Survey of Primitive Money: The Beginnings of Currency*, 1949; R. Firth, 'Currency, Primitive', in *Encyclopaedia Britannica*.
109. Wilmington, 'Aspects of Moneylending in Northern Sudan', in *Middle East Journal*, 1955, pp. 139–46.
110. Bohannan, 'Some principles of exchange and investment among the Tiv', in *American Anthropologist*, 1955, Vol. 57. By the same writer, 'Tiv Markets', in *New York Academy of Sciences*, May, 1957, pp. 613–22, and introduction to *Markets in Africa*, 1963.
111. Moore, 'Labour attitudes towards industrialization in underdeveloped countries', *American Economic Review*, 1955, no. 45, pp. 156–65, and his article, 'Industrialisation et changement social', in *Industrialisation et Société*, Paris and The Hague, Mouton, 1964, pp. 293–372.
112. Cf. P. Bohannan, 'The impact of money on an African subsistence economy', *Journal of Economic History*, 1959, no. 4, pp. 491–503. On the destructive effects of European money upon the potlatch of the Kwakiutl, see Steiner, 'Notes on comparative economics', art. cit., p. 123.
113. Cf. Smelser, 'Mechanisms of change', art. cit. Morgan had already pointed out that kinship systems are stable elements that evolve very slowly in comparison with the changes that occur in the role of the family.
114. W. E. Armstrong, *Rossel Island*, 1927, and 'Rossel Island Money, a Unique Monetary System', in *Economic Journal*, 1924, pp. 423–9.
115. L. Lancaster, 'Crédit, épargne et investissement dans une économie non-monétaire', *Archives européens de sociologie*, III, 1962, pp. 149–64.
116. J. Guiart, 'L'organisation sociale et politique du Nord Malekula', in *Journal de la Société des Océanistes*, VIII, 1952.
117. Daryll Forde says: 'Money of itself does not give a closed economy any link between the present and the future. . . . A community can only be said to save to the extent that durable goods are produced. . . .' ('Primitive economics', art. cit., p. 342).
118. Mauss, 'Essai sur le don', art. cit., p. 199.
119. Boas, *Twelfth and Final Report of the North-Western Tribes of Canada*, 1898, *British Association for the Advancement of Science, 1891–1898*: quoted in Marcel Mauss, *The Gift*, Glencoe, 1954, p. 100).

120. Goldman, 'The Kwakiutl of Vancouver Island', in *Co-operation and Competition among Primitive Peoples*, ed. M. Mead, 1937.
121. See Eisenstadt's article, 'Anthropological studies of complex societies', and the discussion with Banton, Barnes, Gluckman, Meyer Fortes, Leach, etc. in *Current Anthropology*, June 1961, Vol. 2, no. 3.
122. Arensberg, 'Anthropology as History', in *Trade and Market in the Early Empires*, ed. K. Polanyi; and Fusfeld, 'Economic theory misplaced: livelihood in primitive society', in *ibid.*
123. Marx, *Economic and Philosophical Manuscripts of 1844*. See Part II, section I above.
124. See the famous passages by Alfred Marshall: 'Whatever be their climate and whatever their ancestry, we find savages living under the dominion of custom and impulse; scarcely ever striking out new lines for themselves; never forecasting the distant future, and seldom making provision even for the near future; fitful in spite of their servitude to custom, governed by the fancy of the moment; ready at times for the most arduous exertions, but incapable of keeping themselves long to steady work. Laborious and tedious tasks are avoided so far as possible; those which are inevitable are done by the compulsory labour of women' (*Principles of Economics*, 1890, Appendix A: 'The Growth of Free Industry and Enterprise': 1946 edition, pp. 723–4).
125. The idea of progress, like that of rationality, cannot be deduced from *a priori* principles, but assumes many different contents, determined socially and historically. There is no 'true essence' of man that must be recovered, or gradually built up, and constituting both the driving force and ultimate purpose of the evolution of societies, and also the court before which the philosopher or the theoretician summons societies in order to 'judge' them. A speculative attitude such as this has nothing in common with science, and is characteristic of all the 'philosophies of history'. Thus, Morris Ginsberg 'summons economic development before the principles of a rational ethic', in 'Towards a Theory of Social Development: The Growth of Rationality', p. 66. See also E. Seifert, 'Le facteur moral du développement social'. For a discussion of Ginsberg's view see R. Aron. 'La théorie du développement et l'interprétation historique de l'époque contemporaine', in the UNESCO symposium on *Social Development*, 1961, in which the contributions by Ginsberg and Seiffert appear.
126. Cf. I. M. D. Little, *A Critique of Welfare Economics*.
127. Schlippe, *Shifting Cultivation in Africa*, 1955, Part 3.
128. Conklin, *Hanunoo Agriculture in the Philippines*, F.A.O., 1957, and 'Study of shifting cultivation', in *Current Anthropology*, Vol. 2, Feb. 1961, pp. 27–61.
129. Viguier, *L'Afrique de l'Ouest vue par un agriculteur*, Paris, 1961, p. 29.
130. Wilbert, *The Evolution of Horticultural Systems in Native South America, Causes and Consequences*, Caracas, 1961.
131. G. Sautter, 'A propos de quelques terroirs d'Afrique de l'Ouest', in *Etudes Rurales*, 1962: Godelier, 'Terroirs africains et histoire agraire comparée', in *Annales E.S.C.*, 1964, no. 3.
132. Hackenberg, 'Economic alternatives in arid lands: a case study of the Pima and Papago Indians', in *Ethnology*, 1(2), April 1962. Archaeology has begun to provide information of use on the evolution from marginal agriculture to intensive agriculture in pre-Columbian Peru and Mexico, in the ancient Middle East, etc. E.g. D. Collier, 'Agriculture and civilization on the coast of Peru', in Wilbert, op. cit., pp. 101–9, and the commentary by Eric Wolf.
133. Manning, Nash, 'The social context of economic choice in a small society', *Man*, November, 1961, pp. 186–91.
134. If all further development is blocked for certain reasons, such situations can create the conditions for the appearance of 'false archaisms'.

135. Carneiro points out that the nomadism of the crops is not necessarily due to exhaustion of the soil but to the difficulty of working them after a few years of cultivation, owing to encroachment by weeds. Cf. art. cit.
136. Cf. Leeds, *The Evolution of Horticultural Systems*, p. 4.
137. Leroi-Gourhan, *Le Geste et la Parole*, 1964, p. 213, 'Le Territoire': 'The relation between food, territory and density of population . . . is an equation with variable but correlative values'.
138. Awareness of the limiting conditions for balanced functioning of an economic system is perhaps expressed in certain myths of the Siberian hunters, or Tupi-Gursani, the idea of an original pact between the different species of animals and man, by which man undertakes not to kill the animals *without necessity*, without needing to do so, on pain of terrible vengeance by Nature against the human community. Cf. E. Lot-Falk, *Les Rites de la chasse chez les peuples sibériens*, Paris, 1953, ch. IV, 'Les Esprits-maîtres'.

    In another context, Richard-Molard suggested that the economic and social role of the 'master of the land' in the archaic agricultural societies of Black Africa should be analysed in connexion with the need for systems of extensive agriculture to ensure the maintenance of equilibrium between man and the land by vigilant supervision of the periods when land is cultivated or left to lie fallow. 'In the evolution of the tropical agricultural areas of Africa and of their density of population, of their conservation or of their erosion, there are two thresholds, one above the other and quite different, of technical and demographic optimum, separated by intermediate stages that are more or less critical' (J. Richard-Molard, 'Les terroirs tropicaux d'Afrique', *Annales de Géographie*, 1951).
139. *art. cit.*
140. When the 'Pax Gallica' unclamped the grip that enclosed the Kabre of Togo, they invaded the plain and once more practised an extensive agriculture that was much less 'advanced' than the intensive system of their mountain period. Carneiro puts forward the hypothesis that the contradiction between population and production creates the conditions for new socio-economic systems to appear when the area of cultivable land is strictly limited, as in the narrow valleys of the Peruvian coast or in the mountains of the Andes or of New Guinea. This hypothesis seems confirmed by Brookfield's important study of 31 localities of New Guinea with varying ecological conditions, where six forms of agriculture are found, increasing in intensity in proportion to the increasing density of population ('Local study and comparative method: an example from Central New Guinea', *Annals of the Association of American Geographers*, 1962, no. 52, pp. 242–254).
141. Duby, *op. cit.*
142. On the relations between cybernetics and economics, see Henryk Greniewski, 'Logique et cybernétique de la planification', *Cahiers du séminaire d'économétrie*, C.N.R.S., 1962, no. 6.
143. Melvin Ember, 'The relationship between economic and political development in non-industrialized societies', in *Ethnology*, April, 1963, pp. 228–48. See the old work of L. Krzywicki, *Primitive Society and its Vital Statistics*.
144. Naroll, 'A preliminary index of social development', in *American Anthropologist*, 1956, no. 58, pp. 687–715.
145. Murdock, 'World ethnographic sample', in *American Anthropologist*, 1957, no. 59, pp. 664–87.
146. Steward, 'Cultural causality and law: trial formulation of the early civilization', in *American Anthropologist*, 1949, no. 51, pp. 1–25; Braidwood and Reed, *The Achievement and Early Consequences of Food Production*, 1957, Harbor Symposia, pp. 17–31; V. Gordon Childe, *Social Evolution*, chapters 1 and 2.
147. Cf. Sahlins, 'Political power and the economy in primitive society', art. cit.

148. Unintentional does not mean lacking in 'meaning'. Beyond the field of his conscious activities, the domain of the unintentional is not, for man, a silent desert in which he suddenly petrifies into a 'thing' like the rest, but is the other face of his work, in which all his behaviour finds part of its meaning. The unintentional is not merely that part of man that is made up of the sediment of all the 'non-willed effects' of his undertakings, it is the place where the hidden regulators are organized that correspond to the deep-lying logic of the systems of action he invents and practises. The unintentional is not just that which it 'seems' mainly to be, a reality that Sartre describes to us as the 'practical-inert' reverse side and effect of our living projects, it is the hidden aspect of our social relations where part of the 'meaning' of our behaviour is actively organized. It is the elucidation of this meaning that the anthropological sciences undertake to carry out, by revealing the relation between the intentional and the unintentional, discovering the 'laws' of social reality. Cf. Sartre, *Critique de la Raison Dialectique*, 1960, Vol. I: 'De la "praxis" individuelle au pratico-inerte'.

149. Morgan, *Ancient Society*, 1877.

150. Engels's successors forgot that *The Origin of the Family, Private Property and the State* (1884) began with advice to modify Morgan's 'classification' of the facts in the event that 'important additional material necessitates alterations' (FLPH edition, p. 33).

    Marx's text presenting the first Marxist general outline of the evolution of societies is still unpublished in French, having been found only in 1939 ('Formen die der kapitalistischen Produktion vorhergehen', published in the *Grundrisse der Kritik der Politischen Ökonomie*, Berlin, Dietz, 1953 [now available in French as *Fondements de la critique de l'économie politique*, Paris, Anthropos, 1968. The section specially mentioned is available in English as *Pre-Capitalist Economic Formations*, London, Lawrence and Wishart, 1964]). It is to be observed that in this document Marx does not assume, as his successors did, that all societies must pass through more or less the same stages. On the contrary, Western history seems to him to have evolved in a 'singular' way. See my discussion of this work: M. Godelier, 'La notion de mode de production asiatique', in *Temps modernes*, May 1964.

151. Cf. on certain points, J. Steward, *Theory of Culture Change*, 1955, chapter 1. Most often, a schema of the evolution of societies was a speculative construction whose author peopled it with his 'ideas' about the word, and in particular about his own society. Depending on whether he admired the latter or was critical of it, the author either made history advance along the paths of progress and civilization or caused mankind to fall from its original goodness. Good or bad, primitive man remained what he was, a theoretical puppet made up of cultural elements taken from among contemporary 'primitives'. Cf. K. Bucher, *Die Entstehung der Volkswirtschaft*, 1922, chapters 1 and 2, who attributes to the original savage living in a pre-economic stage all the vices that contrast with the alleged virtues of civilized man (egoism, cruelty, improvidence). Cf. O. Leroy, *Essai d'introduction critique à l'étude de l'économie primitive*, 1925, p. 8.

    The evolutionists, instead of studying societies as they found them, seeking in their actual struggle the logic of their functioning, analysed them hastily so as to construct an alleged origin and a pseudo-history for them.

    In order to save the facts, evolutionism had to be rejected, and from Golden-weiser and Lowie to Radcliffe Brown the slogan became 'Sociology versus History'. On the basis of the information gathered, diachronic analyses can now be attempted that are free of all preconceptions about the evolution of mankind.

152. 'Matérialisme et Epistémologie', in *Annali*, the journal of the Instituto Giangiacomo Feltrinelli, Milan, 1971, in the special issue 'Ricera dei presupposti e dei fondamenti del discorso scientifico in Marx', pp. 7–21.

153. We have explained this itinerary at the beginning of *Rationality and Irrationality in Economics.*

154. See pp. 90–102 of this volume.

155. In the introduction to *Sur les sociétés précapitalistes*, C.E.R.M. An extended analysis of Mbuti economy and society will be found in *Anthropologie et Economie*, a work in preparation for the SUP collection of the Presses Universitaires de France, under the general editorship of Georges Balandier.

156. See Engels's still relevant remarks in his letter to Joseph Bloch, 22 October 1890 (from *Marx Engels Selected Correspondence*, pp. 417–9):
    According to the materialist conception of history, the *ultimately* determining element in history is the production and reproduction of real life. More than this neither Marx nor I have ever asserted. Hence if someone twists this into saying that the economic element is the *only* determining one, he transforms that proposition into a meaningless, abstract, senseless phrase… Unfortunately, however, it happens all too often that people think they have fully understood a new theory and can apply it without more ado from the moment they have assimilated its main principles, and even those not always correctly. And I cannot exempt many of the more recent 'Marxists' from this reproach, for the most amazing rubbish has been produced from this quarter, too…

157. See Symmes C. Oliver, *Ecology and Cultural Continuity as Contributing Factors in the Social Organisation of the Plains Indians*, University of California Press, Berkeley, Cal., 1962, pp. 269–71.

158. See Preston Holder, *The Hoe and the Horse on the Plains: A Study of Cultural Development among North American Indians*, University of Nebraska Press, Lincoln, Neb., 1969, pp. 23–8.

159. It is to study this problem in greater depth that we have devoted two texts to the study of John Murra's data on Inca economy and society. We were trying to locate and explain the elements of the earlier modes of production and social organisation which the new, State, mode of production had maintained and transformed to adapt them to its own process of reproduction. See *Horizon*, part 1, chapter 2 and part 5, chapter 3.

160. It is this — in our view fundamental — distinction between these two types of intra- and interstructural contradictions which we set out in the article 'Système, structure et contradiction dans *Le Capital* de Marx', published in the special number of *Les Temps Modernes*, 1966, devoted to 'Problèmes du structuralisme' and which provoked a violent attack by Lucien Sève, and then our reply published in *Horizon*, part 3, chapters 1 and 2.

161. Søren Kierkegaard, *La concept de l'angoisse*, Gallimard, Paris, 1935, p. 224.

162. A complete translation of the *Grundrisse* was published by Penguin in 1973.

163. See *Horizon*, pp. 135–82.

164. We take up Desanti's beautiful formula from his article 'Sur la "production" des concepts en mathématiques' in *Les Etudes Philosophiques*, October-December, 1969, pp. 475–597. Of course Marx's ideas on primitive societies — 'to read in the connection of their context' — first assumes dissatisfaction with the repetition of the same little book of quotations on the topic drawn from Engels' *The Origin of the Family*. On the contrary, what is striking in Marx's and Engels's attitude on this topic is their permanent capacity to receive with great interest, and to think about, the new ideas contained in the works of Maurer, Kovaleski, Morgan, Maine, Taylor, etc.

165. Marx, *Pre-Capitalist Economic Formations*, p. 70.

166. See *Horizon*, part 4, chapter 2, the text requested by J. B. Pontalis for the special issue of *Nouvelle revue de psychanalyse*, no. 2, 1970 devoted to 'Objets du Fétichisme'.

167. We have chosen the example of the Mbuti for two reasons. On the one hand,

since their economy is based on hunting and gathering activities in a generalised eco-system (the Congolese primary forest), it is relatively simple; on the other, and this is the main reason, by contrast with many ethnographies which supply vague indications of the economy of the societies they are studying, Turnbull's ethnography is of exceptional quality and wealth and is happily supplemented by the remarkable discoveries made by Richard Lee, Lorna Marshall and Julian Steward among other hunter-gatherers, the Bushmen, Shoshone, etc. Besides we want to take this opportunity to thank Colin Turnbull who agreed with the greatest simplicity and amiability to answer the many questions we asked him and also to criticise the interpretations we attempted to make of his data and work.

168. It would be interesting to look in the old but still important book by H. Frankfort and Th. Jacobsen, *Before Philosophy* (Pelican, London, 1949) for the list of the various imaginary or real functions performed by the State and its living representative in ancient Egypt and Mesopotamia. It is remarkable to discover in the myths summarised by these authors that the Cosmos itself is represented in the shape of a State and that the forms of the State compose the sociological model which organises representations of the universe. In the myths of American Indians belonging to Stateless societies, on the other hand, it is kinship relations which play the role of sociological model. It must also be noted that what is exceptional work, *extra* work in the form of exceptional hunts among the Mbuti, who then consume the product of their hunt, become *surplus labour*, corvée, in Egypt or among the Incas to celebrate the gods and support their earthly representatives, kings and priests.

'The Economy' in Agricultural Self-Sustaining Societies: A Preliminary Analysis

Claude Meillassoux

This essay, which first appeared in Cahiers d'Etudes Africaines *in 1960, represents a pioneering effort by Meillassoux to elaborate a problematic for the investigation and analysis of self-sustaining social and economic formations or, more specifically, as he himself argues, of self-sustaining societies in which agricultural production is associated with the exploitation of land as an instrument of labour (for he considers other modes of production elsewhere). This theoretical essay and the detailed monograph on the Guro of the Ivory Coast, both based upon fieldwork carried out in 1958 and 1959, constitute works of fundamental importance which have had an enormous influence on later research, both theoretical and empirical, by other scholars. Indeed, several of Meillassoux's own more recent articles – such as the essay 'From reproduction to production' which appeared in* Economy and Society *vol. 1, no. 1, 1972 and the short paper presented to the 'peasants' seminar held at the University of London in 1972 and included in this volume (pp. 159–69) — develop the concepts utilised here and explore further the structures and crucial relationships identified in this 'preliminary analysis'. Like Godelier's essay with which this collection began, Meillassoux's discussion finds difficulty in escaping fully from the imprisonment of an inadequate theoretical framework although it brilliantly points the way out of 'liberal' anthropology towards a Marxist science of pre-capitalist formations.*

INTRODUCTION

In the 1950s the debate on economic anthropology was chiefly centred on what seemed most aberrant to the advocates of the classical school, namely the circulation of goods, a problem which has, at any rate, always dominated liberal economics. It was still very dependent on Boas' interpretation of the potlatch, taken up and embellished by Mauss. Although the potlatch was presented as strange and exotic, not only was it studied independently of any historical context, but interpreted in terms of business concepts such as 'interest', 'credit', 'market', etc. According to Boas it was similar, if not identical, to the Stock Exchange speculation which then dominated Wall Street and the American capitalistic ethic: like any wise young American boy playing the Stock Exchange, a young Kwakiutl could, by 'playing' potlatch, raise his 'cool million' of blankets!

This ethnocentric attitude is indicative of one confusion maintained by liberal economic theory which considers the different systems of production as belonging, in varying degrees, to a generalised capitalist economy. Despite the contribution made by modern anthropologists and often despite the excellence of their data, the tendency to apply concepts and notions borrowed from capitalist theory to problems so obviously different has not been abandoned. Polanyi and his school remain the only non-Marxists who attempted to unearth the qualitative demarcation which separates the market economy from the previous ones. Although the aim of all science should be to strive for exactness — primarily by a comprehensive use of a relevant terminology — social science is today either deeply immersed in analogy or masquerading in mathematical rags borrowed at random. In both cases the error is the same: it comes from the unsupported adoption of conceptual frameworks from disciplines or models relying on different axiomatics. This is more than mere error or sheer ethnocentrism; it betrays the impact of ideology on social science; it betrays the imperialism of the science of Imperialism which wants to submit 'development' to the universal laws of capitalist exploitation, or the reactionary intellectualism which wants to see in primitive societies the realisation of the old dream of religious and clerical domination.

Because liberal economics confuses all forms of production, it is incapable of bringing together related elements pertaining to a single historical system in order to build its model. Since disciplinary specialisation channels the liberal economist within a field of causality restricted to 'economics', he is blind to the dialectic of a concrete complex reality. He can only build contingent or 'stochastic' models in which randomness is substituted for reason. Because of its historical approach, dialectical materialism escaped the limitation mentioned above.

However, when the text below was written, the contribution of Marxism to the study of primitive societies was almost entirely limited to the writings of Marx, Engels and Lenin. At that time, no

English or French translation of the *Formen* had been published and the problem of the specification of the modes of pre-capitalist production, as well as that of the relations of production, was not under discussion. The following model emerges mostly from the need to explain to myself and to my students phenomena which I had the opportunity of observing in the field, and to relate them to the corpus of observations provided by anthropological literature on apparently similar societies.[1] The construction of a logical and comprehensive synthetic model compelled me to specify the type of society to which it applied, restrictively, and therefore to sketch the definition of a mode of production through the understanding of the level of the productive forces and of the nature of the relations of production, as given. This attempt, here still in an early stage of elaboration, is taken up in later studies, e.g. one devoted to the mode of production of the hunter-foragers in opposition to cultivators,[2] another (published in this book, pp. 159–69) to the material basis of the relations of production and reproduction. It is however within this double set of relations that the present paper must be considered, as I attempt to do in later works.

This model has no pretentions to universality, but, before objecting to its generality, we must recognise its theoretical limits (those of the self-sustaining agricultural community) and to exclude from it, on the one hand, societies which exploit the land as a subject of labour (as hunter-foragers) and on the other, agricultural societies which produce for exchange and in which emerge new relations of production, even though they may sometimes remain concealed under the type of relations described above.

'THE ECONOMY' IN AGRICULTURAL SELF-SUSTAINING SOCIETIES: A PRELIMINARY ANALYSIS

Economists have had three different reactions to the apparent paradoxes presented by economic phenomena in traditional societies.

The first reaction is to deny the existence of an economic problem in those societies, either by gratuitously declaring that they have no 'economic systems'[3] or by attributing observed behaviour to a special mentality and to irrational and unexplained customs rather than to economic necessity. This latter view is in line with the thesis of 'primitive mentality': at the economic level 'primitive man' was not quite a man since he was not a 'homo economicus'.

A second, more generous attitude, restores to 'primitive' man his human status by actually bestowing on him some of the more sophisticated attributes of *economic man*. In this view the premises of a liberal economic theory are implicitly or explicitly accepted as valid for non-capitalist economic systems. Theoretically free and equal individuals, liberated from family obligations, are seen to indulge in economic activity. 'Primitive economy' is thus represented as a simplified version of a more complex system observed in a modern economy, the idea being that 'all economic systems belong to a sort of continuum'[4], i.e. that their difference is one of degree, rather than kind. 'Objects therefore become 'commodities', sometimes 'capital' bearing real 'interest'; transfers, gifts and prestations are seen as 'exchanges' giving rise to 'price' formation. Some liberal scholars ascribe the title of 'entrepreneur' to the head of the family and bestow that of 'employees' on those who work for him. Having thus reconstructed a world with which he is familiar the liberal economist inserts into it the legal concepts which are its corollaries: property, contract, corporate persons, etc. as well as his pet theories: law of supply and demand, the maximisation of profits, marginalism, national accounting etc. The analogies are unfortunately powerless to change the nature of institutions and the liberal economist is finally faced with a residue of inexplicable phenomena which he proceeds to explain by the unexplainable (religion, prohibitions, 'customs').

There is little doubt that Melville Herskovits is the most eminent representative of this school. The results of his by no means negligible theoretical work go no further than those of the old classical economists who dramatised exemplary 'savages' and made them rediscover political economy. The premises implicit in these imaginary economic dramas are in fact exactly the same as those which Herskovits develops. On several occasions other writers have attempted to apply liberal economic theory to traditional societies, as for example the English writer Goodfellow[5], with equally disappointing results. Even Raymond Firth, whose contribution to these problems is significant, returns to these concepts as soon as he tries to provide a theoretical explanation for his penetrating observations[6] — although admittedly he is hesitant on this point. The American, Sol Tax, in his study of a Guatemalan village, does not adequately differentiate between those problems which are connected with a recently monetised economy and those inherent in a traditional economy[7]. He is thrilled to discover a 'penny capitalism' at this level, thus providing, according to well-established tradition, further evidence of the universality of the capitalist system.

A third approach goes beyond these two positions and agrees that:
(1) these societies have a form of economy (by contrast with the first approach);

(2) these economies obey laws which are specific to themselves (by contrast with the second approach).

Marx and Engels recognised very early the special character of economic phenomena in 'primitive communities' by relating them to historical and social conditions. In their writings they constantly referred to such economies but always with the intention of contrasting or comparing them with capitalist society, with the result that the latter is illuminated by widely scattered references to the former. In the framework of a dialectical explanation of contemporary society reference to pre-capitalist or primitive economic phenomena is made not from a historical but from a hierarchical point of view[8].

A compilation of the material contained in the work of these authors provides the main lines of what might be a theoretical sketch of traditional economies, and one which the discoveries of modern anthropology would tend to confirm. Marx and Engels' analysis is based on a few basic observations, the most prominent being the importance of kinship and the dependent position of the individual producer within the family or clan community, the absence of *exchange*, in the economic sense, between the members of the community, therefore the absence of transformation of produce into value, and the common ownership of land.

Although he has been discredited because of his conventionally obsolete vocabulary, Richard Thurnwald[9] expressed penetrating though uneven views on these problems, some of which, by no means the best, are often similar to those of Engels in *The Origin of the Family, Private Property and the State* to whom, however, he does not refer. Thurnwald clearly separates himself from the economists and rejects the theoretical postulates of liberal economics. This methodological freedom enables him to restore to social phenomena — family, social status — an importance that had been obscured by the individualist conception of economics and to discover some fundamental aspects of traditional economies. Nevertheless he still insists on using certain concepts with their strictly economic meaning irrespective of the social context (for example capital: 'objects of primary necessity capable of growth by themselves'); and, although he denies it, his work is also cluttered with a form of diffuse evolutionism which stifles and interrupts the analysis as soon as phenomena become complex.

Apart from economists and economic anthropologists some other anthropologists have also made a considerable contribution to the problem of traditional economies by providing a very valuable body of data: Paul Bohannan,[10] Mary Douglas, Max Gluckman, Lucy Mair, Malinowski, Margaret Mead, S. F. Nadel, Evans-Pritchard,

Audrey Richards, etc. (the list grows longer every day). Free from the anxiety of forcing the facts to fit a theory they have often been content to notice that what they observed did not coincide with the models of the liberal economists they have sometimes provided extremely penetrating elements of an explanantion.

Maus[11] occupies a special place among anthropologists who have dealt with economic problems. By considering the gift as a total phenomenon involving the social political and religious structures he placed the study of economic problems in these societies in their correct context. He correctly noticed that goods circulate according to a system of prestation and counter-prestation. He discovered the link that exists between the material transfer of objects and the social hierarchy: 'To give is to show one's superiority. To accept without returning or repaying more is to face subordination.' However, Mauss reduces the various types of transfers to only one: the gift. He does not use the consequences of his observation on the relations between prestations and social status, failing to differentiate between the status of the protagonists and to define the direction of the transfers. This omission leads him to accept the irrational explanation of the potlatch (offering to the divinities) according to the thesis of quasi-absolute reciprocity. In addition, he mistakenly uses modern legal jargon in this context. The terms 'rights' ('circulation of rights', 'rule of right', etc.) frequently occurs in his text; he speaks of 'legal links between the parties', of 'contracts'; he identifies communities with 'corporate bodies'. As a result, his faulty analogies lead him to propose a doubtful historical interpretation in which the gift is thought to be an intermediate step towards modern legal forms of trade; the potlatch, a ritual pre-monetary market without merchants. Lastly Mauss suggests several times that gift exchange is made for the purpose of making a profit and he even quotes rates of interest of '30 to 100 per cent'.

The most positive contemporary contribution to the study of these problems has been made by Polanyi[12] and his interdisciplinary team of researchers. They take as their point of departure the thesis that the mechanisms for exchange in traditional economies are of a different nature and that the laws of the market economy are not applicable to them. They distinguish three exchange models, reciprocity, redistribution and trade, each one corresponding to a social and political structure. With regard to the circulation of goods the authors stress the need to take into consideration the identity of the protagonists, the order of sequence of the gifts and a comparison of this frequency. Their work, which includes a great deal of material and ideas, as yet represents only the critical phase of an unfinished but promising research.[13]

Despite these recent contributions no general model for the explanation of economic phenomena in traditional self-sustaining societies has yet been outlined. This is what we have attempted to do in this essay by taking up some of the concepts and analyses of the above-mentioned authors, chosen from those who have looked at the problem from outside the theoretical framework of liberal economics.

METHOD AND DEFINITION

It is not our intention here to confine ourselves to the vague and questionable definition of economics. We are studying things (objects, means and products of labour) seen as the focus of certain material or personal relationships which link them with individuals or other things, or individuals with each other. The very nature of the economies under consideration will lead us by devious ways through areas usually considered to be outside economics but will, nevertheless ultimately lead us back to it; without these detours our analysis would be discrete and incoherent.

To make the demonstration easier we will describe a series of models corresponding to observable but simplified types of economies. The reader will judge for himself the validity of these simplifications. Models embedded in one another at the most complex stage of the demonstration are presented in a logical progression that can possibly be regarded as an 'ideal' historical production, which does not exclude the hierarchisation of these various models in a structured system.

We will limit our analysis of phenomena observable in self-sustaining societies and to a few of their after-effects in societies with a complementary economy, basing our argument essentially on African economies with which we are most familiar. This is why this essay cannot claim to cover all known cases of the self-sustaining economy in detail. Hypothesis still plays a large part because it has not often been possible to find the information necessary for this kind of study in the available monographs. Relevant observations appear only in a few recent works.

Because of the limitations of an article format we will not encumber our demonstration with references to specific cases. We believe that the readers can themselves supply examples to illustrate this work.

As our starting point we will take the traditional social unit composed of a number of individuals of both sexes linked by kinship ties and grouped territorially or moving around together under the authority of a man regarded as eminent. Such a unit, which we will call a *community*, derives its subsistence from agriculture combined in various ways with food gathering, hunting or herding.

One main economic feature of such a community is self-sufficiency: the group produces all the goods needed for its perpetuation and growth from the immediately available natural resources. We will see how once a social system has been built on it, this self-sufficiency tends to be artificially maintained, resisting changes brought about by complementary trade with other economies.

Such a community is integrated either in a larger formation composed of similar self-sustaining[14] communities or in a more complex and stratified political society.

The other economic characteristics of the community, in the sense in which we define it, are the following:
— all members of the community have physical access to raw materials and land;
— individual means of production are simple;
— relative complexity of production techniques;
— division of labour according to sex and age;
— circulation of foodstuffs in terms of a social hierarchy centred on the notion of seniority.

The phenomenon of the circulation of goods may be illustrated by the following diagram (fig. 1):

Fig. 1

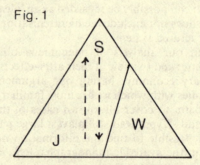

The social unit is represented by a pyramid at the apex of which is the senior (S), i.e. the person who exercises authority over the group, this is concretised by his role in the redistribution of commodities.

At the base of the pyramid are the juniors (J), i.e. all the men who work for the senior and hand over the product of their activity to him. The women (W) occupy a mediating position, which is not symmetrical to that of the men, as we shall see later on.

In a system of this type women work for their husbands who hand over their produce to the seniors; the latter redistribute it to the whole community either directly or through the married men.

If at this stage we deal only with the relations between seniors and juniors we can define two types of circulation of goods:

— *prestation* from the juniors to the seniors;
— *redistribution* from the seniors to the juniors.

This model thus reveals a *dependence relationship* between two categories of individuals which is characterised economically by the fact that one receives the other's prestations and hence supervises the whole of the group's output.

At this stage the problem is to know:
(1) What is this dependence based on?
(2) What is the role of economic fact in the development and the maintenance of this dependence?

STUDY OF THE NATURE OF AUTHORITY

What is the basis of the seniors' authority over the juniors?

(1) It is clearly not *physical strength*: the seniors are not only numerically but also physically the weakest category. It should also be noted that in this type of social system the 'seniors' have no police force available to enforce observance of their decisions if these do not reflect a certain degree of consensus. As we shall see, this does not, of course, imply that there is no antagonism between the two groups, seniors and juniors.

(2) It is often implicitly assumed that the authority of the seniors over the juniors is based on *links of kinship*. Kinship alone, taken in the strictly genetic sense, has no intrinsic virtue likely to ensure social cohesion. The societies themselves prove this. Kinship relationships vary from one system to the next and they are highly flexible within each group. The various classificatory systems of kinship and the different rules governing exogamy result in an individual having differing kin relationships depending on which particular society is being studied. We notice that in all societies adoption is common and there are also frequent fictitious relationships which are sometimes so extreme that they may reverse the sexes and bestow family functions normally regarded as male on a woman and vice versa. Finally these links may be totally broken in certain circumstances sanctioned by tradition; they can also be broken as a consequence of certain economic changes.

Indeed paternal filiation is not an immediately observable fact and the social concept of fatherhood preceded the genetic one: the father being the person who stands in a specific relationship to 'his' children's mother's family. By contrast maternal filiation is immediately perceptible. Because it is impossible to wean the children this filiation continues actively for three or four years. It is therefore likely that kinship links on the paternal side may be distinctly looser than those on the maternal side, at least during this first phase and, as we shall see this has repercussions on the woman's social status with regard to her procreative function.

Consequently we accept that kinship *expresses* the social relationships which form the basis of social cohesion but that it is not itself a cohesive force. We will concentrate on the concept of *social kinship* whether or not it coincides with genetic kinship, without thereby denying that the one may be or seem to be a replica of the other. The study of actual economic or other relationships on which social cohesion is built and which, we repeat, is expressed in terms of kinship, will throw light on the distinction.

In order to simplify still further we will deal with only three social categories: the seniors, the juniors and the women, these terms being given a sociological meaning.

(3) The fact that the *means of production* observed in these societies are simple and accessible means that they cannot be used as a means for controlling the producers. In this way these societies differ fundamentally from societies with a more complex technology where the material importance of the means of production provides its possessors with the most efficient means of exercising control over the producers.

In traditional economies, the means of production are of essentially two kinds: tools and land.

Tools are made of raw material that is directly accessible to all the members of the group. Most of these societies nevertheless use iron tools and this presents a specific problem because this metal is not immediately accessible. Either iron is produced in the society itself or it is imported from outside. In both cases the society is confronted with individuals — blacksmiths or merchants — who possess a commodity which has certain attributes that make it liable, as we shall see, to upset the traditional mechanisms for the circulation of goods. It is only when we have considered these mechanisms and their social function that we will be able to infer the consequences. We can however assert that traditional societies tend to preserve their own system of circulation of goods against these disruptive commodities by all sorts of restrictions and prohibitions and that, consequently, their economic mechanisms can be studied in a first phase independently of this factor, i.e. within the context of self-sufficiency.

Concerning *land* we must immediately distinguish between the control exercised over it regarding its use by members of the community and that regarding its use by persons alien to it. Concerning the latter it is the group as a whole which exercises and sanctions this control: the seniors decide whether or not the stranger shall be accepted on the community's land, but this decision can only be made effective by the force represented by the juniors who are also the warriors. Concerning members of their own lineage the seniors have no coercive power which would allow them to control land physically since they cannot enforce any such control over those very persons who are its collective guardians.

The seniors' control over land is neither direct nor immediate and cannot be taken as the source of their authority over the juniors it is through the intermediary of other methods of social control that the seniors in the group[15] ultimately control land.

The fact that at this stage it is impossible to control the means of production effectively and therefore impossible to control the producer through them, makes control over the producer himself essential, by the development of prior relations of a personal rather than a material nature.

(4) The third observation we have made, on the relative complexity of production techniques, will supply us with the first element of an answer.

The acquisition of technical *skills* provides those who possess them with genuine authority over the layman since the continuation of the group depends on this knowledge. A more or less lasting leadership is conferred on those who show their superiority in particular techniques. The social importance attributed in these societies to 'the one who knows' is easily apparent to all observers.

But the acquisition of knowledge takes time and it coincides, if not totally, at least significantly enough with physiological ageing to support the fundamental senior/junior relationship. Therefore the acquisition and possession of knowledge will result in a greater authority of the older people over the younger.

There are several limitations to this authority. In the first place, if the acquisition of knowledge compensates for physical decline and replaces physical strength, then this advantage is precarious and vanishes with senility. It is therefore not adequate to ensure the seniors' authority definitively. (This might explain the practice of abandoning or liquidating old men which is encountered in certain primitive hunting societies when such means of social control have not yet developed.) Secondly, the quantity of vital technical knowledge in this kind of society is limited and can be mastered in a relatively short time. This is likely to put all men above a certain age[16] on an equal footing.

Moreover knowledge and age do not absolutely coincide. It is distorted by individuals' greater or lesser capacity to acquire this knowledge. Hence the acquisition of knowledge *irrespective* of age weakens the authority of the seniors *unless knowledge is closely identifiable with age.*

In order to perpetuate their authority, the seniors must extend their knowledge beyond fundamental subsistence skills to new fields (social learning, knowledge of customs, genealogies, history, the rules governing marriage) and even further to artificial fields (magic, divination, religious rituals, etc.). They will try to make this knowledge their exclusive province by setting up barriers to regulate its transmission: institutional barriers like initiation which in its most elaborate forms defines the individual's rank until a very advanced age; and esoteric barriers which are placed around magical, ritual (or medicinal) information so that it is only transmitted to chosen individuals. The adoption by 'wise men' of young men who show great interest or inclination for their skills helps to neutralise further possible rivals by creating an artificial link of filiation and hence of dependence. Later the granting of titles or rank to individuals versed in certain 'sciences' will also identify them with the senior group which possesses authority.[17] The need to make age coincide with knowledge ultimately involves a revision of the ideas of age and kinship. If age and kin relations were not accompanied by real social relationships they would be weakened in favour of a social system independent of them. Here the status of a senior appears to be linked more with those attributes regarded as due to age rather than with strict physiological age.

As social organisation becomes more complex other social relationships emerge from the pre-eminence of knowledge and age. But this multiplication of relations, while it strengthens the kinship which expresses them, also weakens it by reason of the autonomy of these relations, that is, the increased opportunities for establishing social relationships independently of kinship. The maintenance of the authority of the seniors over the juniors is thus the outcome of a permanent contradiction between establishing social relationships designed to strengthen the existing kinship system and the ability of these relationships to form autonomously outside the framework of kinship as established at a given moment, and challenging it.

MARRIAGE RELATIONSHIPS AND ASSOCIATED ECONOMIC FACTORS

At this point in our argument, the seniors' authority is based on the possession of knowledge which justifies their *control over the product of the juniors' labour* (see fig. 1). By taking on the task of redistribution, the seniors therefore carry out a useful function which socially legitimises this authority. Control over foodstuffs, which in agricultural societies means control over the granary, becomes in its turn an attribute of the status of senior. Both knowledge and foodstuffs, however, are perishable and therefore do not definitely establish the seniors' authority. As knowledge is slowly acquired by the juniors, the seniors are gradually losing it; foodstuffs can be kept only for a limited time, stocks must continually be replenished but prestations are renewed only if the conditions for social control are perpetuated.

If we now look at the junior's situation at this stage of the analysis we can assume that, despite the obstacles mentioned above and which only develop slowly, it is relatively easy for him to acquire the vital knowledge necessary for the satisfaction of his basic needs, to make the tools necessary for his labour and to occupy a vacant area of land. However the fulfillment of these conditions only provide him with a solitary independence; they do not enable him to achieve a position of authority within his group.

Such authority and, with it, relative independence can only be acquired if the young man has people dependent on him, i.e. if he recreates to his advantage the social model from which he comes and within which he is still in a subordinate position. In other words, and more specifically, he has to take a wife and establish paternal relations with her children.

The strengthening of the seniors' authority over the juniors depends on their capacity to control access to nubile women. The lack of such control would lead to a very rapid segmentation of the group with the result that only small restricted family groups could be constituted. The authority of the senior over such small units would be weak. The inability of such a group to perpetuate itself biologically for more than three generations would result in the disappearance of the old men at a relatively early age.

Above all it is logical in an economy in which the product of labour can only be controlled through the direct control over the producer, to control also — and maybe even more so — the *producer of the producer*, i.e. the procreative woman.

This function of the 'producer of the producer' is reflected in the intermediate position of women in traditional societies where their status is not symmetrical to that of men and where they do not constitute a truly inferior social group. For it is not so much their function as workers which is considered but their procreative function. This procreative power will be the object of the prohibitions, restrictions and controls which surround pubescent women. The sexual relations of young girls are usually very free in many societies because women become subject to tight social control only when they are able to have children, i.e. when a decision has to be made concerning the fate of their progeny. Enquiries concerning possible adultery, and sometimes wars, take place on the occasion of births.

Access to women will therefore be regulated by a number of institutions whose mechanism we shall try to describe so as to better assess the economic features with which they are associated.

THE MECHANISM OF MARRIAGE

Control of marriages between kinsfolk would assume that the senior member of the group should settle each particular case and would preclude the formation of a generally applicable strict rule. Such a system is possible though, being entirely arbitrary, it would be rather inefficient. The senior's still limited authority prevents him from enforcing arbitrariness; the establishment of marriage relationships between homologous groups does permit the development of more efficient institutions.

The problem is to create a system which will allow marriage at the juniors' level only through an agreement at the level of the senior members of the communities concerned.

Where only a few communities are involved, the agreement of the seniors of each one concerned would be sufficient, provided that marriage between individuals from the same community is forbidden so that the young men have to take a wife from the allowed group through the intermediary of their community's seniors. Hence exogamy rules constitute the corollary of matrimonial alliance rules.

In fact, at this level of social organisation, there are few communities which do not simultaneously have institutionalised and hostile relationships either with different groups or alternately with the same groups. Now, while exogamy strengthens the seniors' authority within these matrimonial alliances, this is no longer true of homologous groups with whom there are no such alliances.

Such a situation enables a young man either to abduct a woman from a non-allied community and bring her back to his own group, or to leave his own community and settle with a neighbouring one who will adopt him and give him a wife.[18]

Neither of these processes gives the seniors the possibility of a positive control of marriage. Moreover, they maintain an atmosphere of hostility between rival groups which gives the younger warriors powers likely to encroach on those of the seniors. This will give rise to latent or open tension between those who advocate settling disputes by conciliation — the seniors' speciality — and those who favour settling them by force, the young warriors.

Hence a more inclusive alliance is necessary between the seniors of these neighbouring communities in order mutually to preserve their respective authority.

To this end the means of control already in the hands of the seniors will be exploited. *Of the goods* produced by the community and handed over to the seniors as prestation *some will not be redistributed* but kept over at the level of the seniors to sanction access to wives. *Possession of these goods will testify to the seniors' status:* these objects become the attributes of 'social age'.[19]

Since in self-sustaining economies young men are those who produce these goods, they would be in a position to deal directly with the guardian of the woman they want to marry. It is, in fact, their ambition to achieve such a position. But any senior who would accept such a transaction with an individual without the required status would be weakening his counterpart's authority and consequently his own. It is in the joint interest of all seniors to respect established order.

Indeed this moral restriction is backed by material facts. The goods handed over on the occasion of a marriage are of various sorts and are frequently accompanied by labour prestations performed by several members of the groom's family. The *composite character* of bridewealth testifies to the status of the person able to collect it. It also precludes the possible exploitation of specialisation in the manufacture of a single marriage object.

MARRIAGE OBJECTS, ELITE GOODS, ALLIANCE GOODS

Thus it is that with the institutionalisation of marriage relationships between homologous groups we notice the appearance of specific *objects whose handling is associated with the rank of the person handling them.* We then have the following diagram of the circulation of goods (fig. 2):

Fig. 2

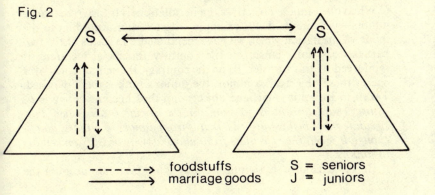

------→ foodstuffs   S = seniors
———→ marriage goods   J = juniors

— The circulation of marriage goods stays at the level of seniors. Juniors are excluded from it, but women are indirectly included in the circuit.[20]

At the economic level, this calls for two observations:

— Here marriage goods are not exchanged for one another. They sanction control by one party over the progeny of a woman from the other party. Women themselves are not 'exchanged' against the bridewealth goods. What is considered in this circuit is the expected progeny of the woman. It would therefore seem more accurate to say that bridewealth circulates, not in the reverse direction from women, but in reverse direction from their children. Indeed, we note that in the case of divorce, bridewealth is frequently kept when the children remain with the father.[21] As we shall see later an understanding of the full significance of this observation leads to a correct appreciation of the concept of *value* in this kind of system.

— The retention of marriage goods in the hands of the seniors represents a levy on the group's production: some of the goods will not be redistributed. They could be considered as a *surplus*. This surplus, however, does not stem from greater productivity but from the establishment of an institution which demands it. Here we are on common ground with Marx and Pearson[22] when they maintain that the surplus is institutional in nature and that it does not necessarily give rise to a new social structure. The level of productivity may be identical in another social system, but it is the *nature of the products* and their *social distribution* which will be different.[23] If this levy is not accompanied by an increase in productivity, the share redistributed will be small and social tension may well be increased.

— Since these goods testify to the social condition of the person who handles them and since the purpose of their circulation is to strengthen the authority of the seniors within their respective groups, *their transfer cannot take place without taking into account the rank of the parties concerned.*

When one of these objects, taken in isolation, is transferred from a junior — who made it, for example — to a senior according to the mode of prestation which we have mentioned, the status of the two parties does not change; on the contrary the social hierarchy is reinforced by this transfer. If, on the contrary, the senior hands over one of these objects to a junior, the junior's rank is thereby raised. Taken in isolation, marriage objects can thus become *elite goods, whose characteristic is to confirm the social order when they circulate from below upwards, that is from juniors to seniors, and to change it when they circulate from above downwards, from seniors to juniors.*

Hence 'exchange' is significant only if we take into account the identity of the parties concerned and the direction of the transfer.

— When these goods circulate on the occasion of a marriage, the person who hands them over and the person who receives them are at the same social level: it is a transfer between equals and in principle the rank of each remains unaltered.[24]

— However, since marriage implies an alliance these goods, again used in isolation, can circulate between equals, irrespective of the circulation of women to demonstrate an *alliance*. The principles governing the circulation of alliance goods can be deduced from what was said above:

1. There is a transfer to mark the alliance between the parties concerned.

2. There is reciprocity because the parties regard each other as of equivalent social rank; if the first gift were not returned, the donor would be placing himself in an inferior social position. This is not strictly speaking an 'exchange' but *two movements with different intentions* (first alliance, then preservation of social prestige). Besides, reciprocity may not be immediate. Often some objects circulating between equals will be 'exchanged' at a rate determined by tradition, a rate which remains constant whatever the supply and demand of the goods concerned. Certain transfers may also represent social challenges: a gift is bestowed on the other party to attest to his social rank and his capacity to return it, or a gift might be requested so as to prove one's ability to take up any challenge.[25]

Reciprocity is not required in the case of a gift made by a senior to a junior. We have seen that in this case the junior's rank is raised while his dependence on the person who gave him the object is reasserted. His promotion to a higher rank is nevertheless accomplished. This promotion may eventually enable him to give a gift to his donor and to weaken or even break that dependence if the latter accepts it. *When reciprocity occurs it implies a recognised or desired social parity between the parties.*

— The accumulation of these elite goods asserts the social superiority of the person who accumulates them. Their ostentatious exhibition is a manifestation of prestige which may in some societies take the appearance of what Georges Balandier has described as 'economic challenge'. One understands that elite goods cannot be given to common people without granting them the attributes of a higher social rank, i.e. without handing over to them some elements of social power. On the other hand the need to preserve social prestige implies an *equalising* reciprocity between peers. Ostentatious destruction of these goods remains the ultimate demonstration of prestige: it means that no-one has a rank equal to oneself. Only food and certain neutral objects will be distributed to people of lower rank according to the redistributive function pertaining to common objects.

— Concerning social organisation, it will be possible to extend the social control effected through the custody and control over the circulation of durable and transmissible elite goods, to a group *wider* than that on which control was exercised through custody of staple goods.

The redistribution of foodstuffs to a large number of individuals can be done only by the establishment of an administrative organisation which is beyond the capacities of a segmentary society such as the one we are concerned with.

By contrast, from the moment when the senior has a simpler and more flexible means of social control through the custody of durable and handier elite goods he can *decentralise the control of staple goods*, by handing it over to adult married men, thus enabling a larger number of individuals to attain a higher social rank — still inferior to his own — and thereby increasing his power. (In an agricultural society it is control of the granaries which will be handed over to the seniors' dependents.) The circulation of goods within the group would be thus represented as follows (fig. 4).

Fig. 4

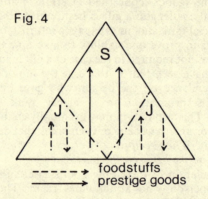

- - - - - → foodstuffs
—————→ prestige goods

But, we shall see later how the expansion of the group, corresponding to the integration of several lineages must also be accompanied by a concept of seniority adjusted to the principle of identification of age and power.

VALUE, LABOUR

By now, we have traced the various modes of circulation associated with the nature of the goods and with the status of the protagonists.

Staple goods are basically the object of prestations by the juniors to the seniors and of redistribution by the seniors to the juniors; marriage goods are the object of transfer and imply both alliance and reciprocity. Elite goods are the object of prestations when they are given by the juniors to the seniors and of gifts when they circulate in the opposite direction. When they circulate between peers, they imply reciprocity.

Apart from reciprocity, which we will consider separately, *these various modes of circulation never enable the products to be confronted with one another*. This is obvious when discussing prestations, redistribution or unilateral gift. Concerning marriage goods, we have already stressed that one of their main functions is to assert the seniors' authority. *The amount of bridewealth* does not reflect the greater or lesser worth attributed to the woman's personal qualities. It reflects a series of more complex considerations, the two most important of which are the concern to *set the bridewealth at a level inaccessible to the junior*, and the need to demonstrate one's *social prestige*. Were 'exchange' to take place, it would be measured against the expected progeny of the woman but this consideration is so remote that it is obscured by the two considerations mentioned above (although gifts are usually handed over by the husband to his wife's family when she has children).

Since none of these modes of circulation makes possible the confrontation of goods with one another, the objects cannot be measured in terms of each other. No *exchange value* can emerge under these conditions.

There could be found in reciprocal gifts some elements liable to give rise to 'exchange value' since reciprocity implies an equalisation of the gifts which must be considered as *equivalents*. This equivalence however is not based on the nature of the elite goods which are nearly always abstracted from their immediate use (loin cloths, mats, etc.) and converted into treasures *without use-value* in the economic sense of the word. Since these objects are considered in relation to their social potential, they acquire no more than a conventional — and constant — value. Lastly, these objects are limited in number and circulate only inside a sphere which has been made as hermetic as possible. Thus while these 'exchanges' may contain an embryonic element of value, this value remains abstract and conventional and since it cannot be measured physically by comparison with other objects it is not universal.[26] The immediate consequence of the non-value of products is the *non-value of labour*: there is no such *commodity* as labour-power.

— Labour cannot by itself be a source of enrichment and social advancement for the person performing it.

— Nor will labour be remunerated. When a young man works for someone who is not a relative, there is in fact a transfer of the kinship relation (since the fact of working for someone else involves handing over to him the product of one's labour, hence making a 'prestation' which, as we have seen, characterises the relationship between seniors and juniors within the community). When repeated this transfer brings with it most of the relationships which accompany the kinship relation. *Vis-à-vis* the person employing him, the worker will be in the position, for example, of a son in relation to his father. The employer will thus have the obligation of a father towards him; in particular he will provide him with food *during* the performance of the labour (and not *afterwards* as is typical of wage-labour). The gift which may be given to the worker afterwards will usually be handed over by the young man to the person whom he is normally dependent on. This gift will not be directly measured by the amount of work performed.

When collective labour is performed for a leading person, food will be provided for everybody irrespective of each person's labour. Some people will even participate in the feast without having taken any part in the labour. The 'value' of the work performed will not be taken into consideration in determining the remuneration, according to the principle of the 'labourers of the eleventh hour'.

THE HIERARCHISATION OF LINEAGES

We have now seen how the authority is backed by the establishment of several social relationships and that the rank of senior is manifest through the possession of certain attributes. These attributes multiply as the society becomes more integrated, enabling the less efficient ones to be abandoned in favour of the more efficient. The relative autonomy of these attributes in terms of age and kinship tends to make seniority a social concept and kinship an *ideological frame of reference*. The possession of more numerous and more efficient attributes and the social relations which derive from them make it possible to extend the seniors' control to wider groups.

We thus see *conditions emerge for a transformation of the society into larger and more highly integrated units* in which the functions of authority will be exercised through more sophisticated social techniques leading towards the building of a society hierarchised according to social class.[27]

The growth of the group however requires adjustments in the concepts of seniority and kinship *which, in their turn, will have further economic repercussions*. Indeed all the economic and social relationships which we have considered are attached to these two concepts (seniority and kinship). They justify the social organisation, give it coherence and establish a frame of reference. At this stage no change can be carried out independently of this ideological system.

If authority is linked to seniority and if this is limited to the lifespan of an individual, this authority can then be exerted only on those descendants born during that period. For the group to increase and include a greater number of lineages it is essential, if one is to respect the principles of identifying age with power, to project into the past the source of authority claimed by the living senior. This projection into the past then justifies the power of the senior over a group more or less proportional to the number of generations which separate the dead ancestor from the living senior. Hence the dead ancestor who would have been forgotten in a more elementary society will here become an object of worship.[28]

In many systems, authority is transmitted from elder brother to younger brother until the generation is finished, after which it is transmitted to one of the brothers' sons. In such cases the rank of senior is not bound up with any single lineage. Sibling succession eliminates the domination of one lineage over the others by virtue of the seniority principle. If authority is transmitted from father to eldest son according to the law of primogeniture this is no longer true. In this case power will *always be located in the same lineage, which becomes a senior lineage.* All the members of that lineage will then have the status of senior towards all the members of the junior lineages, regardless of the real respective ages of the parties. From being *personal, the rank of senior becomes social.*

This can be represented diagrammatically as follows: the death of senior A logically brings about the splitting up of the group into *ab* (fig. 5) unless one of A's descendants, called A1, claims A's authority for his own benefit, which continues to include B.

If the system is one of transmission from brother to brother, on A1's death power will go to B and later to one of A1 or B's descendants: authority does not necessarily remain in the same branch (fig. 6). If there is a system of hereditary transmission by primo-geniture, then authority will go from A to A1 and then to A2; B branch is definitely kept away from power (fig. 7). According to this latter system of transmission, the whole A1 lineage acquires a privileged position associated with statutory seniority. A1's lineage becomes a senior lineage. The privileges and prerogatives of seniority will become, in due course, the privileges and prerogatives of all the members of the lineage. Henceforth we can represent the social system as a hierarchised system (fig. 8).

Economically, hierarchisation will be reflected in a number of

Fig. 5

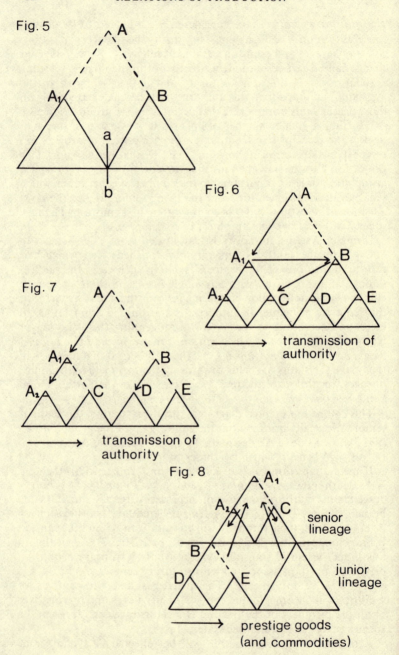

Fig. 6

Fig. 7

→ transmission of
authority

→ transmission of
authority

Fig. 8

senior
lineage

junior
lineage

→ prestige goods
(and commodities)

phenomena:

— The mode of circulation of goods (prestation-redistribution) which operates on the personal level between senior and junior within the elementary communities *will continue to operate between the senior lineage and the junior lineages.* The senior group will receive tribute from the inferior groups and will retain for its own use the prestige goods (and possibly the goods which may be exchanged with the outside world) *according to the ideological model inherited from the previous social organisation* (fig. 8).

A new kind of marriage restriction arises *between classes.* For marriage with women of inferior status would involve giving marriage goods — henceforth 'noble goods' — to commoners. Since the latter do not have free access to these goods neither can they have access to wives from the higher group. This new marriage restriction is not only alien to the traditional rules of exogamy, but it is opposed to them because it sanctions the *endogamy* of a group which claims descent from the same ancestor. The emergence of *deliberate* endogamous practices seems to mark the appearance of social classes.

— An individual belonging to the senior group will be able to establish bilateral relations with an individual from a junior group, which will be the transformation of the original relation between senior and junior at a higher level of social integration. In this relationship, which could be described as a *patron/client relationship*, economic links may be established concerning goods specific to the patron's culture. By entrusting to his client certain goods (cattle for example) the patron raises the client into his own class where the latter finds himself in the position of an adopted junior *vis-à-vis* the senior, irrespective of their actual ages, but by virtue of their social conditions. In a way the social relationship senior lineage/junior lineage is reconverted into a personal senior/junior relationship within the patron's own system.

— We now have the conditions for the *control of land* by one social category in relation to others. We have seen that within an elementary community the seniors could not enforce control of the land over the juniors who were its guardians *vis-à-vis* outsiders. The dominant group, composed of men of all ages, will now be in a position to exert physical control over access to the land, provided that it acquires the appropriate administrative and police techniques.

The control of a means of production as basic as land in peasant societies in due course brings about the disappearance of this type of communal economy. Henceforth, the mode of social control which, as we have seen, tended to be exercised directly over the producer and in which wealth consists of 'status symbol' objects, will gradually disappear, giving place to a more efficient system: the control of men through the appropriation of the means of production. A new society will develop, based on the ideological projection of the segmentary society from which it emerged, to set up the economic foundations of a pre-feudal type of domination.

RELATIONS WITH A COMPLEMENTARY ECONOMY

These *community societies* usually undergo such transformations under the impact of a market economy. We must therefore define these new relationships and try to see how they interfere with the traditional modes of circulation of goods.[29]

In community societies, characterised by self-sufficiency, the circulation of commodities is ensured solely by the functions of prestation and redistribution. A system of circulation is established between communities to regulate marriage relationships, without involving any complementary exchanges. The mechanisms on which social organisation is based are built on the subsistence economy.

This situation of economic insularity may be altered if these communities come into contact with other societies which possess a very useful product, which they themselves do not produce. This is generally the case for metals, including iron which we will take as an example.

Iron combines several characteristics which none of the products of the self-sustaining economy possess:

— It is not directly accessible. On the one hand it requires a comparatively advanced production technique; on the other, iron ore is unevenly distributed. Hence its possession will always be the privilege, either of a group of *specialised* techniques, or of a geographically favoured society.

— It is used for making production goods (tools) or weapons.

— It may be shaped into uniform and aliquot objects, i.e. it can take on some of the functions of money and thus threaten the traditional system through a process already described by Marx.

When faced with this product, the community will take steps *to protect the self-sustaining nature of its economy*, on which its social organisation is based.

In order to specify the mechanism of exchanges following the introduction of an imported product of the nature described above, we will assume that the communities concerned have achieved a certain degree of social integration characterized by the fact that the juniors control the redistribution of foodstuffs within their respective families (see model of fig. 4). We thus eliminate the more elementary communities represented by fig. 1. This distinction is important because the economic and political relationships can differ very greatly according to these two cases.[30]

It is generally the trading group which induces exchange by offering iron against certain commodities produced and valued by these communities (kola, cotton, or ivory, for instance). The seniors will therefore fit these products into the prestation circuit where they will become elite goods within the community.

From this apparently simple but basically contradictory phenomenon, will follow a number of new economic and social consequences which we will briefly summarise for the sole purpose of gauging the practical scope of this theoretical essay.

(1) First, products which have no value within the community economy acquire value as soon as they are the object of exchange and are converted into commodities.[31]

But this conversion takes place only at the level of the seniors: *the two economic systems coexist in the same society but at two different social levels.* As a corollary, the juniors' labour, although it is a source of value when its product reaches the seniors' hands, remains valueless within the framework of the traditional system of prestation.

This situation contains within itself the potential of heightened social stress between seniors and juniors, where the former are in the objective position of exploiters in relation to the latter. This situation will be aggravated as the seniors' levies increase: to marriage goods which move in a closed circuit are added goods which can be sold outside and which, if they are exchanged for nothing but elite goods, simply enrich the seniors. This exploitation will thus be accompanied by stricter social regulations, a strengthening of the rules of etiquette and of religious duties (to the ancestors and thereby to the seniors who represent them), by practices such as poisoning those who accumulate excessively, etc.[32]

(2) Let us now assume that this metal is offered by the merchants in the shape of low-value ingots, they can then be introduced at a lower level of exchange, i.e. that of foodstuffs. These merchants must obtain food while they travel; they may also obtain foodstuffs in exchange for which they will offer their merchandise. At this point the juniors, who dispose freely of these commodities — according to our initial hypothesis — will be in a position *to convert ordinary goods into elite goods* and to acquire, outside the conventional norms the attributes of a social status which is not theirs. The circuit of — non-exchanged and 'valueless' — products, and of — exchange-

able and value laden — commodities can be represented as follows (fig. 9):

Fig. 9

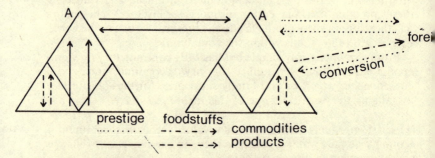

This possibility of conversion therefore threatens the social order based on the traditional circuits. Frequently, the seniors will be unable to recapture the distribution of foodstuffs because they lack adequate administrative techniques.

It will also be impossible for them to deprive iron of its prestigious function henceforth associated with its trading value, its quality as a raw material for the manufacture of means of production, and its potential as currency.

Since the juniors cannot be prevented from having access to iron, bridewealth will be set at amounts of metal inaccessible to those who do not engage in the trade monopolised with *quantity*.[33]

Moreover, bridewealth will remain composite and will include objects which will be traditionally kept out of commercial transactions, objects which are strictly reserved for social transfers, only transmissible by succession. This situation therefore necessitates the *super-imposition of closed spheres of exchange* within which homologous goods only will circulate (beginning of the distinction between patrimonial goods and 'capital'). The possibility of converting products belonging to different spheres will be subject to customary prohibitions invoked by the seniors, but which the juniors will try to circumvent.

(3) The introduction of iron into a self-sustaining society sets off within it a hostile reaction towards those who introduce it. When the society itself does not exploit the ore the foreign merchant offering iron will not be trusted. In order to neutralise the disintegrating effects which he bears with him the merchant will be prevented from becoming integrated into the society and particularly from entering into marriage relationships of the conventional type. *The trading*

relation will usually exclude war which is linked with matrimonial exchanges. The term 'foreign' seems to have been linked more often with individuals belonging to trading societies than with those belonging to culturally different societies.

This attitude is reproduced in iron-producing economies concerning *blacksmiths*[32] whose potential economic power will be neutralised by the prohibition against establishing marriage relations with other social categories. In this respect, the smiths find themselves, at the material level, in a situation comparable to that of the *griots*, for example, at the intellectual level, in spite of the fact that griots are casted because they possess an element of power inherent to social organisation, whereas the power held by the smiths is outside social organisation.[33]

The interference of an exchange economy with a self-sustaining economy brings about many other changes which would lead to the study of such phenomena as slavery, markets, money, land tenure systems, handicrafts etc. at different moments of economic history.

CONCLUSION

At this point, this theoretical essay may perhaps allow us to make a number of remarks on the role of the economic factor in the organisation of traditional societies.

We have seen how self-sufficiency is the economic framework in which the modes of production and of circulation of goods develop: a direct mode of production, involving relations of production of a personal and immediate nature; a mode of circulation without exchange and based on these personal relations which it confirms and extends.

The determining role of economic conditions is not immediately apparent because these societies are based on a weak material infrastructure which gives proportionately greater importance to intellectual phenomena. What baffles those economists who look for simplistic economic determinism, is the fact that the system of circulation of goods which they observe develops by way of the handling of knowledge of non-material phenomenon.

Once the self-sustaining economy is threatened by the emergence of trade, the society which has been built on self-sufficiency tends to be preserved artificially by the neutralisation of the different merchandise which penetrates into the group. The eventual disappearance of the self-sustaining economy brings about the emergence of new social relationships based no longer on strict personal relationships, but on the fact that individuals now belong to statutory hierarchised social categories, and of new economic relations between classes built on the altered model of the former relationships.

The notions of kinship and seniority are maintained throughout these changes and acquire the strength of a kinship and religious ideology.

The society will be in transition between the direct economy and the feudal economy; it will find support in this ideology throughout the period in which, while already hierarchised, it has not yet reached the stage of control of the land by the dominating class.

Because of the contradictions inherent in them the concepts of age and kinship contain within them the seeds of these changes.

The apparent immobility of these societies stems from the fact that they are usually studied at the level of clan organisation. As long as the conditions for self-sufficiency are maintained these societies multiply, spread and duplicate themselves through segmentation without there being any significant transformation in the organisation of the constituent cells.

It is at the demographic and geographical levels that these societies manifest their dynamic. In so doing, they themselves create the conditions for their transformation by creating the possibility of contact with a complementary economy, or by becoming complementary themselves through geographical expansion.

In order to carry this type of study forward, it would be useful to direct fieldwork towards certain observations on, for example, the kinds of goods in circulation and the different levels at which they are placed, the identity of the protagonists, the direction taken by transfers and their sequence in time, the social and geographical origin of the objects of generalised exchange fulfilling certain monetary functions. *Markets* have been the subject of study for several years now. They, doubtless, constitute long neglected privileged vantage points where many economic, social and political phenomena appear in a new light.

In addition, study of collectivities as they relate to one another, often disregarded in favour of localised studies, should lead to the investigation of large-scale economic and geographical units. By exploding the far too narrow framework of monographs it would probably be possible to reveal certain unsuspected coherences between societies which one has exaggeratedly regarded as being more isolated and more self-contained than they are in reality.

NOTES

1. For a discussion of the method used, see 'Elaboration d'un modèle socio-économique en ethnologie', *Epistémologie sociologique* vols. 1–5, 1964–68, pp. 283–308.

2. 'On the mode of Production of the Hunting band' in Alexandre, P. (ed.) *French Perspectives in African Studies*, Oxford University Press, London, 1973.

3. Marchal, A., *Systèmes et Structures économiques*, Presses Universitaires de France, Paris, 1959, p. 210n.

4. Herskovits, M. J., *Economic Anthropology*, Knopf, New York, 1952.

5. Goodfellow, D. M., *Principles of Economic Sociology*, Routledge, London, 1939.

6. Firth, R., *Elements of Social Organisation*, Watts, London, 1951.

7. Tax, S., *Penny Capitalism, A Guatemalan Indian Economy*, Washington D.C., 1953.

8. Marx, K., *Contribution to the Critique of Political Economy*, Lawrence and Wishart, London, 1971, p. 33.

9. Thurnwald, R., *Economics in Primitive Communities*, International African Institute, London, 1932.

10. We must mention here a remarkable study by Professor Bohannan on Tiv markets, which we have received but has not yet been published. Professor Bohannan is at present preparing (May 1960) a symposium on African markets. [Published in 1962 as *Markets in Africa*, Bohannan, P. and Dalton, G. (eds.)—Ed.]

11. Mauss, M., *The Gift*, London, 1966.

12. Polanyi, K., Arensberg, M., Pearson, W. H. (eds.), *Trade and Markets in the early Empires*, Free Press, Glencoe, 1957.

13. To this list must be added the contributions published in number 1 of *Humanités* (no. 95 of the *Cahiers* I.S.E.A.), Paris, November, 1959.

14. See the explanatory models by Thurnwald, 1932, *op. cit.*, and Engels, *The Origin of the Family, Private Property & the State*, Lawrence and Wishart, London, 1972.

15. The role of the chef de terre is described in almost all monographs more or less as follows: 'In *theory* the land chief owns the land, in *practice* he exerts no authority over its distribution.' C. K. Meek, in 1946, in *Land, Law and Customs in the Colonies*, Frank Cass, London, already pointed out and discussed this 'contradiction' between theory and practice. It seems that the expression 'land chief' is a very poor translation, whose vagueness derives from the ambivalence of the word 'land' to which both spatial and jural connotations are attached. If the expression were translated 'priest of the soil' (for example) less importance would be given to discovering the inexistent property rights of this personage. In relation to land, one must acknowledge:
(a) that in the traditional economic system, land is valueless (see below), i.e. without exchange value.
(b) that the authorisation given to a stranger to till the land and to settle in the domain of a given group is a permission to join a neighbourhood, which implies the eventual adoption of that immigrant into the group. All prestations and reciprocal relations between the group and the immigrant are established with this prospect in mind. Therefore the decision to accept the stranger depends on the person who exerts *de facto* social control. In some cases he may be the descendant of the first settler, this 'priest of the soil', but he will not rule by virtue of this single quality.

16. Women play an important role as guardians of vital knowledge (agriculture, food-gathering and food-preparation). While the group is small in size the women's skills are up to its needs, giving them an authority which they will lose in a more integrated group where the problems of political organisation exceed the domestic and agricultural domain to which they will be restricted.

17. In a more organised society, knowledge, the instrument of social power, becomes an intellectual burden which is too heavy to be borne effectively by the dominant class. A social group which becomes the holder of knowledge on behalf of the

reigning families appears. But because they control this instrument of power, these 'wise men' are also subjected to measures aimed at neutralising them politically. They will either be recruited from a lower social class or made into a caste.

18. Notice that the first case corresponds to the patrilineal-patrilocal system: the progeny of the woman belongs to the agnatic group; the wife resides with her husband's kind. The second case corresponds to the matrilineal-matrilocal system: the progeny of the woman remains under the control of the uterine group. The husband lives with his wife's people.

19. The nature of these goods will vary according to the society. In some cases they will be foodstuffs; more often they will be durable and transmissible handicraft goods.

20. An adult male may himself pay the bridewealth for his wife. Usually he will not do this for the first wife but rather for the second or third wife. In dealing directly with the father of his second wife, he places himself socially on the same age-level as his father-in-law. His second wife, for whom he has paid the bridewealth himself will on the other hand be of inferior status to him and to his first wife, who comes from a higher *social* generation.

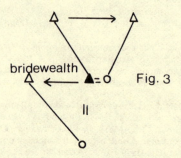

Fig. 3

21. A comparison should be made between the often deplored instability of marriage in those societies and the stability of filiation links established through the marriage.

22. Polanyi, K., Arensberg, M., and Pearson, W. H. (eds.), 1967, *op. cit.*

23. This is flagrant in the context of the colonial economy which was not accompanied by any technical progress in agriculture, but which gave rise to an exportable agricultural surplus by the introduction of new institutions such as taxation or forced labour.

24. The kinship term which is usually extended to the affinal group is that of 'brother' which implies social parity, alliance, reciprocity — the same term is applied to both parties.

25. This type of transaction marks the behaviour of the individuals belonging to these community societies when they come to 'exchange' certain goods, to which they attribute a prestige function, with foreign merchants. In these exchanges which they continue to regard as an alliance relationship between equals, they are always aware of the need to preserve their social status.

26. Those objects which are not introduced into the system of social control will be the object neither of prestations, nor redistribution nor gifts. Therefore they will have neither social 'value' nor economic 'value'. They will be used freely by the members of the group and loaned or borrowed with great ease. They will not be controlled or appropriated. Although the nature of these objects varies according to societies it seems that many household implements used by women fall into this category.

These are generally the goods which will be most easily channelled into the modern trade sector.

27. The immediate economic causes of these transformations will be discussed later.

28. Genealogical depth increases as the authority of the chief or king spreads over a larger number of individuals. If carried to its limits, projecting the ancestor back into eternity justifies universal domination by his presumed representative. The historical content of genealogies is certainly as much affected by the size of the group as by the political pretensions of the person in power.

29. The other causes of transformation may be of historical origin (conquests). As to the process of transformation under the effects of the market economy, a process due mainly to the *valorisation* of labour and manifested in the use of slave-labour, the specialisation of labour, the accumulation of personal property, etc., analyses have been made of it which we will not repeat here (see Engels, 1972, *op. cit.* and Thurnwald, 1932, *op. cit*).

30. The trading population sometimes establishes a paternalistic, protective relationship with an elementary community which, under the effect of a colonial economy, may be transformed into a second-degree colonialism.

31. This originally vague value will be made more precise by the introduction of measures or standards which enable the setting-up of terms of exchange and ultimately of prices.

32. This situation brings about two other consequences which touch on present and practical problems:

Concerning the creation of *co-operatives* within the framework of the traditional economy: the co-operation which is observed in these societies rests at the level of labour where it is valueless. Only the head of the family enters with his goods into the trade circuit where he finds himself in competition with other heads of families, and where he acquires individualistic reactions. Here.the co-operative aspect disappears completely. People work inside the framework of the communal or collective economy; they sell in that of a capitalistic economy.

Concerning *agricultural development programmes*: the encouragement to produce cash crops leads, within the traditional framework, to an increased exploitation of the juniors and thereby to an intensification of social conflicts; the more strongly the traditional hierarchy prevails, the more violent the conflicts will be. It can be assumed from this that in order for an agricultural programme to have best results it should be preceded by a transformation of the traditional family structures.

33. Within the framework of a colonial monetary economy, the money circulating at the level of retail trade and that circulating at the level of bridewealth do not have the same qualitative content. It has been repeatedly observed that there is a resistance to the conversion of one into the other. Bridewealth is deliberately set by the seniors at a level which increases as the juniors have access to money incomes. The attempts made by the colonial authorities to reduce the amount of bridewealth conflicted with the fact that such a restriction would have weakened the authority of these 'notables' who were in other respects supported by the colonial administration.

34. The blacksmiths in question are mainly those who produce the iron from iron ore and rarely those who merely work the iron.

35. In general, groups who, through their 'professional' specialisation, are repositories or producers of the representative elements of the political power of the dominating class, are caste-ed.

The Social Organisation of the Peasantry: The Economic Basis of Kinship

Claude Meillassoux

This brief sketch, which was presented to the seminar on 'peasants' held in 1972 at the University of London and published in The Journal of Peasant Studies, *Vol. 1, no. 1, provides the elements for an analysis which, unlike the earlier 'preliminary analysis' (see pp. 129–57), does not take the relations of production character- istic of the self-sustaining formation as given but seeks to identify the conditions under which those relations are created. It represents in some ways a gloss on, and in some ways a development of, certain themes explored in the essay 'From reproduction to production', which appeared in* Economy and Society, *vol. 1, no. 1, 1972 and was itself a development of Meillassoux's early essay on 'The economy in agricultural self-sustaining societies'. Discussion of the paper at the seminar concentrated on the central question of the existence and nature of class divisions in self-sustaining societies. Meillassoux referred to the fact that, in France, two points of view had emerged on this subject: first, there were those (e.g. Dupré and Rey) who claimed that class antagonisms existed, since the seniors exploited the juniors and had an interest in maintaining this situation; second, others, including himself, held that there was no class antagonism properly speaking. The debate remains open.*

My own knowledge of the peasantry is far too limited to support generalisations suitable to all types of peasant organisation, geographically and historically. The present paper is widely influenced by the field of my investigations which are restricted to West African rural populations, and by the scope of my research through which I try to reconstruct peasant social organisation prior to colonisation and the development of the market, as the point of departure for further change. So-called 'traditional' peasant organisation will provide, therefore, the main part of my paper.

In the first two parts, I will examine the social organisation of the peasant on two levels: that of the productive unit and that of the relations of these units among themselves. In conclusion, I will briefly mention the transformation of the social organisation of agricultural production under the impact of market development and capitalism.

A definition of peasantry requires first a specification of the historical period we are referring to, not as a dated moment of history but as a period characterised by the development of the productive forces. Prior to European colonisation and the development of the market, West African agriculture was, in general, dominated by the following features:
— use of human energy in agricultural work;
— use of individual means of production requiring little labour investment;
— non-methodical division of labour, but rather an allocation of tasks between the members of the productive cells;
— immediate accessibility of land and raw material;
— self-sustenance (the community produces to satisfy its own needs and finds within its reach the necessary objects and instruments of labour and raw material).

In this context, we will define peasants as people living off the land through their agricultural labour, cultivation being the dominant activity. (Dominant because it determines the overall social organisation of the community, other activities, however useful or necessary, being subordinated to the dominant one.) My contention is that the social organisation of the peasantry is built, first around the relations of production as they grow from the economic constraints of agricultural activities, and next, around the necessity for reproduction of the productive unit.

THE ECONOMY OF PRODUCTION

I have shown in a previous paper[1] that the radical difference observed between a foraging-hunting economy and an agricultural economy is related to the fact that the first uses land as a 'subject of labour' while the latter uses it as an 'instrument of labour'. The use of land as an instrument of labour means that labour is invested into the land with the expectation of a later return. For botanical and climatic reasons, the output is delayed, not only until the end of the process of investment but beyond, until the maturity of the crop, that is, for a period of time which is not under the control of the producer. The agricultural cycle is divided into successive productive and unproductive periods. It starts necessarily with an unproductive period, which means that the agricultural enterprise cannot be undertaken unless the cultivators have some resources at their disposal to survive during the preliminary, preparatory work. Such resources come either from subsidiary activities, as gathering or hunting, or more often, from the left-over of the previous crop. Agriculture requires, therefore, either a combination with a different mode of production and/or storage and management of the product.

If we eliminate the first case, we see already the main characteristics of agriculture: delayed production, accumulation and storage of the product, managed redistribution.

Because of delayed production, cooperation in agricultural activities is a lasting one, if not everlasting. Cultivation creates bonds between people on two counts: first, between people who worked together from the time of the preliminary tasks to the time of harvesting and who have a vested interest in remaining together to benefit from their combined labour; second, and this is even more important, between the successive teams of labourers who at each season are depending, for survival during the unproductive period and for preparation for the next cycle, on the food produced during the previous productive period. From this angle, the agricultural cycle appears as a continuously renewed cycle of advance and restitution of food (and seeds eventually) between the producers of each successive season: each successive seasonal team is advancing food (and seeds) to the following one. Of course, in the short term, most of the labourers are likely to remain the same. But as time elapses, the composition of the working team is bound to change gradually: the older ones disappear, while younger people take their place. This amounts, in the long run, to a change of generations.

The changing composition of the team explains the hierarchy that we find in agricultural communities. The actual hierarchy relates 'people who come before' and 'people who come after'. Hierarchy rests on a notion of 'anteriority'. The first are those to whom one owes food and seeds. They are the elders. Among them, the senior member of the community owes nothing, but to his ancestors, while all his junior partners are indebted to him. Because of his apex position within the community, the senior is logically appointed to collect and store the product of the community. He will also be in a position to manage it. The necessity of this management to ensure the reproduction of the productive cycle creates a function while the structure of the productive unit points to the one who must fulfil it. The cycle of advance and restitution which we mention above is going to take place between the senior and his junior partners along a prestative-redistributive circuit which is the dominant mode of circulation within such communities. We have here the relations of production in their essence. They create life-long relationships between members of the community; they generate a hierarchical structure based on anteriority, or age; they contribute to the emergence of well-defined social cells, with a membership, a structure and a leader.

Beyond the reproduction of the productive cycle, the cultivators are faced with the problem of reproducing the productive unit. The perpetuation of the distributive cycle, which means the opportunity for the members of the group to benefit in the future from their past labour, is subordinated to their capacity to recreate the social organisation along a repeated scheme and along the same structures.

One of the main requirements, from this point of view, is to keep within the community a proper balance between the number of productive and unproductive members and, among them, a sufficient number of offspring of both sexes to reproduce the productive unit in number and proportion. Given its limited extent, the agricultural community can hardly find within itself the necessary elements for an harmonious reproduction; coexistence at all times of nubile partners is unlikely. An opening towards other communities is necessary.

THE ECONOMY OF REPRODUCTION

Relations with other communities start from a factual situation: the lack, at a given time, when she is needed to mate with a young male of marrying age, of a nubile woman within the productive unit. A woman of proper age will be sought in a group where she is without a male partner.

Now, there is nothing that can compensate for a pubescent woman in her reproductive function but another pubescent woman. Whoever is yielding a girl expects another one in return. But for the very reason that such a transaction takes place, exchange of women cannot be immediately reciprocated. Most of the deals are time-bargains, regulated by a dowry system. Only people in a position to return a woman in the foreseeable future can enter into such a deal. For this reason, the seniors must keep absolute control on the destination of the women of their respective communities. But if exchange of women requires greater authority over a group of women as large as possible, it also allows for management of a larger group. While management of food might soon become cumbersome when extended to an increased number of people, matrimonial policy is easier and more efficient when dealing with a large population. The social corporate unit is bound to be of larger size and to include several productive units through a decentralisation of the control over subsistence. In other words, segmentation can take place at the economic level while cohesiveness is maintained and increased matrimonially at the level of an exogamic enlarged cell.

If the group could be restricted to the size of the strict productive unit, it would probably not need to enforce incest prohibition since (besides the fact that opportunities are scarce) the authority of the senior rests on the control of subsistence. But because such a unit must reproduce structurally and open itself towards the outside to secure women, the power of the senior shifts from control over subsistence to control over women. From then on, the senior's authority rests on his capacity to deal with the outside, and since marriage is the main and dominant reason for exterior relations, preservation of this authority requires that marriage be prohibited within the group. Paradoxically, this prohibition is all the more necessary as the group becomes larger and its capacity for endogenous reproduction greater. (Preference marriage may be considered as a lead towards autonomous reproduction, although endogamy never becomes the rule in an agricultural community, except in aristocratic lineages for reasons beyond the scope of this paper.)

Assuming at this point that nubile women are available and evenly distributed among the male members of marrying age of the community, a balanced reproduction is still not ensured. It would be still less ensured in the case of strictly endogamous reproduction of the community. The need for exchange of people would be even greater and lead necessarily to relations with other communities. Differential fecundity, unbalanced sex-ratio, premature death are bound to bring an uneven distribution of sex and age. Genetic reproduction is inadequate to fit the reproduction and growth of a functional agricultural community: communities derive from agricultural relations and not the reverse. Genetics ensure the natural reproduction of the population on a large scale, not the structural reproduction of the limited functional unit. Natural reproduction must be corrected ceaselessly through co-option of members born outside the community. Adoption of children, of war captives, clientage, sometimes the gift of a spouse are means to correct an unfavourable balance.

Social reproduction of the community is consequently a political endeavour and not a natural process. It favours on all counts the authority of the senior.

We perceive here the logical gradation of social organisation from the productive unit, which generates the authority of the senior, to the reproductive cell, which grows from this authority on the basis of its capacity to ensure the reproductive cycle. Unlike the productive cycle, the latter is not self-sufficient. In both cases nevertheless, authority rests on the control of the means of human reproduction: subsistence and women.

KINSHIP EXPRESSION OF SOCIAL RELATIONS

Kinship is usually considered as the basis of social organisation in so-called 'traditional' or 'primitive societies'. Often it is understood as an expression of genetic relationships. It is, however, above all the expression of the relations of production and of reproduction of the peasant community as we have defined it. Most of the relationships built on the functional requirements of the group can fit the kinship description.

Cultivation does not require a large group of co-operants and this group can be made up of labourers of various strengths, i.e. various age and sex, such as can be found even in the nuclear family.

Planting agriculture, which does not require seeds, favours a type of disseminated storage of the product in the fields, sometimes in the ground. Women, who are the main cultivators, retain more easily control of production, and we may speculate that matrilineal relationships are perpetuated in this context. On the other hand, cereal agriculture requires stocks and care, and centralisation of the product in the village. Men can exert their control without over-stepping women's prerogatives. Here are possible grounds for a patrilineal family and for the enlargement of the productive unit towards the extended family. Co-operation in agricultural enterprises leads to life-long relationships between the partners, as we find familial relations to be.

The reproduction of the cycle generates solidarity and hierarchy between successive generations; notions of anteriority and posteriority preside over social relations. It does not mean only, therefore, a relation between the genitor and his offspring, but also between older and younger brothers (a reason why the notion of 'brother' as a kinship term is less frequent probably than the distinction between senior-brothers and junior-brothers), patrons and clients, host and foreigners.

Management and redistribution of the product leads to the election of the senior as the logical leader of the family group. He acts, in so doing, as the foster-father of all the junior members. The father is he who feeds you and who has a claim on your labour and your product. In his function as regulator of the social reproduction the father is also he who marries you. If such relations of production and reproduction are severed, so is dependency. Adoption on the other hand carries with it such material and social relations between the parties. In the process of adjustment to the economic requirements, kinship is treated as a social relation extendable beyond sheer natural relationships. Kinship expresses genetic relations only to the extent that they fulfil actual functional relations. But the confusion is not without significance. Beyond the functional relation, kinship expresses also an apologetic of the social system and, as we shall see later, it is loaded with ideology.

THE ORGANISATION OF THE COMMUNITIES BETWEEN THEMSELVES

If the structure and organisation of the community is the ground for centralisation of authority, relations between communities seem on the contrary hardly capable of generating a co-ordinated power structure.

We know, by now, that agricultural activity contributes to the formation of social and political units by the gathering of a number of people around a given product, resulting from their combined labour investment. We also know that such productive units can be incorporated into larger exogamous structures. For demographic or political reasons these units need to open themselves to the outside to secure the means of their reproduction through relations with other communities. If we accept our premise that communities are self-sustaining and therefore without need for economic exchange, this search for women is bound to be the dominant reason for external relations.

The means of securing women can be violent or peaceful. Rape or elopement, though practicable and practised, lead to war and consequently to two dangers: they might bring the death of young warriors and therefore a possible imbalance of the social structure. It is a major concern of people in this type of community to limit war casualties to a minimum and to seek compensation. Captives or hostages are often used to restore impaired demography. Rape and elopement lead also to the increased political importance of the younger men in their capacity as warriors and a correlative decrease of the dominant position of the leaders in their capacity as policy-makers, particularly as matrimonial policy-makers whose purpose is precisely to organise the reproduction of the group. In both cases, war may be self-defeating and a regulated exchange of women between communities is bound to take place.

As we know, quests for women lead to time-bargaining between the parties, based, in essence, on bilateral agreements. The natural evolution of the system is to extend itself to a population large enough to contain mating partners in sufficient number. Through dowries, bilateral agreements evolve towards multilateral agreements. So are constituted matrimonial areas, without definite limits, resting on the intricate and changing networks of these matrimonial agreements. These areas are without political unity or identity. Marriage regulation is left to the unco-ordinated decisions of the numerous heads of exogamous cells constituting the area. Eventually, the numerous claims and quarrels generated by timely marriage transactions lead more often to war than to unity unless they give rise to a precarious procedure of conciliation and to some local Solomons. But rarely do we witness the elaboration of central power on the basis of this judicial function. By and large, the need for matrimonial conciliation does not outweigh self-sustenance and the constitution of separated individual units without corporate interest.

Besides this cause of weakness, agricultural communities are vulnerable on many counts: sedentariness, the necessity to store the product and to protect it, dissemination of adults during the productive period, etc. They are easy prey to external powers. Not that military conquest is easily made — the history of colonial conquest often testifies to the opposite — but they are poorly protected against pilfering, the lifting of people or cattle, sieges, etc. They need protection against those who are after their product and they have to pay for it.

Several exogamous corporate units may cluster into a single residence and constitute a village, sometimes made of related lineages, sometimes of independent ones. The village fulfils several functions: common protection, common hunting enterprises, exchanges of agricultural labour, etc. Common problems are debated between the representatives of the lineages. Still, it is a well-known fact that no concentrated power emerges from the function of arbitration between conflicting interests. Sometimes military protection will be sought through alliances with neighbouring villages, but since proximity and matrimonial relations are usual causes of conflict such alliances may prove uncertain. Efficient protective organisation will probably not come from an understanding between the parties belonging to the same matrimonial area, but from the domination of one lineage (often a foreign one) over the others.

Paradoxically, kinship shows up again at this stage to support an ideology of power. Whenever political domination is established over such communities, it is expressed in terms of kinship, even though the domination is a foreign one. The sovereign is assimilated to a senior (seigneur) or the father. He is entitled to 'eat' his subjects as his own children, i.e. to receive part of their labour or the product of their labour. Conversely he is expected to protect them. A redistributive system of some sort is set up between the leader and his subjects as between the senior and his dependants. In some cases, the leader gives away spouses according to an elaborate matrimonial organisation. In other words the sovereign fulfils at the level of his kingdom the functions — sometimes symbolic — of the senior within his community. Such relations are often supported by an ideology which relates people to a mythical single ancestor and to a common descent group. But once we have a social structure where one corporate group dominates and exploits other corporate groups we are dealing with a class system in which the above rules of social relationships will change again with the change of the productive relations.

Kinship is transformed here into an ideology whose 'raison d'être' is not so much to express the relationships generated from the growth and organisation of the society as to justify and even support a domination imposed from outside. We could relate this ideology to the new rules of kinship which develop in the aristocratic lineages and which are different because they obey political rather than economic constraints.

When kinship reaches a religious dimension, it may gain enough strength to be considered as the basic justification for domination and exploitation. The situation is inverted: people, instead of being kin and dependants because of the relations of production they are in, are integrated into such relations because of an alleged ideological kin relation. Hence the emphasis on 'blood' relationships in some cases, or on religion in others.

THE IMPACT OF MARKET DEVELOPMENT AND CAPITALISM

With the development of exchange and the rise of the market economy, kinship, as the main expression of peasant social organisation loses its actuality. The change can be related to the new relations of production arising from the transformation of the product into a merchandise. While the product, in the self-sustaining economy, is not an object of appropriation (it cannot be alienated but only 'advanced'), it becomes property once it is traded. While products have no exchange-value within the community or between allied communities, it gains one, once it is confronted for exchange alongside other merchandise. The value of the merchandise is soon conveyed to the agents of production. First to the producer himself. Once a product can be sold, the producer can be bought. Man is the first factor of production to whom property is transmitted, due to the fact that control over people is more developed at this stage than control over the other means of production. Slavery, as a mode of production can develop. Slaves are attached to the community on the basis of personal property, the instrument of labour being mingled with its human support. In the capitalist economy the elements of production are dissociated further and each becomes an object of property: land, tools, means of production and the labour force — now distinguished from the producer himself — are becoming merchandise. Relations of production revolve now around the means of material production and not any more on the means of human reproduction; between landlords and tenants, capital owners and labourers. The structural reproduction of the productive enterprise is not related any more to human reproduction but to the reproduction of capital, as a means of perpetuating and enlarging the relations of production.

Furthermore, agriculture is not any more the unique or dominant mode of production. Accumulation of capital takes place in the industrial and banking sections, to which agriculture becomes completely subordinated. The relations of production within the agrarian sector also reflect the relations of this sector to the industrial one.

Change takes place in agrarian communities where production is turned towards the market. Land becomes a matter of business transactions, and kin dependants give way to wage earners. But beyond this change, in the overall process of transformation, the rural sector is also providing the capitalist sector with labourers. In so doing, it fulfils the important function of reproducing the labour-force used by capitalism. Unlike the domestic economy, capitalism does not fulfil all the needs of the labourer. Historically, the economic superiority of capitalism over the feudal economy was that it did not take charge of the unproductive. In underdeveloped areas, capitalism is again applied in its crudest form to realise anew what Marx called primitive accumulation i.e. the transfer of wealth from the precapitalist to the capitalist sector. Through low wages and precarious employment the labourer is periodically expelled from the capitalist sector and sent back to the rural area. The maintenance of an economy providing collective security is an absolute require-ment for these labourers. The solution is either to perpetuate the obsolete domestic economy or set up some form of integrated rural economic organisation able to fulfil such needs. In this case the function of protection will be emphasised and take a religious and paternalistic turn.

Integration of peasant agriculture into the capitalist system is a long and painful process for the reason that while agriculture should provide the necessary surplus to feed the industrial sector and require therefore the highest degree of productivity, its obsolete organisation is *maintained* as long as possible by capitalism as a means of cheap reproduction of the labour force. According to the balance that capitalism realises between these two functions, the degree of integration of agriculture will vary and the social organisation of agricultural production will change from the family to big industrial business.

The key to this transformation is not to be found in 'natural causes' like demography, psychology or ecology, but, beyond their ideological representations and distortions, in the relations of production which are, I believe, a safer lead towards the understanding of the functioning and transformation of society.

NOTE

1. Meillassoux, Claude, 'Recherche d'un niveau de détermination dans la société cynégétique', *L'Homme et La Société*, vol. 6, October–December, 1967

Reflections on the Relevance of a Theory of the History of Exchange

Georges Dupré and Pierre Philippe Rey

This essay first appeared in Cahiers internationaux de sociologie, *volume 46, 1968 and was translated into English in* Economy and Society, *volume 2, number 2, 1973. But it begins in a general sense, where Meillassoux's earliest contribution breaks off (see pp. 129–57 of this volume) — with a systematic critique of the approach characteristic of much liberal economic anthropology, as exemplifed by Bohannan and Dalton's* Markets in Africa *(to which Meillassoux contributed) and an attempt, in line with this critique, to elaborate a problematic that would put exchange in certain forms of pre-capitalist society 'in its place'. They show how the place of exchange within what they term 'lineage society' can be explained only by the role of exchange in the reproduction of the conditions of production — that is, at a different level from that of exchange itself; and establish a framework for the analysis of the articulation between the 'lineage system' and the capitalist mode of production, arguing that the place of exchange in the articulation of these systems will be justified by its role in the process of one system's domination over another — this role being determined in the last instance by the dominant mode of production. The latter part of the discussion parallels, in some respects, the sketch presented by Meillassoux of the 'social organisation of the peasantry' (see pp. 159–69 of this volume), and here the discussion of the control over reproduction and production in lineage-based societies raises the question of whether domination by seniors of juniors constitutes exploitation. Dupré and Rey conclude that it does; which introduces the problem of whether the seniors could be said to constitute a social class, to which they respond with the suggestion that the exploitation of the juniors constitutes a class function but that the seniors do not constitute a class in the full sense of the term. This problem has been taken up recently by Rey in his book,* Les alliances de classe.

INTRODUCTION

Most of what is included in the following text was written in 1967 as part of an attempt to answer a specific need arising out of fieldwork in Congolese societies. At the time, when this research was in its infancy, the problem was to develop a theoretical tool capable of dealing with the information already collected and of making progress in future fieldwork.

Marx's thought had only recently been applied to anthropology; its application developed in the footsteps of Anglo-Saxon economic anthropology and began to take its place when the latter appeared to have exhausted its possibilities, inextricably caught between substantivism and formalism. For those who, in France, started fieldwork at that period, the only expression of Marxist theory on segmentary societies was to be found in the works of Godelier and Meillassoux. Let us say immediately that Meillassoux's work appeared most interesting in terms of what we were looking for. While Godelier's attempt at an attractive synthesis, derived from Marxist concepts and the ideas of Anglo-Saxon anthropology, turned out to be of greater academic than practical use, Meillassoux's research had the incomparable advantage of presenting a theory of traditional economies which was coherent and at the same time of applying this theory to the understanding of a concrete society, that of the Guro of the Ivory Coast. It is for this reason that Meillassoux's research was placed at the centre of a critique which aimed at producing a theoretical tool capable of dealing with the problems we needed to solve. The numerous criticisms we have made of Meillassoux here and elsewhere only show the extent of our interest in his work.

It was this connection between theory and practice which led us to concentrate on Meillassoux's work; in our view this connection needs to be discussed further here both with regard to our contribution and to the rest of this collection. In order to define the scope of our essay, it is necessary to locate it in the history of a specific piece of research in which it appeared as a preliminary to the process of knowledge in which the ideas put forward had to be confronted with concrete information and emerged inevitably transformed by this confrontation. It was more a critique of existing theoretical works that a construction based on concrete information. Indeed there was no lack of data on the concrete nature of the societies under study, but we were at a stage at which the societies were identified only at the global level and only their outline sketched. For this reason this essay must be considered only as a tool meant to answer specific needs. With time, a certain gap has appeared between the tool and the knowledge which it enables us to produce. This is normal and simultaneously justifies both fieldwork and theoretical work. It would not have been possible in a few lines to state all the transformations which have taken place. In our view it is more interesting to provide the reader with a few ideas which will simplify the use of all the texts in the present collection because it is their use which is in question. In this respect, the reader may question the move from the first part of this collection to the second, from theory to fieldwork, and this all the more because the authors brought together appear to be either theoreticians or fieldworkers.

What is under discussion here is the transition from theory to enquiry, the relation to be established between theory and the concrete, i.e. the whole process of knowledge in anthropology. The starting point of the process of knowledge is not, as claimed by empiricism, a specific concrete reality, but the representations and the concepts which already exist within the discipline and which precede any particular study. The result of the process of knowledge is the most adequate reproduction of reality by means of thought, a reproduction which contributes either by confirming or by challenging the theoretical corpus which pre-dates it. This is enough to emphasise the importance of theory for the study of the concrete; but this importance, probably this dominance, must not allow us to forget that between departure and arrival, between the tool and the product, a whole process of production is inserted which is, at the moment, it must be realised, left to the discretion, the honesty (he who comes from afar may lie) and the temperament of the researcher. As a result most fieldwork studies can be judged only by the coherence of the theories that they propose and not by the capacities these theories may have to reproduce intellectually a particular reality. It is clear that the theories have the opportunity of assuming a scientific character as soon as the conditions in which they have been produced are defined other than anecdotally.

The theory of knowledge in anthropology which should, by taking its proper place between the two sections of this collection, establish the necessary link between theory and fact, is only at the preliminary stage. We must be satisfied with a few pointers. The process of knowledge in anthropology must be conceived as a complex production and as such is defined by its constituent elements and by the relations which structure them. These elements themselves are practices of production which may, as a first step, be reduced to three:
1) the social practice which produces social relations between the anthropologist and his field, thus making possible the use of techniques;
2) the technical practice which uses the social relations produced by

the previous practice as one of the conditions for the production of information;

3) the theoretical practice which produces knowledge for the use of the information as one of the conditions of its production.

The anthropologist's role is to reunite the elements of the different practices, to unite these practices themselves and finally to account for the way in which he has articulated them in his own research. Most of the time, however, the process of knowledge is reduced to one or the other of its constituent practices. This reduction of the structure to one of its elements, which is known as fetishism, can take the following forms: There is for example, participatory ethnology, familiar to a whole French school, in which the anthropologist assimilates himself as much as possible to the society which he studies in order to produce, after a number of years spent in the field, a monograph whose guiding line remains, in the final analysis, the ideology of the society studied. A lot could be said concerning the very vague field of socio-economics which appears to be the most barbarous and inadequate fetishism used to account for social reality, the fetishism of techniques. But here it is particularly relevant to emphasise the particular fetish which is most tempting for Marxist researchers as well as for the reader of this volume who is quite rightly attracted by the totalising aspect of the theories represented, and this fetish is dogmatism. Dogmatism consists in disregarding the facts, or rather, in taking them into consideration only to the extent to which they agree with a theory which is never challenged, turning reality into a pool of examples drawn upon only to substantiate the theory.

The reader should bear in mind that the worship of ancestors, however prestigious they may be, whatever status may be dedicated to them, cannot coexist with a scientific process. Given this condition of fundamental and necessary disrespect he will be able to profit from the texts included here and experience for himself the full fertility of Marx's thought.

*   *   *

REFLECTIONS ON THE RELEVANCE OF A THEORY OF THE HISTORY OF EXCHANGE

In recent years the crisis in American economic theory has manifested itself in a number of critical essays which European admirers of this theory have become aware of only after a considerable delay. Some of these essays even question the validity of applying economic theory to developed capitalist society: this is true of the works of Koopmans, Hicks, Shaeffler and more recently,

Dorfman, among the better known. Others emphasise the inadequacy of the marginalist, neo-liberal theoretical apparatus for all societies in which 'the market economy' is not or was not dominant; that is the intention behind the works of Polanyi and Arensberg, Bohannan and Dalton.

The comparison we are making between these two types of research has a precise historical origin: starting with a critique of the liberal economics applied to American society, Karl Polanyi elaborated his substantive view and became the initiator of a renovating trend in economic anthropology.

Koopmans is incapable of leaving the traditional model of Robinson Crusoe on his island (in spite of the fact that he treats him with greater humour than his predecessors) in which we see Robinson the consumer purchasing with the revenue from his labour the commodities offered by Robinson the producer, both seeking a Paretian optimum which would allow equilibrium to occur. In the same way Polanyi and Bohannan, following his lead, cannot conceive of typologies which allow them to classify economic systems in any way other than by the forms of exchange: 'market', 'prestation-redistribution', 'reciprocity'.

In France this internal critique of liberal economics is hardly tempting for those researchers immersed in their mathematical models or those practitioners embedded in technocratic models but, by contrast, it is made use of from 'outside' by Marxist scholars. The present work was the result of fieldwork: it was conceived in Brazzaville in 1967 with the intention of throwing light on certain problems presented by that inquiry. The necessity for this critical and theoretical phase in research imposed itself through two convergent paths. On the one hand, from the very beginning of fieldwork the problematic of economic anthropology was revealed to be incapable of dealing with the real problems because it was weighed down by its preoccupation with the past.

On the other hand, Marx's problematic for the analysis of capitalist society, which has been made more accessible in the last few years by the works of Althusser, made possible the presentation of the problems, and in particular, those which are of primary interest to us: the articulation of the capitalist and the 'traditional' modes of production, in order to clarify the present condition and the economic and political future of Africa.

Our essay reveals this double progression: on the one hand it is a critique of Bohannan's position and of Polanyi's on which his is based; it aims to show that these approaches are impossible, that is, that they cannot achieve their objective. It then suggests another progression whose logic does not necessarily arise from the preceding criticism but which is an attempt to realise Polanyi's project of a substantive view: to place all the economic and social situations on a truly equal footing and to think their articulations.

To do this it is necessary to put exchange back in its true place and this implies the knowledge necessary to determine this place: this is the aim of the second part of this essay in discussing the 'lineage system' and its articulation with other systems, notably the capitalist system.

In this way the theory of the history of exchange which Bohannan and Dalton are indeed trying to develop as much as Polanyi and Arensberg must find its place within a theory of (simple or extended) reproduction of economic and social formations; that is, to use Balibar's terms, of their 'dynamic' and their 'diachrony' (cf. *Reading Capital*).

A. An Idealist Theory

(1) The Introduction to *Markets in Africa*: An Impossible Typology*

Bohannan and Dalton's text begins in the following way: 'To study markets in Africa, it is necessary that the distinction between the institution of the market place and the principle of market exchange be pointed up clearly.'

In relation to various previous theories, the function of this distinction is critical: in asserting the presence of truly economic facts in African societies, it asserts, in opposition to the defenders of a simple projection of liberal economics on to these societies, the existence of a concrete object, the market place, which alludes to the market principle although it cannot be explained by it.

But this distinction is irrelevant: one of its terms suggests shouts, colours, smells, the other refers to equations; the second presents itself as an equation but the first does not. If, however, this distinction has a meaning, it is because the notion of market place is used to indicate unresolved problems: by simultaneously suggesting a similarity and a difference with the market principle, it induces us to develop concepts at the same level as, but different from, the market principle — itself presented from the very beginning as a universally accepted concept of capitalist economics. Once these concepts have been developed, it would then be possible, in a typology, to compare as equals the African societies regulated by them and those regulated by the market principle. At this stage the reader thus expects the rest of the text to suggest a problematic

---

* Bohannan, P. and Dalton, D. (eds.), *Markets in Africa,* Northwestern University Press, 1962.

which would make it possible to deal with the construction of these concepts, and the conclusion to make an assessment of the progress of this construction. But, as early as the bottom of the first page, a three-fold typology — 'a threefold arrangement has proved convenient' — is imposed: societies without markets, societies with so-called 'peripheral' markets and societies obeying the market principle. It is clear that if the difference between the third type of society and the other two is clearly defined, based as it is on a previously accepted concept (the market principle), then, by contrast, the difference between the first two types is far less obvious since this distinction depends on the presence or absence of the so-called 'peripheral' market whose role, as its name suggests, should not be essential in the society. Thus we get the impression that the presence of this market, despite the fact that it is peripheral, is the sign of something more fundamental which allows a distinction between societies in which it appears and those in which it does not. We shall attempt to discover the role of this typology.

The rest of the introduction attempts to place the three suggested 'types' of societies on the same level, but in fact its true object is to discuss the second type (society with a 'peripheral' market) and it is therefore on the excerpts devoted to this object that we shall concentrate our reading.

This reading gives rise to two observations: the first is that whenever societies with 'peripheral' markets are discussed the text always draws our attention to the market place itself; the second is that when our attention is concentrated on the market place the organisation of the article is absolutely incomprehensible.

The first observation is easily made, be it on page 2 (paragraphs 2 or 4) or page 7 where the description of societies with peripheral markets begins: 'societies with peripheral markets differ from societies without markets in that the market place is present, but not necessarily in the sense that the market is more widespread' or pages 15–19 where a long discussion is devoted to the non-economic aspects of market places (this discussion takes up the basic contributions of the twenty-eight pieces presented in the rest of the book insofar as they discuss market places).

The second is at first imprecise: it is unclear how the different paragraphs are connected, and the reader wonders what the authors' aim is. Why end the essay with the long section (pp. 19–24) devoted to western impact on African societies? Why insist in this section in particular on the transitional structures which appear during penetration into the market economy? Why if not because the whole essay, therefore the whole book, is conceived of as having to provide essential answers to these questions and even because the whole essay and the whole book have been written only to ask these questions and begin to answer them? If this is the case, the underlying principle of the suggested typology becomes clearer: we are not dealing with three types of societies located at the same level but with two extreme types and one 'transitional' type.

We will see later how this transition is envisaged. At this stage of understanding, that is, as long as we have not taken our eyes off the market place to look at what is behind it, the progression of the analysis escapes us: why insist on this notion of market place and

Characteristics of the Market in three types of Economy

	Marketless Economies	Economies with Peripheral Markets	Economies in which the Market Principle is Dominant
Major Source of Subsistence Livelihood	Self-production and use; reciprocity; redistribution	Self-production and use; reciprocity; redistribution	Production for sale; factor resources for sale; marketing and trading as occupations
Price Formation for Goods and Services Changing Hands	Equivalency ratios gift exchange	Supply and demand forces qualified by idiosyncratic social influences and controls; absence of factor markets	Supply and demand forces; market principle transacts factor ingredients as well as outputs
Market Price as Integrating Mechanism for Allocation of Resources, Incomes; Outputs	Absent	Absent	Absent
Money and Money Uses	Standard (special Payment purpose moneys) moneyless transactions	Standard (special Payment purpose moneys) moneyless transactions	Exchange (one standard all-purpose Payment money)
External Trade	Gift Trade; Administered trade	*Market place exchange*; Gift trade; Administered trade	Market trade

then state in conclusion (p. 26) that when the market principle develops the market place evaporates? Also to state that the development of the market principle does not usually take place starting from the market but elsewhere (p. 26) or by extra-economic means (p. 22)? Why devote long discussions to the political or religious role of the market place simply to discover that these aspects, in contrast with the political or religious levels, tend to disappear with the increase of economic autonomy, an autonomy which is characteristic of systems subject to the market principle?

Let us cease looking at what we are asked to see. The authors themselves will help us in this task: indeed, they return to their typology in a table (p. 16) which, as it is intended to do, presents all the characteristics at the same level and allows us to take a step in the direction in which we want to go.

A first observation needs to be made on the reading of this table: while, on the whole, the first and second columns have nothing in common with the third, on the other hand, they differ from each other in only two lines out of five:
— the last line, in which market place exchange is added in the second column; it is on this point that our attention has been directed up to now;
— the second line, in which the notion of supply and demand is introduced.

By comparing the fate of these two differences in the course of their transition to the third column, another observation can be made: while the market place has again disappeared in the third column the principle of supply and demand has expanded so much that it fills all five lines of the third column. The situation is thus clear: the market place which appeared in the second column and again disappeared in the third is there only as the sign of something else: the unobtrusive presence of the principle of supply and demand in the second column which is destined to become pervasive. On the other hand, if we read the text from the beginning we find other signs of this reversal. At the bottom of page 7 after the section devoted to the market place we are told: 'Two aspects of peripheral markets, of special interest to economists, concern the process of price formation and the role of market-made prices in the overall economy'; this is followed by a page of discussion of supply and demand in an economy of 'peripheral' markets and in an economy 'dominated by market principles' respectively. By going even farther back to page 2 we find, at the end of the paragraph devoted to societies 'dominated by the market principle': 'It is in such societies that the price mechanism functions as an integrative device to allocate resources, incomes and outputs', which leaves us to understand that the said price mechanism, if it does not play this role in the preceding societies, has at least already appeared there; let us note that this discovery, which can be deduced from the form of expression used in paragraph 3 is not made explicit in paragraph 2 devoted to a society with 'peripheral' markets.

The organisation of this introduction is now clearer: it matters little that the market place has evaporated in the third type of society if it is because the principle which hid behind it, the presence of supply and demand, has penetrated the whole society. As for the political and religious aspects of the markets, they represent a necessary stage in the subordination of the political and religious aspects of the former exchanges to supply and demand. Let us note that it is sometimes said that the participants are unconscious of this subordination: 'some markets are not regarded as primarily "economic" institutions by the people' (p. 18) and that the forces of supply and demand already in action deep down do not yet appear in their entire purity: 'supply and demand forces qualified by idiosyncratic social influence and controls' (table p. 16). This subordination of religious and political phenomena to supply and demand logically precedes their later ejection from the economic sphere, characteristic of western or westernised societies, at least as it is interpreted by marginalist, liberal economists, etc.

Under these conditions the strategic role played by the market under analysis, as well as the fact that it is necessary to devote a book to it are understandable: it is the place where this principle of supply and demand which at a later stage will penetrate the entire society appears visibly for the first time.

One may wonder however about the nature of this supply and demand in the societies with 'peripheral' markets and about the nature of their development. One may also wonder why the authors have not themselves made the principle of their progression explicit.

But if, like the market, supply and demand are peripheral in relation to the functioning of society, they are also peripheral in relation to its transformation; the authors themselves tell us that we have seen that the market economy develops outside the market place and its development is based on direct — forcible — political intervention by the coloniser rather than the independent dynamism of the principle of supply and demand. From then on the relation between systems with 'peripheral' markets and the systems subject to the 'market principle' cannot be considered in terms of efficacy. The initial presence of the principle of supply and demand has nothing to do with its later development. In short, supply and demand are not presented as mechanism but as essence, and the article suggests to us the development of essence as in idealist philosophy.

However, while Polanyi discovers in Aristotle, under the guise of exchange determined by social controls and influences, the essence of the liberal economy which was to develop later, we have seen that Bohannan and Dalton are reluctant to follow this path openly. In short, their essay presents itself as a failure.

We were wondering why this proposed typology was not preceded by a problematic which would justify it and why the introduction has no counterpart in a conclusion setting out the progression made in the book. In fact this would have been possible only if the problematic envisaged at the beginning had been adequate, that is if it had presented the problem of the process of transition. But the idealist problematic could be decomposed only by an attempt to apply it: that is why instead of having both an introduction and a conclusion we only have two superposed introductions: the idealist, coherent introduction which we have read between the lines; and the real and apparently unprincipled introduction which emerges from a confrontation with the facts.

We consider Bohannan and Dalton's failure to be progress compared with the previous achievements of liberal theory applied to non-capitalist societies. This progress has been made possible only by two conditions: first, the information available on the period studied (the colonial period) was sufficient so that not only an initial and a final state of the structure could be known in detail (the pre-colonial and the present economy of Africa) but also the conditions under which there had been a transition from one of these stages to the other; also the authors' intellectual honesty was sufficient to stop them from abstracting the known process of this change and replacing it with an imaginary process which would have corresponded better with their idealist problematic.

This honesty is not as widespread as one might assume; for example, the whole technocratic literature devoted to Africa in the name of multilateral as well as bilateral aid is based on a dichotomy in the presentation of the history of colonisation: on the one hand, the regrettable excesses: the police system, forced labour, massacres; and on the other hand, the positive results: the development of exchange, the birth of a local bourgeoisie, the introduction of this part of the population to the 'American way of life'.

Such a historical view coexists very easily with an idealist problematic which accepts that the market system developed through its own forces, independently of any intervention in any structure other than that of exchange;[1] by contrast, it finds it more difficult to give a scrupulous account of the facts which does not hide the fact that the famous 'market principle' developed only through the violent intervention of the coloniser in the previous mode of production, for then it appears that things could be no different and that, as a consequence, the 'positive' and the 'regrettable' aspects of colonisation were not linked by chance but by necessity. But this type of analysis continues to cause as much scandal as Marx's description of the primitive accumulation of capital, and for the same reasons; that is why American anthropology, like American economic theory (e.g. Koopmans) is ready to criticise its former problematic but not, at least not yet, ready to suggest a new one.

II. THE ORIGIN OF THIS TYPOLOGY

The notion of the market place which is central to Bohannan's problematic appears in Polanyi as the product of theoretical research aimed at an autonomous understanding of economies other than the liberal economy. The market place which Bohannan has used as a key term in his classification of economies is in Polanyi's work the logical result of a project which is derailed from the start because it fails to avoid reference to the market economy. With him then we shall meet no attempt to camouflage internal contradictions: on the contrary in Polanyi the deviation appears in its full clarity.

To make this and all its consequences obvious let us examine Polanyi's two main essays in the symposium *Trade and Market in the Early Empires*, beginning with the one in which he is supposed to give a theory of economies.[2]

At the beginning of this article Polanyi wishes to distinguish himself from his predecessors who projected the definitions and the concepts elaborated in the framework of the liberal economy on to their studies of the economies of archaic societies. He rejects a formal definition of the economy, the application of the logic of rational action to the market economy, as unfit to describe the functioning of other economies. At the same time he proposes the adoption of another point of view for the study of these economies: the substantive point of view. From this point of view, the economy is defined as an instituted process that is a totality of movements of goods and services within the framework of institutions specific to each society.

He reaches an extremely comprehensive understanding of archaic economies: 'The human economy, then, is embedded in institutions, economic and non-economic. The inclusion of the economic is vital. For religion or government may be as important for the structure and functioning of the economy as monetary institutions or the availability of tools and machines that lighten the toil of labour' (p. 250). This assertion concerns both the economies of the western type and those which do not belong to this type. If it is to be truly operative it should help define a single theoretical field in which a problematic common to all economies could be elaborated. When the rest of the chapter is examined to discover whether the development of this concept answers this expectation, we are forced to recognise that it does not, that far from introducing the theoretical unity which we had the right to hope for, it does no more than once again bring up the contrast between market and non-market economies.

A preliminary remark is essential: the market economy can very well be studied without the substantive definition: 'As long as the economy was controlled by such a system [system of price-making markets], the formal and the substantive meaning would in practice coincide' (p. 244). From this moment onward the situation is clear: the substantive definition of the economy does not even begin to question the market system in order to set up a general problematic. It is merely a didactic definition whose ambiguity is immediately revealed: on the one hand it is the only one to be able to include all economies; on the other it is not necessary to the understanding of the market economy which is analysed far more conveniently in the formal way. Under the unifying appearance of the substantive view of economy, the duality remains untouched since the market economy continues to be opposed to the other economies. The rest of the article is constructed on the model of this opposition. The only link between market economies and non-market ones is to be found in their differences and their oppositions. Indeed, after devoting a paragraph to reciprocity, redistribution and market exchange as the three possible modes of integration of an economy, the article continues with the description of the elements which constitute an economy: the forms of trade, the elements of the market and the use of money. The description takes the role of a comparison between the role of these elements in the market system and in the systems based on reciprocity and redistribution, a comparison which takes the market system as its point of reference since there homogeneously and autonomously integrated elements are to be found which present themselves elsewhere as incongruous and unarticulated. The market, money and trade which in one case are integrated through the mechanism of supply and demand, are in the other isolated and independent. 'All-purpose' money is contrasted with various 'special use' monies, fluctuating and regulating prices are contrasted with fixed equivalents, etc. To summarise: at the end of the description of the elements of the economy, two totalities are implicitly set up: that of the market economy and that of the economies based on reciprocity and redistribution.

The failure of the substantive view is complete: the significance of the non-economic merely begs the question since the non-market economy is studied according to the criteria of the market economy.

We shall examine the implications of Polanyi's failure and in particular the historical relations which now appear necessary between market and non-market economies.

Polanyi takes care to specify that the three forms of integration, reciprocity, redistribution and the market do not constitute the stages of an evolutionist model: 'In any case, forms of integration do not represent stages of development' (p. 256). This is hardly surprising since an evolutionist model presupposes something which does not exist in Polanyi's work, namely a theory of the structures of each of the societies taken in isolation (the simplest object), as a pre-liminary to a theory of transition from one stage to the next (the most complex object). He thus places himself at a sub-evolutionist level.

How then is the transition from non-market economies to market economies to be made? In his description of the elements of the economy, Polanyi refers, in order to analyse economies based on redistribution and reciprocity, to a coherence which is external to them, whatever the postulate of the economy embedded in the non-economic may say about this: it is the coherence of the market system integrated by the interplay of supply and demand.

To make the form of this transition explicit, it is then necessary to try and find the first appearance of coherence in the non-market system which, as it affects an element of the economy, would be liable to permeate the whole system by its own impetus and, with time, to transform it into a market system.

On this point many assertions are significant; thus: 'Higgling-haggling has been rightly recognised as being the *essence* of bargaining behaviour' (p. 255); '. . . ancient Greek auction ranked among the *precursors* of markets proper' (p. 268); and later on the same page: 'changing or fluctuating prices of a competitive character are a comparatively recent development and their *emergence* forms one of the main interests of the economic history of antiquity.' The terms *essence, precursor, emergence* which we have emphasised imply a certain attitude on the part of the historian correlative with a certain form of emergence of the market economy from non-market systems. The economic historian's role is to study the non-market economies, to detect in them the germs of the market system — in a word, to grasp the essence of the market system when it emerges locally.

The study of the economy of Aristotle's ancient Greece, the subject of another of Polanyi's essays, will give us the opportunity of seeing how he answers two questions which he considers to be fundamental for the economic historian, 'When and how did trade become linked with markets? At what time and place do we meet the general result known as market trade?' (p. 263). The structure of Polanyi's analysis of the development of Greek society exemplifies market and non-market relations. Because the birth of the market system is understood as an irruption in the non-market, the analysis of historical facts is compelled to shift register at the point of transition and present it as a discontinuity.

The first part of the essay[3] is entirely devoted to setting out Aristotle's economic and political anthropology. The economy is actually described as embedded in the non-economic, in this case the political, and as finding in it its true coherence. From the moment when the germs of the market appear, the analysis which had prevailed up till then is replaced by an analysis following the principles of liberal economics.

For Aristotle 'natural' exchanges are those which within the communities, the city or the *oikos*, allow an equitable distribution of resources in such a way that each community's subsistence is adquately ensured and no more. The rate of exchange for two given products was fixed and dependent on the status of the exchangers.

Exchanges for profit were of little importance and those who practised them, the *kapelos*, were doubly excluded from society: by statute, as they did not have citizen's rights and did not participate in the play of reciprocity (the exclusive privilege of citizens and *oikos* chiefs), and physically, since their activity was exercised at the Agora built in a primitive fashion outside the city. Their small profits were pettily obtained by the sale of foodstuffs and cooked foods.

In the fourth century the introduction of mercenary troops for military expeditions as well as the increased length of those expeditions due to the subjection of the neighbouring cities presented the armies in the field with problems of provisioning. At that time food markets were created in the allied cities. The money which soldiers spent in these markets was given back to them on their return when they sold their booty. The case of General Timotheus in 364 (p. 86) reveals this transitory role of money since he was able to pay for food with copper instead of the usual silver coins by giving the assurance that these coins would be accepted, when they returned, for the purchase of the loot. These markets were temporary and disappeared at the end of the campaign.

The fact that food markets may have given certain citizens the opportunity of making profits appeared to Aristotle to be contrary to the political order. And according to him this new way of exchange should have been kept out of the city, just as the retail merchants of the Agora were.

Polanyi considers this comparison of Aristotle's to be judicious despite the fact that, according to him, Aristotle had failed to see that the relationship between these two forms of exchange were established through the mechanism of supply and demand. Does this mean that the mechanism of supply and demand existed at the time of Aristotle? The answer given by Polanyi clearly shows how he sees its emergence:

1. The mechanism of supply and demand did not exist as such in Aristotle's time: 'The distribution of food in the market allowed as yet but scant room to the play of that mechanism; and long-distance trade was directed not by individual competition, but by institutional factors. Nor were either local markets or long-distance trade conspicuous for the fluctuation of prices.'

2. According to Polanyi, the mechanism of supply and demand was realised only later in the third century: 'Not before the third century BC was the working of supply-demand price mechanism in international trade noticeable. This happened in regard to grain, and later, to slaves, in the open port of Delos.'

3. But despite this, Athens is the precursor of the introduction of supply and demand: 'The Athenian agora preceded therefore by some two centuries the setting up of a market in the Aegean which could be said to embody a market mechanism.'

Thus the link which Aristotle did not make and which Polanyi establishes between the small traders of the Agora and long-distance trade is based only on the fact that the two forms latently contained the market mechanism. In Aristotle's time this mechanism appears only furtively, in the form of its essence sensed through the market place. This essence will only be realised, embodied in economic reality, two centuries later at Delos, without it being known how this historical transition between Athens and Delos took place, if it did.

Using emergence as the mode of transformation from non-market economies is the consequence of a lack of theory, replaced, as a palliative, by an idealist ideology.

The absence of theory also induces an extremely simplistic view of the relations between the two types of system, relations which can then be reduced to an elementary dichotomy: the market and the non-market, or, more precisely, the market or the non-market since the relation between the two terms can be seen only as mutually exclusive. Indeed from the very moment when a single element of the essence of the market is actualised in a non-market economy it then invades, at the same time destroying, the system in which it has manifested itself and replaces it by the market system.

Let us return to Polanyi's general essay[4] to look at the way in which he makes explicit this mutual exclusion of the two types of systems, an exclusion which in the final analysis, is the only logical consequence of seeing the origin of the market as an emergence.

On page 255 Polanyi opposes the exchanges at a set rate of the systems based on redistribution and reciprocity to exchanges at bargained rates in the market system. This opposition is developed, not in terms of structures but atomistically by the mediation of psycho-sociological attributes bestowed on each of its terms. The solidarity of the societies which practise exchange at a set rate is contrasted with the antagonism, the individualism and the desire for profit which necessarily accompany exchange at bargained rates. To complete this intrusion of the psycho-sociological, previously foreign to the analysis, Polanyi presents two postulates: 'No community intent on protecting the fount of solidarity between its members can allow latent hostility to develop around a matter as vital to animal existence and, therefore, capable of arousing as tense anxieties, as food' (p. 255).

This amounts to saying:
1. Societies based on redistribution and reciprocity could not tolerate antagonisms and tensions in their midst.
2. The essential thing for the economy of these societies is the satisfying of basic needs — the sphere of subsistence.

Owing to these fundamental postulates and the intervention of the psycho-sociological, Polanyi's explanatory system finds an apparent coherence; in a non-market economy, when a certain sphere presents possibilities of profit, and especially, the sphere of foodstuffs, as in the Athenian Agora, the antagonism which all the benefits necessarily entail, thus appears as the proof of the appearance of the essence of the market. Because of this the market system and the others are absolutely incompatible; the only possible coexistence is that of the market, a unique form of integration accompanied by secondary transactions of redistribution and reciprocity, which have no integrative role.

Aristotle's and Polanyi's analyses, in spite of their different points of view — the one in terms of economic anthropology and politics and the other in terms of liberal economics — produce superposing categories. What Aristotle rejects as non-political Polanyi takes up again in his category of market.

This conception of market and non-market relations has extremely important consequences for the subject which interests us, the penetration of the colonial economy to the heart of traditional societies. In the usual analyses of this contact, the themes of the idealist ideology are widely used. One element of the market system is sufficient to impose the whole system in traditional societies; for this reason it is an entire mode of comprehension and an entire mode of analysis which are in question because, at the moment when the market is introduced, the analysis which heretofore was anthropological gives way to the principles of liberal economics.

This type of analysis, brought about by conceiving of contact between economies as exclusive, results in the reinforcement of this conception, since it is incapable of grasping compromises or co-existence between the two systems.

B. *The Place of Exchange*

In our critique of Bohannan and Dalton we have shown how the hypothesis of the development of the 'market principle' by a process of diffusion (a hypothesis according to which the previously 'peripheral' market progressively comes to dominate non-market societies) could not be seriously defended by its authors. Besides, this hypothesis is clearly equally unable to explain the development of the market and of monetary exchanges in Greece, and we believe that the few indications given by Marx on the dissolution of the 'ancient mode of production'[5] and 'the mere existence of monetary wealth, even its conquest of a sort of supremacy'[6] constitutes a far more solid scientific basis.

In a similar perspective we shall describe:

— Lineage society, by making explicit the fact that the place held by exchange — just like the place of exchange in capitalist society or the place of the political in ancient Greek society — is to be explained by the role of exchange in the reproduction of the conditions of production, i.e. at a level other than that of exchange itself.

— The articulation of this lineage society and that of the capitalist mode of production. To be complete this second element implies the need to state a theory of the capitalist system which is symmetrical with that of the lineage system: we have merely provided the framework for such an analysis and for the analysis of the last two forms of articulation which we identified; but the description of the first type of articulation does not require a detailed knowledge of the capitalist mode of production and we have therefore developed it at greater length. Just as we find within each particular system, the place of exchange in the articulation of these systems will be justified by its role in the process of domination of one system by another and this role will in the final instance be determined by the dominant mode of production.

I. THE PLACE OF EXCHANGE IN LINEAGE AND SEGMENTARY SOCIETIES

(1) *Control of Matrimonial Exchanges by the Seniors.* In his essay ' "The Economy" in Agricultural Self-Sustaining Societies: A Preliminary Analysis'[7] Meillassoux has attempted to demonstrate

the importance of exchanges between seniors of different lineage groups and in particular the importance of matrimonial exchanges. Noticing that goods which are essentially produced by 'juniors' in the framework of the unit of production (the lineage being based on real or fictive kinship) are entirely controlled by the seniors, Meillassoux asks the following questions:

1. What is this dependence based on?
2. What is the role of economic fact in the development and maintenance of this dependence?

He then surveys different possible answers to this double question:

— Physical pressure which allows the maintenance of the social hierarchy in bureaucratic and feudal societies: but the 'seniors' do not control any police force capable of enforcing such pressure;
— Kinship relations; however 'kinship expresses the social relationships which form the basis of social cohesion, but it is not itself a cohesive force';
— Control of the means of production gives the non-producer control over the producer in the capitalist system, but the means of production in lineage societies are too elementary and too easily accessible for such control to take place;
— The control of technical knowledge: but technical knowledge is relatively rapidly accessible and senility makes this knowledge disappear.

Thus none of the mechanisms which, in other social systems, allow the maintenance of forms of dependence can be used by the seniors. By contrast, they retain for their sole access control of social knowledge (knowledge of genealogies, history, marriage rules) widened to 'artificial fields (magic, divination, religious rituals)' and particularly they retain control over the juniors as well as their own access to women, a control guaranteed by their possession of the 'elite goods' essential to marriage. This final weapon in the seniors' hands is original by comparison with the weapons previously considered: indeed, while all the others were each particular senior's *individual weapons* within his own group, this is a *collective weapon* under the control of all the *seniors from the different lineage groups*. That is what Meillassoux expresses when he wrote (pp. 140-1): 'Hence a more inclusive alliance is necessary between the seniors of these neighbouring groups in order mutually to preserve their respective authority within their communities'; of the goods produced by the community and handed over to the seniors as prestation *some will not be redistributed* but kept over at the level of the seniors themselves who will use them to sanction access to wives';

'But any senior who would accept such a transaction with an individual without the required rank would be weakening his counterpart's authority and consequently his own. It is in the joint interest of all seniors to respect established order.'

Thus the decisive argument which gives the seniors power to dominate the juniors is particularly manifested in marriage exchanges; it is their 'solidarity' which unites them in the face of discontinuous (and even antagonistic) groups of their juniors.

But what is the origin of the importance of this control of marriage exchanges? As Meillassoux clearly shows, the problem is not that of satisfying the juniors' sexual needs in societies in which male-female relationships are very relaxed before marriage. Control of matrimonial exchanges is one of the ways in which the group of seniors guarantees that they retain control over the demographic reproduction of the lineages; reproduction of the dependence relationship of juniors towards seniors is guaranteed as a corollary: indeed it can be said by taking up Marx's[8] formula that to reproduce himself as an 'objectively individual man' that is, as junior of a lineage, the junior must follow a continuous progression in the social hierarchy which allows him to reach, one day, the status of senior: among the Guro of the Ivory Coast, Meillassoux shows that the bachelor, even when he is old stays associated with younger juniors, i.e. placed lowest in the social hierarchy. By controlling matrimonial exchanges, the seniors can slow down or stop this progression for any given junior i.e. prevent this junior's reproduction as an 'objectively individual man'.

(2) *Control over the Exchange of Men.* Control over matrimonial exchanges is not the only way in which the group of seniors exercise control over the demographic reproduction of lineages: they also exercise it by control over the exchange of slaves. There exists in numerous lineage societies a mode of integrating slaves or descendants of slaves into the lineage after a few generations; thus fictive kinship is created, which is either actually presented as being fictive or presented as being true; anthropologists insist on this aspect of things which supports the theory according to which any chief in a lineage society is searching for the largest possible dependence group; but there is a symmetrical aspect to the reinsertion of the slave: the senior has the possibility of reducing the junior to slavery by exchanging him against elite goods provided by another senior.

These two symmetrical and complementary mechanisms are present in the societies of the western Congo in which we carried out our field-work. A senior could not reduce his junior to slavery as he pleased, but such a threat constantly determined the junior's behaviour towards his senior. Indeed in cases of adultery, theft, witchcraft, etc. any man, senior or junior, had to pay a fine of 'elite goods' possessed by the seniors only; a junior then had to rely on his senior and the latter provided the necessary goods only if the junior was usually submissive to him; in general he did not provide them in case of relapse; one of the senior's 'exchange partners' could pay the fine for him and take the junior as slave. Similarly, despite the fact that during the whole period of the slave trade the general tendency had been to transfer slaves from one exchange partner to the next until the coast was reached a fair number of these slaves were nevertheless reintegrated as social juniors in the lineages and now many lineages and even whole clans are entirely composed of descendants of slaves since all the descendants of *mfumu* (owners) are dead. It seems that as a general rule the lineages in which slaves were reintegrated were demographically weak lineages: thus the combination of the two phenomena, putting juniors into slavery and reintegration of slaves as nominal juniors has, at the global level, had the effect of redistributing men from demographically strong to demographically weak lineages.

In this way, even more than by control over marriage exchanges, seniors controlled the careers of juniors in society.

(3) *The Reproduction of the Conditions of Production.* This demographic reproduction appears to be the essential precondition for the reproduction of conditions of production in lineage society. By comparison, other conditions appear secondary; this is so for collective ownership of tools, since these are in general very easy to reconstitute; this is also true for reproduction of land ownership as well as for the reproduction of the lineage unit (or of a wider unit grouping many lineages) as a free and independent unit, whereas in the 'ancient communities' such as those described by Marx[9] these conditions seem to be crucial. Let us explain what we mean by this:

Lineage land is the object neither of exchange nor conquest; in other respects confrontations are sorted out between lineage groups as well as between larger groups (including a number of lineages) in such a way that, after the conflict, each of the groups continues to survive independently. However, there are exceptions: when conflicts oppose groups which had previously had no relationship — as in the case, for example, of the great Fan or Bakota migrations in the Congo Gabon region — land may be conquered and one group either massacred or totally reduced to slavery. But such conflicts assume the absence of links and exclude the institution of reciprocal exchange between those groups for many years. Conflicts therefore end in this way only in exceptional cases; usually conflicts are linked to the first type of reproduction which we looked at, the demographic reproduction of lineages, and in particular to matrimonial problems. The conflict, regulated and limited in its effects, takes place between groups whose seniors are, or may be, linked by reciprocal exchange. The results of this conflict are the same as those of reciprocal exchange between seniors, i.e. mainly the acquisition of men and women; what cannot be acquired by exchange between seniors e.g. land or the enslavement of a whole group, cannot be acquired by war either; the conflict takes place in a realm which is externally determined by exchange between seniors. The conflict appears as the necessary complement of exchange between seniors: in lineage societies only seniors can exchange men, women, elite goods, bridewealth goods. Permanent hostility between groups is a condition of this privilege: the seniors alone can transgress this hostility or rather return it since exchange between seniors retains strongly antagonistic forms.

As we understand them lineage societies can be contrasted both with Nambikwara hordes, wandering through an immense territory in which they hunt and gather and are highly unlikely to bump into a similar group, and with 'ancient communities' as Marx sees them, in which a land deeply transformed by agriculture, division of labour on a greater scale, and a high population density turn the land itself into an object of desire and men whose land has been conquered into 'mere organic appendices of this land'.

A comparison of the processes of reproduction in ancient society as Marx analysed it and lineage society allows us to specify what the dominant mode of reproduction is:

— in lineage society the reproduction of the conditions of production is primarily the demographic reproduction of the production group (the lineage) whereas in ancient society it is primarily the defence or acquisition of land, the preservation of the overall freedom of the community or the enslavement of the defeated community;

— in lineage society this reproduction is achieved primarily by a process of exchange whereas in ancient society primarily by war.

In this way the conditions of production explain why exchange between lineages controlled by seniors takes the first place in lineage societies: it is the dominant mode (one of the dominated modes being armed conflict) of the process of reproduction of the conditions of production.

The control of this process by all the seniors of the group allows them to control the reproduction of each junior as a junior of this group: for the junior the threat of being deprived of a wife or of acquiring one late corresponds to the demographic reproduction of the group by the acquisition of women; for the junior the threat of being reduced to slavery corresponds to reproduction by acquisition of men. It can thus be said that control of the reproduction of the technical conditions of production (demographically adapted labour unit) ensures the reproduction of social relations (dependence of the juniors on the seniors).

Here we have a clear answer to the double question Meillassoux asked about the dependence of juniors:

'1. What is this dependence based on?

2. What is the role of economic fact in the development and the maintenance of this dependence?'

Or at least this is a partial answer if we are right in thinking that the problem really concerns the *mode* of dependence and not the dependence of a particular individual: indeed this explains only the maintenance (or as we have said, reproduction) of dependence; its establishment would demand a very different discussion which would among other things, draw out the mode of transition to lineage society from another form of society. The confusion of these two problems is not without danger.

The 'role of economic fact' is determinant since it is the reproduction of the conditions of production which allows the reproduction of dependence; but this economic fact is not exchange: it is production and it first concerns men and not goods. On the contrary, exchange as we have shown by a parallel with war, appears to be a political fact: as it concerns the slave trade we will see the consequences of the fact that exchange belongs directly to the political level.

(4) *The Function of Elite Goods.* Exchange is primarily the exchange of men and women and only secondarily that of goods; secondarily, but nonetheless necessarily, because large-scale exchanges of men and women which simultaneously maintain the hostility of the groups and the continuity of their relationship at the level of the seniors are inconceivable without an inverse circulation of goods; certainly direct exchanges of men for men exist; for example the direct exchange of dependents (men and young children) among the Tiv of Nigeria as described by Bohannan: but this direct exchange is merely complementary to an exchange of 'elite goods' on a far larger scale; slaves are to be found in this last 'sphere' in which goods are exchanged for one another and eventually for dependents whose circulation is usually in the 'sphere' of direct exchange.

Those 'elite goods' which are not perishable and circulate without being consumed (copper, iron goods, bracelets, kula necklaces, blankets on the north-western U.S. coast, raffia or cotton loin cloths, etc.) tend to be accumulated since they are continually produced and their total mass thus increases ceaselessly (the increase in bridewealth in Africa can be partly explained in this way since money has taken the place of elite goods as long as the sums accumulated and received are not used for other purposes). In many societies a readjustment is periodically made by institutionalised destruction; these destructions, inexplicable in terms of 'rationality' (that is, from the point of view of an economic or non-economic individual or collective subject), are the manifestations of the limits which the structure of reproduction imposes on the economy of such a society. These elite goods are not always directly produced by the juniors but often by caste groups (blacksmiths, weavers) or by the seniors themselves. But even in these cases, all or part of the extra labour socially necessary for the manufacture of these goods is provided by the juniors (or people assimilated to juniors, such as slaves reintegrated into the lineage), who must either produce the food given to the castes in return for these goods, or make prestations of labour or of consumption goods to the senior who is engaged in organising the production of elite goods. The manufacture of these goods often brings into play the most complex techniques known by the society (iron-working, weaving) and the only skills which it is possible to delay the learning of for a long time: juniors or women can then be employed by the senior who possesses these skills, as is done in Banzabi ironwork where the seniors organise the labour and intervene directly only in the final phase.

Iron, whether it is produced by the society itself or imported, is often an elite good; but iron is used to manufacture production goods (tools); among the Guro of the Ivory Coast — iron importers — iron tools are the direct property of the seniors whereas wooden tools circulate very freely in the lineage and even from one lineage to another. The political control which the seniors exercise through reciprocal exchange on the reproduction of the conditions of production is thus doubled at the level of each lineage by direct control of the means of production. Among the Banzabi of the Congo, who are iron producers this doubling is even clearer — the hierarchy of elite goods exactly parallels the hierarchy of production goods:

— at the top are found the smith's hammer and anvil, means of production of the production goods;
— in the middle was formerly the axe and now the imported machete, male production goods of agriculture;
— at the bottom, finally are found simple consumption goods such as raffia loin cloths.

In these two examples however, political control of reproduction is the basis for economic control of the means of production and not the reverse; but a general theory of lineage societies alone makes it possible to assert that this is really the case — consideration of an isolated case does not allow us to make any conclusions.

Even if the seniors do not differentiate themselves from their dependents by any particular consumption, under the guise of 'elite goods' they collectively have at their disposal a surplus directly or indirectly produced by the surplus labour of the juniors and the women and they use this surplus labour to control the reproduction of the lineage groups and correspondingly the reproduction of the dependence of these groups on themselves.

(5) *Is there Exploitation?* Under these conditions is it possible to talk of the exploitation of the juniors by the seniors? Meillassoux himself explicitly denies this in the following way: 'Despite the fact that they represent a relatively considerable amount of labour, the sumptuous character of these treasures (elite goods) is still limited . . . the precise destination of these good restricts their use and does not really allow them to be diverted for personal gain' and he concludes that it is only contact with the market economy which has made it possible for the seniors to transform the community organisation into a system of exploitation.

What is the definition of the concept of exploitation which underlies this argument? It is precisely the one given by Godelier in many articles and which we quote as he formulated it in *Les Temps Modernes*[11]: 'Exploitation begins when the surplus is appropriated without any counterpart.' We believe that this definition is inoperative (according to its terms no society would be exploitative) and that it does not constitute a scientific statement.

Indeed let us attempt to apply this definition to the capitalist system: the development of the productive forces is undeniably a 'counterpart to the appropriation of the surplus'; therefore exploitation takes place only when the bourgeois class squanders the surplus without ensuring the extended reproduction of a the conditions of production. The argument is a return to the concept defended by the classical economists and which cleanses all known capitalist regimes of the sin of exploitation as soon as it is based on a period of time sufficient to eliminate the temporary effects of cyclical crises. It is not uninteresting to notice that this definition of exploitation brings about an understanding which is the reverse of Marx's: indeed it assumes that capitalists exploit less to the extent to which they provide a more important counterpart, that is, insofar as they devote a greater part of the surplus to the development of productive

forces and a smaller part to their personal consumption; but for
Marx[12] the reverse is true. When the capitalists devote a greater part
of the appropriated surplus value to reproduction, the exploitation
of the labour force is increased, not diminished (any trade unionist
knows this too); either because the capitalists thus have the capacity
to exploit the labour force already at their disposal more intensely or
(in the case when the capitalist mode of production has not yet
eliminated the preceding mode of production), because they may
exploit a new one.

Moreover this definition of exploitation is not a scientific
statement; Godelier continues: 'And it is difficult to identify the
precise moment when the community begins to be exploited by the
very people who provide it with services.' This continuity shows that
the author had not placed himself at the correct level to define his
concept: the fact that the surplus product is appropriated without
counterpart at a given moment is merely an external effect of a
mutation in the relation of forces and tells us nothing of the process
which permits the appropriation.

What Marx means by exploitation can be found in an ideological
form in his earliest works: the product turns against its producer and
increases his subjection.

We suggest the following definition of this concept: there is
exploitation when the use of the surplus by a group (or an aggregate)
which has not provided the corresponding labour reproduces the
conditions for a new extortion of surplus labour from the producers.
Thus, according to Marx, in the capitalist system, at the end of the
labour process the proletarian finds himself obliged once again to
sell his labour power which the capitalist will then exploit (more
intensely) thanks to the surplus he has appropriated during this
labour process.

In lineage society, as in all non-capitalist modes of production, the
process which allows the simultaneous reproduction of the technical
and the social conditions of production is distinct from the process
of production itself; we have advanced our analysis of this process
sufficiently to state that there is exploitation of the juniors by the
seniors who control this process of reproduction.

In his discussion on societies 'in transition towards socialism'
Preobrazhensky, in the first edition of *The New Economics* asserts
that, in this phase, the working class must exploit the peasantry. This
refers to an understanding of exploitation which we are questioning
here, as is made clear by the rest of his work. This assertion has been
eliminated in later editions, including the French CNRS one, for
tactical and not theoretical reasons. However the theoretical

problem is more complex in this last case since exploiters and exploited belong to two different modes of production, articulated within the same social formation.

(6) *Do the Seniors Constitute a Social Class?* The seniors' control over production and in particular their control over the means of production (land, tools, etc.) is weak and, when it does exist as in the case of iron tools, it appears to be a consequence of the control these seniors exercise over the process of *reproduction.* This control over reproduction is a 'class function' but the support of this function has no effective existence outside the function itself, at least in real lineage societies. The societies of the western Congo where we carried out our field-work gave us the opportunity to observe the synchronic transformation which turned a group of seniors among the Banzabi, a hinterland people deprived of successors, into a truly dominant class among the Vili of the coast; but this was accompanied by an important shift from real 'seniority' towards social seniority (juniors, called 'grandsons' are the descendants of slaves) and also by a hierarchisation: the Vili kingdom of Loango was an elected monarchy; the king's electors were the chiefs of the main land-owning clans. We believe that this problem of a class function which is not supported by a constituted group can also be found in other socio-economic formations: thus, before the emergence of real feudalism as it is understood by Marc Bloch, the nobles and various magnates took on some of the class functions of the future feudal lords before becoming a real class.

(7) *Lineage Society and the Lineage Mode of Production.* The unit of production on which lineage society is articulated i.e. the lineage cell proper, is not the only possible unit of production in lineage societies, nor is the mode of production of this unit, which may be called the lineage mode of production, the only mode of production which is present in these societies but it is the dominant one. Here we will approach neither the problem of the identification of coexisting modes of production (without one of them tending to bring about the disappearance of the others) within a non-capitalist social formation, nor the analysis of the relations of domination between these modes of production. These problems may, however, be discussed — at least in a preliminary way — in the same way as that of the articulation of 'traditional' modes of production with the capitalist mode of production, during periods in which they coexist within the same society.

II. ARTICULATION OF THE 'TRADITIONAL' AND THE CAPITALIST MODES OF PRODUCTION

We will examine the process through which European capitalism established its domination in the very midst of the African social formations which had previously been dominated by other modes of production. We propose to show that, if their usual interpretation is somewhat modified, the terms in which the history of this 'contact' is usually described, i.e. trade followed by colonial and neo-colonial periods, are able to recover the concepts of a periodisation of this history. We will restrict our analysis of this 'contact' to the lineage social formations on which we have concentrated up to now.

(1) *Homogeneity and Heterogeneity of Trade.* In the western Congo the networks used for the exchange of slaves during the (first official and later illicit) slave trade and commodities during the goods trade are identical: they are chains of 'exchange partners' moving from the hinterland to the coast, from one clan's territory to the next, from one ethnic group to the next.

In his contribution to *Markets in Africa* Meillassoux mentions[13] that the Guro differentiate 'man to man' exchanges or exchanges 'between partners' (they use the French expression 'entre camarades') which distinguish the exchange of slaves from other forms of exchange and particularly their relationship with the Diula. Since trade goods reached the Guro from the Ebrié (a coastal people) by way of the Agni and the Baule, it is very possible that such chains of exchange may also have existed in the Ivory Coast.

The period of the goods trade, which we assimilate to the slave trade, precedes the establishment of concessionary trading companies in the hinterland: when this begins we will speak of the colonial period.

During the whole period of the goods trade, the goods reach the coast through traditional chains of exchange; the trading posts are only set up on the coast and along the first few miles of the banks of the main rivers. Similarly, during the period of the slave trade, the slaving captains land only in the small coastal ports (Ngoïo, Kakongo, Loango, etc.) and the exchange chains bring the slaves to the coast. Each trading post is 'protected' by a local chief who provides it with labour, ensures its supplies and defends it against possible external attacks; besides it is only by using a local chief's network of 'exchange partners' that the trading posts can be supplied with trade goods. Similarly the slaving captains are under the protection of the 'kings' of the trading ports; for example, in Loango, they are assimilated to the royal clan and they depend on the *mafouc* for their supply of slaves.

However, there is an important difference between the two trading periods: while the slave trade (at least while it was legitimate) reached only a few ports, the goods trade took place in a multitude of trading posts spread along the coast. Correspondingly, at the end of the eighteenth century, the ports were capitals of kingdoms which appear to have been centralised; a century later no trace of centralised structure could be found; all the small coastal chiefs were independent of one another and the Loango kingdom, for example, existed only as a memory: thus the protection treaty signed by France with the king in no way committed the chiefs of Punta Negra (the future Pointe Noire) twenty kilometres away, and a new treaty had to be signed with them. Besides it is likely that the kingdom was declining before the installation of the trading posts whose traffic hardly developed before 1880.[14] Also, when the slave trade was outlawed it ceased to be practised in the main ports and the illicit trade developed at various points all along the coast; it was to carry on until the first years of the twentieth century. Our informants state that at that time they knew that a Portuguese whom they called 'Malalou' who bought slaves in Loango Bonde on the coast near the present border of the Congo and Gabon.

At other coastal points, by contrast, the trade seems to have induced a degree of centralisation: in Gabon, for example, the ephemeral Mpongwe 'kingdoms' of King Louis and Denis developed their influence thanks to the trade networks. However this centralisation took place at a much lower level than that of the earlier Loango Kakongo and Ngoïo kingdoms.

The two phenomena are interrelated and they reflect the very contradictions of the trade; on the one hand, as the trading posts multiply, the decomposition of the great traditional political units is speeded up; but on the other hand, for the trading posts to carry out their activities it is necessary that a degree of order be maintained. Thus Brunschwig[15] demonstrates that the problem presented to the European traders by the irruption of the unhierarchised Fan along the Gabon coast could be solved only by a colonial conquest; but at the same time Loango, whose institutions and organisation were praised by all observers at the end of the eighteenth century, now suffers from the looting resulting from the rivalry of small chiefs no longer controlled by any hierarchical authority.

Even at the time of their greatest prosperity the kingdoms of the Congolese coast were not based on bureaucratic organisation. Their basis was an agreement between the chiefs of the principal land-owning clans who elected the king. All these kingdoms split off early from the Kongo kingdom which they survived by over two centuries. Trade certainly contributed to their survival, and for each trading port (as they are enumerated by Desgrandpré) there was a kingdom; all the exchange chains necessarily ended in one of these ports and the role of intermediary which the slaving captains recognised in the kings and their 'ministers' could only strengthen royal power. The termination of the slave trade, at least in its centralised and regulated form, reveals the character of the coastal societies: they are lineage societies headed by a royal power whose main function was to guarantee the cohesion of the class of seniors.

(2) *The Slave Trade: Exploitation of the Internal Contradictions of Lineage Society.* We have made explicit the function exercised by the exchange of men in lineage societies. In western Congo-Brazzaville this function must have been disturbed even before the trading period by an asymmetry between the hinterland and the coast: indeed the coastal groups produced sea salt by craft techniques before the arrival of the Portuguese and the process remained relatively unchanged until the 1930s. Throughout the whole trading period and the beginnings of the colonial period, and until this late date, the salt thus produced remained an essential element of exchange 'between partners' between the coast and the hinterland.

This asymmetry, which was increased by the arrival of European goods during the trading period, re-directed the slave traffic from the hinterland to the coast. Of course, the bottomless pit created by the demands of the trade accelerated this polarisation to a previously unknown extent. Those demographically strong lineages who had no traditional need to reintegrate slaves as nominal juniors developed among themselves exchange chains from the hinterland to the coast, excluding weak lineages for whom slavery could therefore play the role of demographic corrective only to a smaller extent.

Thus, during the whole period of the slave trade, the European commodity economy got its supplies essentially by manipulating the internal contradictions of the lineage social formations (indeed all the descriptions by missionaries of captains show that the direct 'grabbing' of slaves played only a minor supplementary role compared with the mechanism we have described) and in particular by using the contradiction within the social function of the circulation of men controlled by the seniors alone; this contradiction was exacerbated when a hierarchy began to develop in this lineage society.

The fact that the goods trade never developed in a way comparable to that of the slave trade reflects, as Brazza himself indicated, the direct competition existing between these two forms of trade; beyond this it also demonstrates that in the system we have described the transfer of men was easier to carry out than the extortion of a significant amount of surplus value from these same men.

The stability of this first type of articulation is remarkable: in the course of four whole centuries, according to Reverend Rinchon, 13,250,000 slaves were exported from the Congolese coasts (i.e. the two contemporary Congos and Angola). This stability is to be explained by the apparently perfect complementary interests of the chiefs of strong lineages on the one hand, and European ship-owners on the other. This complementarity itself reflects a deeper reality: namely, that in the two modes of production present, the dominant instance acts through the use of exchange. But this complementarity is only apparent because if, in the capitalist mode of production, it is the economic level which acts through exchange, we believe that, in the lineage mode of production, it is the political level which is thus expressed. For the European trader trading is distinct from the political level, while for the lineage society, whether hierarchised or not, such exchange is the main argument of the political level. For the coastal kings in particular, control of trade is the means to control access to elite goods by the chiefs of dependent lineages, i.e. it is control over the control that these lineage chiefs have over the reproduction of their dependence group, and therefore of the dependence of this group.

The durability of the slave trade is thus to a small extent due to a coincidence: that the European traders, by making the type of demands which were at the time necessary for the (extended) reproduction of the capitalist system, thereby gave a boost to the form of political power (monarchy) which most favourable to the pursuit of their activities. But when, as a consequence of the dispersion of the illicit slave trade and later the goods trade, commodity exchanges ceased to take place at the level of hierarchised power, this transformation which is purely economic for capitalism has, on the other hand, directly political implications for the lineage societies: the small local states where the exchange chains now terminate no longer have any use for royal authority and it disintegrates. As a consequence, the political protection necessary to trade disappears and in order to carry on with trade it is necessary to recreate a political order by force. The period of the goods trade, as opposed to that of the slave trade, is an unstable period which makes colonisation necessary. This will take place, however, only under the joint pressure of the need for order combined with the exacerbation of inter-imperialist contradictions.

(3) *The Colonial Period: A Period of Transition.* During the trading period the domination exercised by the capitalist system over the

lineage mode of production is exercised through the intermediary of the dominant level of the *lineage social formation* itself; the latter, however, will remain equally dominated by the lineage mode of production. The object of the colonial period on the other hand — regardless of briefly held illusions about the considerable intensification of production without modification of the mode of production — is to introduce the domination of the capitalist mode of production at the very heart of the colonised society. At the end of this process a new type of social formation is to be constituted in which the capitalist mode of production is dominant; moreover, the capitalism this set up must be dominated by the capitalism of the metropolis, i.e. it must be dependent on it for its reproduction: neo-colonialism.

In short, the two extreme stages have more in common than either of them has with the transitional stage; indeed in stages 1 and 3 metropolitan capitalism merely acts through the control it exercises over the reproduction of the dominant mode of production in the dominated society and it acts by its 'normal' means of domination, i.e. exchange. The difference between stages 1 and 3 resides in the fact that in stage 1 the society's dominant mode of production is not capitalist whereas in stage 3 it is.

Stage 2, that of colonisation, is characterised by ambiguity: its problem is to set up the conditions of the transition to capitalism through the use of the economic base characteristic of the lineage society. The most characteristic examples of this contradictory situation are the building of roads for motorised traffic and the building of railways taking place where there is neither the possibility of a labour market nor a pre-existing infra-structure. The organisation thus established is far more similar to 'oriental despotism' than to capitalist organisation. It implies the forced hierarchisation of segmentary societies (introduction of 'chefs de terre' and 'chefs de tribu') subject to the white 'leader'. Where, as in Madagascar, a centralised government existed prior to colonisation, the comparison between the two 'despotisms' does not, from the point of view of the effectiveness, favour colonial despotism. Overall, this period is not profitable for the capitalist system: it often is not profitable for particular capitalist groups.[16] By contrast, both the trade period and the neo-colonial period are highly profitable.

(4) *The Neo-Colonial System.* As capitalism tends to adhere to its own laws and to manage without the colonial apparatus of political constraints, the administrative and police systems lose their front-line role. They remain in place but the representatives of the colonial

society who directly control production no longer need to control this police organisation personally. The capitalist system continues to prosper even where it is absolutely ineffectual.

During this period the colonised country's social formations appear in the shape of a complex articulation:
— of the lineage system which still operates;
— of the politico-administrative system inherited from colonisation which, on the one hand, is based on the lineage system (tribalism) and, on the other, supports the emergence of local capitalism (bureaucratic capitalism);
— finally of the capitalist system itself under its different forms as they are articulated among themselves (for example, the large trading companies provide capitalist forest exploiters with means of production) and as they are articulated with the capitalisms of the developed countries and in particular that of the former metropolis.

(5) *Overall Interpretation of the Transition.* If we consider the lineage system on one side and the capitalist system on the other we notice that in each of these systems exchange plays a dominant role for the reproduction of the domination of one of these systems over another with which it is articulated. Let us examine a few examples of this as they concern the capitalist system:

During the last two centuries in France the capitalist mode of production has fought against small-scale peasant production; as is clearly shown in some recent works[17] it is by the use of political intervention that small and middle peasant forms of production maintained themselves between 1870 and 1958, but had the 'law of competition' been applied as it has been in other countries (where a bourgeois class under less of a threat from the working class, or less intimidated, could survive without allying politically with the peasantry) their disappearance would have taken place at a far faster rate.

In *The New Economics* Preobrazhensky shows how, during the transitional period before it has established its domination, the socialist mode of production must defend itself against the joint attacks at the level of exchange of small and medium commodity production within the USSR and of international capitalism abroad. This second problem, at least, is still valid today.

The neo-colonial period, particularly in Africa, appears when capitalism, having created a labour market (during the preceding colonial period) and developed an infra-structure adequate to its needs can finally draw the full profit from the (mainly military and administrative) expenditure it made during the colonial period to establish itself; its domination of the previous modes of production and their (very gradual) elimination are ensured through the medium of exchange.

The struggle between the different national capitalisms is *normally* carried out by preference at the level of economic competition.

This is just as true for the *regular* reproduction of the conditions of capitalist production as for the regular reproduction of its domination over other modes of production. Indeed, even in normal times, other levels such as the political or ideological level, play a part in these two reproductions; but it is a supplementary role, the primary place being held by exchange itself.

By contrast, in periods of *crisis* the domination is reversed for both the reproduction of the conditions of production and that of the conditions of domination:

Concerning the reproduction of the conditions of production, this is so, for example, in the case of German capitalism during the 1914–18 war (war economy) or under Nazism; political intervention becomes primary and exchange plays a subordinate role; this is also true for all contemporary capitalist production which some characterise as 'State-monopoly capitalism'.

Concerning domination, this is the case during crises between national capitalisms in the form of hot or cold wars; this is so during the implementation of the direct domination of capitalism over other modes of production either by importation from outside, for example, during the colonial period, or by self-development within a social formation in which it had not existed: it is this latter case which Marx analyses in the chapter of Capital[18] devoted to 'primitive accumulation'.

We may notice analogous phenomena concerning lineage societies: we have shown that exchange played the dominant role in the reproduction of the conditions of production, but other processes, such as armed conflict, play a supplementary role under normal conditions; similarly the ideological level intervenes in this reproduction.

In periods of crisis the dominant element can be shifted: thus during the colonial period exchange of men becomes more and more difficult (though the slave trade for internal use survived the emergence of colonialism by many years) and the exchange of women is disrupted by the monetisation of the economy. At this point the idological level ceases to play a merely supplementary role and takes the first place in the reproduction of the system; it is at that level that the 'retaking of initiative' which is the prelude to the disappearance of the colonial system is manifested.

The fact that under normal conditions in each of the two modes of production (capitalist and lineage) which come into conflict, the dominant level is expressed through the medium of exchange facilitates the interpretation of transition as a continuity such as the one which underlies the introduction to *Markets in Africa*. But this interpretation ceases to be possible as soon as one goes beyond the form of exchange and poses the problem of its role in each of the modes of production with respect to each other and in their articulation.

For four centuries goods produced by different forms of European capitalism were absorbed by the lineage system: they were exchanged from senior to senior as elite goods in the lineage societies and there they partly or totally replaced locally produced items which had previously played the same role: thus these goods of European origin have played an important part in the reproduction of the lineage mode of production (despite the fact that the corresponding losses in men disrupted the demographic reproduction of the weak lineages); but these goods in no way contributed to bringing about the emergence of the capitalist mode of production within the said social formation. Of course, the injection of money into such a system was even less able to transform this mode of production than the injection of goods had been (some of which, e.g., guns and gunpowder, were production goods).

It was necessary to introduce a break to give the capitalist mode of production the possibility of developing besides and in opposition to the lineage mode of production. This break manifested itself as an independent mode of production which was neither capitalism nor the lineage mode of production; this mode of production remained dominant as long as the normal conditions of development of capitalism were not fulfilled. In this transitional system exchange does not play the dominant role: as in other bureaucratic systems it is administrative and police constraints which play this role.

Bohannan and Dalton's problematic does not allow the identification of this transition. But it cannot seriously suggest that it be replaced by the only form of transition it seems capable of imagining — that of the 'peripheral' market — since all historical references show that there is no relation between, on the one hand, the existence of a market at the periphery of non-market society, even if this market is as important and as lasting as the slave trade, which lasted for four centuries on the periphery of Congolese lineage societies and, on the other hand, the transformation of the mode of production which alone allows the market economy to establish itself as dominant within the society.

CONCLUSION

What conclusions can we draw from these analyses of the problems which concern us: that of contemporary relations of forces between the 'traditional' systems and the capitalist system, and that of the future development of the relation of these forces?

It is obvious that the answers to these questions are not univocal: when capitalist domination is studied from the angle of the capitalist system itself there is no doubt about this domination; indeed the problem is presented globally by taking the example of the African country as a homogeneous entity. Dalton was one of the first people to show how this attitude brought about the confusion between 'birth' and 'development', i.e. in the terms used here, between the domination of the capitalist system constantly reinforced at certain points in the territory (ports, main roads, mines, etc.) and the domination of the capitalist system over the whole territory.

It is therefore suitable to present this problem from the point of view of the dominated societies — then the answer is more subtle. Indeed, if one can still talk of the domination of the capitalist system, it is with many different meanings, of which the following can be distinguished:

(a) A mode of domination corresponding to that of trade. The capitalist mode of production plays no part within the social formation under consideration but it controls the reproduction of this mode of production by providing the items (goods or money) specific to this reproductive circuit; the sale of juniors by seniors (characteristic of trade) may be replaced by the temporary sale of the junior's labour power, whose price is to be paid to the seniors.

(b) Typically neo-colonial modes of domination:

— Either the domination of commercial capital which is accompanied by the replacement of the traditional mode of production in agriculture by small commodity or capitalist production (plantation economy);

— or the domination of industrial capital within the social formation under consideration with its contemporary characteristics: urbanisation, large units of production and a labour market. All this is equally true of large industrialised capitalist agriculture. The traditional mode of production is then left with nothing other than a more or less significant supplementary role in certain sectors of consumption and it is subjected to commodity exchange imposed by capitalism.

(c) An intermediary situation between a and b in which capitalism and the traditional mode of production live side by side as in b but in which the domination of the capitalist system is guaranteed only in the same way as in *a*. This is possible when, for example, certain male agesets play only a minimal role in lineage agriculture and can become wage-earners without affecting agricultural production; then this production is not subject to commodity exchange or only insofar as the producers desire it. Symmetrically, the wages can be almost entirely used in the circuit of reproduction of the traditional system (bridewealth, funeral celebrations, and so on). But if the reproduction of the traditional system is then dependent on the money thus earned for its supply of 'elite goods', it is obvious that the capitalist system is equally dependent for its supply of labour power on the only coercion which the traditional system itself can exert; it is therefore a fairly small and unstable source.

(*d*) Finally the establishment of capitalist domination can be ensured by political intervention which, in the neo-colonial phase, takes the form of 'incentive' and 'supervision' rather than that of brute force. The great trading companies can then provide direct or indirect technical assistance to the State which thus intervenes to develop production.

But it is only the *b* form of domination which creates a situation which is always favourable to the capitalist system: the traditional mode of production has indeed an increasingly narrow field of operation and no opportunity of recovering its autonomy. As for modes of domination *a* and *c* they are conceivable only as complements of the *b* mode of domination established nearby. Indeed, here, far from weakening the traditional structure, the presence of the capitalist mode of production tends to maintain it as in the case of the goods trade with an unstable capitalist domination whose access to surplus labour is limited by the traditional system. Except by having recourse to a form of coercion which would bring us back to the real colonial system this type of domination cannot maintain itself in isolation. Finally, in the neo-colonial phase, type of domination *d* always appears to be transitory and of dubious efficacy.

It is thus established that what is ordinarily understood as capitalist domination during the neo-colonial phase is a system of modes of domination articulated around a dominance described in *b*. Types *a* and *c* on the one hand, and *d* on the other, *appear as the sequel* during the neo-colonial period *of the modes of domination which have successively dominated during the trade and colonial periods*. The promotion of the typically neo-colonial mode of domination has not yet eliminated the preceding modes of domination but has relegated them to a secondary function. Thus the history of the types of articulation and the history of exchange, which is part of it, take place in the present as well as the past.

NOTES

1. Besides it is still possible that in a second phase the memory of even the 'regrettable' facts cannot be more or less eliminated, on the one hand by the camouflage or destruction of compromising archives and, on the other, by discrediting those who may formerly have consulted what are happily described as blind, anti-colonialist fanatics. It is also necessary to take into consideration the self-censorship of the scholars themselves who attempt to avoid these problems first to avoid public disgrace and then because they are caught in a Bohannan-type problematic and thus do not know how to fit these facts into their models. If this were so it would be possible to let people believe that the market system developed in Africa through its own internal dynamic just as Marx's predecessors implied that the first capitalists got rich by their own labour. There already exists a whole body of literature gleefully doing just this.

2. K. Polanyi, M. Arensberg and W. H. Pearson, *Trade and Market in the Early Empires*, The Free Press, Glencoe, Ill., 1967, p. 382. The essay to which we refer is 'The Economy as Instituted Process', pp. 243–70.

3. K. Polanyi, 'Aristotle Discovers the Economy' in Polanyi *et al.*, op. cit., chapter 5, pp. 64–94.

4. 'The Economy as Instituted Process', *op. cit.*

5. *Pre-Capitalist Economic Formations*, pp. 123–5

6. *Ibid.*, p. 109.

7. See pp. 129–57

8. *Pre-Capitalist Economic Formations*, p. 94.

9. *Ibid.*

10. See *The Guro*, p. 334 my translation — *HL.*

11. May 1965, P. 2008 my translation — *HL.*

12. See *Capital*, volume 1 part 4.

13. *Ibid.*, p. 290n.

14. See C. Coquery-Vidrovitch, 'L'échec d'une tentative économique: L'impôt de capitation au service des compagnies concéssionaires du Congo français (1900–1909)', *Cahiers d'études africaines*, volume VIII number 29, 1968, pp. 96–109.

15. *Cahiers d'études africaines*, number 6.

16. See Coquery-Vidrovitch, *op. cit.* on the concessionary trading societies of the Congo.

17. See, for example. Gervais, Servolin and Weil, *Une France sans paysans.*

18. *Capital*, volume 1 part 8.

The Concept of the 'Asiatic Mode of Production' and Marxist Models of Social Evolution

Maurice Godelier

Dupré and Rey end their discussion with the construction ·of a framework for the analysis of the articulation of 'traditional' modes of production and the capitalist mode of production, and suggest that 'if their usual interpretation is somewhat modified, the terms in which the history of the "contact" is usually described . . . are able to recover the concepts of a periodisation of this history' (see p.198 of this volume). Godelier's survey of Marxist models of social evolution and his specific analysis of the 'Asiatic' mode of production provides an immensely valuable introduction to Marxist approaches to the principles of social development and to the fundamental concepts essential to the analysis of any determinate mode of production. It broadens the framework of social historical evolution from the rigid and dogmatic schema adopted under Stalin by re-introducing the 'stage' of the 'Asiatic' mode of production and, having located this particular model within the general scheme of historical development, proceeds to reconsider the very notion of historical necessity. Finally, it suggests the need to go even further and to consider the various forms possible within the model of the 'Asiatic' mode of production and the various forms of development from these particular modes of production. The essay was published in the C.E.R.M. volume, Sur le mode de production asiatique *in 1968.*

INTRODUCTION

Since its first publication in 1964, this text has been discussed, at times polemically, in the USSR, Poland, Czechoslovakia,[1] Mexico and Peru. Its re-publication in 1968 calls for a number of corrections.

There has been nothing to invalidate the main theses which were developed then and will be recalled in a moment. However our conclusion was incorrect on a secondary point, that of knowing whether Engels had abandoned the concept of Asiatic mode of production after reading Morgan. A more detailed and *chronological* analysis of Marx's and Engels' correspondence has brought out clearly the fact that neither of them had rejected the ideas elaborated between 1853 and 1877 concerning the existence of 'despotic' forms of the State constructed in Asia, Russia or elsewhere on the basis of earlier agricultural communities.

Drafting the rough copies for his answer to Vera Zassoulitch in 1881, Marx, who had just read Kovalevsky and Morgan, reasserts the existence of a despotic State in Russia. He seeks its foundations not in the necessity for great projects, hydraulic or otherwise, but rather, on the one hand, in the dispersion and isolation of agricultural communities over an immense territory (the same thing he suggested for India in 1858), and on the other, in Mongol domination.

In 1882, Engels, who, together with Marx, had just signed the preface to the Russian edition of the *Manifesto* takes up the ideas of Marx's reply of 1881 to Vera Zassoulitch in his drafts of *Die Fränkische Zeit*. In it Engels suggests the possibility that ancient Germanic village communities might, in a different historical context, have developed towards a 'despotic' society of the Russian type. More specifically, in January and February 1884, four weeks before undertaking the writing of the *The Origin of the Family* Engels wrote to Bebel and Kautsky on the subject of 'State Socialism' arguing that the examples of Java, India and Russia perfectly illustrate how the exploitation of man by man, and a despotic State may find their 'broadest bases' in the existence of primitive communities.

This is enough to show that neither Marx nor Engels abandoned their former hypotheses after reading Morgan. In itself this point is of minor significance since, even if they had been abandoned nothing would prevent us from taking them up today if the present state of scientific information gave them a new topicality.

In fact *The Origin of the Family* put the histories of Asia and America on one side because, as compared with the Graeco-Roman West they did not (in Engels' eyes) develop the *most direct* forms of transition from the ancient clan community to the *typical* forms of the State and class societies.

The Origin of the Family thus scrutinises, in the light of Morgan's findings, one of the two possible forms of transition to the State suggested by Engels in *Anti-Dühring*,[2] namely the western one leading to the generalisation of productive slavery and of commodity production.

The other path leads in Russia, Peru and India to primitive, crude and despotic forms of the State and class societies without breaking up the earlier communal organisation.

There is thus a continuity between the texts of the *Formen, Anti-Dühring* and *The Origin of the Family*. The theses on the Asiatic mode of production remain valid in Engels' eyes and continue to describe *a* form of *transition* from classless to class societies, a somehow unfinished transition which entails slow or stagnant social development.

However, this real continuity must not conceal the unfinished and open character of Marx's and Engels' thought, an incompleteness reflected in the fact that some of their theses remain unadjusted or badly adjusted. For example, when in 1881 Marx, following Kovalevsky, suggests that Hindu, Russian or Germanic communities are the most recent forms of the earlier 'primitive formation' of society and manifest a dynamism and vitality unknown to Greek, Roman, Semitic and other communities, this represents a profound change from the analysis developed from 1863 to 1877. This theory 'rejuvenates' Asia and seems to transform the vision of an Asia vegetating for millennia in stagnation and misery and passively suffering foreign invasions. Marx calls these early forms of primitive communities 'rural communities' and he is careful to note that part of their dynamism is due to the fact that they are no longer totally dependent on the 'strong but limited' set of kinship relations between its members.

Engels, on the other hand, emphasises the persistence of primitive kinship relations and the vitality of clan organisation. To explain primitive history there is a definitive shift from the Hindu to the 'Indian' model of clan society of hunter-cultivators, characteristic of the lower and middle stages of barbarism. All earlier agricultural communities once again become 'gentile' [This term refers to the *gens* and could be translated as 'clan' — *Ed.*] forms of society, and based therefore on kinship relations, and in this way they partly lose the 'new youth' which Marx had discovered in them in 1881. These are the facts.

By sketching the *historical* reconstruction of the archaeological (Schliemann's dig in Troy in 1870-73, in Mycenae in 1874), the anthropological and historical contexts of Morgan's and Engels' texts, and by showing that Morgan's concept of 'military democracy' prevented Engels from readopting the theses of the Asiatic mode of production (insofar as it concerned the Aztecs and Incas), and the analyses in *Anti-Dühring* of the process of the genesis of a tribal aristocracy (a process which is in our view the key problem of the formation of primitive class societies), we performed a useful service, even if we did not prove that Engels had abandoned the hypothesis of the Asiatic mode of production.

But that was not the main point of our text; this can be summarised in three theses which international discussion in the last few years has in no way proved incorrect.

1. THE SPECIFICITY OF THE ASIATIC MODE OF PRODUCTION

The concept of Asiatic mode of production designates *a specific, original mode of production* to be confused neither with the ancient slave mode of production nor with the feudal mode of production.

The very essence of the Asiatic mode of production is the existence of primitive *communities* in which ownership of land is communal and which are still partly organised on the basis of kinship relations, combined with the existence of *State power*, which expresses the real or imaginary *unity* of these communities, *controls* the use of essential economic resources, and *directly appropriates* part of the labour and production of the communities which it dominates.

This mode of production constitutes *one* of the possible forms of *transition* from classless to class societies, perhaps the most ancient form of this transition, and contains the *contradiction* of this transition, i.e. the combination of communal relations of production with embryonic forms of the exploiting classes and of the State.

2. BASIS OF THE EMERGENCE OF PRIMITIVE FORMS OF STATE AND OF CLASS SOCIETIES

Marx replaced the narrow explanation suggested by Engels in 1853 of the emergence of a central authority above local village communities, by a far broader and more fertile hypothesis which is summarised in the formula from *Anti-Dühring*: 'The exercise of a social *function* was everywhere the basis of political supremacy.' The basic change which leads to the emergence of class societies consists in the gradual transformation of this functional power of a social minority into an exploitative power and into domination by an exploitative class.

This formula goes beyond Engels' narrow explanation of 1853 that the main cause of the emergence of despotic forms of State authority was an ecological determinism which demanded the organisation of major hydraulic works. However it is this explanation, criticised and extended by Marx, which Wittfogel mechanically repeats to the point of misleading an uninformed public into believing it to be Marx's true thought (cf. Carrasco, Leach, Murdoch and others).

However, this hypothesis of Marx's goes *beyond* the problem of the Asiatic mode of production by posing the *general* problem of *multiple forms* of evolution of classless societies, organised principally on the basis of kinship relations, towards different forms of class societies and the State. By seeing in the Asiatic mode of production *one* of the possible forms of transition to the State and not the *only* possible form, one avoids inventing a new dogmatism which would restrict itself to *adding* a new 'necessary stage' to those enumerated by Stalin.

Besides, one goes *beyond* the Asiatic mode of production as soon as one follows up Marx's idea that the emergence of exploiting classes is born of the transformation of the functions of a social minority. These functions concern not only the economy, in particular that of the 'Asiatic' peoples, but religion, political authority and kinship relations. To analyse this transformation of functions in depth, it is thus necessary to make use of the knowledge accumulated by the anthropology of religion, social and economic anthropology, archaeology, linguistics and history; to combine these available knowledges; and to develop cooperation between disciplines isolated in different university institutions, and by specialised approaches.

Our inherited nineteenth century hypotheses about the primitive forms of evolution of humanity as well as the postulates and methods of evolutionism themselves must be confronted and criticised in the light of this modern knowledge. Marxism must also transform itself it it wants to play an *avant-garde* role in this great comparative enquiry in which archaeology, anthropology, history and linguistics converge, as they did in the nineteenth century, but on a new theoretical basis.

And, as we indicated in 1964, despite the wealth of Marx's theses on the Asiatic mode of production, this transformation of Marxism is not and cannot be a 'return to Marx'.

3. DEVELOPMENT OF MARXISM, NOT 'RETURN TO MARX'

Contemporary research cannot in any way claim to be a mere 'return to Marx', for two reasons: first, such a return would mean going back to a level of information and theoretical conceptualisation concerning primitive societies which has been *partially overtaken.* Second, our present inquiries demand a *more penetrating* elaboration of certain basic Marxist concepts such as infrastructure, superstructure, dominant structure, causality of a structure, and historical necessity.

That is why if the concept of Asiatic mode of production, or an *equivalent* but better-named concept, can and must be 'reactivated' by modern science, it is on condition that it be *rid* of its *dead* parts, *confronted* with *all* the available information and *enriched* by a *new* theoretical analysis of kinship structures, and of economic and religious structures in classless societies or in primitive class societies.

Among these dead elements, let us mention:

a) The concept of 'despotism' which is not scientific but ideological. It carries with it the philosophical and political conflicts of the eighteenth century, and generally expresses in a distorted and partial way the fact that, in its primitive forms, the State is incarnated in the person of the sovereign and seems to depend on his arbitrary will. As Radcliffe-Brown emphasised regarding the traditional African sovereign, the king is head of the executive, legislator, supreme judge, master of ritual and administrator of the chief resources of the kingdom. This 'fusion' of functions and power in the figure of a single man, has mainly appeared to the Westerner to be the mark of a '*despotic*' power knowing no law other than the arbitrary will of the sovereign.

b) The image of Asia stagnating from millennia in an unfinished transition from classless to class society, from barbarism to civilisation, has not stood up to the findings of archaeology and history in the East and the New World. In fact, if Pharaonic Egypt, Mesopotamia, and the pre-Columbian empires belong to something like the Asiatic mode of production, then it corresponds to the period when humanity opts locally but definitively for an economy of working the soil, invents agriculture, herding, architecture, mathematics, writing, trade, money, law, new religions etc. What was born in Greece was not civilisation but the West, a particular form of civilisation which was finally to dominate it while pretending all the while to be its symbol.

In its original forms, the Asiatic mode of production meant no stagnation, but the greatest progress of the productive forces accomplished on the basis of the earlier communal forms of production and social existence. The Asiatic mode of production does not therefore *necessarily* imply stagnation and despotism. Marx's thesis might however appear to retain a certain validity for the *later* development of societies of the 'Asiatic' type which then became imprisoned in millennial stagnation. Without denying the slow and uneven development of many non-Western class societies, we have suggested that this process of imprisonment appears only in the cases when the contradictions specific to the Asiatic mode of production did not develop, when the earlier communal relations of property and sometimes of production had not been destroyed and replaced by various forms of private property. In other cases, China and Japan in particular, we have suggested that the evolution may have passed through various forms of the Asiatic mode of production to forms more or less analogous to European feudal relations although the State played a role not found in Europe.

c) If discussions of the Asiatic mode of production necessarily involve more general discussion of the structures of classless societies, and of their kinship structures in particular, then other parts of Morgan's and Engels' work will have to be eliminated. Thus we can no longer accept Morgan's reconstruction, accepted by Engels, of the evolution of kinship relations in primitive societies from a stage of primitive promiscuity, and the succession from matrilineal to patrilineal kinship. The binary correspondence between forms of marriage and kinship terminology which he postulated in order to reconstruct the vanished stages of the evolution of the family, simply does not exist. Kinship terminology expresses not only marriage, but also residence and the multiplicity of functions kinship relations assume in a primitive society; this poses a greater problem for Marxism, and marks the point of departure for a new theoretical enrichment.

d) In a primitive society kinship relations are simultaneously relations of production, relations of authority, and an ideological model which partially organises the representation of relations between nature and society.[3] Therefore they are *simultaneously* infrastructure and superstructure and it is because they *unify* multiple functions that they play the role of the *dominant* structure in social life.

This poses a double problem for Marxism. How are we to understand the determining role of the economy in social life and the dominant role of kinship relations in primitive societies?[4] Under what conditions do kinship relations cease to play a dominant role in these societies and slip to a secondary position while the new social structures, *e.g.* the State, develop and occupy the central place left empty?

e) On a philosophical level, present research forces Marxism to deepen the notion of 'historical necessity' as well as those of 'dominant structure' and 'causality of a structure'.

f) Finally, on a secondary but important level, there are many nineteenth century conclusions accepted by Marx and Engels, which must be abandoned or re-evaluated — the chronological priority of nomadic herding over agriculture, the self-sustaining character of primitive economies, the problem of castes, the *direct* evolution of primitive Greece and Rome from 'clan' relations towards class societies.

This bare enumeration is enough to demonstrate that Marxism, purified of any dogmatism, at the price of an immense theoretical effort, in itself desirable, will be able to take charge of the scientific revolutions which are as necessary to our time as social revolutions.

*   *   *

THE CONCEPT OF THE 'ASIATIC MODE OF PRODUCTION' AND MARXIST MODELS OF SOCIAL EVOLUTION

'The manners of the ancient Hellenic world are very similar to the manners of foreigners today'.

Thucydides I, 6, 6.

From its very earliest beginnings,[5] Marxism has presented itself as an attempt to think history scientifically; it has tried to lay bare the essential structures of societies and to explain their *raison d'être* and the principles of their evolution. Marx and Engels discovered and took up a general hypothesis put forward by a number of scholars, i.e. that the history of humanity is that of the transition from classless forms of social organisation to class societies.[6] They enriched this hypothesis by looking for the basic cause of this transition in the development of productive forces and of relations of production. Adopting this approach, they showed that capitalism, by developing the productive forces, created the conditions for the abolition of class societies and class exploitation. Their works seem to convey the more precise image of humanity necessarily evolving through the successive stages of primitive community, slavery, feudalism and capitalism. Necessity was taken by many Marxists to imply that this model, more or less adapted to local 'particularities', would be found in all societies. When confronted with the immense archaeological, anthropological and historical material accumulated since Marx and Morgan, this interpretation became the subject of endless specialist debates on the date of the appearance and development of a 'slavery' stage in China, Japan, Africa, or of a 'feudal' stage among the Mongols, in the Islamic world, etc. All these difficulties came together in the 'periodisation' drama — not that of the chronological succession of events but of the logical succession of the slavery, feudal and capitalist structures.

To avoid this futile game of spelling out the logic of history, many scholars chose not to 'classify' the facts or the societies that they analysed, into one stage or another. Non-western history exploded in a burst of 'empirical' facts saved from absurdity only to be left meaningless. As for non-western history itself — the cause of these complementary theoretical disorders — it seemed to escape the 'necessity of history' because it did not reproduce the necessity of western history.

In the midst of this drama, by a peculiar paradox, there were certain specialists, Marxist or not, who also refused to fit their 'facts' into the categories slavery or feudalism, and instead tried to supply them with a comparative and theoretical meaning by classifying them in a Marxist category which had long been hidden in the shadow cast over many texts by Engels' brilliant *The Origin of the Family*: the category of the 'Asiatic mode of production'. For example, Suret-Canale wrote about pre-colonial Black Africa:

> It seems likely that the dominant mode of production of the more developed areas of traditional Black Africa can be compared with what Marx has called the 'Asiatic mode of production.'[7]

and Métraux, describing pre-Incan states, wrote about the Mochicas, Indians of the north coast of Peru (300 to 800 AD):

> As in Egypt and Mesopotamia, the taming of the desert on the Peruvian coast postulates the existence of an authority commanding respect, as well as a highly organised bureaucracy. Marx already appreciated the bearing of irrigation upon the creation of despotic governments of the Asiatic type.[8]

This remarkable return to a forgotten Marx presented a new series of theoretical problems. The first, apparently relevant to 'Marxology', was to establish the contents of Marx's category by making an inventory of all the scattered texts in which it appeared; then to compare this content with the schema constructed by Engels in *The Origin of the Family*. Having restored the concept, the next step is to relate it to the facts in order to assess its fertility, and eventually to reshape it and put it back into action. This task is in progress. Finally, as an extension of these two steps, a fundamental question inevitably arises: what is meant by a typical line of development of humanity? We will limit ourselves to developing the first point, merely sketching the other two, to which we will return later. But before launching on this journey, we must first make sure we have a clear idea of what is meant by a 'model of the social evolution'.

1   WHAT IS A MODEL OF SOCIAL EVOLUTION

It is a simplified ideal representation of the mechanisms by which societies function, constructed so as to make their possible evolutions intelligible. Such a representation constitutes a 'model', that is, a linked group of hypotheses about the nature of the elements which compose a society, their relations and their modes of evolution. Such 'models' are essential to the natural and historical sciences. In *Capital*, Karl Marx describes the fundamental structure of the capitalist organisation of production in the following terms:

> For here there are only two classes: the working class disposing only of its labour-power, and the capitalist class, which has a monopoly of the social means of production and money.[9]

On the basis of this fundamental relation the other structures which form a capitalist economic system (synchronic analysis) and their movement (diachronic analysis) can be understood simultaneously. But a model only partly corresponds to reality. *Capital* is not the real, concrete, history of any particular capitalist nation, but the study of the structure which characterises them as 'capitalist', abstracted from the infinite diversity of national realities. Marx explicitly warns us of this:

> In a *general* analysis of this kind, it is usually *always assumed* that the *actual conditions correspond* to their *conception*, or, what is the same, that actual conditions are represented to the extent that they are typical of their own general case.[10]

By this method, a 'logic'[11] of social evolution can be grasped. In order not to misunderstand grossly the models of evolution built by Marx and Engels, it is therefore necessary to recognise in advance that they neither want to, nor can, constitute the real history of societies, but rather an abstract history of realities reduced to their essential structures, a retrospective view of the justification of their evolution understood as the development of the *internal* possibilities and incapacities of these structures.

These models are thus configurations of working hypotheses linked to a state of knowledge and reality, simultaneously the point of arrival of theoretical reflection and the point of departure for a further deciphering of the infinite variety of concrete history. It is at this second level that the hypothetical schemas must prove their correctness. It is here that we must revoke the perpetual temptation to transform hypothesis into dogma, making a truth to be demonstrated into a given requiring no verification and which can, *a priori* reign supremely over the facts.

It was in this spirit, that Marx, sketching his first model of evolution in *The German Ideology* (1845), gave us directions for its use, and criticised those who would like to see in it a new philosophy of history, a corpus of first and last truths accessible only to the philosopher and from which history would derive its necessity and its meaning.

At the best its [philosophy's] place can only be taken by a summing-up of the most general results, abstractions which arise from the observation of the historical development of men. Viewed apart from real history, these abstractions have in themselves no value whatsoever. They can only serve to facilitate the arrangement of historical material, to indicate the sequence of its separate strata. But they by no means afford a recipe or schema, as does philosophy, for neatly trimming the epochs of history. On the contrary, our difficulties begin only when we set about the observation and the arrangement — the real depiction — of our historical material . . .[12]

We will see to what extent the ignoring of this grammar of hypotheses in the historical sciences gradually led many scholars into bizarre language through which they invoked reality to enter into the words meant to provide 'rational' meaning.

II THE CONCEPT OF ASIATIC MODE OF PRODUCTION IN MARX AND ENGELS

(a) The Sources

The concept was first worked out around 1853[13] and was present in Marx's work till the end of his life. In *Anti-Dühring* (1877) and *Die Fränkische Zeit* (1882) Engels takes it up again and enriches it but it disappears in *The Origin of the Family, Private Property and the State* (1884). Engels leaves it in volumes 2 and 3 of *Capital* which he edited after Marx's death.

Marx's fullest elaboration of this concept is to be found in a manuscript of 1855-59 which remained unpublished until 1939, entitled *Grundrisse der Kritik der Politischen Ökonomie*. The text of the *Formen* is the most complex model of social evolution which Marx has left us. It must, therefore, be contrasted with Engels' *Origin of the Family* which it precedes by twenty-five years.

b) The Concept of the Asiatic Mode of Production

This concept arose from reflection on British documents[14] describing the village communities and the state of nineteenth century Indian society. This information was supplemented by travellers' accounts of the Middle East and Central Asia.[15] One fact particularly struck Marx and Engels: the absence of private ownership of land. In the *Formen* Marx describes seven different forms of ownership of land, the dominant relation of production between men in pre-industrial societies. The forms succeed one another and end with the capitalist mode of production in which there is total separation of the worker from the objective conditions of production. Marx's text thus is presented as a sketch of the development of landed property for all of humanity and particularly Europe, as well as being a fragment of the analysis of the forms of primitive accumulation.[16] The successive elements of this evolution are: the primitive community, the Asiatic mode of production, the ancient mode of production, the feudal mode of production, the capitalist mode of production. On the modes of production other than the Asiatic, we will limit ourselves to a few words, which we will illustrate with diagrams borrowed from the Hungarian sinologist, Tokei.[17]

The Primitive Community

Based on links of kinship, language and customs, the primitive community appears 'not as the consequence, but as the pre-condition of the joint appropriation and use of the soil'. 'Ownership' of land belongs to the whole community and therefore belonging to the community is the precondition for (individual) 'possession' of land.

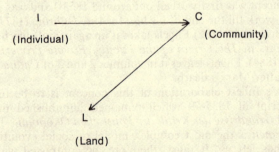

This community corresponds to an economy of 'natural' occupations — hunting, gathering, fishing — and to the first forms of itinerant agriculture, the transition towards the transformation of nature. At this level of the development of the productive forces, the survival of individuals depends entirely on their belonging to a group; and their place in the group depends primarily on the kinship they have with its members on the basis of the kinship system which regulates them:

> The less the development of labour, and the more limited its volume of production and, therefore, the wealth of society, the more preponderatingly does the social order appear to be dominated by ties of sex.[18]

Primitive communities have taken many forms depending on life styles and kinship systems. They have evolved in the course of prehistory and can survive, more or less altered, to the extent that primitive life styles are maintained. Their evolution is linked to the development of new forms of production — agriculture, herding, manufacture — and proceeds in two ways: the extension of individual ownership and possession of goods and the transformation of the old kinship links.[19] It is in the course of this evolution that the Asiatic mode of production emerges.

The Asiatic Mode of Production

It emerges when more developed forms of production allow a regular surplus, which is the condition for a more complex division of labour and for the separation of agriculture from manufacture. This division reinforces the self-sustaining character of production:

> ... a combination of manufacture and agriculture within the small community which thus becomes entirely *self-sustaining* and contains within itself all conditions of production and surplus production.[20]

Production is not aimed at a market, the use of money is limited, the economy thus remains 'natural'.[21] The unity of these communities can be represented by an assembly of heads of families, or a supreme chief, and social authority takes more or less demo-cratic or despotic forms. The existence of a surplus makes a more elaborate social differentiation possible and allows the emergence of a minority of individuals who appropriate a share of this surplus and thus exploit the other members of the community. How does this transition take place? Engels has sketched a model of this process in

Anti-Dühring (1874) :

> They are naturally endowed with a certain measure of authority and are the beginnings of state power. The productive forces gradually increase; the increasing density of the population creates at one point common interests, at another conflicting interests, between the separate communities, whose grouping into larger units brings about in turn a new division of labour, the setting up of organs to safeguard common interests and combat conflicting interests. These organs which, if only because they represent the common interests of the whole group, hold a special position in relation to each individual community — in certain circumstances even one of opposition — soon make themselves still more independent, partly through heredity of functions, which comes about almost as a matter of course in a world where everything occurs spontaneously, and partly because they become increasingly indispensable owing to the growing number of conflicts with other groups. It is not necessary for us to examine here how this independence of social functions in relation to society increased with time until it developed into domination over society . . . and how finally the individual rulers united into a ruling class. Here we are only concerned with establishing the fact that the exercise of a social function was everywhere the basis of political supremacy; and further that political supremacy has existed for any length of time only when it discharged its social functions.[22]

The outline of the embryonic dominant class is extremely imprecise and hard to locate in this context since the same person exercises power derived from his function and power derived from exploitation. The share of the surplus which he receives as the counterpart of his function is indirectly returned to the community which is therefore not exploited in this way by him. Exploitation arises when appropriation takes place without counterpart and it is difficult to determine the point at which the community begins to be exploited by the very people who provide it with services.

Exploitation thus takes the shape of domination not of one individual over another but of an individual personifying a function over a community. Given the nature of the structure of this domination it is easy to imagine the particular conditions which would favour its appearance and maximum development.

These requirements will be satisfied when the development of the natural resources imposes large scale cooperation on the particular communities for the realisation of major projects in the general interest which exceed the forces of these communities taken in isolation as individuals. The hydraulic projects (drainage, irrigation, construction) of the great alluvial valleys in Egypt and Mesopotamia would be a striking example of this.[23]

The realisation of such projects simultaneously demanded new productive forces and a centralised direction uniting and coordinating the efforts of the individual communities under its higher economic command. The 'all-embracing unity' thus appears to be the precondition for local communities to have effective labour and appropriation. It is on this basis that it is possible for power derived from the function of higher authority to be transformed into an instrument for the exploitation of the subordinate communities. This transformation is accelerated when the 'all-embracing unity' takes direct control of the communities' lands, which become the ultimate property of the State, of the higher community which links and regulates all the local communities. Appropriation of land by the State, personified by the king, the Pharaoh, etc. means the universal expropriation of the communities who lose ownership but retain possession of their land.

> . . . in most Asiatic fundamental forms it is quite compatible with the fact that the *all-embracing unity* which stands above all these small common bodies may appear as the higher or *sole proprietor*, the real communities only as *hereditary* possessors.[24]

Having become the ultimate owner of land, the State seems even more to be the pre-condition for appropriation of the natural conditions of production by the communities and the individuals. For the individual, possession of land passes through the double intermediary of the local community to which he belongs and of the higher community which has become landowner.

To represent this double relationship we suggest the following diagram:[25]

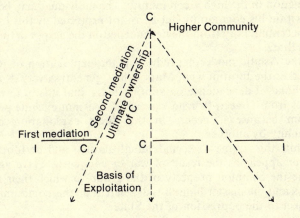

This diagram shows that the emergence of the State and of the exploitation of the communities do not change the general form of property relations; it remains one of communal ownership, this time ownership by the higher community, while the individual remains in possession of the soil as a member of his particular community. Thus a transition to a State society and to an embryonic form of class exploitation has taken place without the development of private ownership of land.

Within this framework the surplus, formerly appropriated by the local communities, now goes in part to the representatives of the higher community:

> Part of this surplus labour belongs to the higher community, which ultimately appears as a *person*. This surplus labour is rendered both as a tribute and as common labour for the glory of the unity, in part that of the despot, in part that of the imagined tribal entity of the god.[25]

The centralisation and the accumulation of this surplus under the control of the State allows for the development of cities and of foreign trade. Here trade is not the expression of commodity production within the communities but the transformation of the surplus into commodities (rare objects and weapons).[27] The trader appears as an official of the State.[28] At the same time forced labour for the State is added to group labour for the communities. The tax in kind levied by the State is transformed into ground rent levied for the benefit of the individuals who personify the State.[29]

The exploitation of peasants and artisans by an aristocracy of noblemen and State officials is done privately since the labour is collective and the ground rent merged with the tax and both demanded by a civil servant not in his own name but in the name of his function in the higher community. The individual may be a free man within his community but he is not protected by this freedom and this community from the dependence on the despot in the name of the State.

In the Asiatic mode of production the exploitation of man by man takes the form of what Marx called 'general slavery'.[30] As it is not a bond of dependence on another individual it is in its essence distinct from Graeco-Roman slavery: it does not exclude personal freedom because it occurs in the direct exploitation of one community by another.

Within this framework, individual slavery and serfdom may however appear as the result of war or conquests. Slave and serf become the common property of the group to which their master belongs and the master himself is dependent on this community and is subject to the oppression of the State.

Slavery and serfdom are therefore simply further developments of property based on tribalism. They necessarily modify all its forms. This they are least able to do in the Asiatic form. . . . Here slavery neither puts an end to the conditions of labour, nor does it modify the essential relationship.[31]

The productive use of slaves cannot become the dominant relation of production. The obstacles are the absence of private ownership of land and the general obligation imposed on communities to create surplus labour. The use of slaves by the king, the priests and the officials is reduced by the use of peasant forced labour and is restricted to the exceptionally arduous activities such as labour in the mines. The inheritance of estates by State dignitaries might offer the basis for productive use of slaves in agriculture but real developments of productive slavery implies private ownership of land within rural communities and this took place in Europe within what Marx calls the 'ancient mode of production'.

Before bringing together the elements described by Marx under the term Asiatic mode of production, we shall briefly describe the modes of production which follow it, according to Marx.

The Ancient Mode of Production

Marx finds it in its 'purest, most complete', form in Roman history. For the residents of the countryside the town or city is the centre. Belonging to the community remains the precondition for the individual's appropriation of land but there the land is divided into two parts: one remains under the control of the community as such — it is the 'ager publicus in all its forms' — the other is split up into plots distributed as private property to each Roman citizen.

Tökei represents this structure in the following way:

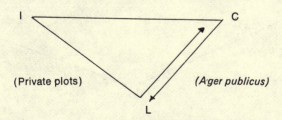

(Private plots)   (Ager publicus)

The individual is thus co-owner of public land and private owner of his plot. The two forms of real estate, State and private, imply and limit each other. In Rome this contradiction will develop to the detriment of State ownership.

The preservation of this structure rests on the maintenance of equality between the small owners. The development of commodity production, conquests, etc. accelerates the growth of inequality between free men.[32] Some of them even lose their property and with it their citizenship. Debt bondage appears. Private use of slaves by individuals becomes widespread as private ownership of land is most conducive to this practice. By its very development, the ancient mode of production creates the conditions for its transition to a real slave mode of production.

The Slave Mode of Production

This thus appears as the development and the destruction of the ancient mode of production which it replaces.[33] The slave mode of production itself evolves and suffers a protracted dissolution in the course of which Germanic forms of ownership develop, to become in turn one of the bases for the feudal mode of production.

The Germanic Mode of Production

Arising out of a lengthy evolution from primitive communal land ownership and linked to the life style of warrior tribes living on slash-and-burn agriculture and mainly herding,[34] the Germanic mode of production combines communal and private ownership of land. In contrast with the Roman *ager publicus*, communal property appears as a functional complement of private property (pastures, hunting lands, etc.), as the 'communal accessory'[35] of private appropriation. It is thus a case of a 'truly communal ownership by individual owners'.[36] The agricultural community is an association of individual owners.

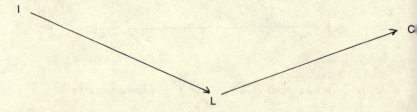

These free peasants slowly lost their personal independence and became increasingly subject to the authority of a new nobility which had developed from Germanic chiefs and their armed retainers and Romanised Gauls who had joined the administration.

Ruined by war and plunder, they had to seek the protection of the new magnates or the Church, for the royal power was too weak to protect them; but they had to pay dear for this protection. Like the Gallic peasants before them, they had to transfer the property in their land to their patrons, and received it back from them as tenants in different and varying forms, but always on condition of performing services and paying dues. Once driven into this form of dependence, they gradually lost their personal freedom; after a few generations most of them became serfs.[37]

This process of the partial subjection of free men converged with the movement of partial emancipation of the slaves begun in the last centuries of the Roman empire and at the end of this multilineal evolution, gave rise to a single form of exploitation of a class of independent small direct producers by a class of noble landowners — to feudal relations of production.

The Feudal Mode of Production

Here the essential relations of production are those which regulate the appropriation of land and its products. They simultaneously bind and oppose the lord to the peasant, the owner of the land and in part of the peasant's person to the immediate producer, owner of the more or less hereditary rights of occupation and use of land and of the other means of production. In its typical form, this structure presents two characteristic features: the lord's ownership is effective but not absolute, since he himself belongs to the feudal hierarchy of lords and is the vassal of an overlord who has ultimate if not effective ownership of the land;[38] the peasants who depend individually on their lord are grouped in village communities,[39] and this economic and social organisation enormously increases their capacity to resist and fight the lord.[40] They are subject to compulsory labour and to rents in kind or money and these dues necessitate the use of extra-economic coercion.

The evolution of the feudal system brought about the development of exchange, towns and commodity production; it laid the foundation for capitalist relations of production which were to become the main contradiction of the system and cause its downfall. In the course of this transformation, many peasants were expropriated from their lands and forced to become wage-labourers.

The so-called primitive accumulation, therefore, is nothing else than the historical process of divorcing the producer from the means of his production. It appears as primitive because it forms the pre-historic stage of capital and of the mode of production corresponding with it.

The economic structure of the capitalist society has grown out of the economic structure of the feudal society. The dissolution of the latter set free the elements of the former.[41]

We have now reached the end of the argument used by Marx to reflect on the stages which led, as a general condition of production, to the separation of the producer from the objective conditions of production, from land, above all; this separation is characteristic of the capitalist mode of production. We shall now look closely at what Marx specifically defined as the 'Asiatic mode of production' and isolate it carefully from other modes of production with which, through one or other of its features, it seems to be confused.

The Specificity of the 'Asiatic Mode of Production': its Scope as Defined by Marx and Engels

We have attempted to locate the theoretical content which, in our view, Marx gave to the concept of 'Asiatic mode of production'. The brief sketch we have given of the other concepts — primitive community, slavery, feudalism — allow us to distinguish it from them, despite the fact that they have one or more features in common.

The primitive community and the Asiatic mode of production both imply the existence of communities governed by forms of communal land ownership. There is no private ownership of land and the individual, as member of a community, has the right to use and occupy the land. But the Asiatic mode of production is not to be confused with the primitive community; the functioning of the former implies and develops the exploitation of man by man, i.e. the formation of a dominant class. It emerges as part of the way primitive communities evolve and dissolve in relation to new forms of production (sedentary agriculture, more intensive herding, the use of metals, etc.).

The Asiatic mode of production is not to be confused with the slave mode of production, except by a misinterpretation of Marx's texts where he writes of the 'general slavery' of individuals under State despotism and shows that at the core of this regime patriarchal slavery can become heavily used. Insofar as he is a member of a community, the individual is free within the limits of freedom as defined by a community existence. This freedom, however, does not protect him against taxation, compulsory labour, expropriation and subjection to the State and its representatives. Slavery can come about by war and conquest but it is the prerogative of a group itself dependent on the State. Within the community, productive use of slaves is limited while at the State level it is restricted by the constant availability of plentiful peasant forced labour.

Does the existence of peasants subject to forced labour allow us to merge the Asiatic mode of production with the feudal mode of production? Are the following features not essential aspects of the feudal mode of production — the State's ultimate ownership of the land of the village communities; its expropriation of the latter, who then retain rights of occupation and of use; the hierarchy of noblemen and officials under a prince who is the incarnation of the community.?

It seems to us that the fundamental difference lies in the nature of the exploitation of the peasants and their state of dependence in each case. In the Asiatic mode of production, the State is owner of the land, inasmuch as it personifies all the communities, and the exploitation of the peasants is collective. The dependence of the individual in relation to a State official is indirect and is mediated by the relationship of dependence of his community of origin to the State which the official represents. By contrast, in the feudal mode of production, the peasants are individually dependent on their lord who owns their land as well as his own estate. The communal organisation of these peasants appears less as a blood community than as the functional complement of the exploitation of individual plots; its existence is derived from the economic constraints to which it responds and its power from the advantages that it obtains (features clarified by the Germanic mode of production).

Thus for Marx the concept of Asiatic mode of production indicated a specific structure whose separate elements (monarchy, centralisation, labour and tithes, etc.) could be found in other structures without merging the Asiatic mode of production with these structures or dissolving it in them.

It seems to us that, for Marx and Engels, the main interest of this concept was to indicate one route by which the State and class exploitation emerge from primitive communities.[42] As Marx and Engels related this development particularly to the achievement of major projects, especially irrigation works,[43] they took this form of development to be appropriate to certain Asian societies and to be the key to 'oriental despotism'.[44] This route would finally have entailed the relative stagnation of these societies; the lack of development of private property and commodity production leads to their 'immutability'.[45]

Defined in this way, the concept seemed to them to be applicable to Ancient Egypt, Persia, Hindustan, Java, Bali, the high plains of Asia, certain parts of Russia, that is, to a number of different Asiatic societies at different periods but organised in response to similar natural conditions.

Following this theoretical reconstruction of the concept of Asiatic mode of production from the widely scattered references to it, and before considering whether such a concept is valid today, we must try to explain the reasons for its disappearance in Engels' *The Origin of the Family*, and the other misfortunes which have befallen it since, among Marxists and non-Marxists alike.

III. THE MISFORTUNES OF THE CONCEPT OF ASIATIC MODE OF PRODUCTION

Morgan was the first person with expert knowledge to *attempt* to introduce *a definite order* into the prehistory of man; unless important additional *material necessitates alterations*, his *classification* may be expected to remain in force.[46]

Until 1882 Marx and Engels often return and add to the concept of Asiatic mode of production. In *Die Fränkische Zeit* (1882), Engels wrote:

The form taken by the power of the state depends on the form taken by social groups at a particular time. Where — as with the Aryan peoples of Asia and the Russians — the social group still tills the soil collectively, or where the social group allocates land to individual families for a certain period, where therefore no land is yet privately owned, the power of the state manifests itself as despotism.

In 1884 in *The Origin of the Family*, Engels discards this concept, for reasons which we shall now briefly outline; our hypothesis is the result of an analysis too lengthy to reproduce here.

What is Engels' aim in writing *The Origin of the Family*? It is to construct a model of the evolution of humanity from classless to state society by grasping the laws and relations of correspondence between the specific evolutions of three sets of structures: the production systems, the kinship systems and the political systems. Basing his argument on the facts of ancient history and on ethnology. Engels establishes that:

1. The law of the evolution of the system of production is the tendency for private property to develop from the means of production beginning with various forms of communal property.
2. The law of the evolution of the kinship system is the tendency for the monogamous family to develop from forms of group marriage and 'gentile' (clan) organisation.

3. The law of the evolution of political systems is the tendency for the State to develop from the forms of government of primitive societies, from primitive democracy.

When the three elements, private property, monogamous family and State are bound up in one society, then it has passed from barbarism to civilisation, from classless to class society. To be civilised thus means to belong to a class society, to a 'contradictory'[48] reality, in which the development of productive forces is necessarily linked to the development of the forms of exploitation of man by man. Slavery, serfdom, wage-labour — 'these are the three great forms of servitude characteristic of the three great epochs of civilisation'.[49] For Engels the typical forms of the transition to class society and of the evolution of class relations are characteristic of western history beginning with the Greeks and resulting in industrial capitalism.

> Athens represented the purest, most classical form. Here the state sprang directly and mainly out of the class antagonisms that developed within gentile society.[50]

The first reason why Engels discards the concept of Asiatic mode of production is because he regards Western history as the prototype of the general development of humanity and explicitly excludes the histories of Asia and the Middle East from his field of analysis.[51]

But that is not the basic reason. We believe it is to be found in Engels' acceptance of Morgan's theses in *Ancient Society* (1877) that it was impossible for a State and a dominant class to develop within the framework of barbaric, tribal societies, and in his acceptance of the concept of 'military democracy' which Morgan took for the final form of organisation taken by classless societies before and during their transition to class societies.

Let us elaborate on these points. Morgan's view, accepted by Engels, is that humanity passes from the upper stage of savagery to the lower stage of barbarism when it passes from the *gens* (clan) to the tribe. Humanity passes from the lower to the middle stage of barbarism when society emerges from the tribe to the confederacy of tribes; and from the middle to the upper stage of barbarism when society passes from the confederacy of tribes to military democracy. A people, in its 'heroic' age, at the dawn of its entry into civilisation, into class society, thus finds itself organised in a 'military democracy'.

> Like the Greeks in the *heroic* age, the Romans at the time of the *so-called* kings lived in a *military democracy* based on the gentes, phratries and

tribes, from which it developed . . . And though the naturally developed
patrician nobility has already gained ground, though the *reges* attempted
gradually to enlarge the scope of their powers — this does *not change the
original and fundamental character of the constitution.*[52]

The Greeks thus pass from the tribe to the confederacy of tribes
and on to military democracy. To understand this evolution it is
necessary to have a clear idea of 'gentile' organisation, its point of
departure. Engels, following Morgan, assumes that 'the American
was the original form of the *gens* and the Greek and Roman the later,
derivative forms'.[53]

He assumes that the Iroquois *gens*, and particularly that of the
Seneca tribe, is 'the classical form of the original *gens*'.[54] Moreover,
in the nineteenth century, the Iroquois had developed to the point of
confederate tribal organisation. The analysis of the Iroquois became
the point of departure for the understanding of Western primitive
history. However, according to Morgan and Engels, the confederacy
of the Iroquois was not the most advanced social organisation
reached by the American Indians.

The so-called Pueblo Indians of New Mexico, the Mexicans, Central
Americans and Peruvians were in the middle stage of barbarism at the
time of the conquest.[55]

Thus the great pre-Columbian civilisations (Incas, Mayas, Aztecs)
were reaching the end of their autonomous history, the point where
the heroic age of the Greeks ended and where their history as a class
society began. For this reason Engels does not analyse them since he
assumes that their institutions are of the same type as those of the
Greeks, but, on the contrary, he analyses the Iroquois *gens* to
explain the transition to military democracy.

What characterises military democracy? It is the fact that a
'gentile' aristocracy has exceptional powers to wage war. But this
power is limited since it is both temporary and granted by the people
or the council of elders. Thus this power cannot become permanent
or escape the control of the members of the community to replace
and dominate it. Thus, the existence of military democracy is neither
the end nor the opposite of a democratic government, but is one of its
forms.[56]

Morgan sees this structure as equally illustrated by the Aztec
military leader and the Greek *basileus*. Engels and Marx also agree
with this:

One word *basileia* used by Greek writers when referring to *Homeric
pseudo-kingship* (because military leadership is its main distinguishing

characteristic) accompanied by the people's council and assembly, only *means* military democracy.[57]

Like the Greek *basileus*, the Aztec military chief has been wrongly presented to you as a prince in the modern sense. Morgan was the first to subject to historical criticism the reports of the Spaniards, who at first misunderstood and exaggerated, and later deliberately misrepresented things; he showed that the Mexicans were in the middle stage of barbarism, but on a higher plane than the New Mexican Pueblo Indians, and that their constitution, so far as the garbled accounts enable us to judge, corresponded to the following: a confederacy of three tribes, which had obliged a number of others to render them tribute, and which was governed by a federal council and a federal military chief, whom the Spaniards had made into an 'emperor'.[58]

This brings us to the heart of a whole host of paradoxes.

By showing that tribal development causes the emergence of aristocracies, Engels has reached the precise point where he could take up the hypothesis of the Asiatic mode of production and in the light of it, interpret the great pre-Columbian civilisations. But Morgan deprives Engels of this theoretical possibility by excluding the hypothesis that the power of a tribal aristocracy might be transformed into absolute power in the hands of a monarch without this transformation destroying the village or tribal communities.[59] The existence of a tribal aristocracy allowed a possibility precluded by the theory of military democracy.[60] A further paradox: Morgan was right not to see the *basileus* of Homeric poems and the Great Inca as feudal monarchs: moreover, as modern criticism has confirmed, the Greek *basileus* was not a king. But Morgan moves from the rejection of the pseudo-monarchy of the *basileus* to the rejection of any monarchy among the peoples of pre-Columbian America and ancient Europe. The strength of the argument on which his first rejection is based seemed to guarantee his second conclusion. Was it possible for Marx and Engels not to follow Morgan on this second matter? No, because in 1880 the archaeology and linguistics of the early periods of Greece and Rome were just beginning to develop. Final paradox: modern discoveries were to restore to the Greeks kings who were not *basileus* but *anax*, thus confirming Morgan on this particular point but invalidating his generalisation.

These Greek kingdoms belong to the distant past of the Mycenean and Cretan periods, to the original core of the oral traditions which from the fifteenth to the seventh centuries BC were laid down layer upon layer containing a great mixture of descriptions of material objects and social realities from the Greek Bronze to Iron Ages.[61] But at the time when Morgan was writing Schliemann had only just excavated Troy (1870-1873) and was beginning to dig at Mycenae (1874). He published a work on Mycenae in 1878 after having excavated Tyrins and, in 1888, he identified the site of the palace of Minos. The decisive stage occurred after Engels' death when, between 1900 and 1905, Sir Arthur Evans discovered the Bronze Age and the Minoan civilisation in Crete.[62]

In 1951 Michael Ventris started to decipher linear B; he was followed by John Chadwick (1953) and discussion about it continues today between Blegen, Palmer and others. But here we have the supreme paradox in this analysis of the fate of the concept of the Asiatic mode of production: the rediscovered Greek kingdoms appear very similar to the great kingdoms of the Bronze Age in the eastern Mediterranean. These societies are contemporaries of the early Greeks but they are societies to which the Asiatic mode of production seemed inapplicable. In the centre of Mycenean society we see the palace and the king who 'concentrates and unifies in his person' all the elements of sovereignty — religious, political, military, administrative and economic. Through administrators and dignitaries, the king regulates the production, distribution and exchange of goods within an economy which knows little of currency or trade. The producers are grouped in rural communities and collectively own lands which may be the object of periodic redistribution.[63] As the conditions of production do not demand large-scale cooperation between communities, their dependence on the kings is not absolute but they are still subject to the king and the warlords who surround and represent yim personified by the *basileus*, at the council of elders in the village *demes*. With the Dorian invasions of the twelfth century.

it is not a mere dynasty which dies in the fire which destroys Pylos and Mycenae in turn, it is a form of monarchy which is forever destroyed, a whole social life centred around the palace, which is definitively abolished, a character, the divine king, who disappears from the Greek horizon.[64]

The Bronze Age is succeeded by the Iron Age, the society of the palace is slowly superseded by the *polis*, the Greek city.[65] Two rival groups confront each other: the village communities and the warlords who control religious and juridical monopolies. Within a society which is in some way less complex and less developed than Creto-Mycenean society, another *basileia* emerges which is in no sense another monarchy or even an heir to the former society and that which thus a discontinuity between the former society and that which succeeds it and gives rise to the *polis* and the slave system.

But, as a final paradox, this new information both invalidates and confirms Morgan's and Engels' description of Greek society and of the origin of the Athenian State. Invalidated since they actually refer to the last and no longer to the first centuries of the evolution of the Greek peoples; but confirmed when they are taken as referring back to the last centuries of this evolution to the moment when private property emerges and a new State appears, serving private interests: the Athenian State, a typical form of an instrument of power for a dominant class. In the context of this later time, the concept of military democracy could be kept to describe a society dominated by a warrior aristocracy but it would no longer prevent us from recognising the existence of monarchies in early Greek times. However Engels' analysis could no longer pretend to show that in Greece 'the State sprang *directly* and mainly out of the class antagonisms that developed within gentile society'.[66] Indeed, prior to the emergence of the Athenian State, the State had already appeared in Crete and in Mycenae, suggesting that military democracy is not the final stage before the emergence of the State but a transitional stage between two of its forms, the 'Asiatic State' and the Greek City State.

To summarise this all too brief analysis of *The Origin of the Family*: Engels discarded the concept of the Asiatic mode of production not for obscure political reasons, as Karl Wittfogel would have us believe,[67] but under the influence of Morgan whose convincing analysis of the Greek *basileus* and the Roman *rex* had led him to question the existence of monarchy in the primitive history of the Greeks and Romans. Morgan's influence reveals the state of scientific information about primitive history[68] in the middle of the nineteenth century; for scholars of that period, it began with the first Olympiad. Nowadays archaeology has extended this history by two millennia and discovered in Europe social relations reminiscent of those of the Near East.[69] The hypothesis of the Asiatic mode of production thus acquires a validity hardly foreseen by Marx, except in the theoretical form of the famous note in *Capital*, which has long remained obscure, in which he located the Asiatic mode of production

after the *primitive form of ownership* of land in common had disappeared, and *before slavery* had seized on production in earnest.[70]

Engels' analysis refers to this period of the ancient mode of production, that is, the time of the real 'Greek miracle' when private property became general and commodity production had developed. Here lies the real inception of the western line of development whose essential elements Engels had grasped.

There remains to give a brief account of the other misfortunes which have befallen the Asiatic mode of production since Engels, and to draw attention to the immense 'ideological' connotations which must be eradicated before it can again become a serious working hypothesis in the hands of the historian or the anthropologist.

There has been an increasing tendency to consider Engels' work as the definitive explanation of the law of the evolution of humanity. According to this law, every society had to conform, more or less, with one of Engels' four stages and more or less reproduce the features of the western society which had provided the prototype of this stage.

However, for a long time Marxists continued to draw on the concept of Asiatic mode of production when clarifying particular aspects of the development of certain societies. Lenin, for example, speaks of the 'semi-Asiatic' system in Russia, thereby extending certain of Marx's hypotheses on the despotic role of the State in Russia in exploiting the village communities. Because of this he emphasises the late and unique character of the development of feudalism in European Russia.[71] The concept is discussed and applied by Marxists in China and Japan.

But the general tendency was to abandon the concept. In *Fundamental Problems of Marxism* (1908) Plekhanov assumes that Marx gave up his former hypothesis after reading Morgan, or at least no longer considered the Asiatic mode of production to be a 'progressive' formation of humanity, as he had done in 1859 in the *Contribution*. Plekhanov's interpretation reinforced the impression that the Asiatic mode of production meant stagnation for millennia.[72] On the other hand, the tendency to see a law of universal development for all societies in the triad, slavery, feudalism, capitalism, obscured the very specific nature of the Germans as described by Engels. In fact Engels shows us the Germanic tribes in his view confederated and organised in 'military democracies' like those of the Greeks and Romans of the 'heroic' period. But although they both start from the same stage of 'upper barbarism' they follow a completely different line of development; after the conquest of the Roman empire, the Germans develop towards 'prefeudal' monarchies. He thus shows us classless societies developing towards a class society and a State *without going through* the ancient and slave modes of production. This makes it clear that the Graeco-Roman evolution was not universal since it appeared as *one* of the forms of transition to class organisation, not as *the* only form. As

Engels' analysis was forgotten, the hypothesis of a plurality of forms of transition to class society faded more and more into obscurity.

Another episode was to make the scientific analysis of Marx's hypotheses more difficult: after the failure of the Chinese revolution in 1927, a discussion was held on revolutionary strategy in Asia. Some of those sceptical of the possibility of a Chinese revolution justified their position by invoking the 'stagnation' of Asia, quoting fragments from Marx on the Asiatic mode of production. They were condemned, and, along with them, the hypothesis of the Asiatic mode of production which seemed to be a theoretical obstacle to a correct analysis of Asian history.[73]

We now come to the final misfortune which was to discredit this concept utterly in the eyes of Marxists. Having been expelled from Marxism, it was to be dug up by the sinologist, Wittfogel, who used it to demonstrate that Marxists got rid of this concept because they were frightened of recognising in it the admission of their totalitarianism, the admission that, on the basis of socialist forms of collective ownership, there could develop a bureaucratic class wielding despotic power.

By the end of this, some Marxists had come to speak of a '*supposedly* Asiatic mode of production, a thought which Marx never developed', of the '*erroneous* theory of the Asiatic mode of production, erroneous because based on a *special* evolution of oriental peoples and on a so-called stagnation', of '*discredited* and reactionary notions',[74] etc. The list is too long to recite here.

But the main point is the way in which the theoretical hypotheses proposed by Marx and Engels to clarify the history of humanity were transformed and degraded. The approach of many Marxists was deprived of the double hypothesis of the Asiatic mode of production and the plurality of forms of transition to class society. Only one path presented itself: to look at the transition from the primitive community (excluding the Asiatic mode of production) to ancient slavery (excluding other forms of class society) followed by an evolution more or less reflecting that of Western society (slavery, feudalism, capitalism). Historical materialism, which had been an open system of hypotheses to be verified was thus stigmatised in *The German Ideology* as being 'a *recipe*, or *schema*, for neatly *trimming* the epochs of history'.

This schema-recipe, the exact opposite of Marxism, found its clearest expression and apotheosis in Stalin's essay *Dialectical and Historical Materialism*. Paradoxically the task of many Marxist historians was no longer to discover history but to 'rediscover' it, to rediscover the stages of slavery, feudalism, etc. But the facts were stubborn, and societies fitted these pre-determined conclusions badly or not at all. Their intransigence heightened the periodisation dramas — dramas not chronological but sociological, i.e., which condone the characterisation of a society by a mode of production (slave, feudal, etc.). Remember the incessant quarrels of scholars when one of them 'discovered' slavery in India, Japan, China,[75] Vietnam or Black Africa. For example, Dange's *India from Primitive Communism to Slavery* (1949) claimed to have rediscovered the transition from primitive communism to slavery in the evolution of the Aryans, without considering the new archaeological sources on the agricultural civilisations of Mohendjo-Daro and Harappa, etc. However, the answer of other Marxist specialists was clear. Kosambi stated:

> Dange is so concerned with the identification of the general stages suggested by Engels, that it is possible to find atrocious untruths on almost each page. . . To join unfounded hypotheses with quotations from Engels is not enough.[76]

In the case of China the analysis was carried on within the theoretical perspective defined by Kuo Mo Jo in the following terms:

> according to Marx's views, the phases of the development of society may be shortened, but not skipped . . . It is not possible for a simple nation to become feudal *without going through slavery* and it is not enough either for it to go through a stage of semi-slavery.[77]

And the *History of China* (Peking, 1958) on Chou society, whose interpretation is still controversial, stated that:

> The Chou were also a slaving society. The exploiting class included the king, the feudal princes and the nobility, and the exploited were the peasants and the slaves.[78]

The setbacks to this dogmatism made it possible to dispute the model of the four stages without actually abandoning it, but questioning it from inside. With no categories available other than slavery and feudalism, many historians who were aware of the non-slave nature of many societies in which forms of exploitation existed, crammed these societies into feudalism. This category was thus expanded beyond measure and the dogmatic model was distorted without being destroyed. To take an extreme case, let us quote a participant in the discussion held in *Marxism Today* in 1961-62 concerning Marxist models of social evolution:

> Nor does Homer, reflecting the Mycenaean civilisation — and finally put

together around 700 BC — paint a picture of either a primitive communal or of a slave society; what is depicted is again rather a feudal society.

In short, in the classical world, feudalism appears to have both preceded and succeeded slavery.[79]

But finally, although the category of feudalism was expanding, it always found itself confined within the schema challenged by its expansion. Paradoxically, this critique of dogmatism led Marxists to adopt the same positions as many non-Marxist historians who invent a 'feudalism' wherever they find an aristocracy;[80] these positions have already been the target of Marc Bloch's ruthless criticism in 1940.[81] Of all these 'exotic' feudalisms he retained only the example of Japan while for the others he awaited more evidence, supporting Marx's thesis in *Capital*.[82]

Finally, faced with the failure of both blind dogmatism and distorted theoretical revisions, many historians attempted 'to save their facts' and recoiled from any theoretical interpretation of them. While amassing immense quantities of new facts, this empiricism arrived at the paradoxical position of protecting them from previous theoretical nonsense and absurdities by simply depriving them of 'meaning'. But were these facts not already deprived of their theoretical meaning when considered in the light of the old or revised dogmatic schemas — were they not waiting for their 'right' or 'true' meaning? Yet all these new facts, accumulated either without theory or on the basis of false ones, represent the total results of all the work of many Marxist historians who devoted their lives to the study of non-western history. Meanwhile, historians continued to make use of the hypothesis of the Asiatic mode of production to throw light on Chinese history (e.g. Welskopf, and Tökei), Japan or pre-Columbian America (Métraux).

In our opinion, this brief analysis of the fate of the Asiatic mode of production illustrates the immense burden of theoretical distortions and contradictory ideologies which this concept has come to bear. We considered it necessary to devote much time and effort to a detailed reconstruction of all the elements of this concept to be found in the works of Marx and Engels and to follow its theoretical misfortunes since *The Origin of the Family*; we have shown that there are many reasons for these misfortunes but they all result from the transformation of the hypotheses of historical materialism into a philosophy of history, a body of dogma-recipes by which the historian operates mechanically on the historical material passed on to him.

Without a clear theoretical grasp of the original contents of the concept and its successive distortions, we consider it extremely dangerous to present it to the public and to ask scholars to compare it with the known facts. On the other hand the idea that merely to read Marx's texts without any theoretical commentary is sufficient to escape the old pitfalls, is to believe it is possible to read *Capital* or a treatise of theoretical physics without any previous preparation; it is to reassure oneself in the good old positivist way by postponing theoretical analysis to some future time.

In conclusion we should like to present a new interpretation of the concept of Asiatic mode of production and, it is unavoidable, put forward some hypotheses on what is called the typical line of development of humanity.

IV HYPOTHESIS ON THE NATURE AND LAWS OF DEVELOPMENT OF THE ASIATIC MODE OF PRODUCTION AND THE CONCEPT OF TYPICAL LINE OF DEVELOPMENT OF HUMANITY

(a) The Nature of the Asiatic Mode of Production

With the concept of the Asiatic mode of production, Marx has shown us societies within which particular village communities are subject to the power of a minority of individuals who represent a higher community, the expression of the real or imaginary unity of the particular communities. This power at first takes root in functions of common interest (religious, political, economic) and, without ceasing to be a functional power, gradually transforms itself into an exploitative one. The special advantages accruing to this minority, nominally as a result of services rendered to the communities, become obligations with no counterpart, i.e., exploitation. The land of these communities is often expropriated to become the ultimate property of the king, who personifies the higher community. We therefore have exploitation of man by man, and the appearance of an exploiting class without the existence of private ownership of land.

In our view, this picture presents a form of social organisation characterised by a contradictory structure. This form of organisation combines community structures and the embryo of an exploiting class. The unity of these two contradictory elements rests precisely on the fact that it is in the name of the higher community that the individual communities are exploited by this minority. A society characterised by this contradiction is thus presented *simultaneously* as a final form of classless society (village communities) *and* an initial form of class society (a minority exercising State power, a higher community.)

Thus we are putting forward the hypothesis that Marx, without having been completely aware of it, described a form of social organisation specific to the *transition* from classless to class society, a form which contains the *contradiction of that very transition.*

In our view, this hypothesis allows us to understand why the concept of Asiatic mode of production is referred to more and more to illuminate the periods and societies of ancient Europe (Creto-Mycenaean or Etruscan monarchies), of Black Africa (kingdoms and empires of Mali, Ghana, Bamoum kingship, etc.) and pre-Columbian America (great Mesoamerican or Andean agricultural civilisations). A common element appears throughout these many specific realities — a common structure which combines community relations and the embryo of class and is related to the same situation of transition to class society. Because of this relation between the situation and structure it is possible to explain the geographical and historical universality of the form of social organisation which emerges when the conditions for the transition to class society develop; maybe at the end of the fourth millennium BC in the case of Egypt with the transition of the tribal Nilotic societies first to monarchies and then to a unified empire,[83] or in the nineteenth century with the birth of the Bamoum kingdom in the Cameroons. By providing many examples of societies in the process of transition to class organisation the archaeological and ethnological knowledge accumulated since the nineteenth century provides the concept with a field of application which Marx or Engels could not have envisaged. In becoming more and more widely applicable both in time and space, the concept no longer applies exclusively to Asia. It may therefore be necessary to abandon the use of the adjective 'Asiatic'.

(b) The emergence and different forms of the Asiatic mode of production

Within the terms of this general theoretical hypothesis, the second task is the systematic study of the nature of transition to class society, of the emergence of the conditions of transition.

For Marx, the Asiatic mode of production is linked to the need to organise major economic projects beyond the means of particular communities or isolated individuals and constitutes the precondition for productive activity for these communities. In this context, appear forms of centralised power which he called 'oriental despotism',[84] a term familiar since the seventeenth century. The State and the dominant class intervene directly in the conditions of production; in the organisation of major projects, the correspondence between productive forces and relations of production is made direct.

Even if this hypothesis provides the key to the typical, most developed forms of the transition to the 'Asiatic' mode of production, it does not exhaust all the possible circumstances. We propose the addition of a second hypothesis to Marx's. Assume the possibility of an alternative route and another form of Asiatic mode of production in which a minority dominates and exploits the communities intervening in their conditions of production not directly, but indirectly, by appropriating surplus labour or produce as profit. In West Africa the emergence of the kingdoms of Ghana, Mali, Songhay,[85] etc. was not the result of the organisation of major projects but seems to be linked to the control exercised by the tribal aristocracies over intertribal or interregional trade in rare commodities, gold, ivory, hides, etc. between Black and north Africa.[86] In Madagascar, alongside the Imerina kingdom which was based on irrigated rice agriculture and had put the marshes in the Tananarive plain to good use, there appeared the kingdom of Sakalava based on nomadic herding and the trading of cattle and slaves.

Our hypothesis allows us to explain the emergence of a dominant class in agricultural societies based neither on great agricultural works nor on herding without incurring the difficulties or contradictions aroused by the expressions 'nomadic feudalism' (mongolian feudalism, etc.).[89]

Comparing these two forms of Asiatic mode of production — with or without major projects — proves that there is a common element: the appearance of an aristocracy exercising State power and consolidating the bases of its class exploitation by appropriating a part of the produce of the communities (either in labour or in kind). What the presence or absence of major projects determines is the appearance of a bureaucracy and an absolute centralised authority known by the vague and antiquated term 'despotism'. Thus, we do not consider it necessary to search mechanically with Wittfogel for gigantic, mainly hydraulic, projects, a bureaucracy and a strongly centralised authority in order to rediscover the 'Asiatic' mode of production.[90] Rather the theoretical task is to draw up a typology of the various forms of this mode of production, with or without major projects, with or without agriculture, and at the same time to draw up a typology of the forms of communities within which this mode of production grows up. Thus it might be possible to reconstitute many models of the way in which inequality is introduced in classless societies and leads to the appearance of antagonistic contradictions and the formation of a dominant class. The collaboration of historians and anthropologists would be essential to this task.

We have tried to define the structure and certain forms and conditions of the appearance of the Asiatic mode of production; now we must approach the problem of the laws of evolution of this social formation.

(c) The dynamic and the laws of evolution of the Asiatic mode of production

If the appearance of the Asiatic mode of production indicates the emergence of an initial class structure whose outlines are still flexible, it also indicates the regular appropriation of part of the communities' labour by this class, i.e. the existence of a regular surplus. From the point of view of the dynamic of the productive forces, a society's transition to the Asiatic mode of production would not mean the beginning of stagnation but, on the contrary, would be a progressive sign for the productive forces. If Pharaonic Egypt, Mesopotamia, the Mycenean kingdoms, and the pre-Columbian empires belong to the Asiatic mode of production, then here we have evidence that it corresponds to the most brilliant civilisations of the metal age, to the period when man definitively wrenches himself away from the economy of land occupation and once and for all passes to the domination of nature, invents new forms of agriculture, architecture, mathematics, writing, trade, currency, law, new religions etc. In our view, the Asiatic mode of production originally meant not stagnation, but the greatest possible progress of the productive forces accomplished *on the basis* of the previous *communal* forms of production. This is amply confirmed in the works of the great archaeologists Childe[91] and Clark.[92]

If the Asiatic mode of production originally indicated a progressive step for the productive forces, what is the law of its evolution? We believe that it is the *law of the development of its internal contradictions*, just as in any other social formation. The internal contradiction of the Asiatic mode of production is that of the co-incidence of community structures and of class structures. The Asiatic mode of production would evolve by the development of its contradiction towards forms of class societies in which community-based (communal) relations have less and less reality because of the development of private property.

The Asiatic mode of production like any other social formation, would stand for stagnation only if it could not be left behind, when its contradictions fail to develop and its structure is petrified, leaving the society floundering in a state of relative stagnation. Although in each case the nature and the timing of a step forward would depend on specific circumstances, it would always mean the obliteration of the former modes of communal social organisation; failure to make this move would on the contrary mean maintaining them.

This permanence and the stagnation which accompanies it are all the more threatening to an 'Asiatic' society, based as it is on self-sustaining communities without any radical separation of agriculture and industry and, if the land is available, likely to allow for their demographic growth by splitting into daughter-communities which will perpetuate the same traditional forms of production and social life. It is this development which is described in Marx's famous text on Indian Communities which has become dogma for the proponents of the secular stagnation of Asia:

> The simplicity of the organisation for production in these self-sufficing communities that constantly reproduce themselves in the same form, and when accidentally destroyed, spring up again on the same spot and with the same name — this simplicity supplies the key to the secret of the unchangeableness of Asiatic societies, an unchangeableness in such striking contrast with the constant dissolution and refounding of Asiatic States, and the never-ceasing changes of dynasty. The structure of the economic elements of society remains untouched by the storm-clouds of the political sky.[93]

Moreover, insofar as the State's exploitation of the communities takes the form of a massive levy of revenue in kind, the structures of production can stabilise since there is no incentive to create a market. Because it is possible for the State to use peasant labour, the possibilities for the development of a market are limited and the transformation of the productive forces is slowed down. Besides, these forms of exploitation can be so intense that they hold back the development of production for a long time.[94]

Aside from this evolution of the Asiatic mode of production towards sinking and stagnation what forms can this development take when its internal contradiction is developed? — forms which lead to its fragmentation because of the emergence of private property. We think there are at least two possible forms of this disintegration.

One would lead to the slave mode of production *via* the ancient mode of production. That would be the path taken by the Graeco-Romans. It would lead to societies based on the combination of private property with commodity production. In this combination lies both the secret of the 'Greek miracle' and of the expansion of the

Roman empire;[95] it also explains the uniqueness of this line of development, the typical character of its class struggles between free men and of their exploitation of slave labour.

Aside from this well known path, we think that another one exists, one which would lead slowly, with the development of individual ownership, from certain forms of the Asiatic mode of production to certain forms of *feudalism, without going through a slave stage.* The appearance of individual ownership within the communities or of personal estates belonging to the aristocracy would transform the communities and, at the same time, the forms of their exploitation by this aristocracy. There is a slow transition from the collective exploitation of the communities to an individual exploitation of the peasants. This evolutionary process seems to be the most frequent and to correspond to the transition to a class society in China, Vietnam, Japan, India, Tibet . . . .[96]

While we cannot substantiate these hypotheses here, we can draw attention to the light they may throw on the development of the last centuries of Inca society. These hypotheses are in tune with Métraux's interpretation of the late development of private estates belonging to the emperor and his caste. The estates were settled by the Yana, people attached to the nobles and the notables of the kingdom by links of personal, and no longer collective, dependence:

> The increasingly important part played by the *yanas* under the empire is only to be explained on the grounds that their efficiency was superior to that obtained by the traditional system of forced labour. By depriving them of some of their members, the Inca weakened the communities and initiated a revolution which, had it continued, might well have changed the structure of the empire. It would have tended to become, instead of a grouping of largely autonomous rural collectives, a kind of 'pre-feudal empire' in which nobles and officials would have owned great estates worked by serfs or even slaves.[97]

This evolutionary path towards a certain form of feudalism is not only the most frequent but the simplest; unaccompanied by a great development of commodity production and currency, it does not break with the 'natural' forms of the economy and for a long time preserves the combination of agriculture and industry. Besides insofar as it remains necessary to control and organise major projects during this transition to private property, central authority plays an important part and the domination by the State and the monarch of the 'feudals' and peasants gives these 'feudalisms' a 'particular' shape where features of the Asiatic mode of production persist.[98] Because of this and other characteristics, extreme caution must be exercised in comparing these 'feudalisms' produced gradually by the Asiatic mode of production with the western form of feudalism born of the decomposition of the slavery mode of production. The main difference between them and the West is that they slowed down the development of *commodity production* and prevented the appearance and the triumph of industrial capitalism. The case of the Meiji revolution in Japan needs to be studied separately. However, it is undeniable that the industrial base, modern productive forces and methods of organisation were imported from the western capitalist countries and were not developed in the Japanese feudalism within which had appeared a certain form of commodity capitalism.[99]

Of the two forms of development of the Asiatic mode of production, one towards a slave system, the other towards certain forms of feudalism, it is the former which seems to us more and more unique and exceptional, and here we differ from the dogmatic conceptions of many writers. The western line of development, far from being universal because it is found everywhere, appears to be universal because it is found nowhere. The mistake of Marxists has usually been the desire to discover a slave mode of production everywhere and failing this, to create it in order to re-discover it. If this is so, why did Marx and Engels consider the western line of development to be 'typical' of the development of humanity? How are we to understand the universality of what now appears to be unique? Is it a remnant of the capitalist world's superiority over the rest of the world, a disguised form of racism, a pseudo-science? This final question brings us to our last hypothesis concerning what is understood by a 'dominant or typical' line of development of humanity.

(d) The forms of disintegration of the Asiatic mode of production and the 'typical' line of development of humanity

To recognise a 'typical' form of development implies a previous awareness of the 'general line' of this development and of *the nature of its movement as a whole.* Is it possible to grasp the general nature of the movement of history in retrospect?

Marx and Engels attempted to do this. We think that since their time no new knowledge has come to light which invalidates the essential point of their conclusions. The *general* movement of history has been the transition of the majority of peoples *from a classless social organisation to class societies.* That is the main point. This emergence requires the development of the inequality inherent in the appropriation of the means of production, and this inequality itself presupposes the disintegration of ancient communal solidarities based on cooperation through labour and living kinship relationships.

Thus, in retrospect, the movement of history appears as the indissoluble unity of the development of two contradictory elements of social reality; a) *the general development of means of dominating nature* and ensuring the survival of an ever-increasing species; b) the progressive breakup of communal solidarities and the *general development of inequalities* between individuals and groups.

Engels made this contradiction central to understanding the nature of 'civilisation':

> since the exploitation of one class by another is the basis of civilisation, *its whole development* moves in a *continuous contradiction.*[100]

Even though it is necessary to abandon the old categories of the nineteenth century Anglo-Saxon anthropology (the succession of the three stages: savagery, barbarism, civilisation) because of its vague and ambiguous nature and because of all its ideological implications, and to replace it with a division between classless and class societies, Engels correctly described the whole movement of transition from one to the other as the fundamental fact of history.

If this is the overall movement of history, then the 'typical' line of development of humanity is that through which the contradiction of the *maximum* development of the productive forces and of class inequalities and struggles is realised.

In recognising the typical line among the various lines of evolution of societies, the criteria consist in looking for the time and place in which the greatest progress of the productive forces took place. The answer is obvious and without mystery; it is the line of evolution which gave birth to *industrial capitalism*, the origin and basis of the most modern and efficient forms of production, of the transformation of nature. Industrial capitalism has appeared only in the line of evolution set in motion by the Greeks. The decisive character of this line of evolution is that it has ensured the maximum development of the productive forces, thus providing immense possibilities for the exploitation of man by man. This development cannot be explained by the appearance of private property alone. It existed in China, Vietnam, etc. In addition it is necessary for private property and commodity production to be combined.[101] Only this combination created the *most favourable* conditions for technical progress, while revealing itself to be incompatible with the functioning of the former solidarities of communal life; it substituted the search for private profit for the submission to common interest, by breaking off the often sacred collective link of the individual with the land of his ancestors.

It seems that this combination appeared for the first time in a pure form among the Greeks: 'Here lies the root of the entire revolution that followed.'[102]

The Romans took it up and generalised it, giving it its universal juridical expression with the theory of the '*jus utendi et abutendi*' which became the legal model in commodity societies based on private property.

The uniqueness of the line of development of the Graeco-Roman societies is becoming clearer. It consists *not* in having overcome certain forms of Asiatic mode of production, and having done it maybe earlier than other peoples, *but* in having overcome them in moving *towards* a mode of production based on the combination of private property with commodity production.

Similarly, what makes western feudalism unique, beyond its similarities of form with what are called the feudalisms of Turkish, Chinese, African, Japanese, etc., what prevents its confusion with them and the basis for their *essential difference*, is that *it alone* created the conditions for the appearance of industrial production and world trade. It alone has allowed the forms of natural economy to be surpassed.

Finally by allowing and imposing the creation of a world market, industrial capitalism has made a universal history possible by subsuming all the less developed societies under its development, which is that of the western capitalist societies.

Moreover, industrial capitalism alone has opened up the possibility of socialism, first in theory, then in practice.

Thus, the western line of development is typical because it is unique in developing the greatest progress of the productive forces and the purest forms of class struggles and also because *it alone has created the pre-conditions for western and all other societies to pass beyond the* class organisation of society.

So it is typical because in its particular development it has obtained a *universal result*. It has provided the practical base (industrial economy) and the theoretical conception (socialism) to extricate itself and all societies from the older and newer forms of exploitation of man by man. It provides the whole of humanity with the conditions for the solving of a universal problem posed since the appearance of classes: how to ensure the maximum development of the productive forces without the exploitation of man by man? It is typical because it has value as a 'model' or 'norm' because it *provides possibilities* which no other single history has offered and gives other societies the possibility of *saving themselves the intermediary stages.*[103]

This perspective provides Engels' remarks in *Anti-Dühring* with their full import:

> But if . . . division into classes has a certain historical justification, it has this only for a given period, only under given social conditions. It was based upon the insufficiency of production. It will be swept away by the complete development of modern productive forces. And, in fact, the abolition of classes in society presupposes a degree of historical evolution at which the existence, not simply of this or that particular ruling class, but of any ruling class at all, and, therefore, the existence of class distinction itself has become an obsolete anachronism. It presupposes, therefore, the development of production carried out to a degree at which appropriation of the means of production and of the products, and, with this, of political domination, of the monopoly of culture, and of intellectual leadership by a particular class of society, has become not only superfluous but economically, politically, intellectually a hindrance to development. This point is now reached.[104]

The true *universality* of the western line of development lies *in* its *specificity* and not outside it, in its difference from not in its resemblance to other lines of development. The unity of universality and of singularity is a contradiction but this contradiction is in life not in thought. When the unity of this contradiction is not recognised, we can take one of two equally futile paths:

(1) a multitude of societies survive and evolve side by side, each locked in its historical singularity by the intransigent scholar. Nothing is comparable with anything else and history remains a mosaic of bits deprived of global coherence;

(2) on the other hand, one can try to see the same process everywhere with the singularities erased and then history becomes the more or less successful application of universal forms to which it is necessarily subject. In fact, these forms which are *sought* everywhere are nothing more than those of the western line of evolution which *must be* sought everywhere since the possibility of many lines of evolution has already been denied.

The typical character of this line of development then finds its root, not in itself, in its own specificity, but in a necessity external to history. But, as we know, the opposite of an external necessity is an internal finality. Within such a perspective, history was a future without surprises, a reality created in advance through which humanity, from its very first entry into primitive communism *was bound to* emerge one day into true communism. This second path was chosen by many Marxists especially after Stalin's treatise on the laws of historical development in *Dialectical and Historical Materialism*, in which primitive communism, slavery, feudalism, capitalism and socialism necessarily follow each other.

Marx, however, had already warned against this error in the *Contribution to the Critique of Political Economy*,[105] where he specified that:

> What is called historical evolution depends in general on the fact that the latest form regards earlier ones as stages in the development of itself and conceives them always in a one-sided manner, since only rarely and under quite special conditions is a society able to adopt a critical attitude towards itself.[106]

From this point of view, socialism appears to be a modern mode of production, just as incompatible with the former pre-capitalist modes of production as capitalism itself and perhaps even more incompatible since capitalism could make use of the old relations of exploitation within the countries it dominated, whereas socialism cannot do this.

Having begun by looking for a lost and even rejected Marxist concept, we have tried to reconstruct it through Marx's and Engels' texts without prejudging its scientific value. Once reconstructed, it was still necessary to find out why it had been lost. Our search led us to discover unmysterious reasons: the relationship between Morgan and Engels, and the state of the most advanced archaeological, linguistic and anthropological knowledge of the second half of the nineteenth century. Pushed into the background by Engels' brilliant analysis, the concept faded away, reappeared to some extent towards 1927-1930 after the failure of the Chinese revolution, then was totally rejected until the night when the renegade Wittfogel dug it up to turn it into a war machine against socialism. At the same time, amputated of the Asiatic mode of production, deprived of the hypothesis of plural forms of transition and evolution towards class society, Marx's model of the evolution of societies ceased to be an open system of hypotheses to be verified and became a closed system of dogmas to be blindly accepted.

Historical materialism cleansed itself of its scientific substance from within and stood like a new philosophy of history, an ideal world in which the philosopher contemplated the historical necessity which moved humanity from primitive communism to true communism. On a practical level, the divorce between anthropology and history, between western and non-western history seemed increasingly definitive. By a strange paradox, innumerable facts have emerged to press scholars to revive a dead concept. If this concept indicates a social formation corresponding to the contradiction of certain forms of transition from classless to class society then perhaps we have rediscovered a historical reality which demands and forms the basis for the collaboration of the anthropologist and the historian (or the archaeologist). In order to understand the specific contradiction of the Asiatic mode of production, it is necessary to be simultaneously an anthropologist to analyse the community structures and a historian to account for the embryo of exploiting classes. The disjointed bits of historical and anthropological knowledge could be reconstructed around this contradictory reality to form a unified whole of anthropological knowledge.

We think that with its revival the Asiatic mode of production has mortally wounded old superseded statements, theoretical corpses which crumbled at the slightest shock, since they were always only pretending to be alive: like the existence of a universal stage of slavery, the impossibility of by-passing stages. But this resurrection is and must be more than a return to Marx since it would then be a return to a superseded stage of historical science. We have attempted, therefore, to put the concept back into working order so that it would become capable of dealing with the problems posed by the comparative archaeology, anthropology and history of today. We have suggested a structural definition of the Asiatic mode of production, assumed a relationship between the structure and certain situations of transition to class society and, at the abstract level, grasped the theoretical possibility of a wider field of application than Marx had been able to predict for the concept. But to move forward it may be necessary to abandon the geographical adjective 'Asiatic', to define rigorously the old word 'despotism' and to search cautiously for 'major projects' and 'bureaucracies'.

It may be necessary to consider stagnation as a possible, but not the only form of evolution of the Asiatic mode of production and to imagine many possible forms of its disintegration whose motive forces should be looked for. We have suggested the hypothesis of an evolution of the Asiatic mode of production towards certain forms of feudalism and considered this path to be a more frequent form of transition to a true class society than the western one. The latter increasingly appears to be simultaneously unique and universal, to have developed to their highest point the characteristic features of a class society, the domination of man over nature and the domination of man by man. Thus, in the final analysis, we think that it is not only the concept of Asiatic mode of production which must be put back into working condition, but the very notion of historical necessity, of historical law. Unless this is done the works of historians will set off blindly, threatened tomorrow with yesterday's fate and, at another level, social practice will develop without knowing where it came from, where it can go or how to get there.

Of course, the analyses and hypotheses we have suggested will be disputed or confirmed by a wider discussion. To accept them without proof would be to abandon the name while retaining the spirit of dogmatism. On the contrary, to look for an Asiatic mode of production in such and such a history, without having previously posed the problems of the theoretical status of this concept is to be nothing but a well-meaning positivist. We therefore suggest research in the following directions:

1. Is it possible to reconstitute the different processes through which inequality is introduced in classless societies and leads to the formation of a ruling class (this question is asked of historians and anthropologists)?
2. Is it possible to draw up a typology of the different forms of Asiatic mode of production with or without major projects or agriculture, etc. and deal with the problem of a typology of the forms of communities by analysing the forms of appropriation of land, the origin and nature of aristocratic and royal powers, etc.?
3. Is it possible to describe different forms of development of the Asiatic mode of production towards class societies?
4. What is the process which introduced a commodity economy among the Greeks and the Romans? How is it possible simultaneously to take the 'Greek miracle' seriously and to de-idealise it?
5. What is the relationship between the concepts of Asiatic mode of production and of military democracy?

These studies will demand the creation of a rigorous language and perhaps the rapid adoption of less loaded, more precise terminology in place of the expression 'Asiatic mode of production'.[107]

NOTES

1. Petr. Skalnik and Timoteus Pokora, 'Beginning of the discussion about the Asiatic mode of production in the USSR and the People's Republic of China', *Eirene*, volume 5, Prague, 1966, pp. 179–87.
2. *Anti-Dühring*, pp. 214–6.
3. See Lévi-Strauss, *The Raw and the Cooked*, Jonathan Cape, London 1970
4. On this point see *Rationality and Irrationality in Economics*, pp. 99–103 and 'Système, structure et contradiction dans *Le Capital*'.
5. Letter from Marx to Joseph Weydemeyer, 5 March 1852.
6. There were many general models of the evolution of humanity constructed before Marx by Ferguson, Adam Smith, etc. See I. Sellnow, *Grundprinzipien*

einer Periodisierung der Urgeschichte and Ch. Parain's commentary in *La Pensée*, number 102, April 1962.

7. J. Suret-Canale, *Afrique noire*, Volume 1, p. 101 [my translation–*HL*].

8. A. Métraux, *The Incas*, Studio Vista, London, 1965, p. 24–5.

9. *Capital*, volume 2, p. 425.

10. *ibid.*, volume 3, p. 143 [emphasis added].

11. Engels, 'Marx's Contribution to the Critique of Political Economy', *Das Volk*, 20 August 1859. On these problems see: Boccara, 'Quelques hypothèses sur le développement du capital', *Economie et Politique*, numbers 79–82; Ilienkov, 'La dialectique de l'abstrait et du concret dans *Le Capital* de Marx', *Recherches internationales*, number 34, 1962; Godelier, 'La methode du *Capital*', *Economie et Politique*, numbers 70, 71 and 80.

12. *The German Ideology*, pp. 38–9.

13. In the correspondence between Marx and Engels, May/June/July 1853 and in Marx's articles on India in the *New York Daily Tribune*, June/July/August, 1853.

14. See Marx's letter to Engels, 14 June 1853. Marx quotes parliamentary reports and Sir Stamford Raffles' *History of Java*.

15. Francois Bernier's narrative on the Great Moghul kingdom, quoted by Marx in his letter of 2 June 1852 to Engels and by Engels in his letter of 6 June.

16. The manuscript's subtitle is *Über der Prozess, der der Bildung des Kapital Verhältnisses oder der ursprünglichen Akkumulation vorhergeht.*
    See *Capital*, volume 1, chapters 16–23.

17. F. Tökei, *Sur le mode de production asiatique*, C.E.R.M. conference, Paris, June 1962.

18. *The Origin of the Family*, p. 156; see also Engels' letter to Marx, 8 December 1882.

19. *The Origin of the Family*.

20. *Pre-Capitalist Economic Formations*, p. 70 [emphasis added].

21. The classic description of the community living in self-sustaining economy is found in the famous passage on Indian communities in *Capital*, volume 1, pp. 357–8.

22. *Anti-Dühring*, pp. 214–5; see also *Capital*, volume 3,

23. Letter from Engels to Marx, 6 June 1853:
    > Artificial irrigation is here (in the great stretches which extend from the Sahara up to the highest Asian plateau) the first condition of agriculture and this is a matter either for the communities, the provinces or the central government, [my translation–*HL*]

    See also *Anti-Dühring*, p. 215:
    > However great the number of despotisms which rose and fell in Persia and India, each was fully aware that above all it was the entrepreneur responsible for the collective maintenance of irrigation throughout the river valleys, without which no agriculture was possible there.

24. *Pre-Capitalist Economic Formations*, p. 69.

25. Chesneaux tells us that this diagram is reminiscent of the ancient Chinese character *Wang* meaning 'king' (*Vuong* is Vietnamese) and about which he wrote in *Le Vietnam*, p. 99:
    > The character *Vuong* in its simplicity, is already a reflection of the social relations which the pupils must absorb studiously: it is made up of three horizontal parallel strokes of which the first is meant to represent the sky, the centre one — the shortest — man, and the lower one, earth; a vertical stroke linking the sky and the earth pierces through man and forces him to accept his condition; this stroke is written from top to bottom because man must obey the

will of the sky and earth receives his labour; only the king's power is great enough to encompass the system of the world.

26. *Pre-Capitalist Economic Formations*, p. 70. For the analysis of the relationship between religious and political representations and the social organisation of ancient societies see H. Frankfort, *Kinship and the Gods*, 1948, *Before Philosophy*, 1946, chapter 3, 'The Formation of the State' and J. P. Vernant, *Les origines de la pensée grecque*, chapter 7 and P. Derchain, *Le pouvoir et le sacré*, Brussels, 1962.

27. *Capital*, volume 3, p. 330, concerning the merchant peoples of antiquity; see Rovere's chapter in K. Polanyi *et al.*, *Trade and Market in the Early Empires*, The Free Press, Glencoe, 1967.

28. Garelli, 'Etudes des établissements assyriens en Cappadoce', *Annales*, 1961.

29. E. Welskopf, *Probleme der Periodisierung des Altengeschichte*, pp. 296–391.

30. 'General slavery of the Orient', *Pre-Capitalist Economic Formations*, p. 95.

31. *Ibid.*, p. 91–2.

32. *Ibid.*, p. 76.

33. See Ch. Parain, 'La lutte des classes dans l'antiquité classique', *La Pensée*, number 108, 1963.

34. Letter from Engels to Marx, 22 November 1882 and *The Origin of the Family*.

35. 'Communal accessory', *Pre-Capitalist Economic Formations*, p. 80.

36. See Marx's letter to Vera Zasulich (second draft) March 1881: 'Cultivable land is privately owned by the cultivators, while forests and pastures remain undivided for common use.' See *The Origin of the Family*, p. 273.

37. *Ibid.*, pp. 275–6.

38. See Ch. Parain, 'Seigneurie et féodalité', *La Pensée*, number 96, 1961.

39. *Capital*, volume 1, pp. 717–8n. 2: 'The serf was not only the owner, if but a tribute-paying owner, of the piece of land attached to his house, but also co-possessor of the common land.'

40. See A. Soboul, 'La communauté rurale francaise', *La Pensée*, number 73, 1957.

41. *Capital*, volume 1, pp. 714–5.

42. This is precisely what Engels asserts in *Anti-Dühring*, pp. 214 and 216.

43. Letter from Engels to Marx, 6 June 1853.

44. Letter from Marx to Engels, 14 June 1853. Article by Marx on India, 25 June 1852; *Capital*, Volume 1, pp. 333–4, 366, 512–5; volume 3, pp. 330 and 384.

45. Letter from Marx to Engels, 14 June 1853; *Capital*, volume 1, pp. 357–8.

46. *The Origin of the Family*, p. 169.

47. *Marx Engels Werke*, Berlin, 1972, volume 19, p. 475 [the following is a loose translation from the French–*HL*]:

    The form of State power is, in turn, conditioned by the form which is, at that time, that of the communities. Where — as among the Aryan peoples of Asia and the Russians — it emerges at a period when the commune still cultivates the land communally, or at least allocates it only temporarily to different families, where consequently, no private ownership of land has developed, then State power appears in the form of despotism.

48. *The Origin of the Family*, pp. 204–5.

49. *Ibid.*, pp. 293–4.

50. *Ibid.*, p. 288.

51. *Ibid.*, p. 257 (Asia), p. 271 (the Orient).

52. See L. Morgan, *Ancient Society*, Oxford University Press, London, 1964, pp. 287–8, concerning the Etruscans and the Romans.

53. *The Origin of the Family*, p. 220. Marx had also accepted this hypothesis.

54. *Ibid.*, p. 221.

55. *Ibid.*, p. 171.

56. Morgan, *op. cit.*, p. 220.

57. Engels quoting Marx (*Marx Engels Archive*, volume 9, pp. 144–5), *The Origin of the Family*, p. 238.

58. *Ibid.*, p. 238n. See Morgan, *op. cit.*, chapter 7, p. 193. The lack of serious discussion on the concept of 'military democracy', its origins and nature considerably limits the scope of Marxist works which use this concept; see J. Varloot, 'La societe homèrique, la famille patriarcale, l'origine de la propriété privée'; M. Rodinson, 'Sur le concept de democratie militaire', *La Pensée*, number 66, 1956. The best study to be found in Sereni, *Communita rurali nell Italia antica*, chapter 9.

59. Morgan, *op. cit.*: 'The kingdom of Mexico . . . is a fiction of the imagination', p. 193.

60. *Ibid.*, p. 254.

61. P. Vidal-Naquet, 'Homère et le mode mycenien', *Annales*, number 4, 1963.

62. See Willets, 'Early Crete and Early Greek', *Marxism Today*, December 1962 and Hutchinson's bibliography, *Prehistoric Crete*, 1962, pp. 355–68.

63. Vernant, *op. cit.*, p. 25.

64. *Ibid.*, p. 2 [my translation–*HL*].

65. *The Origin of the Family*, p. 282; 'The next step brings us to the upper stage of barbarism, the period in which all civilised peoples pass through their Heroic Age; it is the period of the iron sword, but also of the iron ploughshare and axe'.

66. *Ibid.*, p. 288 [emphasis added].

67. K. Wittfogel, *Oriental Despotism: A Comparative Study of Total Power*, Yale University Press, New Haven and London, 1957, p. 411: 'The managerial bureaucratic implications of the Asiatic concept soon embarrassed its new adherent, Marx . . . increasingly disturbed his friend, Engels.'

68. Morgan, *op. cit.*, p. 222: 'When Grecian society came for the first time under historical observation about the first Olympiad (776 BC) and down to the legislation of Clisthenes (509 BC)'; Engels on early Rome, in *The Origin of the Family*, p. 255:

> In view of the utter darkness that enshrouds the whole legendary origin of Rome's historical beginning . . . it is impossible to make any definite statements about the time, the course and causes of the revolution that put an end to the old gentile constitution.

69. Piganiol, 'Les Etrusques, peuple d'orient', *Cahiers d'Histoire mondiale*, volume 1 part 2, 1953.

70. *Capital*, volume 1, p. 334.

71. See P. Vidal-Naquet's important preface to the French translation of *Oriental Despotism*.

72. G. Plekhanov, *Fundamental Problems of Marxism*, (*Questions fondamentales du Marxisme*, Editions Sociales, Paris 1950, pp. 52–4). To our knowledge, there is no text to support Plekhanov's interpretation of Marx's abandoning the concept of the Asiatic mode of production.

73. This was the subject of the famous discussion of Leningrad: 'Diskussia o aziatskom sposobe proisvodstva', 1931.

74. M. Shapiro in *Marxism Today*, August 1962, pp. 282–4.

75. See the discussion in T. Pokora, 'Existierte in China eine Sklavenhaltergesellschaft?'

76. Kosambi, 'On a Marxist Approach to Indian Chronology', *Annals of Bhandarkar Oriental Research Institute*, 1951. By the same author: 'The Basis of Ancient Indian History', *Journal of the American Oriental Society*, 1 and 4, 1955. See also Bedekar's critique of Dange in *Marxism Today*, July 1951. 51.

77. Kuo Mo Jo, 'Conference 1950', *Recherches Internationales*, pp. 31–2.

78. P. 20 [my translation from the French–*HL*]. See *Histoire de l'antiquité*, Moscow, 1962, p. 266: 'It has been firmly established that Chinese society has developed from the communal regime to feudalism, by going through a form of exploitation based on the exploitation of slaves' [HL's translation]. The opposite is asserted on p. 270.

79. B. Tait in *Marxism Today*, October 1961.

80. Ex. Potekhine, 'On Feudalism of the Ashanti', XXV International Congress of Orientalists, Moscow, 1960.

81. Marc Bloch, *Feudal Society*, Routledge and Kegan Paul, London, 1962, volume 1 pp. 56 and 227; volume 2, pp. 383, 446–7.

82. *Capital*, volume 1, p. 717–8.

83. Emery, *Archaic Egypt*, Pelican, London, 1961, 'The Unification', pp. 38–104.

84. See Venturi, 'L'histoire du concept de "Despotisme Oriental" en Europe', *Journal of the History of Ideas*, number 1, 1963.

85. See Sereni, *op. cit.*

86. See Suret-Canale, *op. cit.*, p. 112: 'The emergence of the State accompanies that of the aristocracy which is its instrument and its main beneficiary' [my translation–*HL*].

87. See G. Condominas, *Fokon'olona et collectivites rurales en Imerina*, ed. Berger-Levrault, Paris 1960, p. 29, concerning land-ownership: 'The great king merely transfers onto the sovereign the ultimate right previously shared between the many fokon'dona which composed the country.' [my translation–*HL*].

88. P. Boiteau, *Contribution à l'histoire de la nation malgache*. Editions sociales, Paris, 1958.

89. See Vladimirtsov, *La féodalité mongole*, 1948. Comments by Belenitsky, 'Les Mongoles et l'Asie centrale', *Cahiers d'histoire mondiale*, number 3, 1960, and J. Harmatta's study, 'Hun Society in the Age of Attila' *Acta Archeologica Ac. S. Mong.*, 1952.

90. See Maquet's objections to Wittfogel, 'Une hypothèse pour l'étude des féodalités africaines', *Cahiers d'etudes Africaines*, number 6, 1961.

91. Mainly in *Social Evolution*, Fontana, London, 1950, where Childe was trying to complete Morgan's model by integrating the great Oriental civilisations of the Bronze Age to it.

92. *World Prehistory*: see our account in *La Pensée*, number 7, 1963.

93. *Capital*, volume 1, p. 358.

94. *Ibid.*, volume 3, p. 796.

95. *The Origin of the Family*, p. 285.

96. A. Stein, *La civilisation tibétaine*, 1962, pp. 97–103.

97. Métraux, *op. cit.*, p. 100.

98. See L. Simonovskaia, 'Deux tendances dans la société féodale de la Chine de la Basse Epoque', International Congress of Orientalists, Moscow, 1960.

99. Among a great wealth of documentation see the works of the Japanese Marxist, Takahashi, 'La place de la révolution du Meiji dans l'histoire agraire de Japon', *Revue historique*, December 1953; 'The Transition from Feudalism to Capitalism', *Science and Society*, number 4, 1952.

100. *The Origin of the Family*, p. 295 (our emphasis). There is therefore no possible misunderstanding on the use of the term 'civilisation' by Engels. It does not indicate a hidden racism or the badly disguised confession of a 'moral' or intellectual superiority. And this attitude is shared by many anthropologists who have lived with so-called 'savages' or 'barbarians'.

101. It is the fact of commodity production which provides the key to the scientific study of capitalism, the final stage in the development of western societies. This was emphasised by Marx in the opening words of *Capital* (1867), repeating those

of the *Contribution* (1859): 'The wealth of those societies in which the capitalist mode of production prevails, presents itself as "an immense accumulation of commodities", its unit being a single commodity. Our investigation must therefore begin with the analysis of a commodity.' *Capital*, volume 1, p. 35.

102. *The Origin of the Family*, p. 242.

103. It is in this light that Marx's famous letter to Vera Zasulich, 8 March 1881, is to be understood. 'But does this mean that the historic career of the agricultural community must inevitably lead to this result? Certainly not. The dualism within it permits of an alternative: either the property element in it will overcome the collective element, or the other way round. Everything depends on the historical environment in which it is found. . . . These two solutions are *a priori* possible, but of course, they both require very different historical environments.' In the second version of this letter, Marx is more specific concerning historical environment: 'its historical environment, the existence of capitalist production, provides it with the ready-made material conditions for cooperative labour organised on a vast scale. It can thus incorporate the positive points elaborated by the capitalist system without going through it. . . . It can gradually supplant plot agriculture by industrial agriculture thanks to machines. After having first achieved normality in its present form, it can become the immediate starting point for the economic system towards which modern society is directed, and change thoroughly without beginning by committing suicide. . .' [Translator's note: most of this is my translation from the French.] See Marx's and Engels' preface to the 2nd Russian translation of the *Manifesto*.

104. Engels, 1969, *op. cit.*, p. 334. Our emphasis.

105. See Godelier, 'Economie Politique et philosophie' *La Pensée*, October 1963.

106. K. Marx, *Contribution . . . op. cit.*, p. 211. (Our emphasis-*MG*].

107. We would like to mention A. Caso's important article, 'Land tenure among the Ancient Mexicans', *American Anthropologist*, vol. 65, no. 4, August pp. 862–78 on land ownership among the Aztecs. We read this text after having written our analysis of the Morgan-Engels relationship and it appears strikingly to confirm our analysis. According to the author, Aztec society combined the features of a communal society, tribal with communal land ownership and those of a class society dominated by an aristocracy holding religious, political and military power and controlling the state (p. 875). The king owned lands 'not as an individual, but as a functionary' (p. 868). The clergy and the military were kept by tributes and forced labour, levied on communities of free men. Apart from this state ownership, the nobility and the king owned private demesnes exploited by 'serfs attached to the domain' (p. 870). The existence of such social inequalities and of an aristocratic private property may, according to the author, be understood 'as long as we do not try to do so in terms of Iroquois organisation or Roman property' (p. 874). He concludes: 'it astonishes us that such false conclusions could have been arrived at as those of Morgan (1878) and Bandelier (1880) which were in vogue during the first quarter of this century' (p. 863).

Let us mention Gibson's two articles on 'La transformation des communautés indiennes en Nouvelle Espagne de 1500 à 1820', *Cahiers d'Histoire mondiale*, no. 3, 1955, and particularly 'The Aztec Aristocracy in Colonial Mexico', *Comparative Studies in Society and History*, vol. II, no. 2, January 1960, pp. 169–97 in which the author criticises (p. 171 para. 5) Bandelier's conclusions, concerning the Aztecs in *On the social organisation and mode of government of the Ancient Mexicans*, Cambridge, March 1880; Bandelier is a follower of Morgan's; and F. Katz's *Die Sozialökonomische Verhältnisse bei den Azteken im 15 und 16 Jahrhundert*, chapter 3 and 10, Berlin, 1956.

PART TWO

Fieldwork in Africa

Research on an African Mode of Production

Catherine Coquery-Vidrovitch

The discussion of the 'Asiatic' mode of production, to which Godelier's essay made an important contribution, was initiated in France by Jean Suret-Canale. One of his major pieces of work in this regard was the discussion of the possibility of applying the model usefully to the societies of Black Africa. In this essay Coquery-Vidrovitch draws upon the work of Suret-Canale to explore the relevance of the concept of the Asiatic mode of production in the analysis of social formations of Africa and suggests the model of an 'African' mode of production similar in certain respects to the Asiatic mode and yet distinctive, incorporating lineage society and yet distinct from it as a model. In a sense her essay bridges the first five 'general' essays and the last five 'specific' studies, leading from the formulation of the distinction between the Asiatic mode of production, sensu stricto, and 'another form of Asiatic mode of production . . . in which a minority dominates and exploits the communities, intervening in their conditions of production not directly but indirectly, by appropriating surplus labour or produce as profit' (p. 242 of this volume), to a discussion of the specific historical conditions in Black Africa over the last thousand years. As an attempt to bring together the somewhat divergent work of Meillassoux and Godelier in a specific context and to subject to analysis new data derived from historical researches, Coquery-Vidrovitch's discussion represents a provocative contribution to the elaboration of Marxist models of social evolution. Among other things, it raises the problem of the inherent difference between 'progressive' and 'stagnant' modes of production, and demonstrates the importance of overcoming the limits imposed by the tribal or ethnic framework which tends to confine the more detailed 'specific' studies of lineage societies (e.g. studies of the Guro, Wogo, Alladian, Soninke, etc.).

INTRODUCTION

Within the static perspective strongly influenced by ethnographic works of the first half of the twentieth century, the permanence of 'traditional' African societies (which, when they are not immutable, at least live in the long run at the rhythm of a village self-sustaining economy regulated by slowly elaborated and more or less frozen customary rituals) has long been contrasted with the evolution of western societies which obey the laws of market economies, are more 'developed' and thus are implicitly taken as model and goal because of the impetus of European penetration.

The schematic nature of this model has given birth to a series of platitudes whose banality is equalled only by their inaccuracy. It remains, however, so alive in western thought that a number of problems must still be solved: to what extent is it legitimate to discuss a 'traditional' pre-colonial world? How, in particular, is the technological backwardness of African societies to be explained? And what are we to make of the concepts 'lineage', 'tributary', or even 'Asiatic' mode of production which have been developed with regard to these societies which are apparently reluctant to participate in the contemporary world economy?

Today the people most often accused of ethnocentrism are perhaps those economists who — whatever their ideological position — tend to consider the laws of capitalist development to be absolute and who present the privileged historical experience of England and Western Europe as universal.[1] One example is Bailoch's[2] otherwise fruitful analysis in which he tries to explain the contemporary backwardness of the underdeveloped countries through the history of western development in the nineteenth and twentieth centuries. He attributes the driving force to increased agricultural productivity, but suggests, on the other hand, that demographic pressure results in slow progression or even in the decrease of this production per inhabitant of the Third World. Is it therefore necessary to condemn the latter without appeal? Reference to the western scheme of development, taken as the norm — this has already been denounced by Lévi-Strauss — gives rise to the danger of considering almost all the characteristics unique to under-developed countries as so many obstacles. Would it not be more sensible to elaborate a new force of development, specifically applicable to contemporary history, such as, for example, the potential of the enormous demographic masses which today are underemployed?

Similarly the rigidly maintained schema, according to which

Marxists of the thirties wanted to insert the socio-economic formations of the Third World into one of the three 'classic' stages of development studied in western Europe (slavery, feudalism or capitalism) has turned out to be unworkable. Just because Marx and Engels sketched out the definition of another mode of production, the 'Asiatic mode of production', a concept devised for the analysis of Middle Eastern and Southeast Asian societies, was it necessary to extend its use to the newly discovered African world without any adjustment of the kind attempted by Jean Suret-Canale? He rediscovers the Asiatic mode of production in pre-colonial Black Africa at the culmination of a three-stage development: from the 'primitive community' to the intermediary 'tribo-patriarchal' structures of the so-called 'anarchic' or 'Stateless' segmentary societies in which the fundamental unit is the extended family (the 'lineage'), ending with a well-differentiated class society in which, above the village patriarchy, there emerges a privileged aristocracy which determined the formation of the State.[3]

In its general conception this schema appears acceptable. But, as it stands, it is inadequate, since the structure and development of African 'pre-colonial' societies was unique — in the first place fundamentally different from that of our western societies. The main level of analysis of African backwardness is obviously socio-economic organisation. It also remains to be ascertained whether we ought to look at the level of exchange as scholars have tended to do until now, or at that of production, the prime object of Marxist analysis.

In this respect Meillassoux's theoretical essay on the village self-sustaining community, innovatory in many ways, makes the transition from previous works of the French school, for it is a study of exchange, which is the most visible phenomenon, the immediate manifestation of the life of relationships. But he looks at exchange because it reflects the internal organisation of the society, is the result of the organisation of production and not its cause. He explains the absence of *exchange*, in the economic sense of the word, between members of the lineage community within the spheres of 'reciprocity' and 'redistribution', by the importance of kinship links and the situation of dependence of the producing individuals (the 'juniors') within the family community ruled by the 'seniors'. The transfer of objects is made according to a system of prestations and counter-prestations whose modalities are linked to the social situation of the protagonists: reciprocal gifts at the level of the seniors; real prestations from juniors to seniors, redistribution from seniors to juniors. To give is to manifest one's superiority, to accept without returning is to subordinate oneself. This model based on Guro pre-colonial society in the Ivory Coast, suggests a relatively exceptional degree of economic insularity for Black Africa, even for lineage societies, i.e. societies in which political power is merged with the organisation of the family community.[4]

Moreover, even if it means taking the risk of falling back on the previously rejected schema of 'traditional society' condemned to stagnation since it is assumed to be incapable of reproducing itself except in an identical form, it is important to clarify what process a 'despot', a privileged group, or even a social class was able to use, on various occasions and more or less everywhere on the continent, to make the system change for its own benefit by imposing its political and economic hold on a relatively unconcerned peasant mass.

When these societies are no longer looked at at the level of institutionalised exchanges but at that of production, it is noticeable that they are generally defined by a predominantly agricultural production and characterised by a little developed technology and a weak level of specialisation and exchange, within a community organisation which, among other things, knows no private appropriation of land.

1. Technological Backwardness

To account for the socio-economic specificity of Africa certain writers have stressed, among the criteria mentioned, the low technological level.[5] Indeed, backwardness in this respect, which is indisputable and remained so until very recently, continues to intrigue historians. It is known that until the twentieth century the African peasant used a very small number of even elementary implements — the basic tool remains the hoe and in Casamance (southern Senegal) rice is still picked by hand.

In reality, it seems that this type of speculation is a bad start; it reduces technology to being the driving force of the stagnation/development alternative. But the weak level of the productive forces, though it is the most obvious sign of stagnation, is not necessarily its cause. In Black Africa there has always been a potential agricultural surplus. The reason why it was not exploited was perhaps less the determinism of the natural environment or the ignorance of men, than it was an economic choice resulting from all the social components. When they were adopted, technological improvements were, at best, used by each family not to produce three times more but to work three times less for the same result: has productivity not remained low because of the structure of demand and the absence of division of labour and specialisation, i.e. because the organisation of society in its totality did not lend itself to the extended reproduction of the system? Without, however, neglecting the significance of the intervention of external elements (Arab or European impact) it is important first to look at the role of those internal factors which contribute to throw light on the extraordinary capacity of a relatively balanced society to resist innovations.

It is at this level that the Marxist concept 'mode of production' becomes operative, since it allows me to decompose the examination of the socio-economic system into two stages, through an analysis of the *productive forces* (resources, labour power, and technological level) and of the *social relations of production*, that is, the relations existing between those who produce and those who control the means of production (appropriation of land, relations between seniors and juniors, patrons and clients, masters and slaves, and so on). We must emphasise that the concept 'mode of production' is to be understood as a theoretical model; at the concrete level societies do not produce it in this schematic form. Their organisation reflects a complex ordering of production, in which a whole series of various factors inherited from the history of the group under consideration can interfere, revealing the sometimes contradictory influence that it has been subject to as well as the original institutions which these influences have brought about. At most a 'dominant mode of production' can be defined within a given economic totality which can include characteristics ascribable to another mode of production. Thus we shall attempt to define an 'African mode of production' which does not, in itself, exclude some of the fundamental features of the 'Asiatic mode of production', nor does it deny that some important elements may resemble the slave or feudal type.

2. The Self-Sustaining Village Economy or 'The Tributary Mode of Production'

Since, by definition, in agricultural civilisation land is the dominant element of the economy, the American economist Stephen Hymer discovers precisely in that — in the egalitarian nature of the land tenure system — the key to the relative stability of the system.[6]

In its ideal form this system would define an economy in which all members, linked by blood, language and customs would participate in organised production, distributed within the family according to the principle of reciprocity and redistribution but excluding paid labour, without it being possible to separate economic laws from political and social institutions. This egalitarian form of land organisation is supposed to have thwarted economic progress precisely because, by preventing the separation of the producer from his means of production (the land), it was an obstacle to the concentration of wealth and power and thus to differentiation into social classes which confirms the social division of labour.

On the contrary, a dominant aristocracy, usually warriors since they are capable of appropriating land forcibly in order to make sure they receive most of its revenue, is supposed to have encouraged the development of a craft sector in its service, by using the surplus taken from the land for the purchase of food and other consumption goods (jewellery, materials, etc.) and to have given a more solid base to the agricultural sector expected from that point to feed the whole population, by putting aside a part of its revenue to be used to intensify production (roads, irrigation systems and other works of infrastructure). Thus a whole series of technological innovations are said to have been encouraged which, in their turn, were liable to accelerate the division of labour and to favour, right from the start, the maturation of a 'civilisation' in the western sense of the word, comparable to those of India, China, Egypt or the Middle East — what Marxists call the 'Asiatic mode of production'.

3. Long Distance Trade

This situation sometimes occurred in Black Africa, but it was never based on the agricultural sector. Parallel to subsistence agriculture there developed activities associated with warfare and trading; activities which, at all times, were the basis for the prosperity of vast political entities, from the mediæval Sudanese empires to the kingdoms of Zimbabwe (the 'Monomotapa' of the Portuguese explorers) to modern formations of which there are numerous examples: the Luanda empire, the kingdoms of Kongo and Dahomey, Buganda, the Mossi states, the Hausa principalities, the court chiefships of the Congo river or basin, the Zulu kingdom. Starting with this general observation we have attempted to define an 'African mode of production' characterised by the permanent contradiction between the community and its negation by the State.[7] The particularity of Africa appears to be based on the combination of patriarchal agricultural economy with a low internal surplus at the village level and of the great international, even intercontinental, trade at the State level.

4. The Determining Role of the External Impact

In this way an essential element of African stagnation is made clear: its evolution was conditioned by that of a socio-economic organisation based on a 'dualist' type of structure involving subsistence production and large-scale trade. To go beyond these facts would have implied that the hold which the aristocracy had over the rest of the population, until then indirect (revealed mainly by the exclusive enjoyment of foreign goods), would become direct. But, in such peasant societies, a direct hold would necessitate control over the main means of production — the land. This would, of course, have brought about the disappearance of the community economy.

In fact it is difficult to understand why this step did not take place from the moment when the formation of the State began. Indeed the social organisation was a handicap but, whatever its importance may have been, it should not be turned into a fatal disability: is not the history of all civilisations that of the progressive or violent transformations of its own structures? Even if power was exercised more over men than over land, through control over women and slaves, over guns and horses, it was capable of bringing the peasant communities together around a centralised State.

The solution to the problem seems to recede once more: we must determine why African social structures, already in themselves unfavourable to changes, remained firmly fixed most of the time.

It is because in the modern period they have not found externally any of the incentives to change which they had already been deprived of within their system. Indeed, the mediæval influence of the Arabs encouraged the birth of market civilisations which finally accumulated great wealth throughout the whole continent. What they did not succeed in doing was to make this surplus productive. Why did the transition not take place when, with the decline of the Muslim world, the easy profits of trade became hazardous? It is because at that very moment, Portuguese intervention was about to disrupt the socio-economic situation on the continent.

*   *   *

RESEARCH ON AN AFRICAN MODE OF PRODUCTION

Until now the emphasis has been on the specific character of Black African traditional societies studied in isolation. Economic anthropologists are beginning to define self-sustaining community kinship structures with some precision. But precisely because of their insistence on the mechanism of self-sufficiency, there has been a tendency to underestimate the organisation of production and social hierarchisation within those societies: self-sufficiency, which is not autarchy, excludes neither the division of labour nor the existence of elementary processes of exchange, notably in the form of local food markets. These are not 'class societies' in the sense in which Marxists now use the term; they differ fundamentally from western pre-capitalist societies by the absence of any form of private appropriation of land. However, everywhere in Africa they have gone beyond the stage of 'primitive community'; even among the Pygmies of the forest, economic organisation is always defined in terms of a neighbouring and complementary system (exchange of products from hunting and gathering against the food of sedentary tribes).

Thus is presented the problem of a mode of production which even Soviet historians[9] hesitate to integrate into one of the three stages defined in western Europe (slavery, feudalism, capitalism), despite the noticeable schematism of certain textbooks.[10] Since Marx and Engels had sketched the definition of another mode of production, the 'Asiatic mode of production', the discovery of the African world led Marxists naturally to consider extending the application of a concept elaborated until then on the basis of the societies of the Middle East (Egypt, Mesopotamia, etc.) or of Southeast Asia (China, etc.),[11] to this new field.

On the one hand, the Asiatic mode of production implies the presence of village communities based on a collective productive activity, but combined with a 'higher unity' which, in the form of a State-like regime, is capable of compelling the mass of the population to work collectively: this 'general slavery' reveals the 'high economic command' of a despot who 'exploits these communities at the same time as he leads them'.[12] The State thus manifests itself as an *entrepreneur*, liable to impose, despite a low technical level, gigantic works — hydraulic (the fluvial States of the Middle East), military (the Great Wall of China) or prestigious (the pyramids).[13] But it is obvious that the Asiatic mode of production cannot be found in this extreme form in Black Africa. Even if, at a pinch, it is possible to liken to it certain forms of African despotism, they will always lack its dynamic element — 'general slavery' is found nowhere except maybe (but this is a hypothesis which cannot be checked) in the pseudo-cyclopaeen construction of the southern African 'stone builders' (the Zimbabwe ruins between the Zambezi and the Limpopo, eleventh to eighteenth centuries).

Aware of the fact that some of the features Marx identified in Asia could not be found in Black Africa, scholars have generally avoided drawing their analysis to its logical conclusion. Their uneasiness is noticeable, despite the fact that they tend not to admit it, doubtless out of excessive respect for the great master who, however brilliant, could not include in his analysis societies which were unknown when he wrote.

The most remarkable attempt of this nature was that of Jean Suret-

Canale, who discovers the Asiatic mode of production in pre-colonial Africa at the conclusion of a three-stage development: the *primitive community* (now disappeared), the so-called 'anarchic' or 'Stateless', tribal or *tribo-patriarchal* structure of the segmentary societies in which the fundamental social unit is the extended family (the lineage), which marks the transition towards well-differentiated *class societies, and 'State'* societies in which emerge, above the village patriarchy, privileged aristocracies which determine the formation of the State.[14]

By a process of elimination — African society was neither a slave society (in the ancient sense of the term) nor feudal — Suret-Canale compares this system with that of the Asiatic societies. Forced to recognise the absence of real *despotism*, but despite this, concerned to integrate the African mode of production into the general schema, he falls back on to a loose definition of the Asiatic mode of production: that of the 'coexistence of an apparatus of production based on the rural community . . . and the exploitation of man by man under various forms . . . but which always go through the intermediary of the communities'.

Suret-Canale not only gives the distinction between 'Stateless' and 'State' society an importance which is today debatable with respect to Black Africa;[15] he also bases his definition of surplus value exclusively on the alienation of the villagers' labour by the privileged groups, which, in our view, seems to be a mistake (we shall come back to these problems). But even if it is not correct, this definition of the Asiatic mode of production is too general to be workable; it specifically suppresses what is essential: the driving element of the exploitation of man by man, in other words, the nature of these undefined 'various forms'.

A similar feeling of uneasiness urges Godelier, in a detailed study of the Asiatic mode of production[16] to draw a distinction between 'Asiatic mode of production with major projects' — or true AMP — and 'Asiatic mode of production without major projects' whose nature in our view seems more questionable; once again this definition deprives the mode of production of its dynamic element by eliminating its economic basis, at the very level of production. Indeed major projects which are beyond the means of the small communities, constitute for them the pre-conditions for productive activity: 'The State and the dominant class intervene directly in the conditions of production; in the organisation of major projects the correspondence between productive forces and relations of production is direct.'[17] It is these major projects which determine the emergence of a bureaucracy and an absolute, centralised, 'despotic' authority.

But Suret-Canale had already noticed that the west African states were differently constituted: they are clearly based on the coincidence of a tribal confederation (led by a 'king', 'chef de terre') and of a *market* whose security it ensures and from which it draws an important part of its income.[18] Similarly, Godelier is aware of the fact that in tropical Africa the rise of the empires (e.g. Ghana, Mali and Songhay in the Middle Ages) was not linked to the organisation of major projects but 'to the control of inter-tribal or inter-regional trade, exercised by tribal aristocracies on the exchange of precious products or ivory, hides, etc. . . . between Black and White Africa'.[19]

But to complete this argument Suret-Canale hurriedly and unconvincingly eliminated from African history the dynamic element brought about by foreign contacts, by the use of a local example rather than a scientific argument: his 'proof' was the existence of the Mossi states, in whose emergence 'trade does not appear to have played any role',[20] a suggestion which, moreover, remains to be proven. Godelier, on the other hand, accepts the consequences of his analysis; he suggests 'the addition of a second hypothesis to Marx's . . . that an alternative route and another form of Asiatic mode of production can exist, in which a minority dominates and exploits the communities, intervening in their conditions of production not directly but indirectly, by appropriating surplus labour or produce as profit.'[21]

We agree entirely with this point of view, and the object of this article is to explain why. But we reject the reduction to the 'Asiatic mode of production' of the mode of production observed in at least some African societies (and which, for this reason, we shall call the 'African mode of production'). The only thing shared by these two systems is the existence of self-sustaining village communities. But the former has despotism and direct exploitation through general slavery; and in the latter, on the other hand, as we shall show, the superimposed bureaucracy only interfered indirectly in the community. We do not see the need, one which disregards accuracy, to include two types of production which differ in so many respects in the same framework. In our view it is by taking into consideration the original features of both and by analysing the relations of production in Africa that will make it possible to identify a specific 'African mode of production'.

LONG DISTANCE TRADE

One of the characteristics of African societies is that they have never lived in isolation. The African continent has been affected by two main phenomena: the mobility of its populations considerable long distance trade. Migrations — major movements or progressive incursions — stopped only during the colonial period when the metropolises decided to settle the populations for police or administrative reasons (levying of taxes, allocation of plots of private property, and so on). Previously, African history was indissolubly linked with these migrations which were no doubt partly due to the sparse population density over immense and relatively open spaces; almost everywhere even high mountains are circumnavigated and even the tropical forest is opened up by vast navigable passages, like the Congo basin.

There are numerous examples: the most spectacular was perhaps the Bantu expansion which submerged the previously settled populations (Pygmies) throughout the west and central-southern part of the continent, starting around 1,000 B.C. from a spot located by linguists on the borders of the Cameroons and Nigeria, somewhere in central Benue.[22] After having come from the trans-saharan northeast in the course of pre-historic migrations, the Fulani who had taken refuge in west Africa (Senegalese Tekrur) started in the seventeenth century to move once again, this time in the opposite direction. Until the nineteenth century they created a series of Muslim empires which indicate their progress, ranging from the Futa Jallon (1725) through the Futa Toro (1776), then on the Niger bend (Macina), as far as Sokoto on the east of the river (Usman dan Fodio's Jihad, 1804), and the Adamawa plateau in the central Cameroons. The history of the Fan since the beginning of the nineteenth century is that of their irregular movement from the Cameroons to the Atlantic.[23] Finally, the vast movements which, from the fifteenth to the nineteenth centuries extended from the Egyptian Sudan southwards — through Kenya, the eastern Congo down to southern Africa — can, according to British historians, be compared to the Mongol invasions.[24] In short, there is not one ethnographic monograph which cannot devote a map to the origin of the people studied on which arrows cross each other, symbols of the complex pattern of these successive and often recent moves.

Because of this constant intercourse, African societies have always been subject to external influences, originating from Egypt, the Arab world, Europe or even Asia. Ancient Egypt spread the nilotic heritage southwards to Nubia, around Napata, then Meroë (Kush kingdom, 600 B.C. to A.D. 300) and from there to Axum in Ethiopia. Many early relations were developed between southwest Asia and east Africa which simultaneously offered it a reserve of labour and an area for immigration. From the ninth century onwards, dissidents from persecuted sects took refuge on the coast: Kilwa in Swahililand is said to have been founded in the tenth century by a group of Iranians (*Chronicle of Kilwa*, written in the sixteenth century); the other coastal agencies had a similar origin: Mogadishu, Mombasa, Malindi, Pemba and, further south, Sofala (opposite Madagascar) which, at least until the Portuguese discovery, were the great centres of Arab trading activities in the Indian Ocean. Between the tenth and the thirteenth centuries, the influence of Indian merchants was significant enough to introduce their system of weights and measures and their customary form of currency into the area, as well as to bring to power in the thirteenth century an adventurer of their choice (al Hasan ibn Talut) in Kilwa. In the south even before Islam, Malayan canoes had opened the route to the Comore Islands and Madagascar, and Malacca was, from the ninth and tenth centuries onwards, in regular contact with the western coast of the Indian Ocean. Finally, the Chinese reached east Africa at least twice in 1417–1419 and in 1431–1433, and archæological discoveries of Persian and Chinese potteries are sufficiently numerous for it to be possible to write: 'From the tenth century to the end of the Middle Ages, the history of Tanganyika is written in Chinese pottery under our feet.'[25]

In west Africa, the relationship with the Maghreb was developed earlier still: in 734 the first expedition coming from the Sous reached the Sudan. The contact established then was never broken: in 757–758 the creation of Sijilmasa in the Tafilelt, in southern Morocco, opened the road to the Sudan for the gold caravans. As for Europeans, it is known that their discovery of the coasts ranged from 1434 (when Cape Bojador, opposite the Canaries, was rounded) to 1487 (when the Cape of Storms which later became the Cape of Good Hope was rounded).

These contacts first manifested themselves in the peoples' history in long distance trade (mediæval trans-saharan traffic, Indian Ocean trade, Atlantic slave trade, Arab trade in the Sudan) which cannot be reduced to external factors (Arab conquest, Portuguese discovery, colonial impact); they deeply affected the continent's hinterland by developing the collaboration of the coastal kingdoms (the slaving ones, for example) with 'broker' tribes of the interior who maintained the staging posts. In the Congo basin, goods penetrated long before men, preceding the 'pombeiros', half-caste Portuguese traders who, from the end of the fifteenth century onwards, followed the caravan tracks towards the Pool. In the Gabon hinterland the people of Ogowe owned materials, pearls, and 'neptunes'[26] of European manufacture. The Fan of Woleu-Ntem on the border of the southern Cameroons, an area hardly penetrated before the twentieth century, had guns[27] from trade at a time when none of them had yet seen a white man. Similarly, during the mediæval

Sudanese empires, the forest peoples of the Guinea zone, including the Gold Coast whose mines had been opened towards the middle of the fourteenth century on Manding initiative, had clearly received goods of Maghreb origin (glassware, salt, etc.) in return for the metal, ivory or kola nuts sent northwards.

This trade did not need to affect large quantities of goods to gain considerable influence; this was achieved by the scarcity of the commodities exchanged. However, history shows that it often did reach considerable proportions, as did, for example, the gold and salt transactions in mediæval west Africa, or the copper exports from southern Africa to the harbour of Sofala and the Indian Ocean, through the intermediary of the 'Monomotapa' ruler of an empire located in the Zambezi bend, which interested and then in 1628 was conquered by the Portuguese; finally, also the various activities of the slave trade — from the sixteenth century to the nineteenth, towards the Atlantic (at least ten to twenty million men)[28], towards the north, the Sudanese trade destined for the Ottoman world (approximately ten thousand slaves a year in the nineteenth century, by contrast with seventy thousand to America)[29] or what at the same time drained men from the Congo basin to Zanzibar to the Sultanate of Oman and the Indian market.

CRITIQUE OF THE TRADITIONAL OPPOSITION BETWEEN STATE AND STATELESS SOCIETIES IN AFRICA

Thus the economic life of pre-colonial African society was characterised by the juxtaposition of two apparently contradictory levels: on the one hand localised village consumption, and on the other, considerable international and even intercontinental, trade. This economic phenomenon cannot be separated from the political phenomenon discussed by Balandier[30] — that of interventions which generate a disequilibrium between a tribal and lineage structure based on the family and a territorial organisation with a greater or lesser tendency towards centralisation. Does this mean that self-sustaining 'tribo-patriarchal' 'Stateless' society must be assimilated, as is implicitly done by Suret-Canale, to major trading operations and more or less despotic State power? The analogy is dubious. We shall simply attempt to demonstrate this by a few examples, and leave to historians and anthropologists the task of adding to the case studies likely to verify an assertion which, at the present state of our knowledge, is limited to the presentation of certain research hypotheses.

Anthropologists have certainly shown how closely linked lineage relations are to self-sustaining economic structures. Segmentary societies, hitherto located in the undefined (because little studied) vagueness of primitive 'classless society', turn out on analysis to be very diversified. Once again, it is Balandier who should be thanked for reminding us, in the context of Black Africa, that 'all societies, in varying degrees, are heterogeneous',[31] This primitive community contains 'social stratifications' which already imply 'antagonism, struggle and conflict'.[32] In its simplest form it translates as the predominance of seniors over juniors; the first appear to be the true holders of the means of production, since they exercise an ultimate and discretionary authority over the latter who are 'compelled to give them the product of their labour';[33] the seniors can thus hoard or exchange 'elite goods' exclusively at their level, thus strengthening their predominance — out of this arises the assumption of a process of accumulation liable to produce and increase inequality at the village level. This is only a sketch but it is enough to show the danger of denying to self-sufficiency the right to be a 'scientific, Marxist economic category' because 'it is the place only of an absence, the absence of a market economy and commodities'.[34] In our view such a negative definition is likely to send back 'all precapitalist societies . . . into the vague concept of traditional society'.[35] This would provide a clue to the lack of interest manifested until recently in this problem by many historians, even Marxist ones, affected by eurocentrism. But, in Marx himself, there is no such marked refusal; on the contrary there one can read that:

> [On] the specific economic form in which unpaid surplus labour is pumped out of direct producers . . . is founded the entire formation of the economic community . . . thereby simultaneously, its specific economic form. It is always the direct relationship of the owners of the conditions of production to the direct producers (a relation always naturally corresponding to a definite stage in the development . . . of its social productivity) which reveals the . . . hidden basis of the entire social structure, and with it, the political form of the relation of sovereignty and dependence.[36]

On the other hand, must long distance trade be assimilated to centralised power? This seems far more dubious. Certainly, the most striking examples have been studied in the framework of State societies: Ghana from the eighth to the eleventh centuries and Mali in the fourteenth century saw their rise linked with trade with the Maghreb; Benin and Dahomey's development paralleled that of the slave trade; the Sultanate of Zanzibar flourished in the nineteenth century with the slave and ivory trade in east Africa. But recent works prove that large-scale trade affected the most diverse societies. This is true of the *great Congolese trade*: along the Congo and its main tributaries (Ubangwi, Sangha, Likuala, Alima, to mention only the right bank) segmentary societies turned this trade into their only means of livelihood. Originally, in the sixteenth century, the trade had linked the Portuguese and the Kongo kingdom located on the left bank of the lower Congo around its capital Sao Salvador. But by 1850 it was hardly more than a memory; the trade had gone past the Bakongo of the coastal region, reached the Bateke of the Pool and, upstream, the Bubangwi of the 'country of lagoons' at the junction of the Sangha and Wangari rivers with the Congo.[37]

There the power of the chief rarely exceeded the scope of the village, and more often only a section of the village; but this water people, isolated on earth mounds along the endless network of lagoons, constituted a dynamic whole; since it was impossible to make a living on swampy ground, this society owed its fortune exclusively to the exchange of food combined with trade. In the upper Alima, the Bugangwi (locally known as the Likuba) settled in their temporary dry season settlements, raided as much as twenty tons a day of manioc from the Bateke of the plateau and the coastal Mbochi, and in return they offered the fruits of their industry — mats, pots, paddles, nets, harpoons and above all, dried fish, which they produced in large quantities.

To these activities, essential to the maintenance of their authority over this strategic, unhealthy and infertile area, they added the profitable profession of brokers for the great Congolese trade. In exchange for European goods they received Likuala ivory and further upstream the produce of the Sangha and the Ubangwi — slaves, redwood, ivory and, soon, rubber. All this found expression in important markets, around the Pool and the rivers country (Neunda and Bolobo). Upstream, other, equally segmentary, groups served as further relays for the traffic: Bonga at the junction with the Sangha, exhibited a similar activity, and was supplied by the peoples further upstream. The inhabitants of the forest even knew that the river's source was 'the country of white men' armed with guns, whose description indicates that they were of Arab origin. This fact, among others, confirms the vast scope of the Congolese trade which drained enormous areas of their produce and men.

Whatever the type of society considered, the permanence of this trade demands that the researcher go beyond the traditional opposition between State and Stateless society. In Black Africa, this opposition is likely to appear to be even more formal than elsewhere. Balandier has already shown the coexistence at the political level of apparently contradictory elements in all African societies, whether State or anarchic. In fact all forms of transition from one to the other can be found. Certainly, transition towards a centralised organisation is the indisputable mark of progress; but the difference is qualitative rather than basic. Even in the case of the most 'despotic' societies (the mediæval Sudanese kingdoms, the Kongo kingdom in the sixteenth century, the Dahomey kingdom in the nineteenth century) the sovereign's authority never excluded the tribo-patriarchal organisation; at most it was embodied in a bureaucracy superimposed on, but respectful of, the structures of life in the bush. To account for this feature, common to all African societies, one must look for its economic basis. It seems to us that one of the driving forces in the history of the people of Black Africa is to be found in the dialectical interplay of the relations, or lack of them, between apparently heterogeneous socio-economic levels within the same totality (the coexistence of community clan structures with the territorial system and the superposition of family self-sufficiency and long distance trade); at each moment this force corresponds to a certain stage in the development of the relations governing these elements, which are contradictory and therefore persistently generate disequilibrium and conflict.

TOWARDS AN 'AFRICAN MODE OF PRODUCTION'

It is by taking into consideration these specific features that it becomes possible to identify an *African mode of production* which is not immediately assimilable to the now classic schema of the *Asiatic mode of production*.

Despotism of the Asiatic type, as we have said, was unknown to Black Africa. This does not mean that there was no formation of aristocracies or of privileged classes. But the sovereigns who took power in various places were hastily identified by European observers as 'absolute monarchs'. The levies they took with the help of the dominant classes were not necessarily, certainly not exclusively, taken from the 'labouring peasantry, formed at the same time of free men and slaves' which would in Africa as elsewhere be 'the fundamental exploited class'.[38] Certainly this might have happened; in pre-colonial Senegal, the lineage which controlled State power also had rights over land and over a share of the peasants' labour (but as a collective right — neither exploiters nor exploited were individuals).[39] In Burundi the control over goods (cattle or pasture land) held by the Tutsi at the expense of the Hutu has even given rise to discussion of feudal relations of production.[40]

However it seems excessive to look for the driving force of the development of African societies *only* in the contribution of the productive forces of self-sufficiency. This assertion, as an attempt to rediscover the pair 'exploiters/exploited' within the self-enclosed African society, reveals a lack of observation of the real facts of the country. Black Africa is certainly the part of the world in which agriculture is least likely to produce surplus value: agricultural and craft techniques were particularly rudimentary (neither wheel nor plough — the only tool was the *hoe*); above all it was never felt necessary to improve production with new tools or by recourse to major works. The exploitation of a land which, if not fertile, was at least large, easily satisfied the limited needs of a usually not very dense population. No monarch ever needed to levy food *in quantity* from the village population in order to survive; at most he was content to organise, for his own benefit, domestic-type exploitation under the responsibility of his wives (as in Dahomey, for example) with the assistance of a limited 'domestic' slavery, which cannot be compared with a real 'slave mode of production'. The tributes levied by the most organised despots (the king of the Kongo or the king of Dahomey) in no way appear to have been intended to pay for services, or to provide the labour necessary for tasks of public utility. It is uncertain whether these levies were used to feed the court on a regular basis; there is no indication whatever that they may have been used as an assistance fund to which people in need might apply for help.[41] In the Kongo, the king and the noblemen redistributed what they had just received[42] among the vassals who requested it. In Dahomey the Custom, a grandiose celebration which took place every year from the eighteenth century onwards to honour the royal ancestors, fulfilled the same function; indeed for the sovereign it was an opportunity to receive tribute but mainly to publicise and to present, over many weeks and for all his assembled subjects to see, the wealth and generosity of the dynasty, either by the public sacrifice of hundreds of slaves (a certain loss),[43] or by the distribution of streams of alcohol, of cowries (local money) and of loin cloths thrown by the handful from the top of public platforms.[44] In short, the required prestations were primarily of symbolic value to guarantee social structures. This is not to say that there were no relationships of exploiter/exploited, but that the African despot exploited his subjects less than he did neighbouring tribes — indeed it was long distance trade which provided most of the surplus. From this point of view the celebration of the Custom, to mention this example again, was not a backward institution likely to slow down or paralyse contact with the Europeans. On the contrary, it stimulated the country's economic life; it encouraged the intensive trading activity necessary to supply this 'fair' with all kinds of products (slaves exchanged against European commodities). We should not be blamed here for favouring *the mode of circulation of goods* excessively over *the mode of production*. The fundamental problem was not to transport the merchandise but indeed to obtain it — in some way to 'produce' it. The point in question was obviously a bastardised, immediate and apparent form of production, but one which in fact was contradictory and predatory, since in the long run it made the country barren instead of enriching it. With this end in mind, there were two possible means: war (in the form of slave raids)[45] or peaceful exchanges with neighbouring peoples (e.g. of salt and gold in the Sudan), a form of 'exogenic' circulation which can be assimilated to a form of production by contrast with circulation within a given society.

Jean Suret-Canale has noted the fundamental role of trade in Black Africa as 'the decisive element of consolidation of the first states of tropical Africa'[46] but he has not exploited its significance sufficiently because of his preconceived concern to discover a form of *direct* domination of the aristocracy over the peasantry. But the control exercised by the ruling class manifested itself mainly *indirectly*, by the exclusive enjoyment of foreign goods accumulated by a process analogous to that of the 'elite goods' hoarded by the seniors within the community-based self-sustaining economy, for example, European red cotton which the Bateke chiefs reserved for their funerals,[47] advanced weapons accumulated in the arsenals of the Sultans of the Ipper Ubangwi, and so on. Besides, indirect domination did not exclude its corollary, direct domination, particularly in the case of the arms trade which affected both at the same time: by acquiring arms the sovereign ensured for himself simultaneously power to control military enlistment, payment of tribute and labour on his plantations, which in its turn favoured the accumulation of exportable surplus. (The king of Dahomey, for example, imposed the cultivation of palm oil trees from the middle of the nineteenth century onwards.) But the main levies, let us repeat, were not taken from the village communities: they came from outside the territory, either from annual raids or from peaceful commercial transactions in which the products were acquired at prices well below their value. Thus, life in the Dahomey kingdom was punctuated (just as in the Kongo kingdom before it, and most likely in the Benin kingdom as well) by military expeditions sent during each dry season to Ashantiland in the west or Yoruba towns in the east, to bring back the contingent of slaves necessary to the slave economy. Thus, in central Africa, the Likuba (Bubangwi) obtained the manioc of the Bateke and Mbochi at 'derisory prices';[48] they sold the redwood, the ivory or the slaves bought in quantity for five or six, even ten, times the price in the Pool.[49] Even in the case of empires based on mineral wealth (gold in the Sudan, copper in southern Africa) the sovereign's problem was not how to impose on his subjects a collective effort to extract the metal but rather to obtain at the lowest possible price a metal which was sometimes mined a long way from his territory. Neither the king of Ghana nor the emperor of Mali directly dominated the producers, who probably acted within the framework of a foraging economy; they did not even know them since 'silent trade' was maintained until very late. This frequently described process forbade the two parties from coming into direct contact: the traders who had come from the north laid out their goods (salt) in a predetermined spot and then withdrew. The following morning, opposite each object they wanted to sell they found a quantity of gold dust equivalent to the price offered. If they considered the offer adequate they took the gold; otherwise they touched nothing until something more was added or, if they were considered too demanding, everything was taken away. The only result obtained by the king of Mali when he had one of the traders kidnapped in order to discover 'what kind of people are these who do not want to allow themselves to be seen or to be spoken to', was the interruption of trade for three years.[50] Arab writers also relate absurd stories which circulated in the Sudan about these cannibal producers, deformed savages who collected gold roots after the rain.[51] The fact that in southern Africa the distribution of copper sites ranging from Katanga to the Limpopo does not coincide with that of the ruins left by the 'stone builders', which bear witness to an elaborate political organisation around the cities of Zimbabwe and Mapungubwe (Southern Rhodesia), seems to corroborate an analogous hypothesis of 'production' by means of exchange rather than direct exploitation.

The specificity of the African mode of production thus appears to be based on the combination of a patriarchal community economy with exclusive control by one group of the long distance trade. The form of power at any given moment depends on the nature of this group: if those in charge of trade are also the lineage chiefs at the self-sustaining village level, their predominance is then uncontested. In the case of the Fan or the Bubangwi, it was threatened only by the instability of the small rival groups engaged in the same project; in the middle Congo the system collapsed only under the pressure of external factors — the intrusion of Europeans who confiscated the great trade for their own profit by eliminating the traditional brokerage.

On the other hand if, within a more differentiated political apparatus, a privileged class succeeds in taking control of the long distance trade because of hereditary caste recruitment or as a result of an attempt at capital accumulation, the regime will express a more or less coherent synthesis between the tribo-patriarchal system and the territorial ambitions of a new type. For example, the mediæval Sudanese empires demonstrate the use of traditional animist structures by an Arabised aristocracy in charge of trade, but it would be a mistake to see them as Muslim states because of this (particularly since Ghana was already declining when it came across Islam). The function of these empires was to control and exploit trade between western Sudan and north Africa: their object was the domination of others for profit and this economic objective allows one to account for their political form. It was in fact in the interest of the ruling class, by the organisation of its court and the renown of its pilgrimages to present an Islamicised front which favoured the establishment of good relations with the Maghreb, which was both client and supplier. But, on the other hand, Muslim proselytism was a threat to internal stability; there is nothing to support the theory that Islam had wide support outside the large cities. On the contrary, even within the monarchic institutions, the descriptions we have been left by Arab geographers show that the leaders felt the need to graft their power on to a typically pagan symbolic structure, probably of Manding origin, for instance, the ceremony which surrounded the king, the rituals he had to follow (he never drank in public, did not talk directly to his subjects) the demonstrations of submission by his dignitaries (who bowed their foreheads to the ground or performed sacred dances in honour of the sovereign). Had they not done so the abandonment of traditions would have provoked the hostility of the popular masses attached to patriarchal forces against the notables. The development of the empires was the result of the precariousness of the equilibrium between these antagonistic tendencies; in Songhay, for example, Sonni Ali (1464–1492) the champion of militant paganism, provoked a Muslim reaction to his activities and in fact, subjected the entire Niger bend to his domination, but under his influence the history of the empire became one of continuous competition between pagans and Muslims, which weakened the State and facilitated the Moroccan conquest in 1591. This settled the conflict because all united to resist in the name of animism — but this unity was obtained at the price of economic supremacy.[52]

The history of the Dahomey kingdom reveals another attempt to resolve internal contradictions of the same type. The kingdom developed progressively because of the political vacuum left by the decaying of the Aja ancestral structures, undermined by the introduction of the slave trade. The new concept of a State based on territory in which each subject had to obey the king and no longer only the patriarchal chief, superposed itself on community institutions. The paradox was that the kingdom, originally created to take a stand against the corrosive influence of the slave trade developed into an administrative and economic entity based on this trade: this

was the significance of the reign of Agadja (1708–1740) whose transformation into a slave trader was the cause of expansion in the nineteenth century.[53] Power was closely linked to specific economic
forms; Dahomean centralisation corresponded to the sovereign's
absolute hold over an unintegrated large State trade, little open to
the market economy. It was a massive exchange of products rather
than real trade; the king did not intend so much to make a profit as to
obtain, through exchange, foreign goods: weapons (the pre-
condition of his power and his supply of slaves), the fabrics, alcohol
and petty goods which were the basis of his generosity as exhibited
by the annual parade of the trade treasures accumulated from generation to generation. The celebration of the Custom thus ensured the
periodic regrouping and redistribution of the kingdom's wealth.

The authoritarian administration of trade explains the *stability of
prices* despite the internal disorders and the frantic competition in
which the various Europeans engaged; on the Dahomean side, the
price variations, subject to the law of supply and demand, were
limited by the sovereign who fixed the prices on the basis of
ecological and military factors and conditions of transport. For
example, the standard price of a slave included the calculated
estimate of his faults, the selection of the 'lots' i.e. of the codified and
priced packages of assorted slave trade goods and finally the
relatively stable value of the cowry over a century and a half (in
principle 32,000 cowries = 1 ounce of gold — this shell from the
Indian Ocean was used as currency due to a State policy which
regulated its use and prevented its proliferation by authoritarian
control of its import until just before the colonial conquest).[54]

From that time onwards, Dahomey achieved the surprising combination of a political State with a high degree of monarchic
organisation at the service of the king and his chiefs, but linked to the
most absolute respect for the autonomy of community life in the
bush. Indeed we should not be taken in by the perfection of the
administrative and financial system as described by Herskovits[55]
(counting the censuses, levying of taxes and military enrolment
organised by the palace with the help of stones subtly distributed in
different bags). More recent research tends to emphasise the
schematic character of this somewhat hasty reconstruction by a
European mind.[56]

Finally, the loss by a privileged group or despot of control over
long distance trade brought about the end of their political
power — this was what happened in the Kongo kingdom. In the first
stage its cohesion was due to the monopoly held by the king over a
trade which probably existed in central Africa since the twelfth
century: the blocks of sea salt coming from the coast travelled

towards the hinterland in the same way as the 'zimu' shells fished up in Luanda island which were used as currency in Sao Salvador; in return raffia mats and ivory originating in the dense forest areas arrived from the Pool. As soon as the sovereign lost control over trade with Europe, he lost his authority over his provinces: the chiefs of the Loango coast and Soyo (north of the river mouth) and of southern Angola immediately made use of the remoteness of their capital to take control of the market, with the complicity of the Portuguese merchants of Sao Tomé. Starting in the sixteenth century these peripheral and maritime populations gradually freed themselves from the domination of the interior empire; vassals turned into brokers and derived from trade a power which allowed them to rival the former authority to which they then refused to submit.[57]

On their own the examples given cannot pretend to form a basis for a general law. In the present state of our knowledge, they simply appear as so many unique solutions to the problem of the coexistence of contradictory political and economic elements. What made this coexistence possible was almost certainly the fact that the minorities in power were more concerned with the exploitation of their neighbours than their subjects. No African political regime, however despotic it may have been, felt the need to eliminate within its borders the village community structures which hardly interfered in its process of exploitation. Provided it transmitted its tribute to the district or province chief the village ran its collective life in any way it wanted: the seniors had full control over worship of the clan ancestors; the 'chef de terre' distributed cultivable land on his own authority to each family and each generation and women's associations regulated transactions in the local food markets. It was not even necessary to provide the king with a contingent of labourers for his plantations or porters for his caravans since these duties were usually carried out by the royal slaves who had been captured from other countries. The most frequent obligation was usually only enlistment in the army in case of conflict or, as in Dahomey, the assignment of a number of girls to the king's harem or his 'Amazon' corps of elite women fighters.

Certainly in numerous African societies exchanges played a small part: this is the case with the Guro of the Ivory Coast, even though the presence of kola markets is agreed and their dynamic role recognised. This was the means for the juniors, who took control of them, by which to contest the seniors' supremacy.[58] In any case it seems that everywhere where exchange remained limited nothing threatened the 'tribo-patriarchal' structures since nothing was liable to produce enough surplus. As for the 'military hegemonies' which dominated elsewhere, was the long distance trade as unknown to them as some claim? It seems necessary for example to look further into the role played by the little known caste of merchants in the Mossi kingdoms. Elsewhere, the herding function encouraged the expansion of the Fulani, by favouring the accumulation of wealth in the privileged form of cattle; whatever may be said, their prosperity first manifested itself in active cattle markets (e.g. Kunde on the eastern border of the Cameroons). The Fulani states, heirs of Usman dan Fodio, in the nineteenth century and doubtless earlier had absolute control over the Arab slave trade which supplied the whole Sudan with slaves.[59] It is not, however, a good idea to try to identify everything at any price; it is not impossible that in Africa various types of control by a ruling class over the rest of the population may be found; for example, trade over long distances often implies military power (e.g. Buganda where the State apparatus appears to have been operated as an enterprise for foreign war and hunting for spoils — slaves, cattle, elite goods — for the chiefs, all the military officers and the bravest soldiers; because of all this it tended to mobilise a large section of the population for its two annual campaigns).[60] It would also be necessary to make a distinction between west Africa and the Lakes region. In the former, land was usually under the collective control of the village community (it was only in the nineteenth century that the king of Dahomey argued that he had ultimate right of ownership when he allocated to himself the palm oil plantations created under the influence of the Europeans). In the Lakes region, on the other hand, a phenomenon close to the appropriation of land by the ruling class can be noted early on (e.g. the case of Ruanda).

These examples prove first of all the need to increase the number of case studies, still far too scarce. It would also be desirable to begin a comparison with other so-called self-sustaining economies, beginning with the Maghreb — it seems that there also is found this juxtaposition of two economic systems impervious to one another, at the village and State levels. Maybe it will then be possible to throw light on some of the causes of a dichotomy which has struck all African historians: the *invariance* of the basic self-sustaining communities by contrast with the *instability* at the socio-political level. The second, though it cannot be separated from the first would find the driving force for its development elsewhere; it would first be the result of the complex interplay of heterogeneous constituent elements and among them long distance trade would be the most dynamic but also the most vulnerable since it was subject to external pressures as well as internal factors.

It can be seen how the African mode of production, while irreducible to western pre-capitalist modes of production, is also radically different from Asia, because of the absence of a true despotism aiming at a direct exploitation of the peasant class. A final problem remains: the possible development of this mode of production. It has often been stated that the Asiatic mode of production was doomed to stagnation. Godelier states that, on the contrary, the transition to the Asiatic mode of production, revealing the emergence of a still fluid class structure, would be 'the greatest progress of the productive forces accomplished on the basis of the former communal forms of production'. To go beyond this stage (unless, as is always possible, it is blocked in a petrified form) the society follows the law of development of its internal contradictions: that of the unity of community structures and class structures, the second progressively gaining over the first, as a consequence of the emergence of private property.[61]

Can a similar development be imagined for the African mode of production? Cases of blockage are clearly more frequent than elsewhere, since the productive forces are not real forces. Production, based on war or trade, is sterile; the surplus is certainly restricted to the privileged class but it is an apparent surplus whose price is, in the long or short term, the real impoverishment of the country. The Sudanese empires disappeared without a trace as soon as the trading routes shifted from the north (gold for salt) to the south (gold, then slaves, for European goods) to the benefit of the Guinean zone discovered by the Portuguese. The states based on the slave trade were finally overcome by what had at first given them prosperity — the Kongo from the seventeenth century onward, the kingdom of Benin from before the eighteenth century, the Ashanti confederation (Gold Coast) in the nineteenth century. Does this mean that the African mode of production is condemned not only to stagnate but to disintegrate? In one case at least, that of Dahomey, it was capable of beginning an evolution: around the middle of the nineteenth century King Ghezo gave its congealed structures a shake by agreeing to give up the increasingly uncertain slave trade in favour of a 'legal trade' encouraged by Europeans and based on real production, of palm oil and palm trees. A large accumulation of capital allowed him to impose an increasingly direct domination and exploitation over vast plantations. It was the beginning of a transition to a mode of production simultaneously partaking of the former regime (the labour force was mainly composed of slaves still obtained by annaual raids) and of certain forms close to feudalism; this was brought out in the way the sovereign asserted and insisted on his ultimate right of ownership over this domain: by the carefully maintained confusion between 'lands of the kingdom' and 'king's lands' he was slowly shifting towards private ownership of land. The peasants were compelled to maintain the palm trees and to collect the oil; the *topo* was charged with applying precise regulations; the holders of palm groves were compelled to clean the ground and harvest the fruit or else they would be fined or lose their land; they had no right to cut down a palm tree without royal authorisation. Palm oil enriched the king through the taxes he levied on the trade: his subjects owed him a tax in kind on the commercial produce, estimated to be one eighth of the harvest. Special officials were in charge of the allocation of plots which became more numerous in Dahomey, each town owning some. At Allada, the former capital, any container which went through the town was taxed be it 'a large pot or a small jug'.[62]

Would this development have been possible elsewhere? It seems at least to have been sketched in the Lakes region (a system with feudal tendencies in Ruanda, based on the capitalisation of cattle). Everything was interrupted by the Conquest which perverted relations between colonisers and colonised, and obliged African societies to shift towards an 'adulterated' capitalist system, 'where the capitalist relation of production is closely combined with archaic relations, for the greater profit of the privileged.'[63] These examples seem, however, to indicate that African society, freed from the assimilation of western elements, was just as capable as any other, of overcoming its contradictions, provided it changed the moving force of the economy itself. By substituting the exploitation of palm groves for the predatory trade, Dahomey integrated itself into a renewed economic system without any violent upsetting of its equilibrium. In this way, it began the development of its mode of production.

NOTES

1. I. Sachs, *La Découverte du Tiers Monde*, Paris, Flammarion, 1971, p. 123.
2. *Révolution industrielle et sous-développement*, Paris, SEDES, 1963, p. 370.
3. J. Suret-Canale, 'Les sociétés traditionnelles en Afrique Noire et le concept de mode de production Asiatique', *La Pensée*, number 117, 1964, pp. 19–42.
4. C. Meillassoux, '"The Economy" in Agricultural Self-Sustaining Societies: A Preliminary Analysis', see pp. 127–57 of this volume.
5. J. Goody, 'Economy and Feudalism in Africa', *The Economic History Review*, volume XXII number 3, 1969, pp. 393–405.
6. S. Hymer, 'Economic Forms in Precolonial Ghana', *The Journal of Economic History*, volume XXX number 1, 1970, pp. 33–50.
7. S. Amin, 'Mode de production, formations sociales . . . Introduction aux concepts', seminar paper IDEO, Duala-Kinshasa, 1972 (duplicated) pp. 3, 8 and 62.
8. See Meillassoux above, pp. 127–57.
9. On the beginning of the debate on the AMP in the USSR see Chesneaux, J., 'Ou en

est la discussion sur le mode de production Asiatique-II', *La Pensée*, number 129, October 1960.

10. Such as Mitropolski, Y. Zoubritski and V. Kerov: *Apercu d'histoire et d'economie, I: Formations précapitalistes: La communauté primitive, la société esclavagiste, la société féodale*, Progress Publishers, Moscow, p. 280. (This is the textbook used since 1960/61 by the Asian, African and Latin American students of the Patrice Lumumba University for Friendship among the peoples.)

11. Concerning this, see J. Chesneaux's articles: 'Le mode de production asiatique, quelques perspectives de recherche' *La Pensée*, no. 114, 1964; 'Ou en est la discussion sur le mode de production asiatique?' *La Pensée*, no. 122, August 1965; 'Ou en est . . . II', 1960, *op. cit.*; 'Ou en est . . . III', no. 138, April 1968, pp. 21–42.

12. Chesneaux, J., 'Le MPA Quelques perspectives de recherches' *op. cit* [my translation—*HL*].

13. Parain, Ch., 'Protohistoire méditerranéenne et mode de production asiatique', *La Pensée*, number 127, 1966, pp. 26–27.

14. Suret-Canale, *op. cit.*, pp. 19–42 [all extracts from this article are translated by myself—*HL*].

15. In whatever the type of society under consideration, the political institutions are structured on the basis of the descent principle, the two orders of relations — lineage and political — often seem complementary and antagonistic. Balandier, G. *Political Anthropology*, Allen Lane, London, 1970, p. 56.

16. Godelier, M., *La notion de Mode de Production Asiatique et les schémas marxistes d'évolution des sociétés*, see pp. 209–57 in this volume.

17. ibid., pp. 241–2.

18. Suret-Canale, 'Les sociétés traditionnelles . . .' *op. cit.*, p. 37

19. Godelier, M., *op. cit.*, p. 242

20. 'This hypothesis is invalidated by the existence of Mossi states', Suret-Canale, *op. cit.*, p. 37.

21. Godelier, M., *op. cit.*, p. 242.

22. Greenberg, J. H., *Languages of Africa*, Indiana University Press, Bloomington, 1962.

23. Alexandre, P., 'Proto-histoire du groupe beti-bulu-fang: essai de synthèse provisoire', *Cahiers d'Etudes Africaines*, v, no. 20, 1965, pp. 503–60.

24. Oliver and Mathew, *History of East Africa*, Oxford University Press, chapter vi, 'Discernible developments in the Interior c. 1500–1840', pp. 169–211.

25. Sir Mortimer Wheeler, 1955, quoted by B. Davidson in *Le Courrier de l'Unesco*, October 1959. Besides G. S. P. Freeman-Grenville has carried out important studies on the currencies discovered on the coast, which testify to continuous commercial relations with the Yemen, Arabia and Asia. Cf. 'East Africa coin finds and their historical significance', *Journal of African History*, vol. i, 1960, pp. 31–44. On the history of relations between East Africa and the Indian Ocean, see among others Toussaint, A., *Histoire de l'Ocean Indien*, Paris, 1961; Villers, A., *The Indian Ocean*, London, 1952; Gray, J., *History of Zanzibar from the Middle Ages*, London, 1962. G. S. P. Freeman-Grenville: *The Medieval History of the Tanganyika coast*, Oxford University Press, London, 1962; Duyvendak, J. L., *China's Discovery of Africa*, London, 1949; Synthesis by Mollat, M., *L'Afrique et l'Ocean Indien*, 1965.

26. Large dishes of embossed copper, which were used as currency, particularly for the payment of bridewealth (they were originally introduced by the Portuguese and used until the 20th century).

27. Correspondence of the members of the 'Mission de l'Ouest Africain', Brazza's third penetration mission 1883–1885. Coquery-Vidrovitch, *Brazza et la prise de possession du Congo*, Paris, Mouton, 1969.

28. For a long time it has been estimated to be between 20 and 50 million. In his current researches, the American historian P. Curtin who is working on the accounts of the slave ships and the port registers, estimates on the contrary that a figure of 10 million would be a maximum.

29. Adu Boahen, A., *Britain, the Sahara and the Western Sudan*, Oxford University Press, London, 1965.

30. Balandier, *op. cit.*

31. *Ibid.*, p. 78.

32. *Ibid.*, p. 79.

33. Meillassoux, *The Guro*, p. 217.

34. Suret-Canale, J., 'Structuralisme et anthropologie économique' *La Pensée*, no. 135, 1967, p. 99. He obviously goes beyond his own thought, since he also analysed 'tribo-patriarchal' society, whose *productive forces* based on communal agriculture, he defines: 1964, 'Les sociétés traditionnelles . . .', *op. cit.*, pp. 19–42.

35. Here we have the contradiction in Godelier, who accuses Meillassoux of this while on the other hand accusing him of over-emphasising 'the fact of inequality . . . in most classless societies' in 'A propos de deux textes d'anthropologie économique' *L'Homme*, no. 3, 1967, p. 86.

36. *Capital*, volume 3, page 791. On this subject see also Parain, 1966, *op. cit.*, p. 26.

37. Sauter, G., *De l'Atlantique au fleuve Congo*, Paris, 1965, pp. 215–325. See also C. Coquery-Vidrovitch, 1969, *op. cit.*, and Vansina, J., 'Long distance trade-routes in Central Africa', *Journal of African History*, vol. iii, no. 3, 1962, pp. 375–90.

38. Suret-Canale, 1964, 'Les sociétés traditionnelles . . .', *op. cit.*, p. 30. Godelier expresses the same idea in an analogous form though less categorically, the aristocracy 'ensuring the bases of its class exploitation by levying a share of produce of the communities (in labour and in kind)', 1963, *op. cit.*, p. 30.

39. Deme, Kalidou, 'Les classes sociales dans le Sénégal précolonial' *La Pensée*, no. 130, 1966, p. 17.

40. Maquet, J. J., *Le système des relations sociales dans le Ruanda ancien*, Tervuren, 1954.

41. Lloyd, Peter C., 'The political structure of African kingdoms' in *Political Systems and the Distribution of Power*, London, 1965, p. 78.

42. Randles, W. G. L., *L'ancien royaume du Congo des origines à la fin du 19e siècle*, chapter 5, 'La Fiscalité', Paris 1969.

43. A hundred or so each year, over 500 for the Great Custom, celebrated in the year of the King's funeral.

44. Coquery-Vidrovitch, 'La fête des Coutumes au Dahomey, historique et essai d'interpretation', *Annales*, no. 4, July–August 1964, pp. 696–716.

45. 'War, which is one of the forms of production, entails characteristically what are called military parasite states found in antiquity as well as in the middle ages.' Melekechvili, G. A., 'Esclavage, féodalisme et mode de production asiatique dans l'Orient ancien', *La Pensée*, no. 132, 1967, p. 41.

46. Suret-Canale, 1964, 'Les sociétés traditionnelles . . .', *op. cit.*, p. 36.

47. Sautter, G., 'Le plateau congolais de Mbe', *Cahiers d'Etudes Africaines*, no. 2, 1960, p. 373.

48. Statements by European observers. Coquery-Vidrovitch, 1969, *op. cit.*

49. *Ibid.* A knife bought for four bars of copper in the Ikelemba was sold for 60 bars at Bonga; a slave bought for 20 bars was sold for 400 or 500 bars.

50. A. Ca' da Mosto, *Relation de voyages a la Cote Occidentale d'Afrique*, 1457. (Published in Paris 1895, p. 52 sq.)

51. See statements by Al Bakri, 1068, *Description de l'Afrique*, translated by Alger,

1913, p. 381; Al-Omari, 1338, *L'Afrique moins l'Egypte*, translated Paris, 1927,pp. 70–1; A. Ca' da Mosto, 1895, *op. cit.*, p. 52, etc.

52. Fage, J. D., 'Some thoughts on state formation in the Western Sudan before the 17th Century', *Boston University Papers in African History*, I, 17–34, 1964.

53. Akinjogbin, A., *Dahomey and its neighbours, 1708–1818*, Cambridge University Press, 1967, p. 234.

54. Polanyi, K., *Dahomey and the Slave Trade*, American Ethnological Society series, University of Washington Press, Seattle, 1966, p. 195. The rigour of the system suggested by this author should be adjusted on the basis of work which is being done at the moment on cowries by Marion Johnson: 'The ounce in the eighteenth-century West African trade', *Journal of African History*, vol. vii, no. 2, 1966, pp. 197–214.

55. Herskovits, M. J., *Dahomey, an Ancient West African Kingdom*, New York, 1938, 2 vols.

56. Argyle, W. J., *The Fon of Dahomey*, Oxford University Press, London, 1966, pp. 94–5.

57. Randles, W. G. L., 1969, *op. cit.*, chapter 4, 'L'économie'; chapter 11, 'Les conséquences de l'ouverture de la nouvelle frontière'.

58. Meillassoux, *The Guro*, pp. 263–90

59. The Lamibe from Adamaoua led annual raids against the East beyond the Chari. Coquery-Vidrovitch, 'La politique française en Haute Sangha' *Revue Française d'Histoire d'Outre-Mer*, no. 186, 1965, pp. 29–31.

60. Sperber, Daṇ, *Les paysans-clients au Buganda*, Communication au Colloque du Groupe de Recherches en Anthropologie et Sociologie Politique (CRASP), Paris, 29 March 1968.

61. Godelier, 1963, *op. cit.*, pp. 31–3.

62. Coquery-Vidrovitch, 'Le blocus de Whydah (1876–1877) et la rivalité franco-anglaise au Dahomey', *Cahiers d'Etudes Africaines*, vol. ii, no. 7, 1965, p. 384.

63. Lacoste, Y., *Géographie du sous-developpement*, Presses Universitaires de France, Paris, 1965, pp. 230–1 [my translation—*HL*].

Kinship Relations and Relations of Production

Claude Meillassoux

This contribution is a chapter (originally entitled The Agricultural Community) *extracted from Meillassoux's monograph on the Guro of the Ivory Coast, which was published as* Anthropologie économique des Gouro de Côte d'Ivoire *in 1964. The presentation of a chapter isolated from its total context is always unsatisfactory in some respects but, in this case the discussion of the agricultural community and the analysis of the lineage relations and the relations of production is central to the study as a whole. It also reveals, as do the following three contributions, the importance not only of an adquate theoretical perspective but also of careful and detailed fieldwork. As Dupré has remarked in his introduction: 'Meillassoux's research had the incomparable advantage of presenting a theory of traditional economies which was coherent and at the same time of applying this theory to the understanding of a concrete society, that of the Guro of the Ivory Coast'*: the relationship between 'theory' and 'enquiry' is a complex one and one should beware of any suggestion which presents a crude dichotomy between 'theoretical' and 'empirical' approaches to the analysis of social and economic formations. The starting point of the process of knowledge is not, as has been claimed by empiricism, a specific concrete reality, but the representations and concepts which exist within the discipline and precede any particular study and which are themselves constantly re-formed and re-created by the confrontation with concrete information.*

I. THE HIERARCHY OF AGRICULTURAL PRODUCTS

The Guro do not value all agricultural produce equally. It is divided according to a hierarchy which gives pre-eminence to rice, the

---

* See p. 172 of this volume (they will be referred to hereafter as *The Guro*).

vegetable food *par excellence*. Grown exclusively by women, it is associated with fatherhood and matrimony. Rice is stored in granaries under the direct or indirect control of the head of the family; when it is sold the proceeds always go to him. Rice is offered in hospitality to travellers, and in return for cooperative labour from relatives or neighbours. Without free access to this product one cannot play a prominent role in society. Linked as it is to the authority of the senior and thus an instrument of social relations, rice cannot be compared to any other product.

The yam is second in the hierarchy, particularly in the savannah area where rice is less common, although yams are stored in the fields rather than in the village and are not a food given to honour a guest. However (as with rice) the seniors profit from their sale.

Plantain, a crop valued mainly in the forest area, is not regarded in this way, probably because it is comparatively plentiful. Its weight makes its transportation and sale difficult and the revenue produced usually goes to the women who take the trouble of carrying them to market. The same applies to vegetables such as courgettes, tomatoes, peppers, and so on, which are grown by women and, when there is a surplus, sold for their benefit.

Manioc ranks very low. The seniors show no interest in it but women from savannah villages near the markets grow and sell it for themselves.[1]

We have not specified the precise position of other tubers (taro, sweet potatoes) or maize, which anyway are not commercialised. Among the products acquired by gathering, kola nuts, because of their role in trade with the savannah, are stored by the seniors. Thus it is not primarily commercial considerations (or even taste) which give value to products, but, to a far greater extent, the role they play in relations between communities.

The modes of cooperation observed in agriculture are largely oriented to the cultivation of rice, and to a lesser extent, of yams. It is also true that because of the complementary nature of cultivation, they both determine the production of all other crops. The circulation of rice and yams within or between communities does not follow the same lines as other produce. We can therefore distinguish between high-rated products (rice and yams) and low-rated ones.

Although today coffee and cocoa are the main sources of cash income, they are not considered to have the same social importance as high-rated food products. Modes of cooperation do not operate in the case of cash crops, as they do with subsistence crops. Actually, they vary from one community to the next. Nor is the circulation of cash crops subject to the same rules. Indeed the integration of cash-cropping into the social norms is not yet complete and it remains economically and sociologically a complex phenomenon. As an agricultural activity cash-cropping tends to graft itself onto traditional structures and to make use of the modes of cooperation associated with subsistence agriculture, but as a source of cash and not of subsistence it remains marginal. Even though the money it brings could serve as a universal means of exchange, in the hands of the old traditionalists cash-cropping is reintegrated into the framework of personal relations of dependence by the introduction of money into the content of the bridewealth. Partly escaping from traditional norms, partly exiled from communal forms of cooperation, cash-cropping demands wage-labour, sets up new relations of production and departs from the structures of sub-sistence economy and tends towards those of the market economy. For all these reasons, although cash-cropping cannot be totally isolated from agriculture in general, problems related to it are examined separately. [In Chapter XIII of *The Guro*.]

II. THE MEAL

As Audrey Richards has shown in one of her earliest books,[2] the problem of food is still the main concern in self-sustaining societies. Food consumption, beyond its nutritional and routine functions, takes on the aspect of a real institution: the collective meal.

Among the Guro, agriculture rather than hunting is associated with this institution.

Whereas hunting supplies high quality, but only occasional, nourishment, agricultural products, which are varied and com-paratively more plentiful, form the basis of the daily diet. Hunting is a sporadic activity with an immediate product. Agricultural pro-duction, on the other hand, is the long-term result of a number of complex operations. The former demands the occasional and temporary cooperation of a small group of men brought together to accomplish a single task. The latter demands the regular, continuous cooperation (the amount of which varies according to the tasks), of restricted teams of men and women. Collective hunting, therefore is associated with a large but incohesive territorial group, the village; whereas agriculture is the continuous activity of small but more compact social units: the family communities and their social extensions. Finally, the product of hunting, in its unprepared form, is subject to straightforward sharing out between the participants; the prepared and cooked product of agriculture is consumed during a common meal by those individuals or groups who have cooperated in domestic and agricultural tasks.

One adjustment must be made to this contrast: agricultural

cooperation may also be occasional and bring together many people. It is then followed by a common meal bringing together a large number of people. But this form of cooperation is the extension of that which characterises family communities. We will therefore start by examining the latter, which will lead us to the former.

During periods of abundance, the Guro eat two main meals a day: one around mid-day and the other between dusk and darkness, sometimes continuing into the night. On this occasion, the members of the family which we will call a community (to be defined later, p. 295), come together under a *ba* [a shelter attached to the community] or in the open and divide themselves into distinct groups according to age and social rank. In the forest area, the oldest man, the grandsire, is already assimilated to the ancestor (*tra*) although still living but weak and left with moral authority only; the old man-ancestor eats alone. This is an indication of the respect accorded to him. In the savannah area, the grandsire eats with the other men (*gonenu*). The *gonenu* are all about thirty-five to forty years old; some are married men and some are fathers, others are bachelors or childless divorced men. They eat together with their senior (*kwa*) whatever the generation to which they belong. The non-adult men (*penu*), the adolescents, the younger bachelors and childless men make up a separate group.

Wives and their young children of both sexes eat separately from the men. When the community is large and a more clear-cut distinction is apparent in the hierarchy of men, the wives are separated into domestic groups made up of all the wives of one man or one class of men: the senior's wives, the senior's brothers' wives, the wives of the latter's sons. In this case the wife or widow of the oldest man will also eat separately.[3] Finally, the adolescent girls or young married girls (*blenu*) may also possibly form a separate group.

This division is a formal reflection of the social hierarchy but does not alter the distribution of food. Each domestic group (as defined above) is responsible for a hearth and cooks one dish for the community. This dish is divided into as many portions as there are groups, e.g.: one portion for the old man; one for the men (*gonenu*); one for the young men (*penu*); one for each of the other domestic groups of wives; one for the adolescent girls, etc.

By this rather involved mechanism food products are redistributed to all the members of the community; the collective meal is the end result of the process of agricultural cooperation: everyone's unspecified labour is mingled in a common product. Everyone's labour is blended and each participates in the product of the other's labour.

The functioning of this institution is not rigid. Not everybody attends each meal — some are in the fields or travelling, others, respecting a personal taboo, separate themselves from the community; and anyone in conflict with the senior may form temporary or definitive separate groups. Nor does each domestic group always prepare a dish for each meal, but sometimes takes it in turn.

In Bazré, the *goniwuo* [roughly: 'exogamic lineage'; see *The Guro*, pp. 62–3 for a proper definition] called Diazramo includes twelve domestic groups which would, in theory, mean that twelve dishes are prepared for each meal. When I had the opportunity of observing the meal only eight men were present under the *goniwuo*'s *ba*. The others were either in the fields or travelling. Only four dishes were served and not everyone ate from each of the four dishes: the first arrivals, satisfied after having tried two dishes, left the remainder to the late-comers. The adolescent boys, who formed a small group very close to that of the *gonenu*, were given what their senior had left behind. Despite this practice, the institution remains. It is always described according to its theoretical or ideal functioning, the only one which counts in the eyes of the Guro.

The Senezra Example

The Senezra *goniwuo* of Ziduho provides a concrete illustration of this theory.

Senezra comprises three communities which correspond to the spatial units which have already been described [in *The Guro*, p. 63]: the *dogi*, a unit of production and consumption smaller than the *goniwuo*. The reader will be able to refer to the map of the village [in *The Guro*, pp. 80–1] to locate the territorial distribution of these groups.

The figures in brackets correspond to the number of huts occupied by the main members of the *dogi*. The dates of birth are those recorded in the census.

First dogi

The first *dogi* is that of the *goniwuoza*, head of the *goniwuo*, Zohu bi Kwai (3). The four seniors are grouped together:

Zohu bi Kwai, *goniwuoza*, born in 1906, two wives and one under-age son.[4]

Tuai bi Tra (35), 1904, divorced, two sons, one of them married and childless.

Zehue bi Tua (1), 1915, three wives, six underage sons.

Wane bi Djeti (34), 1905, two wives, two underage sons; his family is not related to the lineage.

The *penu* gather near the house of the eldest among them, who in this case is Guni bi Tuai, who lives in the house of his uncle, Zohu bi Kwai. They are:

Tua bi Ohu, 1940.
Tua bi Vanie, 1943.
Tua bi Si, 1950.
Kwai bi Zohu, 1938.
Guni bi Tuai, date of birth unknown but oldest of them.
Tra bi Irie, 1943.
Tra bi Kwai, 1930, one wife and childless.

Each wife or group of wives of each married man, i.e. Zohu's two wives, Zehue bi Toa's three wives, Wane bi Djeti's two wives, Tra bi Kwai's wife — four domestic groups altogether — cook either each time or in turn a dish for the whole community. It is Tra bi Kwai's wife who cooks for Tuai bi Tra, for her husband and for Tra bi Irie. All the wives gather to eat a portion of each dish. The two adolescent girls of the *dogi* share a portion of the two dishes prepared by their respective mothers, eating alternately in each of their houses. Finally, young children, 'those who walk on all fours', are fed and suckled by their mothers.

Second dogi

The old man, Ba bi Gala (32) 1890, eats with the *gonenu.*
Gala bi Irie (32), 1913 (senior in function, for whom the other men work), two wives, two sons, one of whom is Tra bi Tie, born of one of his wives' past marriages.
Gala bi Ba (28) 1917, one wife, one under-age son.
Gala bi Kanao (30), 1923, two wives, no children. He is the owner of the *ba* in which meals are eaten.
Gala bi Kwai (32), 1919, crippled and unmarried.
Tra bi Tie (54), 1937, he is the son of a divorced woman now married to Gala bi Irie (see above) and adopted by the latter. Two wives and three under-age sons.
Toa bi Irie (51), 1920, two wives, one under-age son; he is the last survivor of a family which is not related to the *goniwuo*, dependent on Gala bi Irie.

The domestic groups are made up of: the wives of Gala bi Irie and Tra bi Tie who form only one domestic unit; the wife of Gala bi Ba, the two wives of Gala bi Kanao, or three groups. Ba bi Gala's wife, being too old, does not cook; like Gala she shares the food prepared by the other women. It should be noted that Kwai's adopted son's wives belong to the group of Kwai's wives. All four of them live in the same house and all the women of the *dogi* eat together.

The four boys and all the bachelors and the four adolescent girls form two other distinct groups. The youngest girls go and eat at each one's mother's house in turn.

Third dogi

Tubwi bi Gonezie here fulfils the function of the senior although he is the youngest of three brothers; one of them came back to the village in 1953 after working on the railway for fifteen years and the last one was a soldier for several years.

The senior group is composed of four *gonenu*:

Tubwi bi Gonezie (80), 1920 or 1924, three wives, eight under-age sons.

Tubwi bi Djei (59), 1913, former railwayman, one wife, one under-age son.

Tubwi bi Dilo (60), 1920 (?), former soldier, one wife, one under-age son.

Boli bi Kwai (79), 1912, client, bachelor.

The domestic groups are made up of: Gonezie's three wives, Djei's wife, Dilo's wife, Boli bi Kwai's mother eats alone because she is 'very old'.

The boys, all unmarried and aged five to twenty, and the girls again form two separate groups.

These examples show that the status of *gonenu* involves two concurrent factors: age and matrimonial status. Marriage alone does not confer the status of manhood on the young and childless (e.g., Tra bi Kwai) but, by contrast, elderly bachelors like Gala bi Kwai and Boli bi Kwai become *gonenu* by sheer virtue of their age.

III. THE COMMUNITY

The individuals who share a common meal make up a community. This is characterised by its permanence and continuity — every day it assembles to join in the common meal.

Its composition is described by the Guro in kinship terms: it is said that sons (*bi*) eat with their father (*ti*) and juniors (*zuoza*) with their senior (*veneza*). More specifically, the community is supposed to include the grandsire, the senior, his younger brothers, his sons, his sons' sons and the dependents of each head of a restricted family — wives, elderly mothers, young children of both sexes and protégés.

The community is made up of one or more permanent production groups which incorporate individuals of both sexes who participate continuously on common fields, either collectively or individually, in the entire agriculture cycle. This production group is sometimes called *nianawuo* (*niana*: labour; *wuo*: concept of following — those who work behind a senior). The composition of the labour cell is also described in the same terms as that of the whole community: the sons work for their fathers, the juniors for their seniors. The difference is that the community also includes infirm old men, cripples, sick people and young children, i.e. those who are unproductive.

Hence in terms of kinship or seniority, community and productive cells seem to coincide precisely and also to coincide both with the lineage (or with the segment of the lineage) — a concept of structural anthropology based on the notion of kinship — and with the *goniwuo* - an actual social group which claims to be the result of kinship or assimilated social relations.

However, a careful examination of the facts reveals that between these two different groupings there are contradictions and shifts indicative of their growth and their social dynamic. It is these differences which we shall try to bring out by studying the modes of cooperation associated with agricultural activities, the composition of the product groups and how they relate themselves to other social units. Here again, there are many variations from one village to the next, and we consider it better to discuss in detail the cooperative organisation of the three villages described earlier before making any generalisations. We shall first study Bazré (N'Goi) in particular detail since its lineages provide an example of greater cohesion which will make it easier for us to understand the more complex structures of Ziduho and Duonéfla.

Bazré (N'Goi)

The N'Goi people number about 1,600 in six villages and claim to have one common ancestor, Kwasi N'Goi. Arriving a long time ago from Baulé country to hunt, he found the place well-stocked with game and so settled there with his brother Go and their dependents. The descendants of N'Goi are said to be the founders of the six present villages.

Such is the tradition as it is related by Bolu bi Bia, a prominent member of the main lineage of Bazré. In fact, although each village claims for itself formal relation to the ancestor, either they are not all able to relate themselves to him or they do so in a manner which does not agree with Bia's representation as pictured in the genealogical model (p. 297). The data collected in each village among the traditional authorities differ in the following way from this version:

Koaddi: According to this version N'goi's son, said to have founded the village was not called Koapoa — the village's presumed

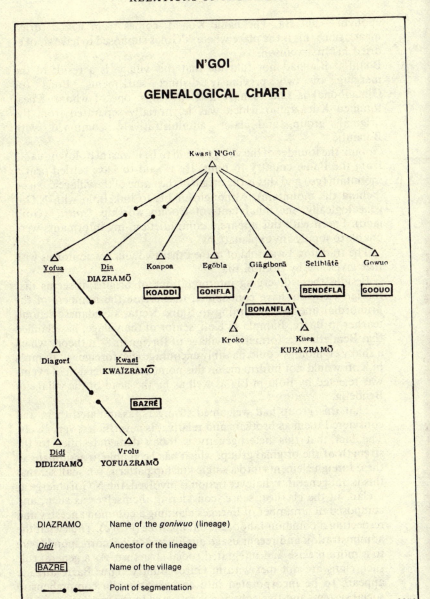

N'GOI

GENEALOGICAL CHART

Kwasi N'Goï

Yofua

Dia
DIAZRAMŌ

Koapoa

Egōbla

Giãgibonã

Seliblãtè

Gowuo

KOADDI

GONFLA

BENDÉFLA

GOOUO

BONANFLA

Kroko

Kuea
KUEAZRAMŌ

Diagori

Kwasi
KWAÏZRAMŌ

BAZRÉ

Didi
DIDIZRAMŌ

Vrolu
YOFUAZRAMŌ

DIAZRAMO	Name of the *goniwuo* (lineage)
Didi	Ancestor of the lineage
BAZRE	Name of the village
	Point of segmentation

eponym — but Ba. The name Koaddi comes from *wikoa* (dried meat), since this is the place where N'Goi is supposed to have smoke-dried his first venison.

Boanfla: Bia had not told me that this village is a result of the merging of two previously distinct settlements. Bona (or Ginagibona) is said to have had two sons, one of whom, Kuea, founded Kueazramo which was territorially separated from the original group and later administratively combined with Bonanflé.

Goouo: the founder of the village is said to be Kwasi bi Bolo who came from the Baulé country to hunt. He is said to have settled near a mountain (*go*) and this is the origin of the name of the village *Go wuo* (behind the mountain). Although unable to link Bolo with N'Goi genealogically, the inhabitants of Goouo worship *Goitre* (Goi's land). Faced with this apparent contradiction, my informants were unable to supply any explanations.

The tradition I was told of in the other two villages conforms with that given me by Bolu bi Bia.

Besides these diverging interpretations of origins, it seems that foreign elements have contributed to increase the numbers of the primordial lineage. According to Sidiki Keita, a Sudanese school-teacher in Bazré, Bampla bi Kofi, senior of the village, has claimed that Bendefla was formerly a village of foreigners — a theory which a shaky etymology could possibly encourage (*be*: foreigner). Bampla bi Kofi would not inform me on this point and this version of events was rejected by Bolu bi Bia as well as by the head of the village of Bendefla.

That this group had welcomed strangers, assimilated them and considered them as brothers and relatives is nevertheless very likely. The fact that this heterogeneity is today denied testifies to the strength of the original group, which has been able to assimilate all these foreign elements into a single kinship pattern. We shall see that this is not general. Whatever fiction is involved, the N'Goi emerge as a clan, in the classical sense, considering themselves as such, and composed of a number of lineages claiming a common ancestry and respecting a common taboo, the chimpanzee (*groga*). Thus what the administration and recent usage qualify as a 'tribe' corresponds here to a more precise and integrated social structure. As a general rule such clans are not met with in Guro country. Thus Bazré already appears to be incorporated into an exceptionally comprehensive social system, and this cohesion is reflected in the institutions of the village.

Bazré is the village of the 'chef de canton', Bolu bi Bia; it is also that of the 'chef de tribu', Yobolu bi Gonekalo. It has, in addition, its 'chef de village'. As a result of revolts against the administration, the size of the N'Goi canton, which had previously included the V'nan and Nana 'tribes' has been restricted to include only the N'Goi 'tribe'. The 'chef de canton' and the 'chef de tribu' thus exercise their authority in the same administrative area.[5]

The fact that the most prominent members of the N'Goi live in Bazré may explain why we find there a better knowledge of the institutions and a greater conformity to social norms. Bazré, by comparison with other villages, gives the impression of being a more rigorous structural 'model'. Individuals such as Bia and Gonekalo, who told us about these institutions and consider themselves to be the guardians and trustees of a tradition which they are perfectly familiar with, can state clearly and without hesitation the genealogies of the whole village and the much more extended one of the whole clan. This clarity, even if it expresses theory more than reality, contrasts with the more confused and sometimes contradictory information gathered in other villages.

The geneological model on p. 297 shows how the inhabitants of Bazré are related to the original stock. Two sons of N'Goi, Dia and Yofua, are said to be the founders of the four *goniwuo* which today make up the village.[6] Each of these is named after an ancestor who is located at the point of segmentation from the original group and which is the point of reference for the *goniwuo*: it is the descendants of this ancestor who constitute the *goniwuo*.

The four *goniwuo* differ in size: Diazramo is approximately twice as large as each of the others. There is also a difference in genealogical depth: Yofuazramo and Diazramo go directly to N'Goi's sons; Kwaizramo to the latter's grandson and Didizramo which appears to be a separate segment of Yofua to the founding ancestor's great-grandson. One of N'Goi's two sons, Yofua, is at the apex of the three *goniwuo*, the other, Dia, of only one. Although they have the same depth, Yofuazramo is several times segmented and cannot be as large as Diazramo which has maintained its unity until now.

The *goniwuo* which have come about as a result of segmentation are obviously the most integrated. Didizramo, the 'youngest' of the four lineages, is considered as a single segment whose members all descend from Gesa, the founder's son;[7] Kofi, the senior, is the *goniwuoza*. The Yofuazramo branch, deprived of Yofua's collaterals and then of Diagore's, is composed on the one hand of Aire's descendants and on the other of Yofua's descendants through women: the present *goniwuoza*, Busu, the last survivor of his generation, belongs to this group.

The members of Kwaizramo are divided into two main segments

descending from Kwasi's two sons: Koble and Guese. Tumbwi bu Bia *goniwuoza* (whose funeral was still being celebrated during our stay) belonged to the first. Although he came from the generation below that of Koble's sons, Bia who was the eldest, claimed the prerogatives of the senior. Hence Bia's authority extended over his father's brothers as well as over Timbue, the son of Guese. It was by virtue of his age that Timbue succeeded Bia, thus causing the authority to ascend a generation.

Diazramo, which descends directly and without segmentation from Dia, one of N'Goi's sons, is also divided into two segments originating from Dia's two sons: Yobolu and Bampla. The *goniwuoza* Gonekalo is Yobolu's son. He is of a higher generation than all his dependents. Most of these belong to a subsegment stemming from Yobolu, through Bolu and Kwame. Gonekalo's successor, Bia, Bolu's son, belongs to this branch. The second main segment is directly related to Bampla, Fia's son. Tone, Nampla's grandson, is appointed successor to Bolu bi Bia. The kinship relations which link the members of this *goniwuo* refer back to a more distant ancestor and are looser than in the other lineages.

These genealogies, in Radcliffe-Brown's phrase 'never give us anything more than the skeleton of the real ordering of relatives in the social life'.[8]

Expressed in Guro terminology relations of dependence conform to classificatory kinship relations: fathers (*ti*) have authority over their sons (*bi*) who have brotherly relations (*bwi*) among themselves. Among brothers (*bwi*) it is the eldest or most senior (*veneza*) who has authority over the others. But this crude terminology does not describe the actual relations which exist between individuals. It is obvious from the above cases that relations of dependence do not correspond to this model: the authority of the senior goes beyond his own dependents to extend not only to his brother's son or to his father's brother's son, but also to his father's brothers.

The kinship system by itself does not ascribe precise relations between the members of the same lineage. Indeed relations of dependence are actually linked in the labour process. Each senior has among his dependents adult men and women responsible for agricultural tasks and who constitute the permanent production group. The composition of this group does not always correspond to the genealogical model and its observations will allow us to perceive how social relations within the lineage are established functionally and organically, and how these relations cut across the kinship relations.

BAZRÉ DIAGRAM

DIDIZRAMŌ

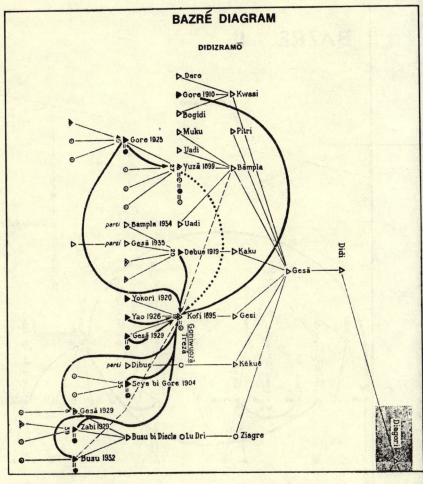

KEY :

Dale 1920   Name and date of birth

▲   Active man

●   Active woman

⧊   Inactive man

☉   Inactive woman

△   Deceased or absent man

○   Deceased or absent woman

=   Marriage links

≠   Divorce

——   Genealogical relations

– – – –   Adoption links

▬▬   Labour relations

· · · · · · · ·   Links of meal sharing

32   Reference to house numbers on the map of the village

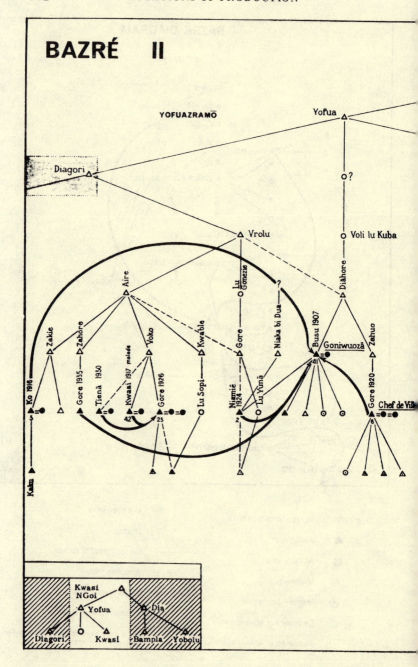

BAZRÉ   II

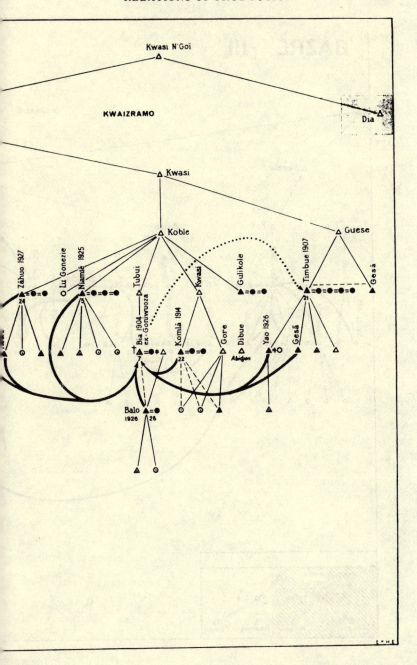

BAZRÉ III

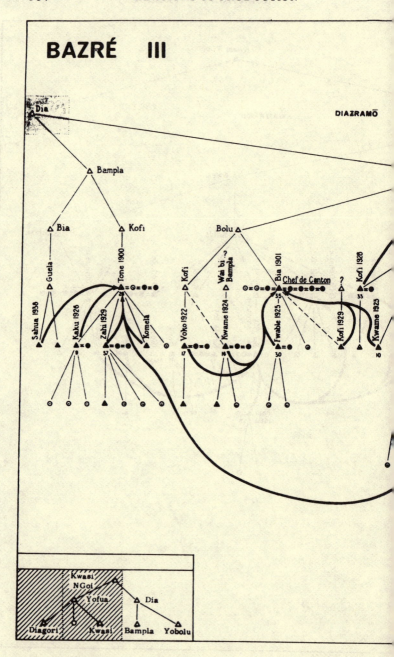

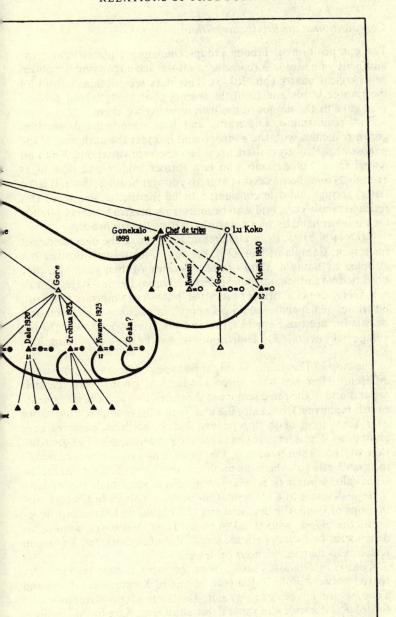

Composition of the Production Groups

The composition of labour groups (*nianawuo*) placed under the authority of a senior is reproduced on the accompanying simplified genealogical charts (pp. 301–5). This data was obtained from all the lineage heads and from the seniors controlling labour groups, who gave us the names of the men working for them.

For Yofuazramo, Didizramo and Kwaizramo, the production group coincides with the *goniwuo* and is under the authority of the *goniwuoza*. However, there are a few aberrant situations: Voko bu Kwasi from Yofuazramo who is a former soldier and now ill, is excluded from the succession as is his younger brother, Gore. It is the latter, though, who is considered to be the titular 'senior' of this residual family core, and who benefits from his two brothers' labour. On the other hand he does not work for Busu the *goniwuoza*.

Bampla bi Yuza, from Didizramo, is placed in the dependence of his senior, Bampla bi Kofi (19), the son of his father's brother but adopted by Bampla, Yuza's father. Because of their great age, they both belong to the council of elders (*wiblimo*) of the village. Yuza's son, Gore, works a little for his father 'but not too much or else Kofi, on whom he depends, would get angry'. In addition to the members of this lineage are Seye bi Gore and his family (a stranger to the village but integrated to Didizramo) who is the protégé of Bampla bi Kofi.

The case of Diazramo, as might be expected because of its size, is different. Here we have three production groups, each centred around one of the three seniors of the previously identified segments or sub-segments. Gonekalo, Bia and Tone thus retain their authority over their immediate dependents, but in addition each includes among his dependents orphans from their collaterals. The distribution of the orphans among the three seniors is, however, made independently of their position in the three lineage segments. Gonekalo, a *goniwuoza* who has no direct adult male descendant, takes in Kwame bi Kofi, son of his brother Yobolu bi Kwame, and the sons of Gore (the deceased son of Yobolu) with the exception of Gesa, the eldest, who is taken in by Tone. Moreover, among his dependents he includes Kiena, son of Yobolu's daughter, Yobolu lu Koks, who married without bridewealth.

Kwame bi Djahore's sons, from the same lineage segment, are shared between Bolu bi Bia (son of one of Kwame's brothers) and Tone, senior of the next segment. The latter adopts Kwadio, eldest son of Kwame bi Djahore and his adult son, Kwadio bi Djahore. Tone includes in his group his three sons plus the son of Guela, who is the son of his father's brother.

Finally Bia includes among his dependents Fwable, his adult son,[9] who returned from Abidjan in 1955; Voko, his deceased brother Kofi's adult son; Kwame, the latter's adopted son who is less strictly dependent on Bia; Kofi adopted by Bia and whose father is unknown; and finally, as we have seen, Kwadio, Djahore's son.[10]

No genealogical chart or kinship relation would be able to inform us *a priori* about this distribution (the only rule which seems to emerge here is that Tone who belongs to the senior segment, despite his official date of birth, is considered to be doyen of the entire family heads). Nor could they tell us the reasons why, for example, Gore's sons, who logically seem to depend on Gonekalo, are divided between the two segments, nor the number of orphans that each of the surviving seniors should take. By contrast a functional reason for this distribution is obvious: the concern to supply each senior with a sufficient number of active men to constitute an efficient labour team. Gonekalo and Tone, who are both inactive, each have seven men among their dependents, while Bia, who is still active, has five.

The following table gives the number of active individuals in each *goniwuo* and reconstituted *nianawuo* (production group), as well as the ratio of the active in relation to the total number of people in each unit.

We can see that the ratio between active people and the total population is comparatively well-balanced between the different labour units. The groups loaded with the most inactive people, i.e. mainly those of Diazramo, have a higher birthrate, and in particular a greater number of girls. We also notice that, insofar as it concerns the three subgroups of Diazramo, this ratio is not the expression of natural demographic growth but the result of a distribution of the members of the *goniwuo* between the three of them.

Each of the seniors, as the head of a small production unit holds, by comparison with his dependents, the largest fields, the largest plantations and some kola trees, sources of produce which go entirely to him. All the men participate in the clearing of the ground and the upkeep of the fields; all the women jointly cultivate a common rice field but split up into smaller units to carry out domestic tasks. The product of the harvests, rice in particular, is stored in granaries of the senior who invests his wife with the responsibility of distributing the grain according to the needs of each domestic group.

Male dependents are sometimes entrusted with a coffee plantation which they cultivate as they like. These plantations are usually small and recent. The product will also be given completely to the senior.

The task of the production groups is to feed the whole community, which as we know, also include the unproductive members. In the

BAZRÉ: DISTRIBUTION OF THE ACTIVE POPULATION BY COMMUNITY

	Men		Women		Total Population	Total Active	1	2
	Total	Active	Total	Active				
Yofuazramo	15	8	12	8	27	16	1/1.7	1/1.34
Kwaizramo	19	9	11	11	30	20	1/1.5	1/3.3
Didizramo	16	10	20	10	36	20	1/1.8	1/3.6
Diazramo	32	20	50	28	82	48	1/1.7	1/4.1
TOTAL	82	48	93	57	175	104		
Diazramo Tone's *Nianawuo*	10	7	18	8	28	15	1/1.9	1/4
Bia's *Nianawuo*	8	6	16	10	24	16	1/1.5	1/4
Gohekalo's *Nianawuo*	14	7	16	10	30	17	1/1.8	1/4.3
TOTAL	32	20	50	28	82	48	1/1.7	1/1.4.1

1: Ratio of active/total population
2: Ratio of active male/total population

case of the first three *goniwuo* the production group coincides with each single community. The three groups of Diazramo, on the other hand, meet around a single collective meal. In this way the food products produced independently by each *nianwuo*, are partly reinjected into the consumption circuit of the whole *goniwuo* (except for the amounts taken by the seniors to fulfil certain social obligations towards individuals outside the community).

While each *nianawuoza* has authority in relation to labour, the *goniwuoza* remains at the apex of the overall economic activity by presiding over the collective consumption of the products. The cohesion of the *goniwuo* is maintained at this level.

It therefore seems that in Bazré the *goniwuo*, as a traditional social group, can be defined as a consumption unit and that segmentation is materialised by new economic connections, entailing a decentralisation of the cooperative organisation and a reorganisation of the circulation of food products.

Now this coincidence between community and *goniwuo* will not be found everywhere and Ziduho provides an example of a far less cohesive village:

Ziduho (Yassua)

The present village of Ziduho (Yassua) is composed of three administratively recognised *goniwuo*: Vahuzrà, Senezra, Ziduhomo. Vahuzra itself is composed of two previously distinct groups: Vahuzra and Kiezra (see map, p. 310).

Vahuzra was created by Ya bi Vadru[12] from T'sienland which he left after internal conflict and war against neighbouring Bete, brought about by a case of adultery. He first settled in Luonu country whence he later emigrated to vacant lands in the Kiapuna forest. Later he moved again to settle near another forest known today as Vahuzrapro.

The history of Kiezra goes back to Balu bi Nianaho[13] who, as a result of a war whose circumstances have been forgotten, left Sienedunufla in T'sienland with his family to settle in Gerahore Gowe (*go* = hill; *we* = palm wine) on the right bank of the Marahue which became the place of sacrifice for the lineage. After the death of Nianaho during a hunting trip, his old slave discovered the Marahue which had previously been unknown and whose fish resources induced the villagers to move *en masse* and settle on the left bank, north of Vahuzura, near a forest since named Kiezrapro. The two lineages, Kiezra and Vahuzra, formed an alliance while maintaining distinct territories and residence. At the time of Zra bi Zrai, a young Yassua woman from Klazra, married in Beziaka (Bueru), died in her husband's family's village. The Yassua and the Buenu were not

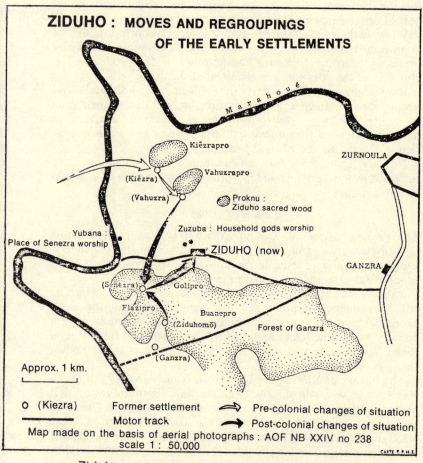

ZIDUHO : MOVES AND REGROUPINGS OF THE EARLY SETTLEMENTS

Marahoué

Kiêzrapro

(Kiêzra)

Vahuzrapro

(Vahuzra)

Proknu :
Ziduho sacred wood

ZUENOULA

Zuzuba : Household gods worship

Yubana :
Place of Senezra worship

ZIDUHO (now)

GANZRA

(Senezra)   Golipro

Flazipro

Buanepro

(Ziduhomō)

Forest of Ganzra

(Ganzra)

Approx. 1 km.

O (Kiezra)   Former settlement   Pre-colonial changes of situation
                Motor track   Post-colonial changes of situation
Map made on the basis of aerial photographs : AOF NB XXIV no 238
                scale 1 : 50,000

CARTE F.P.H.E.

Ziduho : changes of the early settlements

formally allied, and such an occurrence was settled by war, which broke out between the two tribes. It was on this occasion that Vahuzra invited the people of Kiezra to come and join them in their fortified enclosure.

The new village retained the original name of Vahuzra. At first Kiezra maintained its own identity and institutions but today Kiezra is totally absorbed into Vahuzra which represents them in the council of elders.

A bit further to the south of Vahuzra had settled Vanie-bi Kaha[14] from Motifla in Va land; he too had moved after a war against enemies whose name has been forgotten. His settlement on the border of Flazipro was named Senezra after the name of a variety of bird (*sene*) [plegiositagra cullata, p.l.s. Müller, or weaver bird] which were common there. Senezra consists of only one lineage and was fortified.

Finally, a little further east was Ziduhomo founded by Mole bi Za[15] of Guiriafla in T'sien country and said to be related to Ye bi Vadru. He settled on unoccupied lands near the Guanepro and Golipro forests.

After the French invasion around 1915 Captain Foussat brought together Senezra, Ziduhomo and the mingled lineages of Kiezra and Vahuzra, all on the spot where Senezra was located. The new village was given the administrative name of Ziduho. Later, around 1917, when Ziduho was flooded by the rising river, it was moved to its present location (see map, p. 310).

Originally, each of the four settlements housed only one lineage. Two of these settlements were already fortified.

Social factors explain most of the movements and regroupings of these settlements, although ecological causes also play a part. Although begun before colonisation the growth of these settlements into real villages was the work of the military administration.

The map, which is drawn on the basis of a survey of the territory, shows that each settlement was originally located at the edge of a forest in order to exploit both its undercover and the surrounding savannah. All our informants claim that this land was vacant.

By contrast with Bazré the lineages are of varied origins and their merging accident. Each of the four original settlements consisted of one single community but orginally they did not call themselves a *goniwuo*. The term has been imposed in this case by the colonial administration and accepted by the villagers after their regrouping. A *goniwuo* does not correspond exactly to a lineage since two of them are united under the name of Vahuzra. Beside the four main lineages the present genealogies reveal twenty smaller families either foreign, or related by affinity to the main lineages, or of a slave origin.[16] Most of these minor segments have undefined relations with the main lineages. Some are simultaneously claimed by various *goniwuoza*, others claim to be independent, although this is contradicted by seniors of the main lineage.

Since no common ascendance is claimed by all fractions, the arbitrary regroupings of unintegrated lineages leaves chinks within which smaller family cores live and perpetuate themselves. The diversity of origins has not been overcome; on the contrary it seems to contaminate even the main lineages.

The community (all those who consume together) is here limited to segments of lineages, to which occasionally are attached families or individuals of foreign origin; such communities are called *dogi*. The three main lineages or *goniwuo* (Vahuzra, Ziduhomo and Senezra) are made up of several such *dogi*.

Vahuzra

Vahuzra is the name of the village *goniwuo*. It includes 102 members counting Kae bi Bohu, the village head, who belongs to it. It is made up of two major lineages, Vahuzra and Kiezra, and of five secondary families, three of which are associated with Vahuzra and two with Kiezra. (Two other families mentioned in the census are no longer represented in the village.) The main lineage, Vahuzra proper, descends from Hue bi Vadru and is split into four segments regrouped into three *dogi*: that of Kai bi Bohu, the 'chef de village', that of Gala bi Dua and that of Kwable bi Boti.

The dogi of Bohu: The production group which in this case corresponds to the consumption group, is composed of Bohu's immediate kin, those of his sons of working age and living in the village (some have emigrated), their wives plus his own eight wives — a permanent labour force of sixteen hoes (i.e. sixteen women) and five machetes (five men, Bohu's sons plus himself if necessary). Each married son is responsible for a rice field which he maintains with his wife or wives, the produce being handed over to his father. Bohu's wives together cultivate one common rice field which is cleared by the team of men. They also grow such crops as ground-nuts and manioc to sell in the market for their profit. They earth up the manioc themselves or with their husband's help. They each have the use of an individual field for this crop.

The *dogi* is a homogeneous consumption unit. The wives are divided into domestic groups each with its own hearth (as described for Senezra). These hearths are located under the common *ba* belonging to Tra, Bohu's eldest son, where all the *dogi* gather at mealtimes, separating into age and sex groups. The sons cultivate individual rice fields but they have no coffee plantation. They are all supposed to work with their dependents on their father's plantation (seven hectares according to the 1956 land registry) which was started in 1950. However, the family production group, is not required to perform all the tasks involved in the coffee growing; the bulk of the labour is performed by journeymen (there were seven in 1956 according to the registry). During our stay Bohu employed only two journeymen annually, as well as a few pieceworkers. In addition to this permanent family assistance, Bohu also occasionally benefits from the labour of his wives' relatives (*voli*) or from the collective help (*bo*) of the village youth which has been made use of four times since 1950.

The dogi of Gala bi Dua: Gala bi Dua with two wives but no children is in principle Bohu's successor — Gala is Bohu's father's brother's grandson, and replaces him when he is absent. Among his dependents are Bwi, a brother and two of Bwi's sons: Fua who is married and Irie; Zro his divorced second brother and three sons of Kwai bi Kwable (who is now dead), his father's brother's grandsons, two of whom are older than himself. Still Gala bi Bwi does not accept this dependence and refuses to hand over rights over his sons. This situation reflects a conflict of precedence whose origin is obscure and which also extends to one wife, claimed by one and living in the other's house.

This fragmentation is reflected in the organisation of labour: Dua cultivates his fields and his coffee plantation with his two wives, now in the village, with his brother's eldest son and with Gala bi Zro, his youngest brother — three machetes and three hoes.

Bwi with his very young son and his wife make one working team; his eldest son works alternately for him and for his brother. Finally, Kwable bi Tra cultivates his fields with his son and his younger brother.

Kwable bi Irie, Tra's second brother works on his own on the Zuenula ferry.

Each of these men cultivates his own coffee plantation. Except for Gala bi Bwi, who eats by himself, all the other members of the *dogi*, including Bwi's sons, meet around Dua to share the common meal to which they all contribute.

The dogi of Kwable bi Boti: As a veteran who served for five years with the French army, Boti's position in the lineage is marginal. He is approximately forty years old, with two wives, and since his return to the village he has adopted his late brother's two sons, one of whom is married and was previously a dependent of Gala bi Dua. Together they constitute an independent unit. As Kwable bi Boti receives an annual pension of 100,000 CFA, Boti is under great pressure to make gifts and is considering moving to Zuenula.

We should remember that all the *dogi*s described here have a common ancestry. Three other families are associated with this *goniwuo*. The first one stems from Kiabi, who grew up with Hue bi Bohu, the founder of the lineage and who, although not related to him, is considered to be his 'brother'. This segment which includes only three active men is still divided into two *dogi*. Two other families (one of which is related through the wives to Vahuzra) each form a *dogi*.

The dogi of Kiezra: Kiezra, the lineage associated with Vahuzra, is a single *dogi* consisting of the members of the main lineage who all work together plus Irie bi Bwi (the bigamous son of a foreigner who married a Senezra woman) who shares the meal of the Kiezra senior. Finally, Boti bi Vanie, although formally attached to Kiezra, works and eats alone with his two wives. One of his sons, a tailor in Zuenula with only one wife, sends his wife to help with the coffee harvest on his father's plantation but does not contribute to agricultural labour in any other way.

Altogether the Vahuzra *goniwuo* is made up of seven different strands, and is divided into eight *dogi* not counting the two men left to themselves.

Ziduhomo

The people who, according to the census, belong to the Ziduhomo *goniwuo* come from six different stocks redistributed into five *dogi*. The main one is organised around the *goniwuoza*, Tie bi Kua, a member of a small segment founded by his father whose brother, we are told, had been 'chief' of the former village of Ziduho. The widower of four wives and about to marry a fifth one, he is childless but he has welcomed into his *dogi* members of three other families, viz.:

(a) Tra bi Fua, probably of slave origin, bigamous but childless. Despite his age — approximately thirty-seven — Fua is *traza* and *wibliza* of the *goniwuo*: he took over Kua's functions as *goniwuoza* during the latter's absence in 1957. His younger brother Zegbe who recently came back from 'Basse-Côte' is divorced and has a young son; but although he shares Kua's meal he works neither for him nor for his elder brother.

(b) Tia bi Yati and Tia bi Gobue, two brothers of slave origin who were adopted by Tie, Kua's father.

(c) Zo bi Zoati, from a family which is probably of Diula origin, is bigamous and the father of two *penu* sons and his nephew Tie bi Zoati, married to three wives and the father of two young sons.

All these people meet under Gobue's *ba* to take their meals together.

The labour groups are more restricted. Kua's adopted nephews Yati and Gobue are the only two to do routine work in his fields; Gobue, who is married, also cultivates a separate rice field, but no coffee plantation. He works with his brother on the coffee plantation belonging to Kua who does not hire any journeyman. The other family heads of the *dogi* cultivate their own fields with their immediate dependents, sometimes with their wives only. According to Kua they hand over their products to him. They each cultivate coffee plantations with the help of piece-workers and the money-income is theirs.

Besides this *dogi*, two households, those of Zo bi Nati and Irie bi Ya (the brother and nephew of Zo bi Zoati) eat and cultivate independently with their own immediate dependents.

The second important group in Ziduhomo belongs genealogically to the family of the founder of the lineage, Mole bi Za. It is divided into two segments, each forming a *dogi*. All the members of Kua bi Tuei's *dogi* jointly cultivate and consume the product of agriculture; three of Tuei's dependents cultivate their own coffee plantation: they are his son and his two nephews, all three married. The second segment is composed of Gore bi Twi and his three young sons only. Twi is said to be on bad terms with Tuei, his elder brother. He eats with Yali bi Irie from the Senezra *goniwuo* who is himself in conflict with his lineage.

Thus we have here a number of interesting cases: the main group is formed around a man who does not belong to the founding lineage and who is unable to trace his ancestry beyond his father. He has collected around him only individuals who are not genealogically related to him, the descendants of slave or foreign families. By contrast the founder's lineage is withering away and has lost all political and religious functions, these functions having been taken over by the lineage of Tie bi Kwai. A reconstitution of new social units composed of heterogeneous elements came as a response to the disintegration of the lineage organisation. These new units, however, are still loose and fragmentary.

Senezra

The Senezra *goniwuo* is made up of the descendants of seven unrelated ancestors. It is divided up into three *dogi* whose domestic functioning has been described above [pp. 293–5].

The first *dogi* corresponds to the founding ancestor Vanie bi Kae of Motifla in Va land and it includes the *goniwuoza*, Zohu bi Kwai as well as the associated family of Wane bi Djeti, which is of foreign or slave origin and related through marriage with a woman from Vahuzra. They all eat together. Four of them cultivate individually-owned coffee plantations in addition to the *dogi*'s fields; they are (1) the family head, Kwai, helped by his young unmarried son, his sister's son now living with him, and occasionally hiring labourers; (2) Zehue bi Tua, helped by one of his young sons; (3) Djeti who is helped only by his wife. Old Tuei bi Tra's plantations are cultivated by his son Kwai and his wife. The income from coffee growing does not go into the community fund but remains at the disposal of each planter.

The second *dogi* is that of Tubue bi Gonezie, the sixth direct descendant of Moti bi Guone. Although Moti bi Guone is not considered to be the founder of the Senezramo lineage, Gonezie's father, Tubue, is the *treza* (priest of the soil), doubtless by virtue of his age and because he belongs to a lineage of free men (Ba bi Gala, a member of the third *dogi*, who is older, is of obscure ancestry). This *dogi* corresponds almost exactly to the segment of a lineage. Boli bi Kwai, who is not related to it, acts as a protégé. Each of Tubue's three sons cultivates his own plantation; Boli bi Kwai who is older and without dependents only participates in food crops and has no plantation.

The third *dogi*, that of Gala bi Irie, the village diviner (son of old Ba bi Gala whose father married a woman from Senezra) consists of the four sons of Ba bi Gala and of Toa bi Irie, his adopted son and youngest child of a foreign family. Yali bi Irie, whose origin is obscure and who is unrelated to the lineage, used to belong to this community. He has now joined Gore bi Twi of Ziduhomo who, as we have seen, has separated from his own *dogi*. Gala bi Irie's dependents meet under the *ba* of Irie's younger brother, Gala bi Kanao. Gala bi Irie cultivates a coffee plantation jointly with his brother Ba and with the assistance of Kanao and Tra bi Tie (the son by a first marriage of one of Irie's wives). Ba also owns another plantation which he keeps alone with his wife. Gala's adopted son, Toa bi Irie, as well as Yali bi Irie, also grow their own plantations. Bohu bi Fua who is also counted in the *goniwuo* is reputed to be a sorcerer and eats alone with his wife.

At the village level the ratio between active and inactive is almost identical to that which we have calculated for Bazré: 1 active male to 4.1 inhabitants in Bazré compared with 4.2 in Ziduho and 1 inactive person to 1.7 inhabitants compared with 7.5 here. But the fragmentation of the Ziduho *goniwuo* into smaller units works against this equilibrium. The *dogi* with average ratios are those with the largest number of people i.e. between twenty-two and

ZIDUHO: DISTRIBUTION OF ACTIVE POPULATION BY DUGI

	Active			Inactive			Total Population (7)	Male active per persons (3)/(7)	Inactive per persons (7)/(3)
	Men (1)	Women (2)	Total Active (3)	Men (4)	Women (5)	Total Inactive (6)			
Vahuzra									
1. Kae bi Bohu	5	11	16	11	6	17	33	6.6	2.1
2. Kwable bi Boti	3	3	6	1	0	1	7	2.3	1.1
3. Gala bi Dua	5 }8	3 }7	8 }15	3 }6	1 }4	4 }10	12 }25	2.4 }3.4	1.5 }1.7
4. Kwable bi Tra	3	4	7	3	3	6	13	4.4	1.9
5. Irie bi Kue	1	3	4	5	2	7	11	11.0	2.8
6. Tizra bi Irie	3	4	7	3	0	3	10	3.3	1.4
7. Tra bi Zable	4	2	6	2	1	3	9	2.3	1.5
8. Kae bi Ya	4	2	6	0	1	1	7	1.7	1.1
TOTAL VAHUZRA	28	32	60	28	14	42	102	3.6	1.7
Ziduhomō									
1. Kua bi Tūei	6	8	14	6	6	12	26	4.4	1.85
2. Gore bi Twi	3	3	6	1	1	2	8	2.7	1.3
3. Tie bi Kua	6	8	14	6	5	11	25	4.2	1.8
4. Zo bi Nāti	1	4	5	2	3	5	10	10.0	2.0
5. Irie bi Ya	1	2	3	2	2	4	7	7.0	2.3
TOTAL ZIDUHOMŌ	17	25	42	17	17	34	76	4.5	1.8
Senezra									
1. Zohu bi Kwaï	6	8	14	9	3	12	26	4.4	1.9
2. Tubue bi Gonezie	5	6	11	8	3	11	22	4.4	2.0
3. Gala bi Ba	6	11	17	7	4	11	28	4.7	1.65
4. Bohu bi Fua	1	1	2	1	3	4	6	6.0	3.0
TOTAL SENEZRA	18	26	44	25	13	38	82	4.6	1.9
Kiēzra	6	13	19	5	3	8	27	4.5	1.4
TOTAL ZIDUHO	69	96	165	75	47	122	287	4.2	1.75

Table 2

DUONEFLA: DISTRIBUTION OF ACTIVE POPULATION BY DOGI

Dogi no.	ACTIVE		Total Active	Inactive	Total Population	1 male active per . . . persons	1 active per . . . persons
	M	F					
Duo bi Sei, *dogi* no.							
I	2	1	3	1	4	2	1.35
II	4	1	5	6	11	2.75	2.2
III	20	15	35	36	71	3.6	2.0
IV	2	1	3	2	5	2.5	1.7
V	4	2	6	1	7	1.75	1.2
VI	8	4	12	15	27	3.4	2.2
TOTAL DUO BI SEI.	40	24	64	61	125	3.15	1.95
Kiā bi Sei *dogi* no.							
VII	3	3	6	4	10	3.3	1.7
VIII	2	1	3	4	7	3.5	2.35
IX	7	5	12	8	20	2.7	1.65
X	1	1	2	2	4	4	2
TOTAL KIĀ BI SEI	13	10	23	18	41	3.2	1.75
Banene *dogi* no. XI	13	16	29	21	50	3.65	1.75
TOTAL DUONÉFLA	66	50	116	100	216	3.3	1.85

twenty-seven people (except for that of Kae bi Bohu the 'chef de village' whose large number of wives and children disrupts the group's equilibrium). This emerges clearly in the case of the *dogi* of Gala bi Dua and Kwable bi Tra which, when separated, show a strong imbalance, but when merged fall within the average. The ratios of active to inactive in the smaller *dogi* which include at least thirteen people deviate from this norm. The narrowness and imbalance of the smaller units no doubt explain their resorting, here as in Duonefla, to a kind of mutual help which we have mentioned earlier and which we will study later — the *klala* — and which results in the reconstruction of labour teams better adapted to the major agricultural tasks.

Duonéfla — Nianangon

In Duonéfla we find the same tendency towards fragmentation as in Ziduho. To avoid tedious descriptions, we will merely give a short summary of the community organisation.

Three *goniwuo* of different sizes and lacking any common origin are mentioned in the census. Apart from the main lineage, the first two include satellite families of varying depth but each community does not coincide with a *goniwuo*.

Five families make up the main *goniwuo* named Duo bi Sei nene, after Duo, the ancestor of the principal lineage. The *goniwuo* is divided into two segments. Boye bi Kalu, 'chef de village' and *goniwuoza*, belongs to the smaller of these segments. He shares authority with Irie bi Balo, senior of the second segment, although Balo claims ancestral authority over the whole *goniwuo* and argues that it forms a single community over which he presides. But this claim appears to be mainly moral, since the members of the *goniwuo* no longer meet to eat together except on certain ritual occasions. In everyday reality, the *goniwuo* is divided into four *dogi*: the first depends on Boye bi Kalu who delegates his authority to Kwe his eldest son; the second depends on Bangone bi Gore: the third on Za bi Tualo, of slave origin; the fourth on Toye bi Bagone. Each *dogi* counts at least one labour team. Irie bi Balo is said to have charge of the first three *dogi* but he keeps only his nephews Kwaku by Kwe and Fua bi Fua under his immediate authority. Kwaku bi Kwe lives in a farm outside and Fua bi Fua helps his father only with the cultivation of his yams. Balo is a big coffee planter and employs wage-labour on his plantations. Here we can observe a dependence at two levels; Balo has under his authority a small labour team composed mainly of family heads who in turn have authority over the active members of the extended community cooperating occasionally in the agricultural tasks for Balo's benefit. Toye bi Bangone forms an independent household with his brother and two of his father's brother's sons (one being an adopted slave).

Sei bi Ba, doyen of a lineage formerly allied by marriage to that of Duho bi Seinene constitutes, with his sons, a distinct community which includes the entire segment. Living on an outside farm, Ba is somewhat estranged from the life of the *goniwuo*. Two foreign families are associated with the *goniwuo* and are claimed by Kalu as being among his dependents: Tra ba Za whose son is supposed to be working for Kalu, although Za contests this, and Gore bi Baba's family which actually forms a distinct *dogi*. Finally, there is also a foreign household, which is organised as an autonomous group. In this *goniwuo* all the family heads and even a few bachelors grow coffee for their own profit. In these circumstances, considering all these groups as a single community becomes idealistic and is, at the economic level, purely theoretical. Each of them is becoming an independent economic unit.

The *goniwuo* called Kian bi Seinene is allied through a former marriage to Duo bi Seinene. It is made up of four *dogi*, three headed by three sons of Fua bi Bali and one by Boti bi Kie, head of a loosely associated family. Only the seniors of the *dogi* are coffee planters.

Banene, the last *goniwuo*, consists of the main lineage of Voli Bi Dja, subdivided into two other segments one of which is descended from the founder through his daughter Boli, who married without bridewealth; the other, an allied branch formed by the descendance of Boli's husband's brother. The *goniwuoza* belongs to this branch. All the members of Banene form a single community divided into three labour groups. Almost every adult grows a coffee plantation for himself.

Ratios between active and inactive are still very close to those we calculated for the other villages although the smaller number of active women increases the burden of the active males. The division of the *dogi* is less unbalanced than in Ziduho; the more numerous groups still remain among the most balanced.

If we compare the figures for the three villages we are struck by the consistency of the ratio between active and inactive as established for the larger groups, which seems from this to respond to the need of an internal equilibrium. According to our examples the best balanced groups, i.e. with a ratio of less than two people per active member, include between twenty and thirty people. Hence the fragmentation into smaller cells seems to work against this balance. Fragmentation is difficult to explain by endogeneous factors since these should actually make for a better balance. It is more obviously related to cash cropping and individual monetary gains as is explained in a later chapter [Chapter XIII of *the Guro*]. We must also notice that the heterogeneous composition of the villages of Ziduho and Duonefla predisposed them to these divisions, whereas Bazré which is also subject to these same factors has, up to now, maintained more fully the primitive cohesion of its lineages.

IV. LINEAGE RELATIONS AND RELATIONS OF PRODUCTION

Despite the variety of cases described above, each of which seems to be a special case, some trends do show up as underlying the social organisation.

The agricultural community is fashioned on the model of the lineage or of the segment of the lineage. Genealogical relations are the basic pattern on which the relations of production are built, but endlessly modified and renewed. The kinship relations as they are expounded are the product of these changes. Blood relationships were transformed before our eyes into social 'kinship'. The kinship relations of the remotest generations today express this social kinship whether or not it corresponds with blood filiation. On the other hand, present relations between living people are still in the process of changing. Social and real kinship have not yet merged: the father of an individual adopted by another is still known and the adopted son will use either name. It is likely that in a few generations he will be known only by the name of his adoptive father. The genealogical structures with which we are working are already the product of a shift of kinship, of a social reconstruction whose completion depends on the remoteness of generation involved and on the integrative capacity of the social links capable of replacing agnatic descent.

The genealogical model is indeed continuously affected by demographic factors: the variable number of the current group on the one hand, and mortality on the other.

Diazramo of Bazré gives us an example of an expanding group. As the group becomes more numerous the organisation of labour becomes more complex. At the same time, at the political level, it is more likely that classificatory brothers belonging to different segments will be almost identical in age. These two factors act together to favour the distribution of members of the lineage around men of similar age likely to compete for the position of senior of the community. This distribution, while it modifies eventual social strains, makes for a more decentralised organisation of labour by dividing the lineage into smaller, more cohesive groups, each under the control of one directly responsible individual.

Mortality constantly affects the genealogical pattern. At the death of each family head, which does not necessarily occur in order of age and succession, the 'family' centred on the deceased is broken up, to be reorganised either around his successor, if the deceased was the senior of a lineage, or around the seniors of the dead man. Life and death thus act as disrupters and tend to disintegrate the 'natural' families. Economic constraints among others are contributing to the reconstruction of new groups whose members will be linked above all by relations of production and consumption.

In this way functional families whose members are associated more by economic obligations than by relations of consanguinity are substituted for biological families incapable of perpetuating themselves within their strict biological framework. In such a dynamic it is necessary that kinship relations be flexible enough to adjust to these shifts: the terminology of classificatory kinship predicts the relations liable to develop between individuals with the death of a relative linking them to each other.

Such is, according to the Bazré example, the process observed in a homogeneous lineage.

Ziduho and Duonefla, on the other hand, are cases of heterogeneous *goniwuo*, formed from lineages and fragments of lineages which claim no common origin. The dynamics of population in this area, as well as domestic slavery which was more common here than in the forest zone, certainly contributed to this situation. A principal lineage acts as a focus for these groupings. The relations which are set up through marriage alliances, adoption, relations of clientship or slavery take on the aspect of relations of production: the men and their families are integrated into the main lineage and work for the senior of this lineage or give him a share of their product; these material links turn into relations of kinship and seniority which are their jural and ideological expression. Integrated foreigners are always said to be kin (*dri*); the men are the sons (*bi*) or brothers (*bwi*) or at least the juniors (*azuoza*) of him who has granted them hospitality. But the integration does not always seem to be maintained. The cohesion of some of these composite lineages is not carried over from one generation to the next. The guest-family originally dependent, weakens its links with the main lineage as it gains strength. One can observe a tendency for these small autonomous units to merge together. Individually weak, they attempt to recreate together and away from the main lineage the basis for an efficient economic cooperation through a special mode of mutual help, the *klala*. This fragmentation is also communicated to the main lineages whose marginal segments break away and adopt a similar mode of cooperation.

The relations of production set up between the members of the community, the different levels of cooperation and the circuit of high-rated agricultural products is expressed in the social hierarchy as it is apparent in the collective meal. The senior or the oldest man is the apex of this hierarchy.

The *pee* remains under the authority of a senior, directly or through an adult (*gone*) still dependent on the former. He works their fields; he has no one dependent on him, no land which he can cultivate; he does not control any part of the product of his labour which goes entirely to the senior. If the latter still owes labour prestations to his own senior the *pee* fulfills them in his place. Socially we know that the *pee* is either a bachelor or a young childless married man.

His emancipation through marriage and fatherhood, or in some cases merely through age means an easing of the domination of the senior as the young man gradually accedes to the position of *gone* by gaining authority over those who come to depend on him — his successive wives and children. He is first granted a relative freedom in agricultural tasks by being made responsible for fields separate from those of the community (i.e. of the senior). But he is given, rather than a right over land, the capacity to exercise authority over his direct dependents, a responsibility which is manifest, as far as we are concerned, in the fact that he leads a small mixed working team responsible for routine agricultural tasks. This promotion is not necessarily the right to dispose freely of the produce of the land he cultivates. For a period which is sometimes very long, in certain cases lasting until the death of his senior, the agricultural produce remains the community's common property. At a higher level of emancipation, when the *gone* has a second wife or several children, or when, as a consequence of the senior's death, he becomes less strictly dependent on the successor, then the *gone* may be able to use a portion of the product of his dependents' labour. However, through the workings of the system of collective consumption this share returns wholly or partly to the community. Nonetheless being able to make free use of rice is socially significant, since it allows him to entertain outsiders, to establish relations of dependence, to initiate more extended cooperative works for his own profit, and thus to become even more autonomous. Finally, at an even higher stage, when the *gone* has become a senior, he will gain control over the whole of his product.[17]

So a single community is usually split into several labour teams within which still smaller teams can be distinguished. The agricultural tasks assigned to each are different. They stand in a hierarchical relationship according to the nature of the work and the degree of cooperation they require in such a way that the teams are not merely juxtaposed but nested into one another. The smallest teams, composed of one or more monogamous or polygamous households, and corresponding to the female domestic group [see Chapter VIII of *The Guro*, p. 208] do routine work, e.g. binding yams, fencing rice fields, weeding cereal crops, day-to-day harvesting, etc. For these tasks the *gone* may call on the *klala*, a limited cooperative institution, which brings in the help of his relatives or friends.

A community is made up of several such labour teams which come together to undertake the more taxing tasks or those which need to be completed in a short time — clearing, ridging, harvesting, etc. Here the senior of the community can call on a wider cooperative institution, the *bo*, which includes relatives and neighbours.

Thus the social cohesion remains very strong around subsistence agricultural activities. In the final analysis, all the groups participate in each others' work. The smallest group for example benefits from the community work of clearing the ground; it cannot claim that the product of its fields is the fruit of its exclusive labour. On the other hand its cooperation in the larger labour team gives it a claim on the other groups' product. Everyone's labour is intermingled and each person's share is mixed with everyone else's; it is not measurable nor, consequently, is what is owed to each producer. The senior's authority is based essentially on this organisation of the traditional agriculture which, in the final analysis, is of greater concern to them than coffee production. We have seen that young men are liberally allowed to grow coffee, often well before they marry, i.e. before they may grow rice. In many cases the returns from coffee plantations are left to the younger planters even when they are dependents.

The senior of the community is the pole around which circulate high-rated subsistence products, of which a greater or smaller fraction is retained by the juniors in the process of becoming emancipated. Thus a circuit is established between the dependents who produce the subsistence goods and the senior who presides over their redistribution. There is a discrepancy between the composition of the labour groups and that of the whole community. The first includes only young people and adults of both sexes capable of working, i.e. the active population. The second includes the inactive and those who do not participate directly in agricultural production. The children, the sick, the diseased and the elderly participate in the common meal (the sick and crippled sometimes do not mix with the group or sex to which they belong and are served separately). First wives who when they head many domestic groups, are exempt from labour in the fields, nevertheless partake of the collective consumption. Occasionally a craftsman who is detained in the bush or the village by some lengthy piece of work of benefit to the community will be fed by his brothers, and so on[18]. The material security of all the members of the community is ensured through this elaborate organisation strengthened by offering to those who work for it the daily picture of a comforting solidarity.

V. CONCLUSION[19]

The theoretical interpretation of economic phenomena is restricted by the limits imposed in the study of a single society. The traditional economy in Guroland had not developed sophisticated institutions and many of them can be seen only in shadowy outline. Prestations by dependents to their seniors, for example, are embedded in daily routine and do not assume the ceremonial or institutional aspect which they possess in aristocratic societies. The incompatibility of certain economic relations with those based on personal status is far more obvious in the caste system. Similarly the neutralisation of imported goods by the senior in a segmentary society would be the equivalent of the royal monopoly of foreign trade in a dynastic society.

A deeper understanding of these mechanisms should rely on comparative studies of similar societies, and also of societies which have reached different levels of development. Such studies should lead to a classification of the various social systems, not only according to their structural but also their dynamic characteristics. It would also require a theoretical reduction of the observed phenomena in order to avoid undue comparisons since it is always possible to pick out unrelated elements in any society to substantiate the most tenuous hypotheses. Since we are not in a position to undertake this task we have not given this study the theoretical and comparative dimensions it requires.

Instead we have attempted to compare the economic mechanisms of Guro society at different moments of their development.

The history of contacts within Guro society itself, then of contact with the savannah traders, still later with colonisation and finally with the profit economy shows that each economic system is accompanied by specific social relations which are not all compatible with one another. At the same time it shows that the penetration into the self-sustaining economy first by trade and then wage-labour deprives the traditional society of its economic infrastructure and thereby of its capacity of existing as a self-perpetuating social organism.

Orginally, social determinants arose from within the society, i.e. from the interrelations of its constituent units and with the natural environment. During the period of settlement small groups with a rudimentary technology settled freely on unoccupied lands, each practising all the activities necessary for subsistence. Kinship relations acted as relations of production. They corresponded to a social organisation of production which made the labour of each person inseparable from that of all. They fitted a system of redistribution which allowed the apportioning of the common product among all the members of the group according to their needs rather than their labour. In order to maintain the functional balance of the unit, kinship relations extended beyond strict blood relations. In the absence of specialisation and exchange wealth had only a conventional value and its social use was inseparable from the rank of its possessor.

Guro society was in the process of constituting itself by extending to more and more numerous groups common convention, common signs of wealth and common insignia of authority.

Through their relations with the savannah traders, the Guro were drawn into the West African commercial networks. By this contact, products were transformed into commodities and acquired an exchange value independent of the rank of their owner. This contact appears to have brought about a tendency towards fragmentation of the communities, particularly in the area most exposed to trade. But the effects of trade remained limited. The new riches were in demand only to reproduce the old structures. As they penetrated the communities, foreign goods were neutralised and reconverted into treasure. It did not bring about specialisation of labour. Trade relations and kinship relations remained mutually exclusive. Trade was taken on by foreigners, the Fulani, while the social framework of self-sufficiency was not radically affected among the Guro. By contrast the emergence of markets organised into networks provided the inhabitants of the savannah area with a widespread form of political framework, capable of containing a denser and more diversified population.

With the colonial conquest, the Guro were suddenly deprived of their history. Colonisation did not act just from outside: it paralysed trade with the savannah, mobilised men's labour for its own benefit and penetrated inside the functional units by imposing a political and juridical framework taken up from the traditional structures but disfigured and rigid. From then on the society could no longer react but only suffer. During this period it merely vegetated and weakened behind the bars of colonisation.

The disappearance of colonial constraints gave a fresh chance to the Guro to emerge as a living social organism. The lineage community proved itself capable of producing a valuable commodity and bringing it to the market. But this insertion into the market economy was accompanied by a transformation of the exploitation of land. This brought about a progressive relaxation of those kinship relations now incompatible with the relations of production which emerged from the valorisation of the product of labour. Land becomes an object of contract and the nexus of new social relations between employers and wage-earners between owners and tenants which replace the earlier relations of personal dependence.

By selling the product of his labour on the international market, the Guro peasant is also subject to its rules. Still his integration into the capitalist system is the product of a contradictory development. The emergence of cash-cropping, while destroying the traditional structures, is a condition of this integration in the same way as is the maintenance of these same structures which alone are capable of satisfying those basic needs which capitalism refuses to assume, in order, precisely, to integrate family labour into its system of exploitation. In this way the relations of the self-sustaining economy with the capitalist one become organic and not merely peripheral as in the earlier cases.

In such a contingency the persistence of the former peasant society is less dependent on the 'conservatism' or the 'adaptability' of its members than on its position in the international economy, on the transitional and degraded functions which it is bound to fulfil in this wider system, on the still continuing advantages for the capitalist economy in maintaining the traditional sector to make better use of its material and human resources.

Therefore by limiting our observations to the 'traditional' society, we restrict our ability to understand the present situation. 'The colonised society, in its urban as well as its rural aspect, and the colonising society form a totality, a system: to study one single element it is necessary to refer to the totality' writes Georges Balandier.[20]

Indeed, ethnology confines us within a field of observation where we can perceive only a society's reactions to external shocks or stimulations. Given such a narrow perspective most events become contingent.

But where does this totality to which Guro society today belongs, end? What are the limits of this system? At what level can we locate the determinants which influence it?

The colonial and post-colonial situation is closely associated with world affairs such as the organisation of the international market in raw materials, 'aid' to underdeveloped countries, its form and allocation, or more specifically, the application of the Treaty of

Rome, the establishment of 'free trade' between Europe and West Africa, the contents and application of cooperative agreements, and so on.

At this level, Guro society becomes minute and represents merely one society among many others subject to decisions taken at a national level, and through them to the constant pressure towards uniformity exerted by the world economy. It maintains itself only by clinging to staple agriculture, the final bastion of a self-sustaining economy. But its community organisation is already in the process of disintegrating through the spread of trade, the commercialisation of food products and agricultural specialisation. Around cash crops there tends to develop a fragmented peasantry still rooted in former structures and representations which conceal the emergence of a class of landowners. But the new peasantry will be able to recognise the true nature of the new social relations, as the wage-earners push the young villagers away to the city, as the competing immigrant planters ruin local farmers and as big private owners expropriate the village communities.

An alternative outcome does not depend on the development of Guro society, deprived from now on of its concrete bases and therefore unable to act as a support for a new policy. It depends on more fundamental requirements decided at another level, yet dictated by the distant demands of international capitalism.

NOTES

1. Sugar cane which is only found in a few odd villages, is also sometimes a source of income for women. At Goaboifla, a plantation of sugar cane was said to be grown communally by the women and the product sold on the market at Zuenula.
2. A. I. Richards, *Hunger and Work in a Savage Tribe*, Routledge, London, 1932, pp. 59 ff.
3. The organisation of this domestic unit is discussed in chapter 8 of *The Guro*.
4. We will mention only male descendants.
5. In the administrative hierarchy, the *canton* includes several 'tribes' and the *chef de canton* has precedence over the *chef de tribu*. But in the hierarchy of the *goniwuo*, to which both men belong, Gonekalo is Bia's 'father'.
6. The administrative census recognises only three *goniwuo*, Yofuazramo and Kwaizramo being grouped together under the name of the former.
7. See the genealogy of the inhabitants of Bazré, pp. 301–5 ff.
8. A. R. Radcliffe-Brown, *Structure and Function in Primitive Society*, Cohen and West, third impression, London 1959, p. 67.
9. Fwable is now initiated by Gonekalo, the village diviner, into divination through the use of a box of mice.
10. A segmentation of Diazramo, maintaining as they are the functional productive groups, that is of each *nianawuo*, would necessarily bring about a posthumous re-alignment of genealogical relations. The segmentation bringing about the smallest

change would be that of the branch led by Bolu bi Bia. To keep all the men placed under his control, Bia would have to claim the authority of his father Bolu. Even in this case Kwame, Djahore's son, should be adopted by Bia and recognise Bolu as his ancestor. Bia, who would therefore become the founder of a new *goniwuo*, would not in this way become its ancestor. The ancestor would have to be chosen from his ancestors. Bolu, who was merely a modest link between Dia and his descendants, is in a position to achieve the posthumous rank of an ancestor. If the segmentation was to take place between Tone's segment, which seems genealogically predisposed to this split, and the rest of the *goniwuo* it would have to go back to Bampla. Yobolu bi Kwame's descendants who are now dependents of Tone would have to be adopted not only by him, but posthumously by Bampla.

11. By way of comparison, Lombard gives the following ratios concerning the Bariba, the Gando and Fulanji: ratio of male producers to the number of consumers: Bariba: 1/2.79; Gando: 1/3.09; Fulanji: 1/3.49. J. Lombard, 'Les Bases traditionnelles de l'économie rurale Bariba et ses fondements nouveaux. Conclusions à une enquête effectuée dans la région de Bembereke (Nord Dahomey)', *Bull. de l'IFAN*, vol. XXIII Jan–April 1962, no. 1–2, p. 228.

12. Ya bi Vadru bi Ye, Ye bi Bo, Bo bi Kahe, Kahe bi Bohu (present village chief, 50 years old).

13. Balu bi Nianaho, Nianaho bi Kie, Kie bi Gehi, Gehi bi Vo, Vo bi Zro, Zro bi Zai, Zai bi Bua (present elder, 60 years old).

14. Vanie bi Kaha, Kaha bi Gie, Gie bi Drigone, Drigone bi Kao, Kao bi Bua, Bua bi Zehuo, Zehuo bi Toa (35 years old).

15. Mole bi Za, Za bi Male, Male bi Za, Za bi Kwai bi Tra, Tra bi Kua, Kua bi Tunhei (54 years old). Authority no longer belongs to the original lineage.

16. The detection of the slave's descendants is made difficult by the fact that it is forbidden to state that a man is descended from a slave (*lu*). It is only in veiled terms that I have been made to understand the origin of some of these groups.

17. Social promotion often produces a conflict between the head of a community and junior members. The elders of the village are called upon to arbitrate, but it is clear that because of their common interest, in almost every case the *wibliza* of the village council will side with their peers. The junior can either accept the decision, exile himself or face his senior with a *fait accompli* by refusing to participate in the collective meal — this is always a sign of disagreement — or to refuse to work on the community lands and simply cultivate his own fields. A junior will take such a serious step only if he is certain to find support, usually with his maternal family. The following case illustrates this process as well as the significance of the cultivation and access to rice.

Gala bi Tro is administrative chief of the Buavere tribe. He lives in Dobafla married to seven women. Tro has the reputation of being very authoritarian and very jealous of his prerogatives as a senior. All his male dependents, even those who are married and adult, work on community rice fields; none of them has free access to rice. In 1957 Tro bi Tiese, his son, married and about 50 years old, wished to entertain a guest, but because his father had refused to supply him with rice, it was 'impossible' to feed him (this was not, of course, a material impossibility, as Tiese could have fed his guest plantain or yams, but it was 'impossible' to conform to an imperative rule of hospitality). This incident between Tro and his son provoked a conflict which was taken before the council of elders in Dobafla who decided in Tro's favour. For a year Tiese refused to work for his father, settled in a bush camp away from the village and cleared fields for himself on the lineage lands. Tro was hesitant to intervene fearing that Tiese might flee away to his mother's family. Finally, after a year, Tro is said to have forgiven his son.

18. Today wage-labourers, when they are fed, rarely receive high-rated subsistence

goods. If they are not fed they grow their food themselves in their spare time. They only rarely join with the community of the employer to eat.

19. This conclusion is to be found on pages 349–352 of *Anthropologie économique des Gouros de Côte d'Ivoire*.

20. G. Balandier, *Sociologie actuelle de l'Afrique, Noire*, Paris, PUF 1955, p. 11.

The Social Organisation of Agricultural Labour among the Soninke (Dyahunu, Mali)*

Eric Pollet and Grace Winter

This contribution by Pollet and Winter appeared originally in Cahiers d'Etudes Africaines, *vol. 8, 1968; it has subsequently been incorporated into a major work on the Soninke,* La Société Soninké. *It is often somewhat misleading to present a section of a larger work out of its correct context, but in this case, as in the case of the preceding contribution, the detailed discussion of the organisation of labour among the Soninke stands on its own. The major contribution of this essay is its careful delineation of the relations of production in a specific formation and its discussion of the question of slavery and its precise status in the analysis of pre-capitalist modes of production within the context of Marxist models of social development as discussed by Godelier and Coquery-Vidrovitch in this collection. Provocative also is their discussion of the distinction between 'the social' and 'the economic' and the relationship between contradictions in these two 'systems' and contradiction in the articulation of the 'system of distribution' and the 'system of production', which leads them to suggest that in the family organisation of agricultural labour "the social level creates the mechanism of the system and the economic level defines the limit of its application".*

Material for this article was collected in the course of fieldwork undertaken as part of a sociological project by the C.N.R.S. and the Musée Royal de l'Afrique Centrale (Tervuren); this took place in Dyahunu, in Soninke territory, between November 1964 and December 1965. An overall study of Soninke society will be the subject of a book to be published by the Editions de l'Institut de Sociologie (Brussels). We will here limit ourselves to the discussion of a particular topic: social organisation — traditional and contemporary — of agricultural labour; we intend to treat this problem

*This article is part of collective research on African economic systems under the overall direction of C. Meillassoux.

systematically by referring to different ethnic groups in West Africa.

The Soninke (Sarakolle), a people of the Manding group, are settled either among, or more often amidst, other peoples in Eastern Senegal, Southern Mauritania, Upper Volta, and mainly Mali from Matam to Sokolo. Like the Bãmana, Malinke, etc. who are similar, they are organised in classes (free men and slaves), castes and clans; according to tradition, they emerged from the Wagadu kingdom and adopted Islam as early as the end of the twelfth century.[1]

The area under discussion here is densely populated (26,500 spread over approximately 1,700 square km) and ethnically very homogeneous. Dyahunu is a former *dyamane* (a political entity under a clan chiefship, in this case that of the Dukure) situated in the extreme west of Mali, in the Sahelian region, in the contemporary Yelimane district. The Soninke settled there in the twelfth century at the time of the Wagadu diaspora. They spread out into 7 large villages, each populated by thousands of inhabitants; each village was under the authority of a chief who, in his turn was subject to a *tunka*, chief of the dominant village. After having gone back to animism, they were once again islamised by El Hadj Omar, the Toucouleur conqueror in the middle of the nineteenth century. The French conquered the area in 1890.

I. GENERAL FEATURES: AGRICULTURE, LAND TENURE, PRODUCTIVE FORCES

Most of the population's economic needs are satisfied by agriculture, but other supplementary sources of subsistence and wealth have always been exploited: barter during the pre-colonial period, wage-labour of agricultural migratory labourers in Senegal since the beginning of this century.

Up till now agricultural techniques and tools have remained at the primitive traditional stage characterised by a semi-extensive agriculture; land is cleared by fire and axes, sowing and weeding are done by hoe. Only 3/5 of cultivable land is exploited. Dyahunu is watered by an important river the Terekholle, a tributary of the Senegal which, each winter, irrigates an area of 2,400 hectares. These lands, when the water subsides, produce a second crop. The main crop is millet supplemented by maize and ground-nuts. Crop rotation is not practised, but some crops are linked: beans, sweet potatoes, goumbo, gourd, and indigo are mixed with cereals. A field can be exhausted after three or four years. It is then left fallow for an equal number of years, then put back into cultivation. If a field is large it is often split into two halves, alternately grown and left fallow. The lands subject to flooding are fertilised each year, and can be used for 20 years running or more. Each cultivator exploits a little over a hectare. Cultivated lands are distributed into 22,500 hectares of millet, 5,000 hectares of maize, 2,600 hectares of groundnuts, 2,300 hectares of cotton, 110 hectares of rice. The average yield per hectare is 600 to 700 kg for millet, 500 kg for groundnuts, approximately one ton for maize and cotton.[2]

Production and consumption are balanced. It is enough to mention for reference that 0.03% of agricultural produce is commercialised, and that illicit sales of cereals to Moorish nomads is practised; an estimated annual volume of approximately 450 tons is sold in this way. Thus the produce of the crop is essentially allocated to consumption and satisfies it except in very rare cases of difficult bridging.

Tenure and use of land follow a very common model of landholding in West Africa, in which the land is owned by certain clans who are masters of the land (*nyinya-gumme*); their seniors distribute rights of use between family heads in exchange for tribute (*dyaka*, from the arabic *zekat*) in the form of cereals. The title, master of the land, brings social privilege rather than economic advantage: the *nyinya-gumme* is free to give or withdraw the use of land from the cultivators (who are practically always inhabitants of his village) but the *dyaka* which used to amount to 1/10 of the crop is hardly ever paid today. Rents and loans of land exist but are little practised. Land is not sold.

During the pre-colonial period, agricultural labour was done mainly by slaves and to some extent by noblemen. Tradition and archival sources provide us with no information on the numerical importance of slave labour for the period preceding the nineteenth century; the disturbances which took place in the Sudan at that period (Bãmana conquest, the wars of Samori El Hadj Omar and Ahmadu) preclude the extrapolation of such facts to earlier centuries since these events certainly gave slavery a previously unknown boost. Therefore on this point we will limit ourselves to a description which can strictly speaking only apply to the last decades of the nineteenth century. In 1894, Mazillier[3] estimated that the proportion of slaves in the Kayes district, next to the Yelimane district was 30 per cent of the total population (he adds that the census indicated 20 per cent). In certain other areas such as Kingi and Gidyume, close to Dyahunu, which were partly or totally populated by Soninke, this proportion was approximately 60 per cent.[4] To stay inside our area of study, the present inhabitants of Dyahunu remember that a noble family had at most thirty to sixty slaves, but that, in general, families had no more than two, three or four. Such proportions allow us to assume that at that period at least, the Soninke of Western Sahel had the possibility of leaving most agricultural tasks to the care of their slaves: this hypothesis is confirmed by other sources of information. Indeed, many observations made by the French administration on the Soninke and neighbouring tribes give the same impression: 'Between July and December, the Bambara, like other blacks [from the Sahelian area] are engaged in agriculture and free men merely take their slaves to the fields and supervise their labour.'[5] 'They [the Toucouleur, the Moors, the Soninke, the Khasonke] usually do not condescend to work themselves and leave this duty to their slaves.'[6] Our own investigations suggest that these statements should be moderated concerning Dyahunu. The recollections of contemporary family heads indicate that certain slave owners left all the labour to their slaves, limiting themselves to supervision, but others, who formed a slightly larger number, cultivated the land themselves — though with less determination than is done today — with their sons, their younger brothers and their slaves, even if the latter were numerous. A comparison of observations made by the colonial administration on the behaviour of the last slave owners collected among their descendants suggest that the relative importance of agricultural labour performed by free men varied within the same ethnic group from one area to the next, and was not necessarily determined by the number of slaves present.

Whatever the absolute and relative quantity of slave labour may have been, it did constitute the main element of the agricultural labour force and as such represented the economic base of the society. 'Some natives still only use manual labour for agriculture as well as other work, slaves are largely the basis for the wealth of certain countries. The Sarakolles, who are the wealthiest blacks in the Kayes district, and maybe in the Sudan, are those who own slaves.'[7] Slavery not only provided either all or most of the population's needs and allowed a large number of free (nobles and members of castes) men and women to escape agricultural labour, but it also produced a surplus of goods which meant that the economic system extended beyond the strict subsistence level. The slave's consumption was limited to what was necessary to his survival and continued labour. We estimate that it took three years for the owner to absorb his buying costs. The individual's average annual production (300 mouds) minus his consumption (120 mouds plus the value of 80 mouds in the form of various other subsistence costs) is equivalent to the third of a slave's sale price (1 bar of salt, or 300 mouds). The freeman used the profit in part for food and in part for elite goods (horses, jewelry). Millet which was produced by the slave but not exchanged for other goods fulfilled these two functions simultaneously; it is food *par excellence* and nothing entitles the family head to being called a rich man more than a granary filled with the millet of many harvests. Large cattle bought with surplus, also played these two roles.

The status of the trade slave, bought[8] or made prisoner of war, and that of the domestic slave, a descendant of the trade slave, are familiar facts of Sudanese ethnography; besides it is only necessary to deal with the different forms of labour to which each group was subject. This labour was mainly the cultivation of fields. This was done under the supervision of the slave foreman or the owner and his sons. The women helped the wife to pound millet and fetch water, but they also worked in the same way as and alongside the men, cultivating for their owner, though it was considered a 'better custom' (for this reason it was often observed by marabouts) to make them work on the fields of the owner's wife: 'to mix male and female slaves on a same field', informants tell us, was to shame them; but a nobleman who had only one slave of each sex was considered beyond reproach if he made them both work for him. For men the 'best custom' was to make them work in the morning till two o'clock for their owner, from two to four for their foreman, from four to sunset for 'he who comes after the foreman', the owner's younger brother or eldest son, or on his own account on a plot of land loaned by his owner. The foreman was the owner's favourite slave, not necessarily the one who had been there longest nor the oldest, but the one whom he trusted most. He worked with the others and had no right to punish them, but only to correct and threaten them.

The produce of the labour went entirely to the owner. This organisation by which, in the final analysis, all the members of the family benefited from slave labour, thus gave the head of the family total power over the slaves: he owned them, gave them orders and received what they produced. The slave was sometimes allowed to cultivate something for himself or to trade a few goods for his own benefit. Thus he could theoretically own objects which, ultimately, belonged to his owner alone, even when these objects' were themselves slaves: 'the slave is a good (*nabure*), therefore his goods belong to his owner'. Each day the latter gave his slave the food he needed.

The Dyahunanko have nothing special to say concerning the duties of the domestic slave, but there is no doubt that his prestations, though they were less exacting than those of the trade slave, were so only by their quantity. In Khaso, a region neighbouring Dyahunu, it is said that 'usually domestic slaves who had children stopped working for their owners, men when one of their sons was circumcised and able to replace them, women when one of their daughters was married.'[9] In the Kayes district, he was given every afternoon and Thursday and Friday for his own work (while he worked for his owner he was fed by him) whereas, in this area, the trade slave worked in the fields for his owner every day until two in the afternoon, except on Fridays.[10]

The time has now come to locate the description of agricultural labour in its sociological framework and in this way to approach our real subject.

Slavery was part of a social and economic system based on the family community. All slave production was controlled by chiefs of $k\bar{a}$, patrilineal extended families brought together in a single compound.[11] But these family heads ($k\bar{a}$ gumme) also organised and continue to organise their dependents', as well as their slaves', capacities to produce. At a more general level all these inter-personal relations within the $k\bar{a}$ are organised in a hierarchy giving the seniors the use of part or all the labour force of the juniors.

Finally, as we have said it is the $k\bar{a}$ gumme's responsibility to obtain the use of a field from a land master and to share it out in plots between his sons and his younger brothers.

II. THE SOCIAL ORGANISATION OF PRODUCTION AND DISTRIBUTION[12]

I. PRODUCTION

Work groups are formed on a strict patrilineal basis: they mobilise part of or, in some cases, the whole extended family.[13] In relation to one another each participant occupies a particular position: depending on whether he is junior or senior, he will either work for others or others will work for him, or he will even if he is in an intermediary position perform both roles successively in the course of the workday. The group is thus defined by an intricate set of relations of subordination determined by the position occupied by each of its members in relation to every other. Its composition changes with time, because of natural events whose occurrence may be either inevitable or not (as in the case of the death of a senior or the birth of the junior's children respectively). Because of this we will set out an inventory of the existing types of structures by a logical sequence of diagrams. We will thus establish the different modalities according to which the group chooses either to maintain itself, or to split into new units. Therefore these diagrams are all connected by the combined action of natural and social causes in a development which we will reproduce as an ideal diachronic sequence.

Each diagram is composed of two elements: a) a diagram classifying all the workers of the group: fathers and sons, father's brothers and brothers' sons, cousins; b) figures referring to the characters of this diagram, indicating the labouring time-table for each worker, according to the following conventions. The Soninke working day is divided into the *morning* (M); from sunrise till after midday, meal time; the *first half of the afternoon* (PM1) from two to four approximately, the *second half of the afternoon* (PM2); from four to six. For each of these periods we will indicate for whom ((1) (2) (3)) each of the members of the group (1, 2, 3, etc.) is working. For example the sentence

PM1	1	(1)
	2–3	(2)

means that from two to four, member 1 cultivates alone on his own field for himself, and members 2 and 3 cultivate on 2's field.

We will first look at the diagram which is logically the origin of all the others

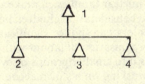

DIAGRAM 1

The work time table is:

M	1–2–3–4		(1)
PM1	1		(1)
	2–3–4–		(2)
PM2	1	(1)	(1)
	2	(2)	(2)
	3–4	(3)	(3)

Possible variant applicable mainly when each of the sons has dependent children:

M	1–2–3–4–	(1)
PM1,2	1	(1)
	2	(2)
	3	(3)
	4	(4)

The work link between the father and his sons is permanent; it lasts till the father's death (the situation in which, when getting older and losing the capacity to work, he frees his sons, making them responsible for his subsistence need not be dealt with since in these diagrams only those of the male members of the family who work are included; therefore the father's retirement is the formal equivalent of his death). This death is therefore the only possibility of ending the relations of this diagram which then takes the following form:

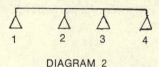

DIAGRAM 2

The tendency towards an individualisation of labour as expressed by the variant of diagram 1 and its cause are equally applicable here.

The development of diagram 2 which necessarily operates through the expansion of the nuclear families can take various forms. There is no need to take into consideration children born to the seniors but those born to the juniors can induce significant changes. Brothers may maintain their organisation of labour without change but more often the group splits into smaller groups or even atomises, each of its former members working on his own account helped by his sons as soon as they are old enough.

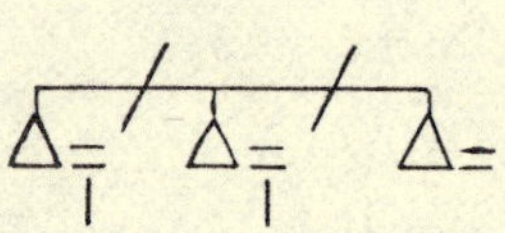

DIAGRAM 3

It is the senior member of the group, the man for whom everybody works for at least some of the time, who takes the decision to split and thus frees his dependents. This shift is due to the fact that each member has wives and children and therefore produces less surplus, sometimes none at all, and therefore his participation becomes at best economically marginal or even possibly a burden for the senior. 'When many brothers work together one may have 6 children, the other only 1. The latter (particularly if he is the senior) won't like working all the time for what amounts to feeding the other's children. They will therefore separate.' This is the main breaking point of relations between workers. . . . It therefore happens that after their father's retirement or death, the sons continue to cultivate together, the juniors working for the seniors; then they all marry and bear children; the senior, rather than take responsibility for the whole family, prefers to let each father be primarily responsible for the subsistence of his wives and children. Viewed formally the basic feature brought out by this dynamic resides in the group's determination to realise its equilibrium on the basis of an optimum number of members; this number, we see, is fairly small, so much so that the mere fact of death is not enough to maintain it within the desired limits and the birth of children to junior members indicates another moment for the group, the socially chosen one of separation.

Let us note here that uterine filiation can, at this juncture, take on a certain importance. A group of brothers who dissociate and choose to form smaller groups will often retain unity between uterine brothers at the expense of consanguines. There are certainly other criteria of selection — the optimum number wanted, the greater or lesser proximity of the kinship links between the members of the new groups which develop etc. — but its operation is observed fairly frequently. The following real example, representing the work groups of a large family (from the Dŏrāme clan at Gori) illustrates this fact:

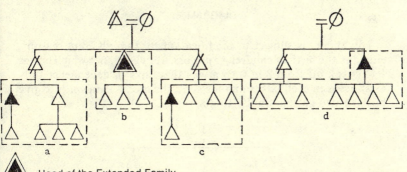

Head of the Extended Family
Head of each of the four Specific Working Groups

DIAGRAM 4

It is clear that the composition of group (d) results only from uterine filiation. It is not necessary to say that filiation through women constitutes a motive for separation, but only that a separation decided on for other reasons finds in it a means for practical realisation.

Brothers may also — diagram 4 enables us to predict this — continue to work together for one another despite the fact that each of them has children. When the latter are old enough to cultivate, the following relations develop:

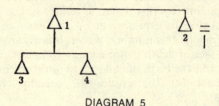

DIAGRAM 5

Later when the sons of the junior brother 2 in their turn begin to work, then the most comprehensive work group known by the society is formed:

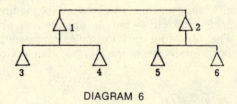

DIAGRAM 6

This model is subject to modification for two different reasons: either by the birth of children to juniors, a circumstance which brings 1 to break off from 2 in such a way that links of dependence only exist between each father and his sons; the model than splits to give birth to two groups similar to diagram 1:

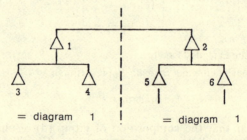

DIAGRAM 7

Or because of the senior brother's death (the junior's only brings about the assimilation of his sons to his senior's) a possibility

emerges which itself gives rise to two possibilities, both equally
practised. If the group remains united, its members will themselves
restructure the frame of the model, which produced their
relationship by a double shift: at the level of the first generation the
junior brother takes the place of his deceased senior, while his place
is taken by the genealogical senior of the second generation. Let us
call this possibility case(a)

M	2–3–4–5–6–	(2)
PM1,2,	2	(2)
	3–4–5–6	(3)

But the group can also split and one of its sections form diagrams 2
and another diagram 1, this is case (b)

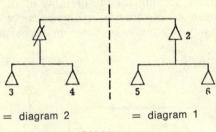

= diagram 2   = diagram 1

DIAGRAM 8

What is the future of case (a)? In other words, after the death of 2
will 5 and 6 work for their cousins 3 and 4? Never for more than one
or two years and this is true even if no external event (e.g. births)
intervenes. Of all the links we have noted this link which unites
cousins is that which connects the most distant relatives; it represents
the limit of the size of the group and its ephemeral character only
manifests a sociological split which, in truth had already taken place
in the preceding generation between brothers 1 and 2 on the birth of
2's children. The contradictory and recent fact that the junior
cousin[15] works for the senior cousin[16], and this only for a short
period of time, is explained by the meeting of two opposed
principles: work is performed according to the general tradition
according to which the juniors owes prestations to his senior; its
termination must be understood in terms of the junior's father's
behaviour, by ceasing to work for his own senior brother. The true
break in labour relations, we repeat, takes place between brothers
and that between cousins is merely an echo of the first.

Besides, the implications of relationships between members of one generation for relationships between their respective sons is recognised by society. Certain informants explaining the attitude of cousins emphasise the first stage and state positively, 'I worked for my father's younger brother, because he himself had formerly worked for my father'; others, taking up the second phase, express it negatively: 'I have stopped working for him because he too once stopped working for my father'. The most aware are obviously the latter since, if the two statements are logical and conform to reality, only the negative one stands — it alone answers a relevant question. Because to work for one's senior cousin has always been the custom, as a consequence of the reciprocity explained above; and at the level at which the answer must be — that of mechanisms — it is not the custom which must be explained but, on the contrary, the reason for its obsolescence.

These diagrams account for the plurality of the existing work groups. Obviously various complex examples can be observed. Here is an example in which junior brother, junior cousin and son work for *ego*:

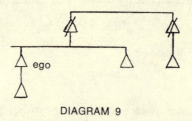

DIAGRAM 9

The distribution of labour time in these special cases is the result of agreements reached by the parties.

As it is essential to the maintenance of social order that no young man, no bachelor be autonomous, his labour must remain that of a dependent. This social demand is clearly manifested when a man loses, before marriage, the patrilineal relative who traditionally controls juniors. This absence will be filled according to the possibilities provided by circumstances. The bachelor whose father is deceased, will, until marriage, work for a distant relative (often only in the morning) such as a cousin of his father's, even if this cousin will never work for him; the orphan may also have to work for a senior uterine half-brother or his mother's second husband.

On the other hand, an old man who has been deprived of his dependents by death can ask his sister's or even a friend's unmarried son to leave his work group in order to assist him.

This outline must be completed by the statement of two rules which apply to all the diagrams.

1) The 5th and 6th days of the week (which correspond to Thursday and Friday) have special work regulations. Depending on the family there is either a shift in the order of prestations (on those days nobody works for 1 in the group who is replaced by 2, 3 taking the place of 2 etc. . .) or each member of the group works on his own account (there is an infinity of intermediary cases, and we will mention only the two main ones, of which the others are no more than variants). Depending on whether he is married or not the junior brother benefits from this favourable system for two days or only one; the son for both or neither except if he is given permission (an infrequent occurrence) by his predecessor who may allow him a day of free labour. Member 1 himself does not work on Fridays, the Islamic day of rest.

2) Any man who works for another must give him, each year, a *dyaka*, a share, usually 1/10 taken from the totality of his crop (the produce of his and his dependents' labour). The *dyaka* is offered as a token of subordination. It even goes beyond the work organisation and is given between cousins, from junior to senior, whether the former regularly cultivated on the second's field or not, and in general by all dependents to their dominant relative, even if they have ceased to work for him.

Use of fields and ownership of granaries

The family organisation of labour which we have just described is made materially possible by the partitioning of fields and the distribution of plots among the members of the work group as well as by the system of ownership of granaries.

The *kā gumme* usually has the use of one piece of land, sometimes two; each of his dependents, whether he works alone or with his own dependents, is allocated a plot determined by his cultivating capacity, and he owns its produce. To say that a man is working for his father in the morning, for his senior brother during the first half of the afternoon, and for himself for the second, means that every day (except Thursday and/or Friday) he works on three different plots of land which are most frequently subsections of a single piece of land. The father cultivates his own field all day, helped in the morning by both his sons; the senior brother works on his own all afternoon, helped by his junior brother from two to four and the latter works on his own field from four to six. On the *kā gumme's* death or retirement his successor takes over the section of land (the *soma-n-tē* senior's field, or *te khore* large field) which is always sufficiently large for a portion to be cultivated, the remainder lying fallow; the *kā gumme* himself never needs to ask the *nyinga-gumme* for land except when the one he cultivates is 'exhausted'. The other members of the group and in particular the juniors reaching working age receive (the son from his father, the junior brother from his senior brother) a plot of land, sometimes cleared sometimes not, depending on the possibilities of the moment (and when it needs clearing then the father or the brother respectively assists his dependent at this task). If the *kā gumme*'s land is too small to provide for the family's needs, it can also happen that one of the group or another has to approach through the *kā gumme* the *nyinya gumme* to obtain the use of a new piece of land. When a group splits up the plots which it previously cultivated are redistributed according to the needs of new sub-groups.

If, however, the family is dispersed in two or more villages, the *kā gumme* remaining in the mother village and one of his brothers or sons settling in an agricultural village for example, the link of subordination manifested by labour relations continues to exist but circumstances change its form. It is only when the *kā gumme*'s field and his dependent's are close to one another that the normal system will continue to operation, but most of the time prestations are replaced by a gift which the dependents extracts each year from his crop and gives his senior; it also infrequently happens that he sends his own son to work the *kā gumme*'s field on Saturday and Sunday as a form of replacement, he himself only working on his own account.

Every man when he marries is entitled to own his own granary, and if he doesn't always get it then he will build one at the birth of his first son. The granary is almost always privately owned. Each member of the family who owns one uses it to store the harvest of his plot, i.e. the fruit of his labour and part of his dependents' total labour. This system prolongs and contributes to the efficiency of the distribution of plots and the social control of labour. But each person who works for himself (even if it is only a few hours a day) does not necessarily have the right to store his millet in his own granary, e.g. the young bachelor who cultivates his own plot from four to six. Thus the granary has a special social significance, that of a secondary sign of the individual's relative autonomy. The granary is, in the sphere of labour, at least an indication of partial independence which is the result of personal family responsibility. Until then, the young man must store his crop in his mother's granary. There are a few examples of a bachelor owning his own granary but this is extremely rare; it may take place when a man whose father is deceased is responsible for his mother, particularly if,

without being from the same family, he works for her second
husband; but even in these circumstances he may be denied this right
and compelled to give his mother his crop directly.

In the large families who live in the same compound and are
divided into many work groups, granaries are collective: there is one
only for each group (in the example given above of the Dŏrāme from
Gori, the compound only includes four granaries belonging to men).

*Historical development of the family organisation of labour. Social
significance of this organisation*

The organisation of production such as we have just described it on
the basis of contemporary rules, has not always been regulated in the
same way: the dislocation of the extended labour group into smaller
units has not always been necessary. Formerly its limits were those of
the *ka* itself. The reason for this profound change is to be found in
the elimination of slave labour. The slave was the bond of the link
which united brothers (and their respective dependents). The *kā
gumme*, sole owner of slaves, concentrated all the family's
agricultural goods under his control. Any son or junior who wanted
to benefit from their use had to take orders from his superior and
work for him. To take one's wives and children and leave him was to
become rebellious, to isolate oneself and become impoverished.
Under the previous organisation of society, agricultural labour
organised and expressed the hierarchical interdependence of all the
members of the *kā*. In those days, a *kā gumme* who had many young
children and nephews (brother's sons) was as now, responsible for a
burden rather than provided with a source of wealth, but his slaves'
contribution compensated for this and allowed him to retain the
social advantage he obtained from his dependents' labour. Today
the mouths to be fed are relatively greater consequence: thus the *kā
gumme* prefers in order to unburden himself, to break the unit of
labour which the brothers formed together, even if this means losing
the prestige and authority which he obtained from running it.

The dislocation of the labour groups is thus due to two causes; the
first, historical, is the abolition of slavery; the second, contemporary
and a consequence of the first, is the senior's refusal to provide for
the subsistence of a large number of women and children. These
reasons, the first of which is not consciously recognised by the
society, are economic, but the seniors and the marabouts deplore the
disintegration of the family in moral terms. They deplore the fact
that large families, uniting many brothers and their sons, sharing the
same compound and working for one another exist today only

exceptionally. These complaints can be explained as long as the organisation of production is not reduced to mere economic terms, and the social significance which upholds it is brought out. Labour done *for* a relative is the sign of subordination *par excellence*; more especially, cultivating land ('it is not the same to give money') is the one sign of subjection. It is a consecration of the son's and the junior brother's dependence.

The individual's slow development towards autonomy in the family situation is reflected, at each step, in his position as labourer. A boy is employed from the ages of eight or nine in protecting the fields from plundering animals and cattle; he starts to cultivate towards the ages of thirteen or fourteen. Until his marriage, he is the one who is available: he works all day (except between four and six, a short space of time during which he may often work for himself) for his father and senior brothers; he may even be loaned to a poverty-stricken distant relative. On his marriage, he builds himself a granary and finds in it the first symbol of oncoming autonomy. He obtains greater freedom on the birth of his children: he then becomes the head of and responsible for his nuclear family, while continuing to work part of the day for his father until the latter's death. The father never frees his son of this duty; on the contrary, it is expected that the son should suggest to his father that he 'should rest'. Only disagreement may put an end to these relations of dependence (if a dispute arises, the father deprives the son of the use of his field).

Sexual distribution of agricultural tasks

If we have been able to present the entire system of production regulating men's labour without ever needing to refer to female labour, it is because in agriculture a distribution of tasks takes place. This is first defined by the nature of the tasks, as well as of the plants grown; men and women always working on different fields.

But this sexual division is even deeper than that; indeed, it manifests two distinct socio-economic entities. We have examined the male sphere of agricultural labour at length; that of women, far less important materially, is very simple in its organisation and can be rapidly characterised. In contrast to the rules we have just described, female labour is based on the principle of individuality: the wife, having been loaned the use of a plot by her husband, cultivates it alone and is sole owner of the product of her labour. She thus disposes of it freely to her own advantage, consuming it, selling it — be it to her husband — as she likes. Whether the members of her residential *kā* benefit from it free depends on her own agreement.

Job	Men	Men assisted by wives	Women	Women assisted by husbands
Clearing	x		x	x
Sowing		x		
Weeding	x		x	
Cutting the grain	x			
Harvest the grain			x	
Threshing	x			
Storing		x		
Winnowing			x	

Picked or cultivated plants	By men	By women
large millet	x	
small millet	x	x
maize	x	x
groundnut	(x)	x
rice		x
indigo		x
calabash	x	
tobacco	x	
gum	x	
cotton	(x)	x
kapock	x	
roselle	x	
tanin	x	
baobab leaves	x	

2. DISTRIBUTION

The distribution group, the entity of relatives within which food is distributed daily, unites the men composing the labour group, their wives and their children. Each male participant is compelled to contribute to the subsistence of all the members. But if the organisation of labour is strict and duly observed, the rules which define the quantity of cereals which each must 'bring out' of his granery, are fairly variable.

The most frequently used procedure is for the senior to provide the millet and maize for the whole group for five days a week; the married juniors have to give their share only on the other two days, on Thursday and Friday and to supplement by paying for meat (which is a rarely eaten dish) and providing the spices. That is to say, that the senior keeps the family, the dependents only contributing to expenses in a supplementary way. The surplus which remains at the end of the agricultural year in each granary becomes the property of its owner.

Another form of distribution quoted merely for reference since it is rare, is to empty each granary in turn, starting with the senior's.

The bachelor gives his crop to his mother who, as compensation, buys him or makes him clothes; he occasionally contributes to family expenditure by providing the millet necessary for the morning porridge.

In those large families composed of many work groups, the senior of each group brings out of the collective granary the quantities necessary for the daily needs of his family.

These rules are an ideal statement of the system. Were they to be strictly followed, it would be enough to emphasise the compatibility between the relations of production and the relations of consumption, each individual participating in collective expenditure to the extent of the labour performed on his own account (this is even manifested in the detail of the parallel allocations of Thursday and Friday). In fact this system of contributions is applied as long as the quantities of cereals which are necessary to its operation are effectively to be found in the granaries, but if the millet or the maize come to be lacking in one, the necessary share will be collected from the other crops. At this point another difficulty arises: in the ideal statement of the principles applicable to these levies, there are differences between the informants. Some assert that the senior alone would be responsible for supplementary obligations, others claim that all are equally responsible for them.

It is our duty to qualify all these rules and to interpret them. Let us first mention that there are here two disagreements, the first bringing about the distinction between the strict definition of the custom and the effective reality of its application, the second (at a lower level, namely that of the rules which should be followed to apply it) dividing opinion between the parties on how the obligation is distributed. We can summarise them thus:

— Custom: the importance of individual contributions is related to the organisation of production.
— Reality: in case of need, increased contributions are made to provide for the needs.
— Theory: they are owed by the senior.
— Practice: they are owed indiscriminately by all granaries which are full.

Each of these rules has a precise sociological meaning. According to tradition, each person's obligation to contribute follows the rules of his labour. The complete process of production and distribution from then on is formed into a single system regulated by the *principle of redistribution*: the senior who, because of his dependents' labour has the major part of the crop at his disposal, finds himself, at the same time and for this very reason, the main provider of the group. It is unnecessary to insist on the unequal orientation of this model which gives the person invested with authority social control over the family's economic life. But if, according to tradition, the system is defined on the basis of the social terms of production and in conformity with the principles of pre-eminence which underlie them (a system which could briefly be characterised by the formula: 'from each according to his social place in production'), reality, by the correction it makes in case of deficit, reveals the emergence of a subsidiary system dependent on the *principle of reciprocity*[17] because it is defined in terms of consumption, that is to say — since everybody, insofar as possible, must eat enough to feed himself — in an egalitarian way ('to each according to his needs'). The first difference, bringing about the distinction between tradition (which remains the normal system of distribution) and the real sharing which takes place in case of inadequate production, can be explained historically. The first term effectively seems to be the real tradition, excluding any additional arrangement, the tradition which was known and practised unfailingly by the society during the period of slavery: thanks to slave labour, the senior's granary was always sufficiently full to face the expenditure he was responsible for. The second term — the adjustments made in reality — is only, in this perspective, a palliative determined by the sole necessity of poverty.

The other disagreement which we have mentioned between different informants — some putting the responsibility for supplementary payments exclusively on the shoulders of the seniors, others wishing to share them out according to everyone's capacity — is, at its lower level, merely the transposition of the first difference. These relate to each other term for term. There is no attempt either to remain as close to pure tradition as possible by ensuring that the system stays under the seniors' authority (be it at their economic disadvantage) or to deny this tradition by setting up equality between the junior and the senior (even if it only concerned the reciprocity of their obligations).

The fact that these points can be formulated only in a way which is contrary to the habits of western economic thought in no way invalidates the convincing value of the demonstration. The point is that the senior's supremacy must be evaluated in social terms of control and authority and not according to the notion of profit.

Similarly those informants who burden the senior with the whole weight of such an obligation are laying down a rule of principle which never applied and whose inspiration can have been found only in a rigorous application of the logic of the system. (The counter-informants are empiricists; they describe the tradition on the basis of practical observations.)

Observation of the relations of production has led us to separate sociology from economics. It has demonstrated that at a given moment of the history of each family, when women and children consume as much or more than their husband and father, the second of these terms, the economic one, which represents a negative determination, wins at the expense of the sociological (let us recall that the senior prefers to give up his power rather than have too many dependents for whom he is directly responsible).

The analysis of the relations of distribution, by leading to a similar observation, confirms this alternative. In both sectors, the norms are conceived in sociological terms and economic reality, to some extent, compels their infringement. In both cases, the senior's power is the theory which practice partially reduces.

We still have to consider the relations maintained between these two systems which have converging characteristics. In this way, we will be able to define the general conditions of agricultural labour. We will try to bring out the fact that the contradiction within each of them is not the only one but also that, considered in their totality and in the final analysis, the system of distribution and the system of production themselves develop contradictory tendencies towards one another. Since, in the end, each member of the group may be called upon to contribute, according to his means, to the satisfaction of the needs of the whole family, it must be noted that the economic significance of the system is, when it comes to it, negligible. The junior's obligation to produce for the benefit of the senior has neither the function nor the object of increasing the latter's wealth; its significance comes from the sole fact that one works on the other's field and he received from his hand most of his subsistence.

It follows from this that in the family organisation of agricultural labour the social level creates the mechanism of the system and the economic level defines the limits of its application.

In these conditions, since all the needs can be satisfied only at the expense of serious infringements of traditional community principles, and since these latter remain the basis of the economic and social organisation and the only type of explanation by which the society tries to account for itself (we have seen what contradictions this brings about), we must conclude that the organisation and the explanation are more dependent on the social domination of one group over another than on economic efficiency. What is, in our view, most interesting about contemporary Soninke organisation is the fact that it betrays the ideological function of the kinship system all the more powerfully since this system is no longer totally adapted today to the needs which it claims to satisfy.[18]

CONCLUSIONS

The sociological analysis of the subsistence sector (the dominant sector) of the Soninke economy and more specifically of the labour relations in their organisation of slavery as they were and continue to be regulated by the kinship system must allow us to elaborate certain theoretical conclusions.

These two types of relations of production, whose study is generally carried out separately must be defined and analysed as they present themselves in reality: as systems which were coexistent and, in some of their secondary characteristics, interdependent. To our knowledge, the theoretical conditions of their compatibility, the influence which they may have had on one another and finally the consequences of the suppression of slavery on family organisation have never been clearly defined. The characteristics of Soninke society brought out by our study (and which can also be extended to other major Sudanese groups, the Manding in particular) must allow us to attempt to answer these questions.

1) The primary determinants of the economic and social formation are the low level of production techniques and the sufficient quantity of cultivable lands for all the members of the society.

2) The social system is based on a community of composite type (clan and family). The family has access to the use of land through the intermediary of a clan, a land-holding unit. The individual works and consumes the product of his labour because he belongs to a family unit of production and distribution. Access to land and work are thus defined through a network of primary and compelling social relations.

3) The slave, removed from the sphere of kinship, belonged to an individual, head of a free family, and worked for him under his exclusive authority. His production belonged to his owner. Such characteristics, which contrast with the social mechanisms described in 2) did not have the ability to compromise their maintenance. In the absence of any means of subjecting one part of the community to another within the society, slave labour was necessarily of foreign origin; its activity operated outside kinship relations and its whole social existence remained excluded from the community by the endogamy rule. Under these conditions, slavery was compatible with

family relations of production;[19] it had no hold over them since it was socially isolated, but also because, at the economic level, it only occupied a marginal position: slave labour was never more than the extension of the labour force of free men, given the self-sufficiency and the solid character of the determinations of the social and economic formations defined in (1).

4) Not only did slavery turn out to be compatible with the family system, but it also had the effect of strengthening its cohesion. Because it increased the senior's economic and social power, the juniors were all the more dependent on him. The negative proof of this lies in the consequences of the suppression of slave labour on the size of the production unit and the operation of the distribution unit; in both these sectors, the importance of the head of the family is reduced.

5) The special sociological situation of slave labour in community societies poses delicate theoretical problems which can only be rapidly sketched in these particular conclusions. It does not seem possible to us to provide single answers to these questions. This is particularly brought out by two fundamental questions: is slavery, as it exists among the Soninke, a mode of production? Do slaves of this type form a social class?

In a recent article[20] Suret-Canale, discussing African slavery in general, thought he could decide on these problems negatively. Basing his argument on the almost complete absence of latifundiary slavery the author asserts that 'the conditions of slavery . . . had an essentially legalistic character and did not imply the determined role in production which characterises a social class.' Slaves and particularly domestic slaves were 'incorporated' in the family mode of production, and it was as united within the same class that slaves and free peasants found themselves exploited by a tribal, military, or bureaucratic aristocracy.

If we are in agreement on the differences which separate the African from the ancient slave mode of production, we cannot follow Suret-Canale in the second part of his argument. In addition to the fact that before its nature can be defined precisely the form of slavery which he discusses should be subjected to a sociological analysis concerning the relations existing between slaves and free peasants, its characteristics do not cover all the African modes of slave labour. The kind of slavery studied in this work gives us the opportunity to realise this. Indeed, here we are not concerned with a system of three groups within which one aristocracy exploits free men and slaves at the same time and in the same way, but with the last two groups only, in which the first exploits the second. Besides it would be incorrect to suggest that the relations between the two may only be defined in juridical terms. Their condition is radically different and this difference comes out of a sociological analysis: a) the owner-slave relationship is an exclusively economic instrumental one, resulting from a purchase giving the buyer full rights of ownership over the slave's person, his labour force and the product of his labour. The relation of subordination existing within the free class subjects the junior to a quite different set of determinations: between the senior and himself there is a social relation based on kinship (ascendance and seniority) and conferring on the senior rights of management and redistribution; b) control over land takes place at the level of clan relations from which slaves are totally excluded. Consequently they are deprived of any control of the principal means of production.

Finally let us note that the condition of domestic slave hardly escapes these determinations — maintained by the endogamy rule — and that the juridical language which we rejected when distinguishing a purchased slave from a free man, is here sufficient to distinguish the domestic slave from the trade slave.

But if this type of slavery is different from the Ancient mode of production and if it cannot either be included in the terms of the family mode of production, we must wonder what criteria must be used and how it should be qualified. In our view, this formulation of the question cannot be answered; it is necessary to give up attempting to define any and every economic and social formation in terms of a single mode of production.

For this reason, we suggest that the use of certain concepts should be made more precise. A specific mode of production is the result of the conjunction of a form of relations of man towards nature ('productive forces', material, technical modes of exploitation) — which will indicate by the sign A — with a form of relations between men ('social relations of production') — sign B.[21] These two terms are linked by a certain relation of determination, the technical-economic basis which conditions social relations.[22] Within the classic sequence, primitive communism — Asiatic society — slave society — feudalism — capitalism, these stages are characterised by the transformation of these two terms AB changing to A′B′ which in turn become A″B″ etc. . . In each of these social and economic formations B,B′,B″, . . . represent only the *principal and dominant* type of relations of production, those postulated respectively by A,A′,A″, . . . but no account is taken of the possible coexistence of subsidiary types of relations of production. Therefore whenever one of the terms in the first series produces different terms in the second, the concept of mode of production, as it is used by Marx and in so far as it indissolubly links the two series, does not appear to be useful for the definition and analysis of these terms when they are contingent, rather than essential to the very existence of the formation.[23]

The classification of types of relations of production into dominant and subsidiary types also leads to the discussion of the implications of another concept, that of social class.

There is no doubt that free men and slaves occupy specific and antagonistic positions (based on exploitation) in the relations of production and that this definition which is economic, exhausts the reality of their relations. These conditions are sufficient to define these groups as social classes. But because these classes are organised on the basis of subsistence agriculture, they present specific characteristics which theory does not usually associate with them: 1) the class of slaves is not a constituent part of the social system; its absence would not change anything essential to its characteristics (that is, after all, what the suppression of its economic role has demonstrated); 2) the consequence of the contingent nature of the slave class is that the antagonism which opposes it to the free class cannot be dialectical (see (3) above, p. 351).

N.B.: at the time of going to press, we have just found Suret-Canale's new article ("Problèmes théoriques de l'étude des premières sociétés de classes" *Recherches Internationales*, 57–58, 1967) in which the writer is led to specify, concerning 'patriarchal slavery' that it is 'a marginal and not a fundamental phenomenon in the relations of production.' (p. 7). Our account shows that this point of view is also the one we have adopted. It is in fact the marginal character of this type of slavery which prevents it from being the primary element of a social and economic formation and not the supposed 'incorporation' of slave labour into family labour.

NOTES

1. See Delafosse, M., *Haut-Senegal – Niger*, Paris, 1912, I, pp. 254–78; II, pp. 1–60 and 162–73) and Mauny, R., *Tableau géographique de L'Ouest Africain au Moyen Age*, MIDAN, 61, Dakar, 1961, pp. 72–74 and 508–11.
2. Annual report of the Yelimane district, 1964.
3. Capt. Mazillier, Rapport sur la captivité, 1894, Arch. du Sénégal, Dakar, E14.
4. *Ibid.*
5. Cdt. de Lartigue, Notice geographique sur la region du Sahel, (1896) Arch. du Senegal, Dakar, I G–156.
6. Cdt. Panier des Touches, Colonne du Gidimakha, 1894, Arch. du Senegal, Dakar, I D–158.
7. Mazillier, 1894, *ibid.*
8. According to Dyahunu tradition purchase was the only mode of acquisition of a servile labour force. The Soninke bought Fulani from Macina, Bobo, Senufor and Mainly Bamana, chiefly at the markets of Segou and Keruane.

9. Monteil, C., *Fin de siècle à Medine* (1897-99) BIFAN, series B, XXVIII, 1-2, 1966, p. 113.
10. Mazillier, 1894, *ibid.*
11. Since the establishment of agricultural villages, a consequence of French termination of Moorish raids, the compounds have split up. The term *kā* retaining its social meaning of extended family, because of this, took up a second, territorial meaning, that of habitation unit — the compound — whether it included the whole family or, what is more frequent, only part of a family.
12. The inquiry on this topic was carried out among the population of three villages, Hungu, Dalisilami and Dyakhadoromu, in which all the families (numbering respectively 20, 16 and 10) were, on the basis of their genealogical tree, subjected to a systematic enquiry on the labour relations they practiced over a period of 3 generations. Some particularly large families were also studied in detail.
13. Threshing of millet is the only task carried out by the villagers collectively: all the crops are brought together in one or many threshing floors.
14. In this case, what is happening is clearly a change in the family group rather than the labour group, but as we will see the point is precisely that the first of these terms conditions the second.
15. These terms refer not to age, but to genealogical location.
16. Idem.
17. We apply the typology proposed by K. Polanyi ('The economy as instituted process' in Polanyi, K., Arensberg, C. M., and Pearson, H. W., (eds), *Trade and Markets in the Early Empires,* The Free Press, Glencoe, 1957, pp. 250-6) but it is necessary to specify that here it concerns a special case of reciprocity insofar as its practice is irregular and contingent. There is no compulsory practice of an organised succession of gifts and countergifts but the application of a principle thanks to which, within a community he who owns pays for he who, at a certain moment, does not own anything.
18. A final observation will give this fact its full impact. Formerly the produce of slave labour favoured the full application of tradition; today non-agricultural produce needed by the society is provided principally by the monetary gains of the migrant labourers young and dependent men.

    Each year a considerable number of young men go to Senegal to grow groundnuts and bring their wages back home. This practice seems to have no serious consequences, either at the economic level, since there is no possibility of useful investment, or at the social level, since the migrants are reintegrated into the family and the village environment without having the possibility of changing them, but on the contrary themselves fall back into the traditional authority from which they had in reality never escaped.

    On this point let us mention that among themselves Soninke cultivators practice a form of occasional wage labour, working for a few half days for one family head of their acquaintance or another when they need to earn some money quickly; but this is only a sporadic form of labour without any possible influence on the nature of the society. The occasional agricultural labourer of course retains the use of his own field.

    It is because wage labour has, from the sociological point of view, this marginal and accidental position that we haven't gone into it further in this study.

    On the one hand it seems that the system of seasonal labour should not be considered as a cause of the dismantling of the work groups. It is, as we have seen between the senior and the junior brother that the links are broken, and the migrant labourers are almost always in the position of having to work not for their senior brother, but still for their father. On their return home, they all rejoin their labour unit and the links of dependence that it organises.
19. Compatibility between slavery and a society of a community type can also be

established by defining the nature of labour not from the angle of relations of production but from that of the relations which man maintains with nature. See K. Marx, *Pre-capitalist economic Formations*, p. 87.

20. J. Suret-Canale "Les sociétés traditionnelles en Afrique tropicale et le concept de mode de production asiatique" *La Pensée*, 117 1964, pp. 21–42.

21. K. Marx *Pre-Capitalist Economic Formations*, Lawrence and Wishart, London, 1964, p. 94.

22. K. Marx, *Contribution to a Critique on Political Economy*, p. 273.

23. Balibar, E., 'The basic concepts of historical materialism' in Althusser and Balibar, *Reading Capital*, New Left Books, London, 1970, p. 292 has stated identical demands, but he limits their application to the *transitional period* of economic and social formations. We notice however that the simultaneity of different kinds of social relations of production may, when it takes place within traditional societies maintain itself there for centuries and in a non-dialectical way precisely because these societies in themselves contain no possibility of development.

Marriage among the Wogo

J.-P. Olivier de Sardan

Olivier de Sardan's contribution to this volume is, like those of Pollet and Winter and of Meillassoux, taken out of its context: it was originally a chapter in his monograph Systèmes des relations économiques et sociales chez les Wogo (Niger) *which dealt elsewhere with the economic structure and relations of production. Nevertheless, his detailed description and analysis of the Wogo marriage ceremonies and prestations provide an excellent example of the way in which relations of production lie behind the concrete forms of reciprocity and transfer that accompany marriage. The piece also demonstrates the extreme difficulty for a Marxist anthropologist of breaking away fully from the epistemological traditions of conventional 'liberal' anthropology. De Sardan's introduction and auto-critique is a telling statement of the difficulties that faced the Marxist anthropologist in the mid-1960s and a clear indication of the possibility of overcoming those difficulties. The powerful and continuing influence of Mauss, mentioned in the introduction, is apparent in the text itself.*

INTRODUCTION

This is essentially a critical introduction to the chapter on marriage from my book *Systèmes des relations économiques et sociales chez les Wogo (Niger)*.

A scholar who bases his work to any extent on Marxism, must practise self-criticism on his own theoretical work.

This self-criticism is limited in its scope: it is not produced as the result of any reaction or pressure from the masses who are, at the moment, very removed from this kind of debate, but by the author's retrospection. However, this retrospection is not entirely subjective and isolated; it is a reaction as much to the general development of the political and ideological conjuncture as to developments of the theoretical problematic.

The two following factors make a large proportion of these pages written in 1967 obsolete.

1) Firstly, May 1968 in France and the western interpretation of the Chinese Cultural Revolution have again challenged the organisation and the finality of knowledge; today it is no longer possible to be an anthropologist, even a Marxist one, in the same way as before. Marxist intellectuals are not immune to bourgeois academicism or to an aristocratic understanding of knowledge; their references to Marx are not enough to preserve them from the influences of bourgeois ideology and 'science'.

These features are present in the following text. Thus the quotation from Lévi-Strauss on marriage by purchase, the criticism of Radcliffe-Brown concerning joking relationships are not based on logical and justified criticism, but they are mere concessions to traditional anthropology, polite references to 'authorities'. Even the references to Althusser and the *rapprochement* with Mauss, though they are more rigorous, form a group of doubtless correct generalities which it was probably not necessary to argue again: certain concepts should now be taken for granted, and this argument from *Capital* or that exposition from *Reading Capital* should no longer be argued step by step.

But essentially, the concrete problems which the Wogo peasants face today are noticeable by their absence; indeed, they are better dealt with in other chapters from the same book; however, even in discussing marriage, the following factors should have been taken into account: the economic weight of bridewealth for young farmers overwhelmed by taxes, threatened with famine, obliged to migrate; the bitterness that this produces in them; their resentment against the marabouts and powerful chiefs who monopolise women; the different situations in relation to marriage, depending on the socio-economic statuses in the villages; the contradiction born of the disintegration of the traditional systems of values and relations, etc. In this respect, the analysis given here of recent changes is more concerned with formal changes in the *old* type of marriage than with the real place of contemporary marriage in the peasant world. Unfortunately, in general, Marxist anthropology often tends to give preference to theorisation on pre-colonial societies ('fill the gaps left by Marx' . . .) over the creative analysis of contemporary contradictions; the first approach is useful to the second, but cannot systematically be given priority.

Finally, the interpretations given by the concerned parties themselves of the *social significance* of marriage have not been collected systematically : division of labour in which the informant describes and the anthropologist explains. . . . However, in all fields, there is (are) one (many) popular ideology (ies), which, in its own way, accounts for each social phenomenon. Explanations suggested by the group or its different sections are themselves raw material for the anthropologist's analysis: they must still be looked for in the realms in which they are not spontaneously expressed.

2) As for the theoretical problematic, today we can go further. The analysis below is based on contradiction senior/junior borrowed from Meillassoux. Since his work there have been other attempts to push the analysis further (i.e. by Terray and Rey). Our study of traditional slavery has led us (in fact, fieldwork has compelled us) to give an increasingly large place to the class opposition between slaves and freemen, and to its political and ideological aspects as well as its economic ones.

This chapter contains no in-depth study of the differences in marriage determined by the slave or free status of the marriage partners: even from a purely descriptive viewpoint, there is no discussion of the role of slaves in the ceremonies of a noble marriage, the discussion being mainly concerned with groups which activate the senior/junior relationship. In the final analysis, marriage is discussed here only from the point of view of the nobility, and of contradictions between seniors and juniors which divide them in a secondary way, but not in relation to the main noble/slave contradiction. The problem is indeed discussed in another chapter, on social structures, but there the slaves are made into 'perpetual juniors', since they are always refused access to noble women. Similarly, the confusion between the roles of marriage at the economic or the ideological level places limitations on this work.

Finally, let us mention that the thoughts about cross cousins and joking relationships ignore a basic fact: the joking *relationship* has a far wider scope than just the relationship between two betrothed cross cousins, as it also appears between two *unrelated* groups as well as between slave and master: it is primarily based on *inequality* and is therefore irreversible; in the case of related groups or of cross cousins (real joking relationship) one of the partners is by definition sister's son (therefore inferior) and the other brother's son (therefore superior); the first explicitly plays the role of the slave, the second that of the master. It is therefore possible not to discuss the joking relationship in terms of marriage (by reversing Radcliffe-Brown's explanation, we stayed on his ground, that of narrow functionalism), but, on the contrary, through all joking relationships to link it with the assertion of social or political differentiation.

Whatever the case may be, by showing how this text is *dated*, we want to avoid formal remarks ('this work is outdated', 'this is only a chapter isolated from its context') and instead, reach the context of its production: a certain state of the problematic, which it is not alone in expressing, which is as much a manifestation of the syncretism between traditional anthropology and the first steps of a Marxist (or a dissenting) anthropology as the inability to question the latter's functions and methods.

*Marriage among the Wogo**

KINSHIP

The Wogo kinship system is identical to that of the Zerma Songhay group.[1] It is therefore impossible to write about the kinship *system* and it is necessary here to repeat what has been stated about the problem of political organisation (absence of lineages, clans) in this group: kinship and kinship relations can make up the framework of economic and social relations, but they cannot be structured into a true system, which would be more dependent on a certain type of political relations.

Because of this apparent poverty, there has been no study devoted to Songhay kinship. Despite this, two related questions arise:

a) Is it really that barren?

b) If such is the case, we must however ask what is its role (and if it is secondary, why and how?) in the systems of social relations and relations of production which, as has often been repeated, are supposedly based on kinship in so-called primitive societies?

We can, unfortunately, only provide here a few descriptive indications in answer to the first question. To answer the second one, it will first be necessary to study the mechanism of production and the system of exchanges that it implies. (See chapters 6 to 9 of *Systèmes des relations économiques et sociales chez les Wogo (Niger)*).

Kinship terminology, shown in table 1, is of a very simple form. On the whole, father, father's brothers, father's and mother's male cousins are called *baba*. Mothers, mother's sisters, father's and mother's female cousins are called *nya*. Brothers, sisters, parallel and

---

*The Wogo are members of the Songhay civilisation; they are rice growers who live on the islands of the Niger River.

distant cousins are called *kayne* (little brother), *bere* (elder brother) *weyma* (sister). Finally, *izo* usually refers to one's own children, nephews and cousin's children; *hamma* the latter's children, *hana sidi* the children of their children.[2]

There appear to be two types of exceptions:
1. The mother's brother and the father's sister are respectively called *hasey* and *hawey*. Their children, i.e. cross cousins, are called *baso*.
2. The sons or daughters of a 'sister' (*weyna*) or of a female *baso* i.e. the real, or distant nephews through women are called *tuba*.[3]

The first case is particularly interesting, since we have been able to notice a relative preference for marriages between *baso*, cross cousins (*hawey-hasey izo*) linked by a joking relationship which is often found in Africa (this relationship can sometimes be extended to a whole tribe, for example the Sorko and the Bella, who are therefore said to be *baso*).

This must be interpreted in relation to all the preferences which rule Wogo marriage. Apart from the taboo on incest (only with a real sister) there seems to be no law to regulate marriages.

Everything seems 'possible' except, of course, marriage between a slave and a free woman. However, the Wogo clearly form an endogamous group. Of 100 marriages observed in Tessa, 99 involved two Wogo. There is no doubt that the unity, the cohesion of the group, which mark it off so strongly from various Kado chiefships, comes from this endogamy.

A Wogo, therefore, prefers his daughter to marry another Wogo; but it is even better if he is also a kinsman. Of these 99 marriages, 66 took place between two related people. Thus Wogo endogamy is no more than an extension of the preference for marriage within the family to the tribal level. For the Wogo, marriage is not an opportunity to create links with others, to extend the field of their relationships, but it is used to consolidate the family or the ethnic group. This is true both in reality, and in the consciousness of the people, who express pleasure when their daughter marries their nephew (*tuba*) and disapproval if she marries a stranger. An attempt is made to maintain as much geographic and cultural closeness as possible: parents want to be familiar with the villages in which their daughter will reside, and with her husband's family, and thus be reassured that there are no sorcerers in the area; the young married woman will easily be able to come home to her family for a few days once or twice a year, and in the case of a quarrel or divorce, she will always find an easy refuge there. Similarly 'herds will stay in the family'.

Reality then seems to conform to the ideal, since only one in three of marriages take place outside the same family. On the other hand

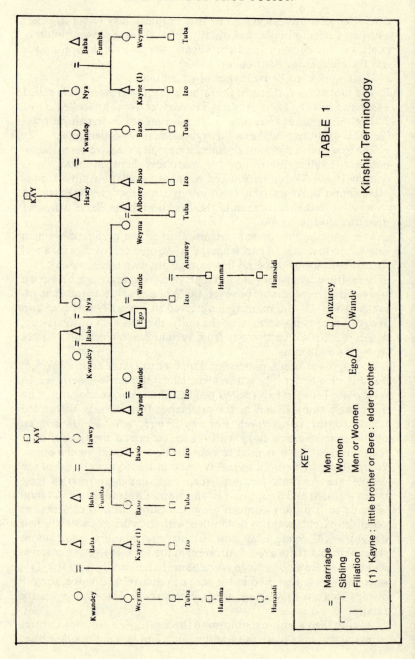

TABLE 1

Kinship Terminology

KEY

=	Marriage
⌐	Sibling
│	Filiation

(1) Kayne : little brother or Bere : elder brother

nearly one in three involve two people living in the same village, and over one in three people living in villages which are immediate neighbours (map 1, p. 388).

These preferences do not prevent Wogo marriage from being classified in the category of generalised exchange which Lévi-Strauss calls marriage by purchase (*lobola*).

> The process whereby the woman provided as a counterpart is replaced by a symbolic equivalent is better adapted to the conditions of a society with a high population density than is direct exchange. Indeed, it is possible to conceive of two formulas of real exchange. One formula is that by which the exchange takes place directly between two individuals, or two restricted groups of individuals, and then there is the risk of marriage never joining more than two groups at once, and of linking them into pairs of families, each pair forming a discrete totality within the general group (restricted exchange). The other formula is that by which the exchange takes place among several sections of the community, presupposing the intentional or accidental realization of an overall structure, which is not always given. In the absence of a structure of this type (exogamous moieties or marriage classes), the practice of *lobola* establishes a flexible system, because the exchanges, instead of being present and immediate, are potential and deferred.[4]

The overall endogamy of the group, its unity, the absence of lineage structures, the practice of bridewealth, thus form a coherent whole: restricted exchange would threaten social cohesion, true generalised exchange would imply the presence of categories which are absent, linked to a minimum of demographic and historical stability which does not exist here.

The existence of a relative preference for marriage between cross cousins (the vestige of an earlier system?) is perfectly compatible with this formula, since it is not matched by family exogamy (which would be the taboo on marriage between parallel cousins, in a patrilineal society). 'If cousin marriage remains sanctioned, purchase will simply reconstitute a simple formula of generalised exchange.'[5]

TRADITIONAL WOGO MARRIAGE[6]

Today, the majestic matting tent (*tende*) which is in the National Museum of Niamey, labelled "Wogo bridal tent" is no longer found anywhere in the district. The whole marriage ceremony, which, despite certain common features with the surrounding peoples', used to be very specific to the Wogo, has suffered considerable changes.

Let us attempt to reconstruct it through the recollections of the elders.

The Participants

Let us rapidly introduce them:
— The fiancé, *ar-higyi* (the man who marries) and his close friends (*ar-higyi tyoro*).
— The bride-to-be, *wey-higyi* (the woman who marries) and the slave who will look after her for seven days, *wey higyi kono* or *girbiye* (seven days).
— The *wadde*, the fiancé's 'age-set' members of his age-set.
— The *weyma*, the fiancé's 'sisters'.
— The *weynya* 'bride's mothers', that is the bride-to-be's female kin.
In fact, originally there used to be a distinction between:
— *weynya* (male and female kin of the bride-to-be's mother)
— *weybaba* (male and female kin of the bride-to-be's father).

Since only women play an active role in the ceremony, *weynya* in fact means, by contraction, the women (mother's sisters, and sometimes sisters-in-law, father's sisters) who act as intermediaries and assistants.

Wadde, weynya, weyma are the three main groups which will also be found in action at other celebrations and events which punctuate everybody's lives.

Aside from the fiancé's future parents-in-law (already called *anzurey*) all the other characters appear, *arhigyi borey*, members of the fiancé's family, *weihigyi borey, kwara borey* (the inhabitants of the village in which the marriage is taking place), the griots (*geserey*); the public crier (*fekaw*), the marabout (*alfaga*).

The Prologue

It takes a long time for a marriage to be settled. Long before the ceremony, the two families have engaged in a series of reciprocal prestations, during a period which could be described as engagement, which may last a year or even longer.

First of all, the fiancé's father will go and ask the bride-to-be's father for her hand in marriage. If no problem arises, he will send the *sugyi* a few days later:

The fiancé's age-set and their younger brothers bring the father-in-law or three bulls which are slaughtered, and provide the opportunity for a large feast: the father-in-law has arranged for the *weynya* to prepare rice and sauce; they eat on one side, the *wadde*, the bride-to-be and her friends all eat elsewhere; finally the bride-to-be's relatives, who have come for the occasion, and the people from the village join in the meal. But there are no griots, so it is not a real celebration. After this the engagement is firmly on.

A few weeks later, the bride-to-be's mother sends the *farminari* (food from the fields) to the fiancé's mother; it is brought by the *weynya*, driven by a canoer chosen by the district chief (*kure*). Husked rice (*monari*) goats, spices, oil, these are the products of female labour given by one mother to another. Of course the *weynya* are given a meal (for which sheep are slaughtered) before they go back.

At harvesting time, the fiancé responds with the *hegyehari* (water for the ox of burden, *hegye*, given from the bridewealth cattle?). His age-set have each brought one or two bundles of millet, or a *kokondo* (basket) of paddy (*mo kopto*), produce of male labour; to these the millet and the rice given by the fiancé himself are added, and the leader of the age-set, responsible for the collective labour team that it constitutes, selects three young men in it to carry these gifts to their destination. In their turn, the messengers are received as the *weynya* had been.

But the bride-to-be's father does not keep these gifts for himself. 'He doesn't sleep on the *hegyehari* (*a si kani heygyehari bo*) 'he doesn't eat it'; when the wedding day comes, they will in turn bring loin cloths, mats, blankets to make up the bride's presents (*kambuza*) and to equip the wedding hut, as well as the food which will contribute towards many generous meals.

The final episode takes place a week before the wedding. The fiancé's friends (*hangasine*), those members of his age-set with whom he has a closer relationship, takes his father and the marabout who accompanies him, to the bride-to-be's village for the *tiraw*. The marabout only says *alfatia* and a sheep, the *higyi alman*, is given. This latter is the symbol of the real bridewealth which the father has not brought, but which he keeps in his house at the disposal of his son's father in law. Usually a few bulls, one or two heifers and/or a slave or two, as well as sacks of rice. Again a meal is prepared for the visitors and sheep are slaughtered.

Finally, throughout this whole period, the fiancé works for his father in law; he often comes and works on his fields, alone or preferably with his friends, his companions and at least once he brings with him his age-set's work team, the *bogu*, which is then called *anzurey bogu*. On each occasion, the fiancé fasts so as not to eat his father-in-law's food and does his best not to meet him. This avoidance relationship, which is frequent elsewhere in Africa also, was strict before the marriage, and considerable distance was maintained even later, though, then, greetings are allowed. It must be noted that marriage between *baso* weakened this rule since, for example, the uncle (*hasey*) was his nephew's father-in-law (*anzurey*) and already well-acquainted with him. If (a tempting but risky suggestion[7]) the existence of a former marriage rule between cross cousins is assumed, it would then be possible to reverse the explanation and make father-in-law/son-in-law avoidance the necessary consequence of a change in status in personal relations, aimed at making the mother's brother disappear in order to replace him with the wife's father. Radcliffe-Brown[8] rightly notices the relation which exists between cross cousin joking relationships and preferential marriage between them as being a *pre-marriage* institution of the necessary type of relationship between a man and his wife's brothers (these relations are one element of the system, the other being the avoidance relationship with the parents-in-law; this system aims, by one method or another, to avoid all possible sources of conflict between the two distinct family units thus put together). But if a joking relationship between cross cousins is made out to be an exceptional case of the joking relationship with the wife's brother then the second relationship can just as well be seen as an extension of the first. In this case, it is no longer necessary to avoid hostility between two distinct social units 'condemned' to meet (the new and necessary 'social conjunction' must cohabit with the old and still existing 'social disjunction'), but it is necessary to try and convert past and present relations linking the *same* people: my uncle becomes my father-in-law, and my cousin my brother-in-law (the new social disjunction must emerge in the face of the old social conjunction). In fact, preferential marriage between cross cousins cannot be interpreted as a particular case of marriage between two unrelated families (and, as such, simply demanding lack of respect between potential future brothers-in-law) since this case is much too unusual: the parties involved are *already* related, and closely so.[9] The *change* in status between two (already linked) people is quite different from the *creation* of a status between two other people (who previously did not know each other).

The Celebration

It lasts from Thursday to Sunday,[10] without interruption.

Thursday (alkamisa zaro)

The *weynya* and *weybaba* bring their gifts which are used to build and equip the wedding hut (*bundu* wood for the framework; *tabama*

(Kurtey-type mats) and *tari kyare* (Wogo wedding mats), for the blanket and the roof; *dari, dima, tagara, furkanga*, bed, carpet, floor mats and cushions for inside). The father and one or two rich relatives provide the beautiful *kunta arkila*, wool blankets which are the speciality of Wogo weavers, true bridewealth gifts. All these are the *kambuza*.

That day the *tende* is built in the bride-to-be's father's compound. The bride-to-be's elder brothers, the *bere*, put up its framework of wooden arches and pliable roots, standing on a hut (*tatolo*) put up as scaffolding. Finally, they help the *weynya* to put the roof up in two layers, the *tari kyare*, long coloured mats made of doum leaves, the product of endless labour by Wogo women, and the *tabarma diri*, stem mats made of long pliable herbs tied together, bought from the Kurtey, which make up the outside layer. The mosquito-net-blanket (the *kunta arkila*) is attached to a small inner roof, (the *kare kabe*), also made of *tabarma* and *tari kyare*, which covers the bed and isolates it in the hut.

Thursday Evening (alzuma kino)

The bridegroom, his friends and age-set, and his sisters (*weyma*) arrive, bringing bulls. These are immediately slaughtered by the bride's father, for the *yarendi* (to honour). He also kills his own sheep or bulls and asks for the innumerable dishes of rice which the *weynya* have been preparing during the day. The latter eat on their own, so do the *weyma*, the bridegroom's age-set and himself. Meanwhile the bride remains in her mother's house.

The bridegroom and his age-set then go into the *tende* (=*hurendu*). It is now the bridegroom's turn to receive the *kambuza*, on the occasion of the *didigari* or *didigi* (fitting of the turban): a door made of plaited grass mats (*homey dala*) is set up on the ground at the entrance of the house and the young man sits on it;[11] his age-set fit him with the *botabe didigi*, a large white wedding turban with red borders (the same as that worn by the chief when he has just been named). A *fekaw*, public crier, stands beside him, and shouts the nature of the gifts which are given and praises the donor's generosity.

Friends and relatives walk past: sheep, goats, baskets and bags of rice, tobacco, millet, sorghum, sometimes land, heifers and bulls, more rarely a slave, as well as water pots and thalers, are really or symbolically put at his feet. The total amount is considerable; the bridegroom's father is the true recipient, but he will give some of it to his son.

The celebration proper has then started, the griots are there, they will play and sing all night; the *weykuru* (prostitutes) join the young men grouped around the bridegroom in the *tende*, the whole village is assembled and couples who will get together the next day, are formed. The celebration lasts all night, so does the feast; throughout the night the griots' pockets are filled with the constant flow of gifts with which the bridegroom, his age-set and all those present rival each other.

Friday (alzuma zaro)

In the morning the bridegroom's age-set brings bulls from his village for the *baddi* (sentiment).[12] They will be slaughtered by the age-set, eaten by them and the *weynya*, while one or two beasts are slaughtered for the griots, and the tam-tam, flute, violin and guitar players.

In the morning the bridegroom starts his fast (*mehaw*, tied mouth); his two or three friends stay with him all day in the *tende*. Meanwhile the *weynya* prepare food for the evening, they take a break towards the beginning of the afternoon to receive the griots' greetings and to thank them with the customary gifts.

The bridegroom must also make these gifts, when, at the end of the day he comes out and goes round the village to greet the inhabitants before going to break his fast in the bush (*me feri*, unbound mouth) with his age-set, once the turban has been removed.

Friday Evening (asipto kino)

At last the bride comes out of her mother's house and comes to spend the night in the wedding tent with one or two friends and the slave woman who looks after her, there the bridegroom and his *tyoro* are waiting for her. It is the *metemela* evening, a night of sexual license, where couples come together in huts, partitioned by a mosquito net, a night when it seems that not only young men and women but also married men and women give themselves over to chance meetings and desires. This last point is, however, subject to controversy; some Wogo defend themselves against this custom despite the fact that it is the basis of their reputation among the Songhay, Zerma and Bella people who know them. Nowadays, if the freedom of this night is no longer 'official', it certainly seems to have remained quite real.

Saturday (asipto zaro)

The celebration goes on, the griots and the *weykuru* fill their pockets more and more. It is usually on this day that the bridegroom sends an ox to the weaver who made the mosquito-net-blanket (*kunta arkila*) which covers the wedding bed. Usually the *kunta* has been given by the father himself, so it is possible that the weaver is his slave. In any case the bride would never agree to go to her husband's village if this bull had not been given (=*kunta kura,* the hide of the *kunta* 'to pay for the defloration blood which will stain the *kunta*').

Saturday Evening (alhado kino)

For the third time, bulls are slaughtered. It is the *hubanda* ('behind the hut').

Sunday (alhado zaro)

This is the day of the *zulo*, the bride's departure. The *tende* is taken apart, the bride and the *weynya* follow the bridegroom and his kin by canoe. On arrival, a bull is slaughtered in their honour (*yarendi*) and a smaller *tende* is rebuilt; the following morning, the *weynya* go back, the wedding itself is over.

The Epilogue

For the next seven days the bride will stay in the *tende*, helped by the *weyhigyi kono*. The bridegroom will do the same for three days, if it is a first wedding (when a women is remarrying, she will stay only three days).

On the first morning, the village women will come and greet the new arrival, wish her good luck (*barka*) by bringing her small gifts 'to open her mouth'; it is on this condition that she replies to their greetings.

After seven days, the age-set brings the defloration sheep (*fumbia kabakayo*[13]) chosen from the husband's animals, slaughter it and eat it, while the latter, ashamed, hides in the bush.

The last important prestation is the *zulinari*, food of the *zulo*. It is brought by the bride's mother's slave, a few days after the *zulo*, the departure for the husband's village. It is made up of *kokondo* of ground rice for the bridegroom's mother.

Before the next rainy season, the *tende* will be replaced by a *bukka* (a more solid house) or later, a house with a base of dried mud. On this occasion, the wife's mother comes to build her a *tongo-tongo*, a kind of inner *tende* which, from now on, belongs to the man, since it is no longer made of matting which is women's property (and this entitles them to ownership of the *tende* and the *tongo-tongo*).

Finally, a year later, the husband's mother 'gives her daughter-in-law her cooking pot' (*kusu yeri*). The latter then no longer cooks 'behind her mother-in-law' like a slave, but works independently, but she is still subject to the authority of the wife of the compound leader. From now on she owns her own tools, calabash, ewers, pots, mortars, which her mother has brought her on this occasion.

SOCIAL SIGNIFICANCE OF MARRIAGE

Different types of goods are exchanged; the exchanges concern people of different statuses. The study of these exchanges must give us the opportunity to make apparent the precise function of marriage in the system of traditional economic and social relations.

1. Prestations of Labour and of Daily Consumption Goods:

The techno-economic often has intervened only to the extent to which it visibly indicated the superstructure of matrimonial practices and rites . . . So that one is better informed of prestige exchanges than of ordinary ones, or ritual prestations than of ordinary services, of the circulation of bridewealth monies rather than of vegetables, more familiar with the thought of societies than with their body[14]

The study of marriage is a good illustration of the common denominator of certain analyses, which are merely concerned with the internal logic of rituals and ceremonies, their apparent or hidden structures, but not with their place in the total system of exchanges and thus 'miss' an essential part of their meaning. On the contrary we wish to study marriage to the extent to which it refers back to the social structure itself, rejecting the barriers set up between economic exchanges and social relations, rituals and daily activities; these barriers have been put up in two ways: by the above-mentioned process, allowing techno-economic factors to intervene only as hindrances, as external constraints which must be rapidly dealt with; this is an underestimation of the role of economic phenomena. And secondly, in economic anthropology itself, by separating daily exchanges from ritual ones; there is no doubt that this distinction between the spheres of circulation of goods (the simplest one is between subsistence goods and elite goods) corresponds to the reality of many societies.[15] The danger here is of turning this into a general rule for all pre-commodity societies lacking a universal equivalent, and particularly to miss the role of 'ordinary' goods on occasions when ceremonial goods seem to take priority. In societies in which there is only simple reproduction, the process of acquisition, circulation and consumption of subsistence goods is, in the final analysis, the basis of social organisation, even when the intervention of other types of exchanges is a *necessary condition* of their functioning, despite the fact that the latter, by their very nature, are more fascinating for the observer. These spheres are not equivalent, there is no simple process of conversion to deal with the links between them. Their location is not what distinguishes them from one another, but it is their functions and the complementary nature of these functions which usually go unnoticed, while their particularities are emphasised to the maximum:

> The compartmentalising and hierarchical arrangement of goods arises from their use for the functioning of distinct social relations — kinship, politics, religion — relations that each possess a distinct social importance. . . .
> The category of scarcest goods contains those that enable men to attain the social roles that are most highly valued. . . .
> Competition within the group begins beyond the level of problems of subsistence. . . .[16]

It is therefore impossible to isolate a sphere of subsistence in which everybody participates without distinction, from 'further' spheres in which the hierarchisations which form the basis of social status intervene. This social control, indicated by control over elite goods or women, is first manifested by control over subsistence goods. And it is the quantity and organisation of goods necessary to social reproduction which determine, for example, the share of work which may be given over to other activities, the relationship to other forms of labour and the relations of their respective product.

In Wogo marriage, we see that most of the exchanges it gives rise to are extremely commonplace: *hegyehari, farminari, zulinari* involve the immediate product of labour, which regularly circulates in precisely this way in social life; the *anzurey bogu* is an element in a well-structured system of labour relations in the front line of the process of production.[17]

Let A be the bridegroom, B the bride. *Hegyehari* and *zulinari* go from B's mother to A's mother. The sexual division of labour is extended to the division of exchanges. Women give only what is produced by their labour: ground rice, ground millet, spices, oil, goats they have bought. . . . The intermediaries are the *weynya*, women who are also B's 'mothers', who thus legitimately represent the giver.

In fact, the departure of the married daughter corresponds to her insertion in a new economic unit, that of her husband's family. But her relationship with her own family will continue and will be expressed by gifts and counter-gifts among other things. B's mother's gifts to A's mother are the beginning of a series of exchanges between the female 'parties' of the two production units linked by marriage, exchanges whose form will essentially consist of gifts given by B (from now on integrated in the same production unit as A) to her mother (the production unit to which she used to belong). *Hegyehari* and *zulinari* in fact testify to the new authority that A's mother will have over B. B does not escape economic subjection (in the feminine sphere; she moves from being subject to her mother's authority to that of her mother-in-law). The relationship senior/junior female. At the same time B will provide her mother with the counterparts of *hegyehari* and *zulinari* by going to visit her each year, bringing in her turn ground rice, millet and spices.

The *farminari* and the labour prestations for the father-in-law in the shape of *bogu* (work parties) concern the male 'parties' of the two units of production. In both cases it is not only A who comes but this whole age-set which joins him to go and cultivate B's father's fields, or to gather the scores of millet bundles which will be given to him. These gifts assert the youth's lack of economic independence, his existence as primarily a member of an age-set and thus his subjection to the authority of senior age-sets, of seniors, who, for their part, have an independent economic existence. Thus there is no exchange between equals, between two men, but between a group, the *wadde*, (i.e. the age-set), and senior, an *anzurey*. This too is the beginning of a process and, many years after his marriage, A will continue to go and work with his age-set at his father-in-law's.

Thus for women as well as for men, the 'ordinary' gifts, linked to marriage are the beginning of a series of exchanges which express the different status of seniors and juniors, intending to decrease the liberating implications of marriage for youth: the seniors are compelled to give the juniors access to women, and thus to take a first step towards political autonomy and an active role in production, but this contradiction is concealed as well as possible in an attempt to effect as long a transition as possible. Prestations from a daughter to her mother, from a man towards his father-in-law will continue for a very long time; their necessity must be obvious and therefore implies that they should be present at the very heart of marriage, that signal of this maintained, but modified dependence,[18] should be given at the very place when it appears to end.

In marriage, the exchanges whose content has no ceremonial aspect are therefore neither superfluous, nor must they be reduced to their ceremonial form. They are fundamental insofar as they introduce a certain type of relations and rectify in advance an order disrupted by marriage. As for the 'extraordinary' exchanges, which concur in destroying this order, and in emphasising the social importance of marriage and the break that it represents, we will see that they too respond to specific demands.

2. The Role of Cattle and of the Bridewealth Goods

A distinction must be made between the bulls destined to be slaughtered on the one hand and the lasting goods, heifers or slaves, given by A's father for the *higyi alman*, on the other.

The value of the slaughtered cattle was considerably higher than that of the bridewealth cattle. *Sugyi* before the marriage and *yarendi, baddi* and *hubanda* during the celebrations are just such occasions; the beasts which the bridegroom's father gives for them are thus always meant to be eaten, and not to be capitalised on. It is possible for the bride's father to slaughter bulls himself, particularly for the *yarendi*, the welcoming of the 'strangers'. Thus the important than the fact that the cattle must be given. And the seniors purchase of the women. The share of these riches which is destroyed is larger than that exchanged.

Is it then possible to see in this some kind of 'potlatch' by imagining a wholesale dichotomy, in terms of which competition in a commodity economy is based on the search for profit and in a 'primitive' economy on the importance of the gifts given and of the wealth destroyed?

In fact, Wogo marriage feasts do not directly correspond to the social meanings which Marcel Mauss had found in the potlatch:

> The motive of such excessive gifts and reckless consumption, such mad losses and destruction of wealth, especially in these potlatch societies, are in no way disinterested. Between vassals and chiefs, between vassals and their henchmen, the hierarchy is established by means of these gifts. To give is to show one's superiority, to show that one is something more and higher, that one is *magister*.[19]

This is the assertion of the parties' unequal status through the inequality of their gifts. It is a process of social differentiation between the two camps.

Here, on the contrary, there is no competition between the two seniors whose children are getting married. At best, each will try to 'maintain' his social place through the generosity of his gifts or of the meals he offers. But, in our opinion, the function is not the establishment of a hierarchy between the two, but rather the manifestation of their common position as seniors. The destination of the cattle given away (whether a meal or entry into the herd) is less important than the fact that the cattle must be given. And the seniors are the only people who have enough cattle herds to make the celebration of a marriage possible. In these slaughters of bulls, the donor does not attempt to do better than his host, but both assert their control over the circulation of cattle, the circulation of women, and marriage. The social value of herds in most African societies, in which they constitute the chief 'sign' of wealth, cannot be dissociated from the function of cattle in the exchange of women. It is indeed possible to convert ordinary consumption goods into cattle. A cow can be exchanged for a number of millet granaries. But the possibility of operating the conversion remains in the hands of the seniors who control the compound's granaries: therefore the junior who makes a profit on his personal field does not threaten the system.[20]

Just as one aspect of the condition of senior is to own herds, another is to slaughter bulls, or to give heifers (or slaves — only seniors own cattle and slaves). It is possible to do these things outside marriage ceremonies but, by their importance, these are their location *par excellence*: and it is not by luck, since marriage, the first step of the young men towards the condition of senior, must be under the seniors' strict control. Besides, it is always the 'dependent' groups (*wadde* = husband's age-set, *weyma* = women) who are the direct recipients of the slaughtered beasts. Here again, the meaning is brought out by Mauss: A's father (who gives the bulls) and B's father (who receives them, and has them slaughtered) are associated in the obvious and ceremonial destruction of these riches, for the benefit of the subjected categories (youth and women) who thus see the reaffirmation of the social hierarchy and the power-prestige of the seniors.

3. Gifts to the Bridegroom and the Bride (didigi and kambuza)

Here, at last, appear the parties to the marriage. For their change of status must not be forgotten. The gifts they receive from the seniors show this. The bridegroom in particular receives considerable goods for the *didigi*. Through them, his whole family recognises that he has now started the evolution which will later turn him into the head of a family, a holder of cattle, granaries, land. But this is only a distant prospect, so his father will decide on the distribution of these goods: he will leave his son a few head of cattle, (the nucleus of his future herd) and extra field, and the bags or baskets of millet or rice which will be, during the celebration, the main source of his gifts to the griots, the women or his age-set.

The gifts received by the bride are fewer; they are entirely her own and will be used to furnish the house which is her responsibility. Indeed, the new 'couple' form an independent residential unit, even though it is dependent in production and consumption (for which it is integrated into the extended family, cultivating, eating and clothing under the authority of the head of the family). Thus, for a while the only real autonomy of the couple depends on the woman alone since she owns the furnishing of the house. This may not be unrelated to the astonishing independence and freedom of thought of Wogo women nor, similarly, to the frequency of divorce.

Neither the sexual division of labour and of exchanges, nor the fact that women represent a means to rise to higher social status, must allow us to forget the existence of woman as producer and reproducer; the symbiosis of knowledge and of techniques which takes place in the couple turns it into the basic social cell (in the past only potentially, at the beginning of the union). Woman is not only a good, or a means of acquiring goods, she is also just as essential to the economic survival of the group as any person taking her place in the network of interpersonal and affective relations, and this is as true today as it was in the past.

RECENT CHANGES

The suppression of slavery first started a process of levelling of marriages between slaves as well as between free people. Indeed, as we have seen, the former did not have the same precise and decisive social function. They were therefore far less 'marked'. The owner provided the necessary animals (slaves did not own any cattle: 'the owner would take it away', 'their sons do not inherit') and sheep were used instead of bulls depending on the owner's own good will. The prestations of millet and sorghum alone came from the slave's granary (thus of his labour on his personal field) and constituted the *higyi alman*, bridewealth proper, as a substitute for the oxen and slaves which circulated in 'real' marriages. In fact, marriages between slaves used to be a far poorer, simplified imitation of marriage between free people. If everything seemed similar (a *tende* was also built for example, but it did not contain a *kunta arkila* — too expensive for slaves) it was precisely the difference in scale which changed the function.

The economic autonomy of former slaves and the changes which occurred in the modalities and significance of marriage were to unify these two levels of marriage slowly.

We will start with the result: the present state of Wogo marriage.

Kiamali Mamadu's marriage (Tessa)

Kiamali asked his father to go and speak to the parents of the girl he wanted to marry. It is then that the sum of the bridewealth must be determined, nowadays fixed at 15,000 CFA by the government. A month later, his father gave 7,500 CFA, the first part of the bridewealth, to Kiamali's friends who took it to the house of the bride-to-be. That is the *sugyi*. A large meal was given to the young people, the friends of the bride-to-be participated, and in the evening Kiamali's age-set went back home. This *sugyi* will be distributed by the father of the bride-to-be among his relatives and the mother's.

Ten months later two of the aunts of the bride-to-be came to bring the *farminari*: one *kokondo* of ground rice, a sheep, a litre of butter. The *weynya* ate in the village and went back with 2,500 CFA given by Kiamali to greet (*fo nda gweye*) and thank his mother-in-law. That evening Kiamali and his age-set slaughtered the sheep and cooked the rice.

At harvest time, Kiamali sent two of his age-set, chosen by his *bogu* leader to take the *hegyehari* twenty bundles of millet, mostly given by his age-set and one sheep which the father of the bride-to-be slaughtered immediately for the two carriers, to whom he also gave 500 francs and some kola. Meanwhile, during the cultivating season Kiamali brought his work team (forty youths on one occasion, fifteen on the other) twice to his father in law's and went to work there three times with two friends.

In February, six days before the wedding, Mamadu (the father) a friend and a marabout set off for the *tiraw*. They brought the rest of the bridewealth or 7,500 CFA (the *higyi alman*); Kiamali's father in law pays the marabout (500 CFA) for his *alfatia*. On the other hand he keeps the 7,500 francs ('eats it', 'sleeps on it').

On the eve of the marriage, Kiamali and his age-set built a straw hut (*bukka*). Two of them went in a canoe to fetch the bride (the *zulo*) who came accompanied by her *weynya*, bringing the *kambuza* received from her kin (who give to the extent to which her father has redistributed the *sugyi* to them) fifteen ordinary blankets (from Dori) six loin cloths, one bed, many mats, and a large *kunta arkila*, a gift from her father.

In the evening Kiamali surrounded by his age-set, wearing a turban (*didigi*) received gifts from his family, from the village people. The total is impressive: 55,000 francs, five cows, ten sheep, two horses, three fields given, one by his father, the second by his father's brother, the third by a mother's brother.

The next day, Kiamali fasted, but stayed with his age-set and griots in a hut, while the *weynya* settled the bride's things in the *bukka*. Kiamali gave 500 francs to the men who put up the bed.

During the celebration, all the participants spent a lot on the griots who left with their pockets full (15,000–30,000 francs). Eight sheep were slaughtered, millet and mainly rice consumed in quantity; altogether Kiamali gave 4,000 F to the *weynya*, 2,000 F to his age-set who received again as much from the *weynya*.

The day after the fast everybody went away. On that day the village women came and greeted the young bride with a few coins; she had gone out on the first day. However, she spent most of her time in the house for three days, a friend (*girbyie*) at her side.

Finally, a week later, the *weynya* brought the *zulinari*: one *kokondo* of ground rice, two goats, a litre of oil, two loincloths. He gave them again 4,000 F for his mother-in-law.

Thus on the one hand gifts of cattle and the slaughter of bulls have disappeared, while money now circulates at all times. On the other, the place and the importance of the ceremony have changed.

From bulls to money. Bridewealth

In order to maintain the livestock the colonial administration very early forbade the slaughter of bulls.

But the traditional social system still functioned: either the regulation was got round, or practices with the same function were substituted for it. Thus, instead of slaughtering bulls, the habit was developed of giving them, for the *sugyi* and for the celebrations themselves (which goes to prove that the main thing was the existence of livestock as 'good destined to marriage' and not its specific use). Thus the situation was analogous to that described by de Garine for the Massa: 'It is not the herds which are converted into money to allow an improvement of housing or diet, according to criteria exterior to the society, but money which is converted into cows in order to allow men to obtain wives whose possession will give them an improved social status.'[21]

In itself, money did not at first replace cattle, since animals were not archaic monetary symbols. It is only the transformation of family structures and consequently of the significance of marriage which allowed the progressive substitution of money for cattle.

But, and here we see the resistance of traditional social relations, the increase in the monetary level of bridewealth was only a reaction to this irruption of money, that from now on everybody could acquire. It was necessary to determine the sums asked for at a level such that young people had to continue to go through the seniors. This is obvious when the sums nowadays received for the *didigari* are seen. They considerably exceed the sum of the bridewealth and of the expenses attached to it. In this sense, marriage costs nothing but is a source of profit. However, the father has had to make an investment, which he alone can make.

The organisation of ceremonies

For the last thirty years, the District Officer has forbidden the building of the *tende* in the bride's family's compound; the celebration had to take place where the bridegroom resides. The Wogo, whom the officer had consulted, are supposed to have said that it was pointless labour to build this large tent only to pull it down four days later.

In fact, it seems that the District Officer had also been subjected to pressures from the colonial administration; the slaughter of bulls continued despite the ban and they wanted to 'break' the traditional celebration and its wastage.

Despite this, the celebrations continued for a while, and the slaughter of bulls simply took place at the bridegroom's. But, this practice died out after a few years, a small *tende* only was built in the bridegroom's compound, and today there is no *tende* at all (a mere straw hut built by the bridegroom's age-set on the eve of the *zulo*, the bride's arrival) hardly any *kunta arkila*, and the celebration lasts only one day.

This defeat of the custom cannot be attributed to mere administrative intervention. It might have been possible to evade it, as it had been for a while, or the ban could even have given birth to a movement of cultural resistance, like those which sometimes appeared elsewhere in colonised Africa. But the impetus for such resistance had disappeared of itself, because the former significance of marriage had disappeared: the atomisation of the extended family, the introduction of commodity relations linked to the extended use of money, the emergence of new needs, the demands of taxation and the possibility of selling rice; migrations to Ghana; individual appropriation of land, all these things contributed to subvert the traditional control exercised by the seniors over the juniors, and the means of this control. Not that it has totally disappeared: but from now on, marriage constitutes total emancipation, and not just its promise. The bridegroom keeps the *didigi* for himself, since he will constitute an autonomous unit of production now, and the *didigi* provides him with his initial capital (according to the same principle as when formerly the creation of an autonomous living unit implied that the bride kept for herself the furniture which was given to her as *kambuza*). In this can therefore be seen the most decisive innovation made to marriage.

The system of labour and food prestations has maintained itself and still continues beyond marriage, *farminari* and *anzurey bogu* for the young man, *hegyehari* and *zulinari*, and later, gifts from the bride to her mother, for female relations. (As far as this last topic is concerned, it must be noticed that the young bride today still continues to 'cook behind her mother in law' for a year; and remains under her relative authority afterwards, so that when the mother-in-law is too old, she will pound for her). Indeed, both the system of labour teams (*bogu*) and that of exchanges and daily gifts today remain in full strength: thus the prestations of this kind which take place in marriage are only elements of this totality and as such are capable of a far stronger 'resistance'.

CONCLUSION

We will have the opportunity to reconsider a number of these problems; we have, however, chosen to mention them now and to devote a whole chapter to marriage, in order to illustrate the presence of the past in the present structures. These cannot be understood without such a reference to history, to previous relations of production, to the cultural configurations which have been inherited.

And, in our view, marriage constitutes the crystallisation by unification in time and place of the different levels of social reality, of their respective rhythms, which Mauss had suggested should be called the total social phenomenon. Unfortunately, this widely accepted expression has sometimes been deprived of the necessary rigour, used indiscriminately and has lost its meaning that 'everything is included in everything else'. To give these words their whole value, to turn them into a scientific concept, is at the same time necessarily to determine their limits precisely. For this let us go back to the source:

> In these *total* social phenomena, as we propose to call them, all kinds of institutions find simultaneous expression: religious, legal, moral (and these are political and kinship ones as well) and economic — and these imply particular forms of production and consumption, or rather of prestation and distribution; in addition, the phenomena have their aesthetic aspect and they reveal morphological types.[22]

Wogo marriage seems to fit perfectly into such a definition. Let us look at some key-words.

Institutions *express* themselves in it. By institutions, it seems that should be meant the levels at which the different social practices and their respective structures are established (for Mauss, religious, juridical-moral and economic phenomena). Thus the study of marriage is not the study of these levels, these structures, these institutions, but the study of one of their *expressions*.[23] The specific character of this expression is based on its simultaneity: in marriage emerge 'simultaneously' religious, political, kinship, economic structures. . . .

To understand marriage *is not* to understand, for example, the relations of production which are manifest within it. *On the contrary, it is the knowledge of the relations of production which allows us to understand marriage and its function within these relations.* Similarly the ideological configuration of a society, the structures of its knowledge can be realised in marriage and it is only their previous study which allows the study of marriage and its role *from that point of view* (but such research could not be part of our project). One of the main errors in the interpretations of the 'total social phenomenon' has been to assimilate it to an 'essential section' in which could be read obvious social structures of all types.[24]

'In these *total* social phenomena . . . all kinds of institutions find simultaneous expression . . .' but the total social phenomena are not the institutions; they merely illustrate them and emerge at the level of social life. Their analysis is at the same time beyond and beside the analysis of social structures: beyond, they are examples of the functioning of these structures, beside, they are processes of location; they allow us simultaneously to ask questions and to check. But they do not own the field of answers. That is what, in our view, has justified the crucial role of marriage, to illustrate simultaneously traditional relations of production, and introduce those which have replaced them.

Finally, we have intentionally limited our interest to one type of question only (one type of 'institution' only, one level of social practice only): those which involve economic and social relations more specifically. Mauss very rightly speaks of economic 'institutions' which 'imply particular forms of production and consumption, or rather of prestation and distribution. 'This clearly says that the economic structures imply 'particular forms of production and consumption' which can only be socially determined. Economic and social structures overlap. To separate the economic system from the social relations which cement and organise it, is thus to make a second mistake in terms of Mauss's criteria among others. Such is the case of Godelier who radically isolates two types of structures, productive forces and relations of production[25] whereas relations of production are themselves an element of productive forces and productive forces exist only through these relations of production (and not beside them).[26]

Thus, by now studying in succession productive activities and relations of production, this is nothing more, in our view, than a way of describing a field ranging from the techniques used to the relations which put these techniques into action; and it is not a recovery operation of the unfortunate dichotomy between productive forces and relations of production, whose relationship must be grasped far more subtly.

NOTES

1. See Rouch, J., *Les Songhay*, pp. 33–7.
2. A person's name comprises his Christian name, followed by his father's name.
3. This could be a remnant from a matrilineal system, insofar as, in Bourra, elders have told us that formerly chiefship went, not to a chief's son, but to his *tuba*. It seems that the term *tuba* was reserved to the *weyma izo*.
4. Lévi-Strauss, Cl., *The Elementary Structures of Kinship*, Eyre & Spottiswoode, London, 1968, p. 470.
5. *Ibid.*, p. 471.
6. Main informants: Aissata Yacouba, Ganda Idrissa, Haddou Kandagomi and Manou Idrissa, all from Tessa. See 'La Bouche Déliée' a film made in 1967 which reconstructs traditional marriage with the help of the Tessa village.
7. 'It is the essential weakness of conjectural history that its hypotheses cannot be verified.' Radcliffe-Brown, *Structure and Function in Primitive Society*, Cohen and West, London, 1952, p. 57.
8. *Ibid.*, pp. 91–3.
9. On the other hand, this is no longer true if the problem is no longer located at the level of status and role, but at the more general one of exchange, where marriage between cross cousins is first of all an exogamous relationship: 'These difficulties are clarified if cross-cousin marriage is seen as the elementary formula for marriage by exchange and if exchange is seen as the *raison d'etre* of the system of oppositions.' Lévi-Strauss, 1968, *op. cit.*, p. 129.
10. The names of weekdays, taken from the Koran are: *attino* (Monday), *attalata* (Tuesday), *alarba* (Wednesday), *alkamisa* (Thursday), *alzuma* (Friday), *asipto* (Saturday), *alhado* (Sunday). The evening and the night are named with the following day and not the one that has just gone by as in English. For example, Thursday evening (or Thursday night) is said *alzuma kino*.
11. He is told 'so that you should do the *homey dala* well later, for otherwise your wife will divorce you . . .'.
12. The bulls to be slaughtered are never all brought at once: each day, when it is necessary, the members of the age-set go and fetch them except when people from Tonditihiyo (Bourra, in Mali) come to marry in Sinder, in which case, obviously, they bring all the cattle at once.
13. No doubt from *fumbu*, (stinking, rotten) and *bakaw yo*, (those who are friends).
14. Leroi-Gourhan, A., *Technique et langage*, p. 210. [Translator's note: my translation].
15. See particularly Bohannan, P., 'Some principles of exchange and investment among the Tiv'; Firth, R., 'Human Types'; Thurnwald, R., 'L'économie primitive'; Godelier, M., 'A propos des Siane de Nouvelle-Guinée'.
16. See above, passim.
17. See chapters 7 and 9 which take up and develop the study of the system of

internal exchanges, labour relations and prestations, such that they can be seen today as remnants from the past which are still functional now.

18. This dependence is modified in the following way: by giving B to A, B's father allows him gradually to escape his father's authority: by compensation. A will owe him respects, gifts and labour. Similarly B's labour power will no longer be expressed for her family but primarily for A's and then, by giving him children for A himself, whom she will give the opportunity of reaching economic independence: by compensation, during her whole life she will maintain close links with her family, to whom she will bring the greater part of gifts received from her husband. A still goes on working for his father, but is 'indebted' to his father-in-law. B from now on labours for her in-laws and her husband but is 'indebted' to her mother.

'Consequently, the bond between fathers and sons is tied up with the bond between allied families. The groom works for his parents-in-law, and he receives the counter-prestation of his gifts from his wife in the manifold forms of cooking, gardening, procreation of children and sexual gratification.' Lévi-Strauss, 1968, op. cit., p. 467.

19. Mauss, M., The Gift, London, Cohen and West, 1966, p. 72.

20. 'The goods handed over on the occasion of a marriage are of various sorts and are frequently accompanied by labour prestations performed by several members of the grooms family. The composite character of bridewealth testifies to the status of the person able to collect it. It also precludes the possible exploitation of specialisation in the manufacture of a single marriage object.' C. Meillassoux above p. 141.

21. de Garine, I., Les Massa du Cameroun, p. 125. [Translator's note: my translation].

22. Mauss, 1966, op. cit., p. 1. [Translator's note: the English edition is abbreviated; I have translated part of this quotation myself.]

23. This term is used by Radcliffe-Brown: 'The social values current in a primitive society are maintained by being expressed (O.S. emphasis) in ceremonial or ritual customs.' Radcliffe-Brown, 1952, op. cit., p. 28.

24. See the basic criticism made by L. Althusser of this process of 'essential section' in Althusser Reading Capital, New Left Books, London, 1970, pp. 94–6.

25. 'The productive forces are a reality completely distinct from the production-relations and not reducible to them'. Godelier, M., Rationality and Irrationality in Economics, New Left Books, London, 1972, p. 87.

26. See on this Balibar 'The basic concepts of historical materialism in Althusser and Balibar, 1970, op. cit., pp. 227–9. Indeed, these 'fundamental concepts' (in particular those of mode of production, relations of production, productive forces) have been drawn out and used to analyse a history linked to the development of social classes. For this reason, some ethnologists and anthropologists recognise their theoretical interest: 'The theory of this evolution has been drawn out a century ago by historical materialism' (Leroi-Gourhan, op. cit., p. 238 [translator's translation] but this implies two consequences:

a) that the phases of history preceding this development have not yet been the object of such theoretical treatment (despite the fact that periodisation and the methods of approach defined by Leroi-Gourhan pose the problem decisively).

b) that there can be no rigorous separation between these two theoretical objects; this would lead to errors of the type: peoples without history and peoples with history; or, history starts with the merchant economy. That is to say that, to the extent to which they provide a correct analysis of class societies, it must be possible to use the concepts of historical materialism for the analysis of classless societies, as long as they have been organised in 'basic concepts' drawn from their original specifications, then re-specified in function of their new object. Similarly, technological analysis, for example, uses the same fundamental concepts, whether to deal with a mere drill or a modern pneumatic tool.

But the precondition for such a procedure is the refusing of mechanism and simplism. Analysis of the 'history of class struggles' does not instantly provide the fundamental concepts used to develop it, but these must be found. Most of this work remains to be done. For example, what 'modes of production' existed in pre-colonial Africa? And to what extent does the use of this concept to deal with such a reality demand the reconstruction, the remodelling of the concept itself? This is quite different from the summary application of ready-made categories, such as that of 'Asiatic mode of production' to objects whose nature is *a priori* different (societies of Sahelian Africa for example) which save the researcher from making the effort of previous theoretical reflection, which, however, is the effort of previous theoretical reflection, which, however, is indispensable, on the nature of a mode of production, as a *combination* of given social and economic relations.

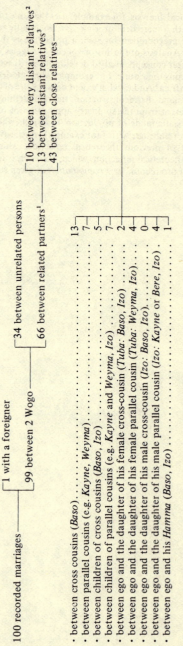

Table 2
TYPES OF MARRIAGES

100 recorded marriages

- 1 with a foreigner
- 99 between 2 Wogo
  - 34 between unrelated persons
  - 66 between related partners[1]
    - 13 between very distant relatives[2]
    - 13 between distant relatives[3]
    - 43 between close relatives

- between cross cousins (*Baso*) 13
- between parallel cousins (e.g. *Kayne, Weyma*) 7
- between children of cross cousins (*Baso, Izo*) 5
- between children of parallel cousins (e.g. *Kayne* and *Weyma, Izo*) 7
- between ego and the daughter of his female cross-cousin (*Tuba: Baso, Izo*) 2
- between ego and the daughter of his female parallel cousin (*Tuba: Weyma, Izo*) 4
- between ego and the daughter of his male cross-cousin (*Izo: Baso, Izo*) 0
- between ego and the daughter of his male parallel cousin (*Izo: Kayne* or *Bere, Izo*) 4
- between ego and his *Hamma* (*Baso, Izo*) 1

Notes: 1. *I Ga Margu*: they are assembled; they are related.
               2. Filiation unknown, or too difficult to trace.
               3. Known filiation, but more than 6 times removed.

Table 3
GIFTS AND COUNTER GIFTS OF MARRIAGE

Name	Nature	Giver	Receiver	Redistribution	Circumstances
SUGYI	money	Father A[1]	Father B[1]	Most of it goes to B's relatives	Brought by A's age-set members
FARMINARI	ground rice, goat, spices	Mother B	Mother A		Brought by B's *weynya*
	money	A		Part to B's *weynya*	Given to the *weynya* who have come for the *Farminari*
HEGYEHARI	bundles of millet, paddy	A and his age-set	Mother B		Brought by A+'s age-set members
HIGYI ALMAN	money	Father A	Father B	A small part to the marabout who says the *alfatia*	Brought by A's father gone to B's for the celebration of the *Thraw*
KAMBUZA	loin cloths, bed, blankets, mats	B's relatives	B		On B's departure (*Zulo*)
DIDIGI	money, cattle, fields	A's relatives	A	Some to A's father, immediately spent on the griots, gifts to the *weyna* and the age-set	On the evening of the wedding day ++
ZULINARI	ground rice, oil, spices	Mother B	Mother A		Brought by the *weynya* a week after the wedding +
	money	A	Mother B	Part to B's *weynya*	Given to the *weynya* come for the *zulinari*

Notes:
1. A and B are respectively the fiancé and the bride-to-be.
+ A meal (slaughtered sheep) is offered to receive those who have come.
++ Large celebration with griots.

Table 4
EXAMPLES OF GIFTS AND COUNTER GIFTS IN MARRIAGE
(3 CASES IN TESSA)

	HAMEY MAGARI	SUMANA GANDA	KIAMALI MAMUDU
Sugyi	10.000 F (in June)	7.500 F (in November)	7.500 F (in November)
Farminari	2 baskets ground rice 1 goat 2 bottles of oil 2 large calabashes of spices (Sept.)	No *farminari*, since it is given only during winter, and Sumana married four months after the *Sugyi*	1 basket ground rice 1 sheep 1 lb butter (September, 10 months after the *Sugyi*)
Counter-gift to the *weynya*	3.000 F		2.500 F
Hegyehari	20 bundles of millet 3 baskets paddy (December)	13 bundles millet. (November)	20 bundles millet. (November)
Labour presta-tions before the wedding	Once 15 people (*Bogu*); twice 3 people (friends); once 2 people (friends)	No agriculture between *sugyi* and wedding day	Twice 40 people (*Bogu*) three times 3 people (friends)
Tiraw and *Higyi alman*	7.500 F (January)	2.500 F (February). The rest will be paid during the marriage celebrations	7.500 F (February)
The couple's house	straw hut (Bukka) built three days earlier by age-set	Somana already had a solid house	Bukka built on the eve
Didigi	received: 6.500 F 26 sheep 3 goats 3 horses 3 cows 1 *kunta*	received: 44.000 F 7 cows 14 sheep	received: 55.000 F 5 cows 10 sheep 2 horses 3 fields
Expenditure during the celebration	6 sheep slaughtered 2.500 F to friends 3.000 F to griots 5.000 F to *weynya*	4 sheep slaughtered 2.500 F to age-set 2.000 F to *weynya* As much given to griots. Pays the 5.000 F of bride-wealth owed.	8 sheep slaughtered 4.000 F to *weynya* 2.000 F to age-set 4.000 F to griots

Table 4 (*continued*)

	HAMEY MAGARI	SUMANA GANDA	KIAMALI MAMUDU
Zulinari	2 baskets ground rice 2 bottles oil 1 calabash couscous 1 he-goat		1 basket ground rice 2 goats 1 litre oil 2 loin cloths
Counter gift to *weynya*	4.000 F	4.000 F	4.000 F

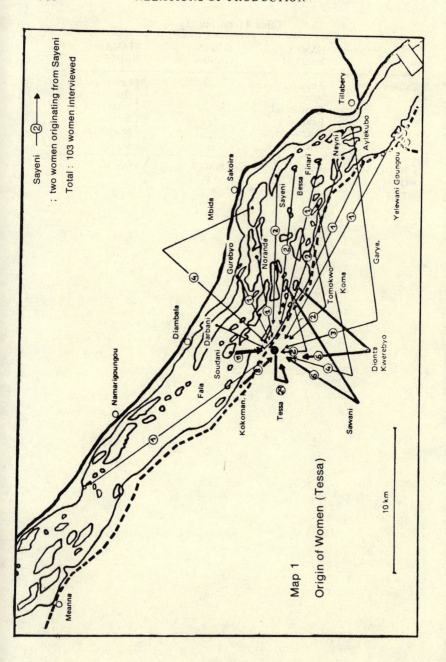

Sayeni ——②——→

②: two women originating from Sayeni

Total : 103 women interviewed

Map 1

Origin of Women (Tessa)

10 km

Status, Power and Wealth: Relations of Lineage, Dependence and Production in Alladian Society

Marc Augé

Olivier de Sardan notes in his introduction that the interpretation given by members of the society studied by the anthropologist of social behaviour, their own explanations, are important material for analysis. In this contribution Augé explicitly considers the representations of the Alladian, particularly with respect to authority and wealth, and the distinction between an 'ideo-logic' and the functioning of an 'ideology'. The central concern of the essay is the nature of the connection between relations of production and relations of dependence and in his introduction Augé relates his discussion to the debate regarding the point of application of the concepts 'reciprocity' and 'exploitation' and the status of the relations they characterise (e.g. the relationship between father and son, which may be characterised as 'exploitative', is represented in the local ideology as 'reciprocal'). It is clear, from this contribution as from the collection as a whole, that the relationship between infra-structure and superstructure is not the simple cause and effect that vulgar Marxism would suggest. Readers are referred back again to the quotations from Marx and Engels which precede the introduction.

INTRODUCTION

This text, first published in 1969, emphasised two aspects of the relations of dependence in Alladian society; it distinguished between dependence based on age, which manifests itself in economic prestations from juniors to seniors ('fathers' or 'uncles') and dependence based on birth. In its essentials, the latter corresponded to the relations between slaves and their owners. The integration of male and female slaves in the matrilineage allows the inclusion of a relationship of dependence no longer linked to age within the language of kinship. In his relationship to the same person the slave accumulates the duties of son and nephew. In some ways these analyses support those of Meillassoux who, in 1964, showed how, among the Guro of the Ivory Coast, the kinship link was transformed into a purely social filiation.

My more recent research (fieldwork between April 1968 and April 1969, short stays in 1970 and 1971) gave me the opportunity to extend my enquiries to other lagoon people (Avikam, Ebrie) and to look more closely at the problems of representations and ideology. This specific viewpoint has, I believe, allowed me to develop some of the observations I had made previously, and in particular those which are discussed in this article. I will deal with three of them:

(1) The father's role in lagoon societies is ambivalent. It would, at first sight, be tempting to say that the father/son relationship is ambiguous: if the son's relations with his father are usually relaxed and conform to the model of stereotype attitudes which Lévi-Strauss puts forward concerning matrilineal societies, yet the father has considerable and formidable authority. In lagoon ideology an infraction of the father's authority is considered more serious than one of the maternal uncle's and the father's power of invoking curses is considered to be particularly efficient. But these stereotypes refer back to the father's two separate roles, the unique father/son relationship (father as father) and the father as representative of his matrilineage (the father as 'ally'). Analysis of the representations that the Alladian have, on the one hand, of the practice and transmission of the power of self-defence, *seke*, and, on the other hand, of the practices and transmission of the power of damnation, *aveda*, clearly reveals this distinction. The power of self-defence, like the name, is inherited in paternal line; the power of damnation is passed on to the father's heir (in the father's matrilineage); and even the prestations due to the father e.g. in the redistribution of the fishing catch, are largely due to the father as representative of his matrilineage (a lineage 'allied' to that of the son's mother and consequently to the son himself). It is thus possible to discuss whether as groups the lineages (mother's lineage, father's lineage) define as many structures of exploitation which are represented as such in the ideology (witchcraft is practised within the matrilineage), while reciprocal relations are the prerogative of extra-lineage relationships — in this case the patriline along which the beneficial power is meant to be transmitted; the strict father-son relationship discussed by structuralists is indeed represented in the local ideology as being a reciprocal one in which the son returns to the father an equivalent of the services he received in the course of his childhood. The debate on the concepts of exploitation and reciprocity has been launched again by P. P. Rey's criticisms of M. Godelier, Rey expressing doubts on the pertinence of the latter; in my view it seems to have a factual

existence in local ideology and it should be analysed as a representation.

(2) The discourse of the society, or rather the speeches of its specialists are made in the singular. The anthropologist and those whom he studies converge in their discussion of the father/son and uncle/nephew relationships. In fact, the ideological level gives preference to a certain number of individuals who are simultaneously its subject (in the sense in which the French word is understood to indicate the object of a study or a treatise) and its subjects (in the sense in which the only people who can use this language with impunity and, for example, make accusations of witchcraft, are those very people who constitute its privileged subject: father, uncle, son, nephew, i.e. the seniors, not by their age but by their genealogical status). The theories of heredity, of the person and of witchcraft form a coherent whole, an ideo-logic or logic of representations but, at the same time they draw the lines of power which combine lineage seniority with individual seniority to base the inter-lineage hierarchisation on an egalitarian language (they speak in the singular). The expression social senior (a potential senior because of his genealogical status regardless of his age) is the counterpart of that of social junior (applied to the younger representatives of branches located in the junior lineages or even more, to slaves or descendants of slaves).

(3) The ideological level constitutes a particularly interesting point of observation; but the language of instances is likely to falsify interpretations which might be based on this observation. Poulantzas has emphasised the diversity of the areas of ideology; diversity does not mean heterogeneity, and at least when discussing lineage societies it is possible to assume a degree of coherence between the different forms of representation of a true ideo-logic. Religious ideology is not the whole of ideology; what M. Godelier has suggested concerning the nature of kinship (that it is at the same time infrastructure and superstructure) may, in other words, be extended to other types of organisation: social organisation and political organisation can simultaneously be understood as organisation and representation. When the empiricists are discussing the connection between religion and social organisation they are in fact discussing the relationship between two levels of representation; they are describing an ideo-logic, not the functioning of an ideology. The problem of the coherence of all the representations of a society has been, however blindly, discussed for a long time already. The main thing is to discover (and this is my present aim) whether or not the contents of the ideo-logic discourse represent both its audience and its beneficiaries. The problem of the

function of the ideo-logic is inseparable from that of its coherence. Because its function is interpretative and because it speaks in the singular, the ideo-logic of the lagoon societies functions as an ideology: it measures individual order with social order; the individual's history of his illnesses, his misfortunes, etc. — is explained by reference to the social order of which it is a part (genealogy, heredity, alliance) and in relation to which it is well or badly located (respecting or ignoring the rules, the institutionalised forms of behaviour, etc.). The reproduction of the individual is the cause as well as the effect of social order.

In this respect current events are revealing; at the moment the 'prophetisms' of the Ivory Coast are responding or attempting to respond, to a double request: the first fits in with lineage order, the second is caused by the appearance of new conditions and fits into the apparent neo-colonial disorder; the study of the new 'prophetic' messages and of the reception they get, by looking at the successes and failures encountered by these prophets, experimenters in ideology, is interesting for two reasons: on the one hand, because the prophets are trying to develop a new ideo-logic (freeing the individual from the framework of his lineage, ridding him of his self-definition in terms of relationships, attempting to confront him with his 'nation'), they educate us on the nature of the previous, and still current, ideo-logic; on the other hand, by their failures and the contradictory requests that are made to them, they testify to the complexity of the relations between economy and ideology within the framework of an accelerated transformation of the relations of production; by attempting to make this transformation meaningful, they implicitly bring up its objective meaning; in their attempt to justify the new order of things, to explain (and answer) all the questions which they are asked (be they of lineage or neo-colonial order), they implicitly discuss the beneficiaries and the victims of this change. The contents of the message, which goes beyond its author, once again discusses those who believe in its stability and is revealed as the product of a situation which it claimed to account for.

STATUS, POWER AND WEALTH: RELATIONS OF LINEAGE, DEPENDENCE, AND PRODUCTION IN ALLADIAN SOCIETY

The Alladian are one of the societies who reside in the lagoons of the lower Ivory Coast. There are fourteen villages whose population is entirely made up of Alladian, they are all along the narrow coastal strip between the sea and the lagoon, between the west of Abidjan and Grand Lahou. Since completion of the canals of Vridi and

Asagny, this coastal strip has become a real island. There has never been a chief whose power controlled all Alladian, but at the religious level, Grand-Jacques has dominated; this predominance had important economic consequences, since it appears that for a long time Grand-Jacques held the monopoly of trade with Europeans until Jacqueville became the most active centre of this trade; towards 1880 the French entrusted the representation of Alladian country to the chief of Grand-Jacques; but, after a number of incidents, they withdrew it in 1890 to give it to Adje Bonny, 'King Bonny', chief of Jacqueville, the richest trader in the whole coastal strip. It was in 1905 that the three districts of Addah, Jacqueville, and Akru were really created and, until recently, they remained administratively connected to the subdivision of Dabu (Lagoons area). Jacqueville became a *sous-préfecture* in 1961 and since then a fourth district brings under the authority of the *sous-préfet* of Jacqueville the Aizi villages of the northern and southern banks of the lagoon.

Traditionally, in each village a chief was chosen from among the members of the founding lineage, usually the matrilineal heir of the preceding chief. The chief's powers were mainly judicial; he also made decisions about war and peace with non-Alladian villages. But on the whole his authority was no different from that of the head of a lineage; it also happened, when two lineages were the founders of a village, that the chiefship would, at least in theory, be taken up by each of them in turn; this is the case in Grand-Jacques, Jacqueville and Avagu.

In this society no hierarchies are articulated around chiefship as such. It is the kinship system which appears to be the principle, the model and the language of most relations of dependence. Since, however, among the Alladian, the principles of residence and of descent are both equally basic to the structure of village society, the lineage system as pure descent system is far from making up the totality of the social system: first of all age-set organisation brings together the population of each village simply on the basis of their age independently of lineage organisation. It institutes precise economic relations between the leader of a set and its members; with time, each set acquires an increasingly great influence; it has its own internal hierarchy and can, in case of war, have decisive responsibilities. Secondly — and most importantly — on the basis of the model of son/father and uterine nephew/maternal uncle relations, links are established which have only the appearance and the language of kinship relationships; on the one hand they are the links between slaves, sons of slaves or foreign women married with bridewealth and the buyer or giver of bridewealth in the same court, and on the other, the links between descendants of slave or foreign women and full blooded Alladian within the same lineage. Thus differences of status between individuals and the precise socio-economic relations to which they correspond are based on the principle of a stratification of the lineage in sections of unequal status.

If one wanted to look at all the relations of dependence to be found in this society, it would then be necessary to distinguish between lineage and village relations; within the first, between relations of personal and lineage dependence, and within the second, relations between villages, relations between the chief and his villagers and intervillage relations linked to the existence of age grades or age sets (*esuā*). Of all these type of relations, the most important and significant is the relation of personal dependence at the lineage level: on the one hand it stratifies the whole of Alladian society; on the other, as we will try to show, it reveals indirectly the development of Alladian society throughout the last century, particularly at the economic level. It is thus on this type of relation we will concentrate here, after we have located it within the totality of social relations characteristic of Alladian society.

I. VILLAGE AND LINEAGE. PUBLIC AND PRIVATE LIFE

As a first approximation it might be tempting to define those relations determined by the residence principle as public and those determined by the descent principle as private; the village would thus be the basic political unit, the clan or maximal lineage the most extensive descent unit. But it will be noticed that at the different levels of analysis demanded by the various types of relations under discussion the concepts of public and private interfere with each other, in the sense that the same institution or social category can as such alternatively play a public and a private role. In a recent work[1] the political scientist Freund writes:

> The private and the public are both social relations, but in one case the relation is based on the autonomy of the people in so far as they have the freedom to join a group, to leave it, or to abstain; in the other it is based on the collectivity's freedom to make up a group, which is independent of other collectivities of the same type, and contains within itself the relations of dominance and subordination.

Freedom to abstain does not really exist for the traditional Alladian, but the possibility, in case of need, of 'playing off' their matrilineage against their paternal kin, or the reverse, is effective; it will be seen that at the lineage level, lineage segments, without breaking all ties with their original lineage, have come to join the representatives of the richer founding lineages, of other villages (Grand-Jacques and mainly Jacqueville). Facts of this nature make explicit the private character of lineage relations; but the identification between founding lineage(s) and leadership of the village, between village elders — whose agreement was necessary for the nomination of the village chief — and heads of lineages and lineage segments, is enough to reveal the public and political roles of the units of descent. Any promotion within the lineage had repercussions at the public level and, in the long run, at the political level; but on the contrary, relations based on the eminently public institution of age-sets or *esubã* (which include all the villagers and which, independent of lineage or status, are formed only on the basis of age) can take on a more marked private character than that of lineage relations: between the leader of an *esubã* and its members, agreement is more contractual than that between father and son, insofar as an *esubã* leader is expected to compensate his group for the services that they provided him with in the course of their youth; on the other hand *esubã* companionship can create close links of friendship and cooperation between its members.

The constant interpenetration of the public and the private fields, and also the extremely limited, purely private field can be related to the relatively weak institutionalisation of power. From village to village, between chief and villager, the balance of power can be extremely demanding; it was not the subject of a clearly formulated theory and except in religious matters no village gave orders to any other. Within the village, it was inconceivable that a chief might act without the agreement of his peers — the court chiefs, the seniors of lineage and lineage segments represented in the village. But, far from corresponding to any kind of anarchy or to a democracy, this weak level of institutionalisation was the reflection of the extreme diffusion and non-specialisation of power. If by power is understood 'the social basis of leadership insofar as it rests on one or many layers of classes of the society'[2] it will be easy to see that, in traditional Alladian society, power was held by all the court chiefs of the villages; the privilege of age was the constituent principle of village as well as lineage hierarchy — chiefship belonging in principle to the most senior of the senior clan. Insofar as a potential senior could be found in every full Alladian (in contrast with the descendants of slave women), he could adhere only to the accepted ideology of family (son/father and uterine nephew/maternal uncle) and political relations (significantly the village head is also called *ama nizi*, father of the village'). Precisely because power was not very institutionalised, it appeared to be strongly personalised; this personalisation went so far that, at Grand-Jacques itself, the list of the traditional chiefs reveals serious infringements of legitimacy. Thus the most prestigious chief Grand-Jacques had in the last century, Kagui Digré, turned out not to belong to the clans who hold legitimate leadership (the Bodo and Moumbro clans) but had become famous because of his enormous fortune; moreover, he was overthrown because he seemed to be more concerned with trade than with the honour of the village: he tried to postpone a punitive expedition against the Adyukru so he could complete his trade with the European ships. We can thus see how wealth or competence could in politics limit legitimacy based on heredity. On the whole, the equation authority = power = wealth = prestige has always been confirmed in Alladian society; however the principle of this equation, which as we have seen has justified some usurpations, is sufficiently clear in the eyes of legitimate authorities for them to have substituted for it the also very generally accepted identification between *auctoritas* and *potestas*. Even the creation of administrative chiefship by the French failed to destroy this identification, as it often did elsewhere, and in general the administrative chiefship has been 'retrieved' by the lineages who traditionally hold chiefship. In Alladian society concern for formal legitimacy and for efficiency go together.

The theory of 'witchcraft' agreed by all the members of the society, emphasises the diffuse, equivocal and personalised character of authority; it is very remarkable that it does not create a negative picture of the true balance of forces in the society, a system of compensation, but rather a system of explanation of these relations.

Awa is a maleficent, ambiguous or rather ambivalent power, attributed to certain people, the *awabo*. Beliefs are unanimous concerning the organisation of *awabo* society, their modes and means of action. *Awabo* society, which we will not describe here in greater detail, makes up an imaginary world in which problems are solved and the private-fantasies of a given individual are expressed; but this is a structured world whose laws are codified, whose hierarchies are listed, a distorted image of village society, whose geography in fact includes the area of the village and its surroundings. *Awabo* society can only be understood on the basis of village lineage society, and the situations in which the *awabo* are implicated (such as can be analysed in the confessions made at Albert Atcho's[3] or, conversely on the basis of accusations or suspicions concerning this or that person) are typical, classifiable and socially significant situations. The system thus created is a system of universal explanation in which all events, from a headache to a bad harvest or death, is liable for judgement: far from systematically reversing the balance of forces of the real world, it accounts for it, explaining power and wealth by the possession of *awa*, poverty by the action of the *awa onõ* (onõ 'man') who has pierced his victim's hand. It inserts this balance of forces in another network of causality where legitimacy, authority, happiness, fortune are no longer causes but results or signs. Thus the *awa* system is in essence 'totalitarian' in the scope it claims, in which the boundary between the public and private fields is eliminated.

No moral judgement is really made on the *awa*. It is admitted that the powers of the sorcerer and those of the counter-sorcerer are not essentially different. It is admitted that neither wealth nor health can be acquired lastingly by someone who does not have the strength: this strength is not given a name but it is well known to be essentially identical to *awa*. The wealthy, the seniors, the powerful are always but quietly under suspicion of possessing the strength which explains their success precisely. *ɔso*, 'hardness', is a quality attributed to a few prestigious and dreaded men: somehow it constitutes the public and social variety of a secret talent whose presence is suspected since people think they perceive its signs.

II. CRITERIA OF SOCIAL DIFFERENTIATION

1. Differentiation based on age

A young Alladian male belongs to his mother's lineage (*aciɔkɔ*); a number of *aciɔkɔ* make up an *ɛme*; the difference between an *aciɔkɔ* and an *ɛme* corresponds to that established by Radcliffe-Brown between a lineage and a clan; in relation to his father's *aciɔkɔ* an Alladian is *ɛbiüi*. An Alladian male lives in his father's court; he may however be called upon to change residence to succeed his maternal uncle or his own elder brother to the throne of a court. Heads of courts and its other inhabitants in principle do not belong to the same lineage; thus the term *abü* 'court' has two different meanings depending on whether it is meant in its residential or its social sense: the *abüüi* are the living members of the *aciɔkɔ*, born of the *abü* in its social sense (i.e. the women of the *abü*) and they distinguish themselves as such from the *ɛbiüi*, sons or daughters of the men of the *abü* in its social sense who may reside in the *abü* in its residential sense (for example in the case when they are the children of the court and lineage head).

The different stages in the life of an Alladian correspond to his gradual emancipation from his father's guardianship, which culminates in a greater integration to his matrilineage and relative economic independence. At first the father has total authority over his son except in one respect: only his maternal uncle has the right to put his uterine nephew into bondage. Such a procedure, morally and normally permitted only by concern to preserve the interests of the lineage as an organic group, logically belongs to the man responsible for these interests; in other respects and later, the relations of dependence of the son to his father and of the uterine nephew to his maternal uncle have an essentially economic content. It must be added that, traditionally, breaking the rules which defined these relations entailed sanctions at the sacred level and the action of a quasi-immanent justice: in particular the damning of his son by the father meant the former's disappearance or misfortune.

For a male the development of these relations of dependence is translated into changes in residence and in the destination of the produce of his labour. The first stage corresponds to the young man's marriage: his father allows him to build a house. His wife comes to join him each evening, but she spends her days with her mother, in whose kitchen she prepares her husband's meal, which he eats alone. At the same time as the right to build his own house, he has obtained that of planting manioc on the land of his father's *aciɔkɔ*.

As yet, he owns neither a kitchen nor the right to redistribute his fish himself. It is only at the birth of his second or third child that he obtains from his father the right to have a kitchen in the latter's court. His wife then comes to join him.

It is still much later, at the birth of his fifth or the sixth child that he can hope to obtain his 'fishing rights' which correspond to an increase in his personal share, and in general to a different allocation during the redistribution of his catch.

Finally, at the death of his uncle or his elder brother, if they were court chiefs, he will change residence and will receive from the inhabitants of his new court the prestations they owed to the preceding chief.

2. Differentiations based on birth

(a) Slaves, descendants of slaves and foreign women

Marriage policy among the Alladian in the nineteenth century aimed at and succeeded in the elimination of the opposition ʃbiüi/əbüüi; the acquisition of slave and foreign women belonging to patrilineal tribes was the instrument of this policy which was so systematic that today many residential courts are still composed mainly of people belonging to the same *aciɔkɔ*. We will call the policy of systematic union with women whose children remain in their father's lineage pseudo-endogamy of *aciɔkɔ*.

In terms of social status as they are expressed in the language and system of kinship, a slave is distinguished from a 'free' Alladian less by a special social status than by the accumulation of many statuses linked to the rules of descent.

The acquirer of a slave (of either sex) would, as soon as he got him, take him to his father (or, in his absence, to his father's heir). The latter summoned the members of his *aciɔkɔ* and those of his son's *aciɔkɔ*. After having praised the merits of his son whose labour had brought him an acquisition which he himself would profit from, he chewed three kola nuts, then spat them in the slave's face, ordering him never again to turn his head towards whence he came. Everybody drank and the father returned the slave to his son. From then on he behaved like the slave's grandfather, his son being the father (slaves of both sexes used their owner's name as first name).

On the whole the slave was considered to be his owner's son in daily life and his nephew if the need was felt: he could be resold, or like the nephew, put into bondage by his uncle. The slave's duties to his owner did not imply any compulsory counterpart; son or nephew, male slave and descendant of a female slave were perpetual *juniors*, having no right to inherit in the direct line; in practice, slaves often married other slaves of Alladian women of the *abü* in its social sense, which entailed the maintenance of the *abüüi* in the court and, when the time came, an increased share for the court chief in the re-distribution of the fishing catch. A slave could, if he gave satisfaction, accumulate personal goods (the male and female slaves of a given court considered themselves to form a separate *aciɔkɔ* and inherited among themselves); in some genealogies collected in Jacqueville, there are examples of slaves having themselves acquired slaves. Obviously a disliked slave could have a difficult time in old age, his owner not having given him a wife and the owner's heir not being interested in him; it was therefore in the slave's interest to show himself to be a particularly keen 'son'.

In Alladian a slave is *owõ onõ*, 'man of shadows'; a slave woman *owõ yii*, 'woman of shadows'. The shadow in question is that from which the slave owner is profiting: it is the slave's labour which allows his owner to stay in the shade of his house, his trees, his goods. One also says *owõ yii üi*, slave's son or daughter, or *owõ yii kiki*, children of the grand-daughters in the female line of a slave woman. The descendants of slave women of the same lineage are addressed as *akore bo* 'hand people' after the hand which has taken and holds them.

The children of foreign women for whom bridewealth has been

paid (*ɛnoku yii üi*, from *ɛnoku*, 'foreign') had the right to inherit if there were no direct heirs (*aciɔkprɔɔ*, by contrast with the *eciɔkɔ* without any other specifications, of which descendants of slave and foreign women are a part). The children of a woman in bondage (*aoba yii üi* from *aoba*, 'wage') had the same status as the children of a slave woman. A person who was put into bondage was considered to be a slave but could be bought back.

In practice two kinds of slaves had a lower status than those discussed above: prisoners of war and people handed over as 'spoils' after a defeat (*ɔorɛciebo*, from *ɔore*, 'debt').

We still have to examine two particular cases of adoption. Traditionally a married man entrusts his first child to his father, who benefits from his domestic services and later treats him with particular consideration. Conversely, if a young bridegroom could not pay the total sum of bridewealth — an infrequent case since it is so low — his children remained under his wife's mother's authority. This fact explains the solidarity of 'fathers' since a young man's ability to pay this sum depended totally on his father's goodwill. *Impko* is a real case of adoption. It happens that parents, following the death of a number of new-born children want to get rid of the child they have just had. Indeed the mother sees in her previous misfortunes the sign of the maleficent will of the *awabo* (if Bregbo's confessions are to be believed, making women abort, making them sterile, or killing their young children are among their favourite tricks). The parents jointly agree to 'sell' the child; they put a bit of rope round its neck and walk it around the village, asking only for a stem of manioc and two dried coconuts. The point is to protect the child from the action of the *awa onõ* (who can act directly only in its matrilineage) by formally denying that it belongs to its family of origin; however the child theoretically keeps its rights in his *aciɔkɔ* of origin, but the rights and duties connected to the father/son relationship are transferred to the adoptive father/adopted son relationship. It is the adoptive father who will receive the share of matrimonial prestations usually due to the father in the case of an adopted daughter; it is he who will provide the sum of these prestations in the case of a son. If the adoptive father dies, it is his heir who takes charge of the child and who benefits from his services.

(b) Cross lineage differentiations

This is not the place to give a detailed description of the Alladian lineage system; we must however make a note of the original processes of splitting and recomposition of the lineages, which, in the course of the last century, together with the policy of pseudo-endogamy of *aciɔkɔ*, appear to have manifested and contributed to the success of certain lineages and villages. There are two such processes and we propose to call them respectively *dissociation* and *dissimilation*. By *dissociation*, we mean the action by which a kinship group leaves its lineage and village of origin to settle in another village with another lineage, without however, ignoring its links with its original *ʃme*; we call *association* the alliance which this group forms with the receiving lineage. Dissociation must be distinguished from the original phenomena of segmentation which induced the creation of Alladian villages. A single *ʃme* can be considered the founding clan in many villages; but even then it is remembered that one village came before the other. By *dissimilation* we mean the process at the conclusion of which a group is born from a lineage in the village, through the intermediary of the slave or foreign women attached to one or many members of this lineage; by contrast, *assimilation*, refers to the process by which, for one reason or another, foreigners of different origins come and integrate into the lineage of a village without maintaining any contact with their place of origin: slavery is the most obvious and important case of assimilation.

These phenomena are directly relevant to our argument insofar as their frequency and their location are a manifestation of the predominance of the principle of residence over the principle of descent in the two trading villages of the last century (Grand-Jacques and Jacqueville). The units which are the result of the association of groups originating from other villages with a founding clan still call themselves *ʃme* within it, but each of them is aware of its real origin (for example, it participates in the funeral of a member of the *ʃme* from which it dissociated). The *ʃme* of Jacqueville are first of all village units, but this reality is partly concealed by the large number of matrimonial exchanges which take place between their constituting groups (pseudo-endogamy of *ʃme*). As for dissimilation, it testifies to the demographic overabundance of certain courts in the last century and to the necessity of ordering this overabundance within the framework of the village by increasing the number of courts and court chiefs.

What was the relationship between the head of the founding *ʃme* and the chiefs of the associated or dissimilated *aciɔkɔ*? First of all it must be remembered that, of course, any association or dissimilation from the *ʃme* first needed the agreement of its chief; secondly, if it is now easy to distinguish the sections of forest which, within the great *ʃme* forest, were attributed to each *aciɔkɔ*, it is clear that these allocations were not automatic and that the *ʃme* chief determined them freely. The forest however played an essential role in the life of the villages, since it provided the trees necessary to the building of canoes and, in the first type of trade, the wood sold to Europeans; finally it seems that the right to trade with European ships originally depended on the chief of Grand-Jacques and later in Jacqueville on the chiefs of the two founding ɛ̣me. Dissimilated ətiɔkɔ were more dependent; originally, the chief of the founding ɛ̣me could create many courts of slaves and descendants of slave women in which he was represented; as a rule sections of forest were not usually definitively allocated and any initiative in economic matters had to be agreed by the ɛ̣me chief. Judging by contemporary courts, we can see that in certain cases, associated or dissimilated əciɔkɔ have been more successful than the representatives of the founding clan, but in general, the latter have maintained their control over the wealth provided by trade,[4] and to a lesser extent, over the possibilities of promotion in fields born of upheavals of the 20th century.

III. RELATIONS OF PERSONAL DEPENDENCE AND RELATIONS OF PRODUCTION[5]

The true content of the statuses previously recorded is better understood when the process of production and reproduction of Alladian society is studied not only in its traditional activities (fishing, food crops, canoe building) but in its more recent activities (industrial agriculture) in which these statuses are used as the basis and justification for the creation, establishment or increase of certain fortunes. In this last case, the language of legitimacy can perfectly adequately express fortune and power, but it also sometimes conceals serious upheavals (when, for example, former slaves or descendants of female slaves take over the throne of a court after having 'made a fortune' as planters or civil servants).

Together with salt manufacture and trade, fishing seems to have been the first activity of the Alladian who settled on the coastal strip. A large number of religious ceremonies concerned the sea and fishing and it may be because of its eminent role in these ceremonies that Grand-Jacques originally succeeded in controlling commercial operations with the Europeans. Fishing was obviously not a mere supplementary activity. In view of the importance of the resources drawn from it, it can be said that for Alladian villages the sea was a genuine public domain, without boundaries or owners; but its users had no right of usufruct by contrast with what is found in certain cases of 'public domain'. Only a senior, a court chief by principle and the 'owner' of the canoe (because he gave permission to pull down the tree out of which it was dug and cut) had the right to redistribute the fishing catch of his sons or of the sons of the man whose heir he was.

The distribution of the catch[6] follows precise rules which vary with the nature of the fish, the fisherman's age and matrimonial situation; these rules are very precisely defined. We will discuss this in the present tense, since, as the role of canoe fishing is obviously predominant today the rules of redistribution have not changed.

Until his marriage the son gives his whole catch to his father. The latter does not have to give him back a share; it must be said that then the son is fed by his parents, unless, as is often the case, he takes his meals at the house of one of his married sisters. When his father gives him a share, he can, in some cases, give it to his sister (if he eats at her house) or to his grandmother. his mother's mother, who smokes it, and after a succession of sales or exchanges will make up a small capital for him, often in the form of small livestock (sheep, kids, etc.).

After his marriage (while his young wife cooks at her own mother's) the son has the right to a share in the redistribution which is still done by his father, or in the latter's absence, by his heir. Five shares are made:

(1) one share for the father himself;
(2) one share goes to the son (the fisherman) and naturally, his wife;
(3) one share is reserved for the son's wife's mother;
(4) one share is reserved for the fisherman's father's father or his heir;
(5) finally one last share goes to the father's close maternal kin.

The fisherman's sister has no right to a share, nor does his brother. But if they come they receive a share. When the fisherman is single, shares 2 and 3 go to his father.

When the fish is large (for example *etru*, 'tuna') the shares are slightly different. The first (*ɛ̃iriciã*, 'marriage fish') goes to the fisherman's wife who gives it to her mother. The second (*eziciã*, 'father's fish') goes to the fisherman's father who gives it to his own father or to the latter's heir; to this share, chosen from the most fleshy part of the fish, is added half a head, the head being sliced from top to bottom. The third share (*əbüciã*) goes, with the second half of the head, to the father's maternal kin. The fourth share is reserved for the father's age-set, who themselves determine its size; the fifth share — if the father's age-set have left one — is for the father who can, if he wants to, give his son some of it.

One day the fisherman's father decides to give him his entire 'fishing rights'. On that day he makes his final, larger than usual distribution; that evening the father and son drink together. At that moment the son also acquires the right to work on his uncle's fields if necessary and to hunt on his own account; on this occasion his father often gives him a machete and a gun.

It is now the son himself who distributes his fishing catch. He makes four shares: one for his father, one for his own maternal kin, one for his wife's mother and a last one for his father's maternal kin. He keeps the rest.

If the father's father, or his heir turns up during the distribution, he receives a share; but he doesn't have the right to a reserved share.

The sharing of a large fish is done more or less in the same way as before, but the distribution is based on the fisherman himself and not on his father. Share 1 goes to the fisherman's wife, share 2 to the fisherman's father or his heir, share 3 to the fisherman's close maternal kin, share 4 to the fisherman's age-set (*esubã bo*), share 5 finally to the fisherman.

If instead of following the circuit of distribution starting from the producer, it is followed from the redistributor, we notice that, in the case of redistribution done by the fisherman's father, only a small share of the fish comes back to the producer, the fisherman's father and his mother-in-law keeping another share, and the rest 'going up' to the paternal and maternal ascendants of the fisherman. When the son does the distribution, there is no 'going down' and the fisherman's maternal relatives (the fisherman's father's allies) appear among the beneficiaries; except for the share kept by the son, all the distribution goes 'upwards'.

These different forms of distribution and redistribution of the fish call for a few remarks.

First of all they are the manifestation of certain particularly marked solidarities within the network of kin relationships: father/son solidarity, of course, the son returning in kind to his father the technical (learning of fishing skills) and material (supply of the canoe) advantages which he has gained from him; solidarity between daughter and mother, the former providing the latter, through her husband, with an important alimentary contribution, which can be taken to be the counterpart for the education she has been given by her mother in the domestic field and in that of food agriculture, and for the services which she benefits from during the first years of her marriage (use of the mother's hut and house, in whose house she eats); finally the more discrete solidarity between brother and sister (the fisherman's sister, if she comes, always receives a share of fish — the shark's head is reserved for her; on the contrary, a man has no right to refuse his wife permission to cook for her unmarried brother, her brother is an effective ally against possible ill-treatment from her husband).

The final stage in the fisherman's career corresponds to a *rapprochement* with his maternal kin; the maternal uncle becomes the object of marked care from his nephew as soon as his father gives up part of the authority he had over him. This 'disengagement' of an already mature man from his paternal court towards his maternal one (*əbü* in the social sense) can be the preface to an effective change of residence in case the uterine nephew is called upon to succeed his maternal uncle to the throne of a court.

Lineage pseudo-endogamy resulted in the homogenisation of the courts in the village in making the residential *əbü* coincide with the social *əbü* in the destruction of the *ɛbiüi/əbüüi* opposition. At the same time, it limits the number of people who benefit from the re-distribution, or rather it entails the accumulation by certain indi-viduals of many statuses linked to kinship and, by this very fact, an increase in the share of each of these beneficiaries; for example a slave accumulates the statuses of son and nephew *vis-à-vis* his owner who, conversely plays towards him the roles of uncle and father. In a court whose composition is the result of many pseudo-endogamic alliances, the same person finds himself to be at the end of many circuits of redistribution, not only because he has many descendants, but because he alone possesses towards the same fisherman many of the titles which gave him a right to a share in the redistribution.

The court in the residential sense thus appears as a unit of pro-duction. Until an advanced age the *ɛbiüi* give their fishing catch either to their father, or to his heir: to the court chief anyway, since, apart from its chief and his descendants, the agnatic descendants of the previous court chief also reside in the same court. Together with the throne the heir also inherits rights over the descendants and the clearest expression of these rights is formulated in economic terms. From the point of view of production, the court in the residential sense has a cohesion which it has neither in theory at the level of lineage composition nor in fact from the point of view of con-sumption, since each household is in principle autonomous (apart from what it receives of the redistribution of the fish from the court chief, the chief of another court, or a mature man from another court); it consumes its subsistence production, and uses its own kitchen or, in the case of a man who hasn't yet obtained that right, a kitchen outside the court. This is also the case of the relatively aged bachelor who goes and takes his meals at the house of his married sister.

If a court is considered in principle to include the representatives of three generations, each generation can be characterised by its role in production and its place in distribution. The generation of court chiefs is generally composed of people who no longer have the physical strength to go to sea, but who receive either the next generation's whole catch to redistribute or, if certain members of this generation have received the right to distribute their fish themselves, a share of this fish to redistribute, a share of the fish distributed by that generation and eventually a share of the fish redistributed by that generation. In a court there can also be sons of the preceding court chief who belong to the same generation as the new chief (for example uterine nephews of the preceding): in certain cases, these *Ɛbiüi* owe a share of what they receive to their father's heir, but anyway they are no longer themselves producers. The generation of seniors does not produce, it redistributes and receives.

The next generation is composed of fishermen who have the right to distribute their fish themselves, and when necessary to redistribute their son's catch or the catch of fishermen who have not obtained the first right, but benefit from the second if their sons are old enough to fish. The people in this generation produce, either do or do not redistribute, but in principle anyway receive, since their father's heir owes them a share of their own fish as soon as they are married, which they usually are.

Finally, the next generation is composed of people who have no right to distribute their fish and who, depending on whether or not they are married, have or do not have the right to a share in the redistribution made by their father.

From the non-producer who receives and redistributes to the producer who neither distributes nor receives, all the possibilities are thus covered, and each of them can in general only happen within the same generation.

	Production	Receiving	Redistribution
1st generation	−	+	+
2nd generation	+	+	+
	+	+	−
3rd generation	+	+	−
	+	−	−

It will be noticed that, for various reasons, a person may receive a larger or smaller share of fish because it is granted to him, or because he is entitled to it and it is taken from his own catch, or because he takes it himself from his own or his son's catch or because he benefits simultaneously from his son's and his grandson's catch and eventually from that of his brother or his maternal uncle's descendants' catch. It is quite obvious that it was rare for a slave or even the descendant of a female slave to get past the stage of the redistribution of his son's catch or of participation in the distribution by his son of his own and his grandson's catch: it was a much more infrequent favour to grant the right of distribution of fish to a slave than to a son. Moreover the descendants' share reserved for the father's father or for the father's maternal kin went more or less regularly to the slave's acquirer or his heir. Fairly naturally the slaves had a much more important role in production than in distribution; tradition excluded the possibility that a slave could take over control of production in a court. Conversely an old court chief who had 'liberated' his sons and received a share in their fish without any longer redistributing it himself, had permanent control over his younger and more 'exploitable' offspring through his slave women.

The distribution and redistribution of the fishing catch is the model for more important economic activities and helps us to understand the mechanism of accumulation which has allowed certain $\mathcal{E}me$ to become powerful economic units originally based on the manufacture of salt, then on trade with Europe.

Each social court — each $aci\jmath k\jmath$ - owned and still owns a 'fund' or $\jmath b\ddot{u}$ wakre, concerning which all informants agree that it has been made up through the labour of the $\mathcal{E}bi\ddot{u}i$; responsibility for the $\jmath b\ddot{u}$ wakre was transmitted, with the court's throne along the direct matrilineal line of the $aci\jmath k\jmath$ leader. It was traditionally made up of loincloths, gold, $\xi kedi$ pearls, shackles. Obviously fishing could not on its own supply the $\jmath b\ddot{u}$ wakre, even though, it seems, that very early on there was a certain commercialisation of fish, based particularly on exchanges with the Adyukru who provided yams, bananas and palm oil. On the other hand the goods which make up the $\jmath b\ddot{u}$ wakre do not really belong to an exclusive sphere based on reciprocity. If indeed they could be used for the acquisition of foreign or slave women, they could in no way come from the reverse phenomenon: the Alladian did not export women, and the relatively low bridewealth they demanded was made up of consumption goods.

The fortune of the big Alladian courts is based on the manufacture and trading of salt. On this point tradition confirms Dapper's testimony. The Alladian claim to have to some extent commercialised it themselves as far as the Tiassalé (Baoulé) region where they used to exchange it for gold, loincloths, slaves, shackles presumably appearing in the eighteenth century. These south-north currents were doubled by the current produced by the first slave trade with the Europeans: the products provided for the Europeans came from the coastal strip itself (wood) or from the north (slaves, ivory, rubber). The specific situation of the coastal strip seems to have consolidated the position of the Alladian as exclusive traders with the Europeans; it is known that in general the coastal peoples all jealously guarded their monopoly, but anyway the Alladian's geographical isolation constituted a natural protection against the activities of the hinterland. The Dida and the Avikam found an outlet on the sea in the area of Grand Lahou, and the Ebrié in that of Vridi Bassam; the Adyukru, then first profited from the slave trade by serving as relays in the exchanges between south and north. Later they provided the raw material (palm oil) of the form of trade peculiar to the nineteenth century, which corresponded to an unprecedented increase in the activity and profits of Alladian traders. All the same the Adyukru have always manifested considerable resentment and jealousy towards a partner who made important profits from them and towards whom they were heavily indebted, for example, accepting advances in kind on goods which later they could not provide in sufficient quantity. In Alladian tradition all these quarrels with foreign areas connected with trade concern the Adyukru with whom, up to the last century, armed conflict seemed to have been relatively frequent. The most marked vestige of this state of affairs is the considerable presence in the genealogies of Alladian courts of Adyukru women put into bondage or handed over following a conflict, as we have already mentioned.

It was the *ɛbiüi* of the large *aciɔkɔ* who provided sea traffic and transport by lagoon for them; like sea fishing this work was owed to the father or his heir, but, if the produce of this labour, elite goods, was destined to the *əbü wakre*, in other words to an *aciɔkɔ* in principle different from the one of the *ɛbiüi*, they, as individuals, were its first beneficiaries, not only because as good sons they could claim their father's favours — and particularly the right to own early an autonomous house and kitchen — but because they were directly concerned by the destination of the *əbü wakre* goods. These goods, hoarded and kept by the *aciɔkɔ* chief, could only be used to the benefit of the *aciɔkɔ* as a solidary organic group; in fact the *aciɔkɔ* head did not decide on such a use on his own but assembled the *aciɔkɔ* elders. There were originally three conceivable uses: the payment of 'bridewealth' for a foreign woman from a patrilineal group, the purchase of male and female slaves, and the reimbursement of *aciɔkɔ* debts and the recovery of an *əbüüi* from bondage. But as we know the father opposed in principle the idea that the maternal uncle might give his son money for 'bridewealth'; it was thus the *ɛbiüi* who could receive free foreign or slave women from the chief of their residential court. The *aciɔkɔ* as a group was the medium term beneficiary of such an investment; the analysis of the system given by the parties themselves justifies the use of these terms. The payment of the relatively modest sums necessary for marriage with an Alladian woman did not affect the *əbü wakre*: the loincloths given to the woman were meant to clothe her and did not come into the category of hoarded goods. The demands of trade implied the maintenance outside the *əbü wakre* of a large number of shackles and these were not reserved goods like Baoulé loincloths, gold and pearls. As compensation for this payment, the father was certain to receive the services of the son's first child and he or his heir would receive shares taken from his grandsons' fishing. But the 'bridewealth' provided for a foreigner or the payment given for the acquisition of a slave woman had long-term consequences for the activity and growth of the lineage; added to the usual advantages obtained from the son's descendants, was the return of the father's descendants to his own *əciəkə*; moreover we have seen that in the field of redistribution slaves and descendants of slave women cannot claim a role equivalent to the one they played in production. The only people who could expect to control the management of a social court were the representatives of the *əciəkəprəo*. The *əkorebo* had all the duties but none of the virtual rights attached to the condition of the *ʄbiüi*[7] except that of being put into bondage by their mother's owner when they were *owő yii üi*. Thus the policy of marriage with foreign women, slaves or descendants of slaves tended to reproduce the dependence structure *əciəkə/əciəkəprəo*.

It can thus be said that, among the Alladian, as in other societies, genealogical relations formed the basis of the relations of production, and that in the course of the development of their society, to take up Meillassoux's[8] expression, the link of kin can be seen to transform itself into a purely social filiation. But the situation is less one of the substitution of social filiation for kinship relations than it is a juxtaposition, which at first sight is all the more in-distinguishable because the inter-play of interlineage alliances increases its forms and the language of kin unifies its appearance, but which is however all the more real and ascertainable because it possesses a precise economic content as the expression of an in-disputable social stratification. The technical basis of the seniors' power — their former role as educators, their experience, and the proof given by their age of their aptitude at controlling or mani-pulating the forces which weigh on society — was paralleled by a hierarchy linked to age; the couple *ʄbiüi/əbüi* was not a form of stratification from the point of view of village society, since in principle each individual was both in relation to two different *əciəkə* but, with the use of the *əbü wakre* to matrimonial ends or for the purchase of slave women, the substitution becomes that from an unchangeable socio-economic status based on birth, to an enduring socio-economic status linked to age. In the new system the distinction *əciəkə/əciəkəprəo* becomes more relevant than the distinction ʄbiüi/əbüüi. Thus, the Alladian provide the example of a society in which lineage relations have very consciously and very explicitly been used as framework for the relations of production.

The importing of women and the intensification of trade with Europeans in the nineteenth century had two important consequences: the growth of the lineages on the one hand and on the other certain opportunities for individual enrichment. These possibilities of enrichment seem to have existed for a very long time: originally for each person they were dependent on his age, the son progressively obtaining a larger participation in the benefits of the salt or slave trade. It is however unlikely that this increased participation had in some cases resulted in a complete individualisation of trade. However it favoured the creation and the increase of personal fortunes, naturally distinct from the əbü wakre of the residential and social courts (to the increase of which they could however contribute).[9] Similarly, the court chief was not bound to put back into the əbü wakre all the profits of the əbü, but merely a share equivalent to that reserved, in fishing, either to the fisherman's maternal kin or to the fisherman's father's paternal kin. Gold — in the shape of jewellery or powder — shackles and weapons made up the main part of these personal fortunes.[10] a father celebrated the acquisition by his son of a slave or a gun: such a celebration happened only when the son was himself the real acquirer of these goods. Alladian tradition distinctly separates inheritance of the 'throne' and personal inheritance, a prestigious chief often having a personal inheritance which was more important than the əbü wakre of which he was in charge. The monetisation of the economy and the appearance of new sources of revenue have strengthened this distinction. They have not created it.

Personal fortunes and demographic pressure have also expressed themselves in the creation of dissimilated aciɔkɔ, which, at first, needed some human investment. The creation of a new aciɔkɔ gave an individual access to the dignity of court chief earlier than expected — he might also possibly never have reached this status — and the possibility of himself organising to some extent for himself, the productive and commercial activities of the new court.

It must be noted that by creating the conditions for individual enrichment, trade made a new substitution possible: that of economic criteria for social criteria based on the membership of direct or indirect lineages. The new substitution which moreover is not general, the aciɔkɔprɔo having always been concerned with the maintenance of their socio-economic status, may have been made easier by the development of modern activities (plantation agriculture) and the appearance of new sources of revenue, but it found favourable ground in the ambiguous conception the Alladian have of the reciprocal relations between power, wealth and legitimacy.

Besides, it is in this ambiguous understanding — manifested by the belief in the *awabo* society and among other things translated by certain specific functions of the *esubā* apart from the ceremonies linked to illness and death — that one of the clearest signs of the forces which simultaneously make up and threaten Alladian society can be found. The definition of the individual's status in terms of descent but also by reference to his economic situation (without this language necessarily being inadequate for this reality); the definition of large village units as *ɛme*, when, by the interplay of dissociations and associations, the most powerful among them are territorial units; the effort of the *aciɔkɔ* chiefs to turn these into residential and economic units despite the patrilocal rule; in the final analysis all these facts testify, in the specific language of a society, to the impact of the economic changes linked to the European commercial intervention on its social organisation.[11]

NOTES

1. J. Freund, *L'essence du politique*, Paris, 1965 My translation—HL.
2. *ibid.*
3. Ebrie land healer (cf. H. Memel-Fote, 'un Guerisseur de basse Cote d' Ivoire: Josue Edjro', *CEA*, 28 VII-4, 1967, Pp. 547 605).
4. The 'permanent' houses built in the last century by the British for the rich traders belong to very specific courts and in this respect their imposing ruins are an interesting sign.
5. This argument is taken essentially from Chapter V of our study, *Le rivage Alladian*, Memoires, ORSTOM, 1969.
   We talk of distribution to describe the fisherman giving his father the catch, the sharing out of the catch by the fisherman himself among the different members of his family and, in general, the circulation of this produce from the producer. We will talk of redistribution to describe sharing out by the fisherman's father of his son's produce and in, general, the circulation of this catch centred around its redistributor.
7. According to informants, slaves or descendants of slave women were, in particular, involved in the handling and transport of oil barrels along the coastal strip. In other words, the Alladian needed a larger labour force at a time when, because of the abolition of the slave trade, slaves ceased to be an exportable commodity.
8. *Anthropologie économique des Gouro de Côte d'Ivoire*, Paris, Mouton, 1964.
9. More than his rank in the lineage of potential heirs, it was the value, the reliability of an individual which got him chosen to succeed a deceased court chief. A reasonable — not too ostentatious — generosity was a proof of reliability.
10. Recourse to money seems to have appeared very early on the coastal strip. Captain Gouriau, in a report in 1862, indicates that a barrel of oil cost 250 francs when it left Jacqueville.

11. We are here merely locating the place of the problem of structural causation (cf. L. Althusser, 'The Object of Capital' in Althusser and Balibar, *Reading Capital*, London, New Left Books, 1970). Our argument was simply to show the remarkable convergence existing between the explicit and the implicit ideology of the Alladian as it manifests itself in the system of *awa* and in the ideological function of the descent structure, and the objective evolution of their social organisation.

Select Bibliography

Works in English

L. Althusser, *For Marx*, Penguin Books, Harmondsworth, 1969

P. Anderson, *Passages from Antiquity to Feudalism*, New Left Books, London, 1974

P. Anderson, *Lineages of the Absolutist State*, New Left Books, London, 1974

T. Asad (ed), *Anthropology and the Colonial Encounter*, Ithaca Press, London, 1973

R. Blackburn (ed), *Ideology in Social Science*, Fontana, London, 1972

M. Bloch (ed), *Marxist Analyses in Social Anthropology*, Malaby Press, London, 1975

F. Engels, *The Origin of the Family, Private Property and the State*, Lawrence & Wishart, London, 1972

A. G. Frank, *Capitalism and Underdevelopment in Latin America*, Monthly Review Press, 1969; Penguin Books, Harmondsworth, 1973

M. Godelier, *Rationality and Irrationality in Economics*, New Left Books, 1972

B. Hindess & P. Q. Hirst, *Pre-Capitalist Modes of Production*, Routledge & Kegan Paul, London, 1975

K. Marx, *Pre-Capitalist Economic Formations*, Lawrence & Wishart, London, 1964

K. Marx, *Capital*, Lawrence & Wishart, London (vol. I, 1970), 1972

K. Marx, & F. Engels, *The German Ideology*, Lawrence & Wishart, London, 1970

C. Meillassoux (ed), *The Development of Indigenous Trade and Markets in West Africa*, International African Institute, Oxford University Press, London, 1971

M. Sahlins, *Stone Age Economics*, Tavistock, London, 1974

E. Terray, *Marxism and 'Primitive' Societies*, Monthly Review Press, 1972

* * * * * * * *

P. Anderson, 'Components of the National Culture', *New Left Review*, 50, 1968

T. Asad & H. Wolpe, 'Concepts of modes of production', *Economy and Society*, vol. 5, no. 4, 1976

J. Banaji, 'The crisis of British anthropology', *New Left Review*, 64, 1970

R. Firth, 'The sceptical anthropologist? Social anthropology and Marxist views on society', *Proceedings of the British Academy*, vol. lvii, 1972

J. Friedman, 'Marxism, structuralism and vulgar materialism', *Man*, vol. 9, no. 3, 1974

P. Hirst, 'The uniqueness of the West', *Economy and Society*, vol. 4, no. 4, 1975

E. Laclau, 'Feudalism and capitalism in Latin America', *New Left Review*, 67, 1971

C. Meillassoux, 'From reproduction to production', *Economy and Society*, vol. 1, no. 1, 1972

C. Meillassoux, 'Are there castes in India?', *Economy and Society*, vol. 2, no. 1, 1973

J. Taylor, 'Marxism and anthropology', *Economy and Society*, vol. 1, no. 3, 1972

J. Taylor, 'Pre-Capitalist Modes of Production', *Critique of Anthropology*, no. 6, vols. 1 and 2, 1976

E. Terray, 'Long distance exchange and the formation of the State: the case of the Abron kingdom of Gyaman', *Economy and Society*, vol. 3, no. 3, 1974